HOSPITALITY AND HEALTH

Issues and Developments

HOSPITALITY AND HEALTH

Issues and Developments

Edited by
Jaime A. Seba

Apple Academic Press

TORONTO NEW JERSEY

Apple Academic Press Inc.
3333 Mistwell Crescent
Oakville, ON L6L 0A2
Canada

Apple Academic Press Inc.
9 Spinnaker Way
Waretown, NJ 08758
USA

Exclusive worldwide distribution by CRC Press, a Taylor & Francis Group

International Standard Book Number: 978-1-926692-92-0 (Hardback)

Library and Archives Canada Cataloguing in Publication

Hospitality and health: issues and developments/[edited by] Jaime A. Seba.

Includes index.
ISBN 978-1-926692-92-0
1. Globalization–Health aspects. 2v. Travel–Health aspects.
3. Communicable diseases. 4. World health. I. Seba, Jaime

RA441.H67 2011 362.1 C2011-905424-8

Apple Academic Press also publishes its books in a variety of electronic formats. Some content that appears in print may not be available in electronic format. For information about Apple Academic Press products, visit our website at **www.appleacademicpress.com**

Preface

All over the world, technological advances are being made at the speed of light, and the hospitality and tourism industry is growing and changing just as quickly. Customers can get a special rate when they follow a hotel on Twitter. They can book tour reservations online with a simple click. Cruise destinations around the world can be explored without leaving home, and bloggers on different continents share dining recommendations. Travelers can even plan a vacation that allows them to commune with nature while printing e-mails from their smartphones.

In order to stay competitive in an international market, businesses must adjust to these emerging social trends and respond to the ever-changing needs of their customers. The traditional focus on customer service and guest loyalty has become intertwined with rapidly progressing technological enhancements influencing all areas of the industry, including sales, marketing, human resources, and revenue and asset management. The result is a visitor experience personalized to each specific guest, through strategic data collection, market trend research, and the capabilities of integrated online self-service. This means knowing what matters most to consumers and recognizing emerging innovations that will be the next big thing for the next generation of customers.

Health issues are another growing concern within the hospitality and tourism industry. How do local health concerns impact tourists to other countries? How do tourist sites impact local health? The answers to these two questions cannot be separated from one another, since they intertwine. Tourists must be protected from disease exposure, while local populations must be equally protected from the possible negative impacts on health created by a resort or other tourist destination.

We live in an interconnected world today, and this reality has enormous bearing on the hospitality and tourism industry. Considering these impact and meaningful trends, the future of the industry will depend on a skilled workforce that can react quickly to rapid changes at the forefront of global culture.

— Jaime A. Seba

List of Contributors

Abdullah S. Ali
Zanzibar Malaria Control Programme (ZMCP), Zanzibar Ministry of Health and Social Welfare, P. O. Box 236, Zanzibar.

Yvonne Andersson
Department of Infectious Disease Epidemiology, Swedish Institute for Infectious Disease Control, 171 82 Solna, Sweden.

Bianca Maria Are
Hygiene and Preventive Medicine Institute, University of Sassari, Sassari, Italy.

Antonio Azara
Hygiene and Preventive Medicine Institute, University of Sassari, Sassari, Italy.

Michael G. Baker
Department of Public Health, University of Otago, Wellington, New Zealand.

Elizabeth Barnett
Division of Travel and International Health, Boston University Medical Center, Boston, MA, USA.

Ron H. Behrens
Travel Clinic, Hospital for Tropical Diseases, Mortimer Market, London, WC1E 6JB, UK.

Mark A. Bellis
Centre for Public Health, Liverpool John Moores University, Castle House, North Street, Liverpool, L3 2AY, UK.

Jiri Beran
Travel Clinic, Hospital for Tropical Diseases, Mortimer Market, London, WC1E 6JB, UK.

Franchette van den Berkmortel
Elkerliek Hospital, Helmond, the Netherlands.

Olivier Bouchaud
Travel Clinic, Hospital for Tropical Diseases, Mortimer Market, London, WC1E 6JB, UK.

Kelly S. Bricker
University of Utah, Salt Lake City, Utah, USA.

Robert S. Bristow
Geography and Regional Planning, Westfield State College, Westfield, MA, 01086, USA.

Marcelo N. Burattini
Department of Pathology, School of Medicine, University of Sao Paulo and LIM 01-HCFMUSP, Rua Teodoro Sampaio, 115, CEP: 05405-000-São Paulo, S.P., Brazil.

André Busato
Institute for Evaluative Research in Orthopedic Surgery, MEM centre, University of Bern, Stauffacherstrasse, Bern, Switzerland.

Edmond J. Byrnes III
Department of Molecular Genetics and Microbiology, Duke University Medical Center, Durham, NC, USA.

Martin Camitz
Swedish Institute for Infectious Disease Control, Solna, Sweden.
Department of Medical Epidemiology and Biostatistics, Karolinska Institute, Solna, Sweden.

Department of Sociology, Stockholm University, Stockholm, Sweden.
Theoretical Biological Physics, Department of Physics, Royal Institute of Technology, Stockholm, Sweden.

Damian Lopez Cano
Support Unit for Research, Evaluation and Accountability (Red IRYSS), Hospital Costa del Sol, Ctra Nacional 340, km 187, 29600 Marbella, Spain.

Manuel Carrasco
Support Unit for Research, Evaluation and Accountability (Red IRYSS), Hospital Costa del Sol, Ctra Nacional 340, km 187, 29600 Marbella, Spain.

Bernadette Carroll
Travel Clinic, Hospital for Tropical Diseases, Mortimer Market, London, WC1E 6JB, UK.

Dee A. Carter
Department of Molecular Genetics and Microbiology, Duke University Medical Center, Durham, NC, USA.

Joan C. March Cerda
Support Unit for Research, Evaluation and Accountability (Red IRYSS), Hospital Costa del Sol, Ctra Nacional 340, km 187, 29600 Marbella, Spain.

Catharine Chambers
British Columbia Centre for Disease Control, Vancouver, British Columbia, Canada.
University of British Columbia, Vancouver, British Columbia, Canada.

Ted Cohen
Department of Epidemiology, Harvard School of Public Health, Boston, MA, USA.
Division of Global Health Equity, Brigham and Women's Hospital, Harvard School of Public Health, Boston, MA, USA.

Jan Copeland
National Drug and Alcohol Research Centre, University of New South Wales, Sydney, NSW 2052, Australia.

Francisco A. B. Coutinho
Department of Pathology, School of Medicine, University of Sao Paulo and LIM 01-HCFMUSP, Rua Teodoro Sampaio, 115, CEP: 05405-000-São Paulo, S.P., Brazil.

Roel A. Coutinho
National Institute for Public Health and the Environment, Bilthoven, the Netherlands.
Academic Medical Center, Amsterdam, the Netherlands.

Gary M. Cox
Department of Molecular Genetics and Microbiology, Duke University Medical Center, Durham, NC, USA.

Nadja Curth
Department of Public Health, Copenhagen University, Copenhagen, Denmark.

Leon Danon
Department of Epidemiology, Harvard School of Public Health, Boston, MA, USA.
Department of Biological Sciences, University of Warwick, Coventry, UK.

Maria Grazia Deriu
Hygiene and Preventive Medicine Institute, University of Sassari, Sassari, Italy.

Marco Dettori
Hygiene and Preventive Medicine Institute, University of Sassari, Sassari, Italy.

Paul Dillon
National Drug and Alcohol Research Centre, University of New South Wales, Sydney, NSW 2052, Australia.

Jaap T. van Dissel
Leiden University Medical Center, Leiden, the Netherlands.

Sabine Dittrich
National Institute for Public Health and the Environment, Bilthoven, the Netherlands.
European Centre for Disease Prevention and Control, Stockholm, Sweden.

Gerard J. J. van Doornum
University Medical Center, Rotterdam, the Netherlands.

Scott F. Dowell
Division of Global Disease Detection and Emergency Response, Centers for Disease Control and Prevention, Atlanta, Georgia, USA.

Martin Eichner
Department of Medical Biometry, University of Tübingen, Germany.

Petra Emmerich
Bernhard-Nocht-Institute for Tropical Medicine, Hamburg, Germany.

Lukas Fenner
University of Zürich, Zürich, Switzerland.

Fidel Fernandez-Nieto
Support Unit for Research, Evaluation and Accountability (Red IRYSS), Hospital Costa del Sol, Ctra Nacional 340, km 187, 29600 Marbella, Spain.

Eleni Galanis
British Columbia Centre for Disease Control, Vancouver, British Columbia, Canada.
University of British Columbia, Vancouver, British Columbia, Canada.

Anna Gallofre
Support Unit for Research, Evaluation and Accountability (Red IRYSS), Hospital Costa del Sol, Ctra Nacional 340, km 187, 29600 Marbella, Spain.

Jose A. Garcia-Ruiz
Support Unit for Research, Evaluation and Accountability (Red IRYSS), Hospital Costa del Sol, Ctra Nacional 340, km 187, 29600 Marbella, Spain.

Peter Gates
National Drug and Alcohol Research Centre, University of New South Wales, Sydney, NSW 2052, Australia.

Johan Giesecke
Department of Infectious Disease Epidemiology, Swedish Institute for Infectious Disease Control, 171 82 Solna, Sweden.

Edward Goldstein
Department of Epidemiology, Harvard School of Public Health, Boston, MA, USA.

Philippe J. Guerin
European Programme of Intervention Epidemiology Training (EPIET).
Department of Infectious Disease Epidemiology, Norwegian Institute of Public Health, 0403 Oslo, Norway.

Stephan Günther
Bernhard-Nocht-Institute for Tropical Medicine, Hamburg, Germany.

Gonzalo E. Gutierrez
Support Unit for Research, Evaluation and Accountability (Red IRYSS), Hospital Costa del Sol, Ctra Nacional 340, km 187, 29600 Marbella, Spain.

Christoph Hatz
Travel Clinic, Hospital for Tropical Diseases, Mortimer Market, London, WC1E 6JB, UK.

Simon I. Hay
Spatial Ecology and Epidemiology Group, Tinbergen Building, Department of Zoology, University of Oxford, South Parks Road, Oxford, OX1 3PS, UK.
Malaria Public Health and Epidemiology Group, Centre for Geographic Medicine, KEMRI, P. O. Box 43640, 00100 GPO, Nairobi, Kenya.

Joseph Heitman
Department of Molecular Genetics and Microbiology, Duke University Medical Center, Durham, NC, USA.

Urban Hellgren
Travel Clinic, Hospital for Tropical Diseases, Mortimer Market, London, WC1E 6JB, UK.

Morten Hesse
Aarhus University, Centre for Alcohol and Drug Research, Copenhagen Division, Købmagergade 26E, 1150 Copenhagen C, Denmark.

Peter J. Hotez
Sabin Vaccine Institute and Department of Microbiology, Immunology, and Tropical Medicine, George Washington University Medical Center, Washington, DC, USA.

Karen E. Hughes
Centre for Public Health, Liverpool John Moores University, Castle House, North Street, Liverpool, L3 2AY, UK.

Tomas Jelinek
Travel Clinic, Hospital for Tropical Diseases, Mortimer Market, London, WC1E 6JB, UK.

Alberto Jimenez-Puente
Support Unit for Research, Evaluation and Accountability (Red IRYSS), Hospital Costa del Sol, Ctra Nacional 340, km 187, 29600 Marbella, Spain.

Birgitta de Jong
Department of Infectious Disease Epidemiology, Swedish Institute for Infectious Disease Control, 171 82 Solna, Sweden.

Enrique Navarro Jurado
Support Unit for Research, Evaluation and Accountability (Red IRYSS), Hospital Costa del Sol, Ctra Nacional 340, km 187, 29600 Marbella, Spain.

Jay S. Keystone
Division of Infectious Diseases, University of Toronto, Toronto, Canada.

Amy D. Klion
Laboratory of Parasitic Diseases, National Institute of Allergy and Infectious Diseases, National Institutes of Health, Bethesda, Maryland, USA.

Marion P. G. Koopmans
National Institute for Public Health and the Environment, Bilthoven, the Netherlands.
Leiden University Medical Center, Leiden, the Netherlands.
University Medical Center, Rotterdam, the Netherlands.

Martin Lajous
Center for Population Health Research, National Institute of Public Health, Cuernavaca, Mexico.
Department of Epidemiology, Harvard School of Public Health, Boston, MA, USA.

Melissa A. Law
Laboratory of Parasitic Diseases, National Institute of Allergy and Infectious Diseases, National Institutes of Health, Bethesda, Maryland, USA.

Jeffrey V. Lazarus
WHO Regional Office for Europe, Copenhagen, Denmark.

Department of Public Health, Copenhagen University, Copenhagen, Denmark.

Jessica Leahy
University of Maine, Orono, Maine 04469.

Fabrice Legros
Travel Clinic, Hospital for Tropical Diseases, Mortimer Market, London, WC1E 6JB, UK.

Yonathan Lewit
Department of Molecular Genetics and Microbiology, Duke University Medical Center, Durham, NC, USA.

Min Li
British Columbia Centre for Disease Control, Vancouver, British Columbia, Canada.

Wenjun Li
Department of Molecular Genetics and Microbiology, Duke University Medical Center, Durham, NC, USA.

Fredrik Liljeros
Department of Sociology, Stockholm University, Stockholm, Sweden.

Ettie M. Lipner
Office of Global Research, National Institute of Allergy and Infectious Diseases, National Institutes of Health, Bethesda, Maryland, USA.

Marc Lipsitch
Department of Immunology and Infectious Diseases, Harvard School of Public Health, Boston, MA, USA.
Department of Epidemiology, Harvard School of Public Health, Boston, MA, USA.

Susanne Lorentz
Parasitus Ex e.V., Vollbergstrasse 37, 53859 Niederkassel, Germany.

Louis Loutan
Travel and Migration Medicine Unit, Department of Community Medicine, Geneva University Hospital, Geneva, Switzerland.

Laura MacDougall
British Columbia Centre for Disease Control, Vancouver, British Columbia, Canada.

Rafael Cortes Macías
Support Unit for Research, Evaluation and Accountability (Red IRYSS), Hospital Costa del Sol, Ctra Nacional 340, km 187, 29600 Marbella, Spain.

Lydia Martin
Support Unit for Research, Evaluation and Accountability (Red IRYSS), Hospital Costa del Sol, Ctra Nacional 340, km 187, 29600 Marbella, Spain.

Maria Dolores Masia
Hygiene and Preventive Medicine Institute, University of Sassari, Sassari, Italy.

Eduardo Massad
Department of Pathology, School of Medicine, University of Sao Paulo and LIM 01-HCFMUSP, Rua Teodoro Sampaio, 115, CEP: 05405-000-São Paulo, S.P., Brazil.

Srdan Matic
WHO Regional Office for Europe, Copenhagen, Denmark.

Klazien Matter-Walstra
Institute for Evaluative Research in Orthopedic Surgery, MEM centre, University of Bern, Stauffacherstrasse, Bern, Switzerland.

Meg McCarron
Influenza Division, National Center for Immunization and Respiratory Diseases, Centers for Disease Control and Prevention, Atlanta, Georgia, USA.

Brigitte Menn
Parasitus Ex e.V., Vollbergstrasse 37, 53859 Niederkassel, Germany.

Joel C. Miller
Department of Epidemiology, Harvard School of Public Health, Boston, MA, USA.
Fogarty International Center, National Institutes of Health, Bethesda, Maryland, USA.

Bruno Moonen
The William J. Clinton Foundation, 383 Dorchester Avenue, Suite 400, Boston, MA, 02127, USA.

Andrew Mowen
The Pennsylvania State University, Pennsylvania, USA.

Nikolai Mühlberger
Travel Clinic, Hospital for Tropical Diseases, Mortimer Market, London, WC1E 6JB, UK.

Elena Muresu
Hygiene and Preventive Medicine Institute, University of Sassari, Sassari, Italy.

Bjørn Myrvang
Travel Clinic, Hospital for Tropical Diseases, Mortimer Market, London, WC1E 6JB, UK.

Torsten Naucke
Parasitus Ex e.V., Vollbergstrasse 37, 53859 Niederkassel, Germany.

Marco A. Navarro Ales
Support Unit for Research, Evaluation and Accountability (Red IRYSS), Hospital Costa del Sol, Ctra Nacional 340, km 187, 29600 Marbella, Spain.

Thomas B. Nutman
Laboratory of Parasitic Diseases, National Institute of Allergy and Infectious Diseases, National Institutes of Health, Bethesda, Maryland, USA.

Karin Nygård
European Programme of Intervention Epidemiology Training (EPIET).
Department of Infectious Disease Epidemiology, Swedish Institute for Infectious Disease Control, 171 82 Solna, Sweden.

Justin J. O'Hagan
Department of Epidemiology, Harvard School of Public Health, Boston, MA, USA.

Agneta Olsson
Department of Infectious Disease Epidemiology, Swedish Institute for Infectious Disease Control, 171 82 Solna, Sweden.

Albert D. M. E. Osterhaus
University Medical Center, Rotterdam, the Netherlands.

Emilio Perea-Milla
Support Unit for Research, Evaluation and Accountability (Red IRYSS), Hospital Costa del Sol, Ctra Nacional 340, km 187, 29600 Marbella, Spain.

John R. Perfect
Department of Molecular Genetics and Microbiology, Duke University Medical Center, Durham, NC, USA.

Andrea Piana
Hygiene and Preventive Medicine Institute, University of Sassari, Sassari, Italy.

Chad Pierskalla
West Virginia University, Morgantown, WV, **USA.**

Sergi Mari Pons
Support Unit for Research, Evaluation and Accountability (Red IRYSS), Hospital Costa del Sol, Ctra Nacional 340, km 187, 29600 Marbella, Spain.

D. Rebecca Prevots
Office of Global Research, National Institute of Allergy and Infectious Diseases, National Institutes of Health, Bethesda, Maryland, USA.

Youliang Qiu
Department of Geography, 3141 Turlington Hall, University of Florida, Gainesville, Florida, 32611-7315, USA.

Carrie Reed
Influenza Division, National Center for Immunization and Respiratory Diseases, Centers for Disease Control and Prevention, Atlanta, Georgia, USA.

Tine Reinholdt
Aarhus University, Centre for Alcohol and Drug Research, Copenhagen Division, Købmagergade 26E, 1150 Copenhagen C, Denmark.

Steven Riley
School of Public Health and Department of Community Medicine, University of Hong Kong, Hong Kong, People's Republic of China.

Francisco Rivas-Ruiz
Support Unit for Research, Evaluation and Accountability (Red IRYSS), Hospital Costa del Sol, Ctra Nacional 340, km 187, 29600 Marbella, Spain.

David J. Rogers
Spatial Ecology and Epidemiology Group, Tinbergen Building, Department of Zoology, University of Oxford, South Parks Road, Oxford, OX1 3PS, UK.

Oliver Sabot
The William J Clinton Foundation, 383 Dorchester Avenue, Suite 400, Boston, MA, 02127, USA.

Patricia Schlagenhauf
University of Zürich, Zürich, Switzerland.

Sanna Schliewe
Aarhus University, Centre for Alcohol and Drug Research, Copenhagen Division, Købmagergade 26E, 1150 Copenhagen C, Denmark.

Markus Schwehm
ExploSYS GmbH, Institute for Explorative Modeling, Leinfelden, Germany.

Heli Siikamäki
Travel Clinic, Hospital for Tropical Diseases, Mortimer Market, London, WC1E 6JB, UK.

Dave Smaldone
Division of Forestry and Natural Resources, West Virginia University, Morgantown, WV 26506-6125, USA.

David L. Smith
Emerging Pathogens Institute, University of Florida, Gainesville, Florida, 32610-0009, USA.
Department of Biology, Bartram-Carr Hall, University of Florida, Gainesville, Florida, 32611, USA.

Frank von Sonnenburg
Department of Tropical and Infectious Diseases, University of Munich, Munich, Germany.

Giovanni Sotgiu
Hygiene and Preventive Medicine Institute, University of Sassari, Sassari, Italy.

Robert Steffen
University of Zürich, Zürich, Switzerland.

Andrew J. Tatem
Department of Geography, 3141 Turlington Hall, University of Florida, Gainesville, Florida, 32611-7315, USA.
Emerging Pathogens Institute, University of Florida, Gainesville, Florida, 32610-0009, USA.

Aura Timen
National Institute for Public Health and the Environment, Bilthoven, the Netherlands.

Sébastien Tutenges
Aarhus University, Centre for Alcohol and Drug Research, Copenhagen Division, Købmagergade 26E, 1150 Copenhagen C, Denmark.

Kees M. Verduin
Elkerliek Hospital, Helmond, the Netherlands.
St. P.A.M.M., Veldhoven, the Netherlands.

Leo Visser
Travel Clinic, Hospital for Tropical Diseases, Mortimer Market, London, WC1E 6JB, UK.

Ann C. T. M. Vossen
Leiden University Medical Center, Leiden, the Netherlands.

Jacco Wallinga
Epidemiology and Surveillance Unit, Centre for Infectious Disease Control, National Institute of Public Health and the Environment (RIVM), Bilthoven, The Netherlands.

Matthew Weait
Faculty of Lifelong Learning, Birkbeck College, London, UK.

Rainer Weber
University of Zürich, Zürich, Switzerland.

Marcel Widmer
Institute for Evaluative Research in Orthopedic Surgery, MEM centre, University of Bern, Stauffacherstrasse, Bern, Switzerland.

Nick Wilson
Department of Public Health, University of Otago, Wellington, New Zealand.

List of Abbreviations

ACT	Artemisinin-based combination therapy
ADHD	Attention-deficit hyperactivity disorder
AFLPs	Amplified fragment length polymorphisms
AIDS	Acquired immune deficiency syndrome
API	Annual parasite index
BC	British Columbia
BCs	Buffy coats
BCYE	Buffered charcoal yeast extract
BNI	Bernhard-Nocht-Institute
CAA	Civil Aviation Administration
CDC	Centers for Disease Control and Prevention
CGB	L-Canavanine, glycine, 2-bromothymol blue
CI	Confidence interval
CNS	Central nervous system
CoH	HSAo with a constant hospitalization pattern
CSHD	Costa del Sol Healthcare District
CST	Certification in sustainable tourism
CT	Computed tomography
CTO	Caribbean Tourism Organization
CVBD	Canine vector-borne disease
CZ	Control zone
DEC	Diethylcarbamazine
dEIR	Daily entomological inoculation rate
DMEM	Dulbecco's Modified Eagle's Medium
DR	Dominican Republic
E.W.G.L.I.	European Working Group for *Legionella* Infections
EATG	European AIDS Treatment Group
ELM	Elaboration likelihood model
GBID	Georgetown Business Improvement District
GHB	Gammahydroxybutrate
GMS	Gomori Methenamine Silver
H1N1	Influenza virus A
HIV	Human immunodeficiency virus
hosp_ar	HSAo hospital(s) admission rate
HP	Human pressure

HSAo	Orthopedic hospital service area
IAS	International AIDS Society
IFA	Immunofluorescent antibody
IFAT	Immunofluorescence antibody test
IPS	International passenger survey
IRs	Incidence rates
JCI	Joint Commission International
loc_ar	HSAo local residents admission rate
l-res	HSAo local residents
LSD	Lysergic acid diethylamide
LUMC	Leiden University Medical Centre
MARV	Marburg virus
MATα	α Mating type allele
MDA	Mass drug administration
MHF	Marburg hemorrhagic fever
MLS	Multilocus sequence
MLST	Multilocus sequence typing
MOU	Memorandum of understanding
MRI	Magnetic resonance imaging
MS	Murashige and Skoog
MSW	Municipal solid waste
NGOs	Non-governmental organizations
NHP	National Historical Park
nloc_ar	HSAo nonlocal residents admission rate
nl-res	HSAo nonlocal residents
NTDs	Neglected tropical diseases
OR	Odds ratio
ORF	Open reading frame
PAHO	Pan American Health Organization
PBS	Phosphate buffer solution
PCR	Polymerase chain reaction
PETS	Pet travel scheme
PICTs	Pacific Island Countries and Territories
PLHIV	People living with HIV
PT	Phage type
RDTs	Rapid diagnostic tests
RegA	Regular areas
SARS	Severe acute respiratory syndrome
SB	Sunny beach

SeH	HSAo with a seasonal hospitalization pattern
SIOM	Sistema Integral de Operación Migratoria
SPC	Secretariat of the Pacific Community
SPSS	Statistical package for social sciences
SSA	Sub-Saharan Africa
STIs	Sexually transmitted infections
STs	Sequence types
TPB	Theory of planned behavior
TRF	Tandem repeat finder
VFR	Visiting friends or relatives
VI	Vancouver Island
VNTR	Variable number of tandem repeat
WHO	World Health Organization
WSA	Winter sport area
Zantel	Zanzibar telecom

Contents

Chapter 1

Prevalence Study of *Legionella* Spp. Contamination of Cruise Ships

Antonio Azara, Andrea Piana, Giovanni Sotgiu, Marco Dettori, Maria Grazia Deriu, Maria Dolores Masia, Bianca Maria Are, and Elena Muresu

INTRODUCTION

In the last years, international traffic volume has significantly increased, raising the risk for acquisition of infectious diseases. Among travel-associated infections, increased incidence of legionellosis has been reported among travelers.

Aim of our study was: to describe the frequency and severity of *Legionella* spp. contamination in ferries and cruise ships; to compare the levels of contamination with those indicated by the Italian ministerial guidelines for control and prevention of legionellosis, in order to assess health risks and to adopt control measures.

A prevalence study was carried out on nine ships docked at the seaports of northern Sardinia in 2004. Water samples were collected from critical sites: passenger cabins, crew cabins, kitchens, coffee bars, and rooms of the central air conditioning system. It was performed a qualitative and quantitative identification of *Legionella* spp. and a chemical, physical, and bacteriological analysis of water samples.

Forty-two percent (38/90) water samples were contaminated by *Legionella* spp. Positive samples were mainly drawn from showers (24/44), washbasins (10/22). *L. pneumophila* was isolated in 42/44 samples (95.5%), followed by *L. micdadei* (4.5%).

Strains were identified as *L. pneumophila* serogroup 6 (45.2%; 19 samples), 2–14 (42.9%), 5 (7.1%), and 3 (4.8%). *Legionella* spp. load was high; 77.8% of the water samples contained > 104 cfu/l.

Low residual free chlorine concentration (0–0,2 mg/l) was associated to a contamination of the 50% of the water samples.

Legionella is an ubiquitous bacterium that could create problems for public health.

We identified *Legionella* spp. in 6/7 ferries. Microbial load was predominantly high (> 104 cfu/l or ranging from 103 to 104 cfu/l). It is matter of concern when passengers are subjects at risk because of *Legionella* spp. is an opportunist that can survive in freshwater systems; high bacterial load might be an important variable related to disease's occurrence.

High level of contamination required disinfecting measures, but does not lead to a definitive solution to the problem. Therefore, it is important to identify a person responsible for health safety in order to control the risk from exposure and to apply preventive measures, according to European and Italian guidelines.

Tourism has played an important role in economic growth in Developed and Developing Countries.

According to the data of the body representing the private sector in all parts of the travel and tourism industry worldwide, that is the World Travel and Tourism Council, travel and tourism industry contribute 10.9% of gross international product [1, 2].

Tourism has contributed significantly towards the Italian economic development; the impact on economy is estimated at 350 billions Euros in the next 10 years [2].

However, an increased risk for acquisition of diseases, such as those related to infection, is inevitably associated with the international traffic volume, as well as with the modern high-speed transport (high disease burden in developing countries).

Among travel-associated infections, increased incidence of legionellosis, infection caused by the bacterium *Legionella* spp., has been reported among travelers; at least 48 species of *Legionella* have been identified, with 18 of these species linked to human diseases [3]. *L pneumophila* is the most frequent cause of human legionellosis.

Legionellosis refers to two distinct clinical syndromes, namely, Legionnaires disease, which most often presents as severe pneumonia accompanied by multisystemic disease, and Pontiac fever, which is an acute, febrile, self-limited, viral-like illness [4].

Legionella are gram-negative, rod-shaped bacteria that are ubiquitous in freshwater environments. Transmission occurs through aerosolization or aspiration of contaminated water [5]. Infection depends on the water contamination level by bacteria, host factors (advanced age, tobacco smoke, chronic degenerative diseases, state of immunodeficiency), and the virulence of the particular strain of *Legionella* (enhanced by protozoa- or amoeba-bacterium relationship).

Most cases of Legionellosis are sporadic but outbreaks can occur due to contamination of hot and cold water systems, evaporative condensers, spa pools/natural pools/thermal springs, respiratory therapy equipment. Biofilm formation can provide a means for survival and dissemination of *Legionella* bacterium [6, 7].

Cases might be linked to nosocomial-lethality rate: 30–50%- or travel-associated infection (tourist accommodation, vessel, etc.).

Owing to the possibility of environmental exposure to the organism, legionellosis is a public health problem, investigated by numerous health organizations, such as the World Health Organization (WHO), European Working Group for *Legionella* Infections (E.W.G.L.I) [8], Italian Istituto Superiore di Sanità.

On this basis, to assess the impact of *Legionella* spp. contamination in vessels, Hygiene and Preventive Medicine Institute of the University of Sassari, Italy, involved in the surveillance of nosocomial legionellosis in the last years, together with Maritime Health Office of Porto Torres, Italy, undertook an epidemiological investigation of ferries and cruise ships.

It addressed two aims:

- to describe the frequency and severity of *Legionella* spp. contamination;
- to compare the levels of contamination with those indicated by the Italian ministerial guidelines for control and prevention of legionellosis, in order to assess health risks and to adopt control measures.

MATERIALS AND METHODS

The survey was carried out on nine ships docked at the seaports of northern Sardinia in 2004; seven ferries belonged to two Italian shipping companies while two cruise ships belonged one to an Italian shipping company and another come from Bahamas. Epidemiological investigation was divided into three distinct types of activity:

- selection of suspected contaminated areas and their critical sites; particularly, five different areas were identified: cabin where people sleep, cabin where crew sleep, kitchen, coffee bar, and room of the central air conditioning system. Water samples were collected from showers, washbasins, kitchen sinks, and evaporative condensers of air conditioning systems.
- water sampling: two samples were collected from every sampling site in a single time-point (total amount = 90; 10 samples were collected from every ship, five for qualitative and five for quantitative identification of *Legionella* spp). The first water sample was collected for qualitative evaluation, without flaming and immediately after the tap was switched on; the second sample was collected for quantitative analysis, after the water ran for at least 5–10 min, being more representative of the water flowing in the system.
- qualitative and quantitative analysis of *Legionella* spp, according to methods described in the guidelines for prevention and control legionellosis [9–11]; furthermore, determination of water quality was carried out in order to enumerate total and fecal coliforms, fecal streptococci, sulphate-reducing clostridi. Total microbial counts were evaluated at 22°C and 37°C. Water temperature and residual free and total chlorine were determined at the time of sample collection.

Briefly, 1 l water samples were collected in sterile containers containing 0.01% sodium thiosulphate to neutralise any chlorine; they were kept at ambient temperature and protected from direct light. Water was processed on the day of collection and sample concentration was conducted using 0.45 μm cellulose membrane filters.

After concentration, the membranes were aseptically removed and placed into sterile screw-capped containers with 10 ml sterile distilled water. The material of the filter membrane was vortex-mixed (3 times for 30 sec).

Then, a 0.1 ml of each sample was inoculated onto two GVPC-selective agar, a medium containing cycloheximide, glycine, polymyxin B, and vancomycin.

The remaining 9.9 ml was centrifuged at 3,000 R/min for 20 min; all the supernatant was removed but 1 ml; then, the sediment was resuspended and incubated at 50°C in a water bath for 30 min; afterwards, 0.1 ml was spread on duplicate plates of GVPC agar. These plates, laid into candle jars, were incubated at 36–37°C in a humidified atmosphere with <5% CO_2. Plates were evaluated for 10 days before reporting them negative.

Gram stain was performed in case of suspected colonies; weakly staining, gram-negative bacilli were observable. Suspected colonies with a mottled surface or an iridescent and faceted cut glass appearance, were counted from each sampling. All colonies from plates with ≤10 and 10–20 random colonies were subcultured on buffered charcoal yeast extract (BCYE) agar (with cysteine), charcoal yeast extract agar (CYE Agar Base—Oxoid), blood-agar and McConkey agar plates.

These plates were incubated at 37°C in a humidified environment for ≥2 days. Only colonies grown on BCYE were subsequently identified by two agglutination tests (i.e., *Legionella* Latex Test, Oxoid, and *Legionella* Immune Sera "Seiken", Denka Seiken Co. Ltd). The first test allows a separate identification of *L. pneumophila* serogroup 1 and serogroups 2–14 and detection of seven *Legionella* species (*Legionella* spp. group), which have been implicated in human disease: *L. longbeachae* 1 and 2, *L. bozemanii* 1 and 2, *L. dumoffii, L. gormanii, L. jordanis, L. micdadei, L. anisa*. The second test identifies *Legionella pneumophila* serogroup 1, 2, 3, 4, 5, 6 and *L. bozemanii, L. dumoffii, L. gormanii, L. micdadei.*

DISCUSSION

Legionella is an ubiquitous bacterium that could create problems for public health; most cases of Legionnaire's disease are sporadic but nosocomial or community outbreaks can occur, such as those related to tourist accommodations [12–15].

We conducted a prevalence study in order to evaluate the presence of *Legionella* spp. in passenger vessels, that is ferries and cruise ships, because of the increased navigation traffic and poor national and international medical reference.

We analyzed two cruise ships and seven ferries; *Legionella* spp. was identified in 6/7 ferries. Microbial load was predominantly high (> 104 cfu/l or ranging from 10^3 to 10^4 cfu/l).

However, we did not identify *Legionella pneumophila* serogroup 1, which is responsible for more than 90% of clinical cases.

This finding might be related to differences in environmental prevalence among *Legionella pneumophila* serogroup 1 and non-*pneumophila* species. Several reports, evidenced that the high frequency of *Legionella pneumophila* serogroup 1 isolation from clinical samples is not strictly linked to environmental predominance but might be due to higher infectivity or more efficient intracellular growth. The low incidence of non-*pneumophila* species among clinical isolates associated to their high environmental frequency implies that these species are less virulent and pathogenic than *Legionella pneumophila* serogroup 1 [16].

It is matter of concern when passengers are subjects at risk (smokers, older people, immunocompromised individuals, etc.); *Legionella* spp., in fact, is an opportunist par excellence, that can survive in freshwater systems; high bacterial load might be an important variable related to disease's occurrence in association to long-term exposure.

Although cruise ships were *Legionella* spp.-free, ferries to Sardinia are frequently used for cruising during all seasons but summer.

Therefore, it is important to analyze the risk of acquiring infection with regard to water supplies and hosts in order to provide preventive interventions.

According to recent Italian guidelines targeted to administrators of hotels and thermal baths, contamination level is high in 77.8% of our samples, requiring disinfecting measures and later evaluation, regardless of disease's occurrence; the remaining samples (22.2%) have to be surveyed, requiring decontamination measures if one or more cases of legionellosis are identified [10].

Prophylactic measures, as stated by EWGLI, imply that all water services should be routinely checked for temperature, water demand and inspected for cleanliness and use [8].

Principal items include the reduction of the possibility of using contaminated water by disinfecting (chemical disinfection), filtering and suitably storing the water; keeping cold water cold and hot water hot; avoiding the dead ends in pipes; properly cleaning and disinfecting spas; periodically cleaning or replacing the devices that might promote dissemination of *Legionella.*

RESULTS

An elevated number of samples was collected from areas and critical sites at risk (cabin where people sleep; cabin where crew sleep; showers, washbasins, kitchen sinks), considering the modes of transmission of *Legionella* infection.

A total of 34 (37.8%) samples of 90 were collected from cabins where people sleep, 32 (35.6%) from cabins where crew sleep, 16 (17.8%) from kitchens, 6 (6.7%) from coffee bars, and 2 (2.2%) from air conditioning system rooms; a total of 44 (48.8%) samples of 90 were drawn from showers, 22 (24.5%) from washbasins, 22 (24.5%) from kitchen sinks, and 2 (2.2%) from evaporative condensers of air conditioning systems.

Legionella spp. was identified in all but one ferries (66% of the total ships), while cruiser ships were not contaminated. An average of four samples (range, 0–10) was positive per ship.

A total of 38 (42.2%) water samples of 90 were contaminated by *Legionella* spp. (Table 1): 50% (17/34) collected from cabins where people sleep, 53.1% (17/32) from cabins where crew sleep, 12.5% (2/16) from kitchens, 33.3% (2/6) from coffee bars; it was not identified in water samples collected in the air conditioning system rooms.

Positive samples were drawn from showers (24/44; 54.5%), mainly those located in cabins where crew sleep, from washbasins (10/22; 45.5%), mainly those located in cabins where people sleep (60%), from kitchen sinks (4/22; 18.2%), mainly those located in coffee bars (33.3%).

Legionella pneumophila was isolated in 42/44 samples (95.5%), followed by *L. micdadei* (4.5%). (Figure 1)

Strains were identified as *L. pneumophila* serogroup 6 (45.2%; 19 samples), 2–14 (42.9%), 5 (7.1%), and 3 (4.8%). (Figure 1)

Legionella spp. load was high: 22.2% contained 1×10^3—1×10^4 Legionella per liter, while 50% 1×10^4—1×10^5, 22.2% 1×10^5—1×10^6, 5.6% 1×10^5—1×10^6. Then, 27.8% contained > 100,000 Legionella per liter which is judged the critical level for environmental decontamination in absence of Legionnaires' disease, according to Italian guidelines.

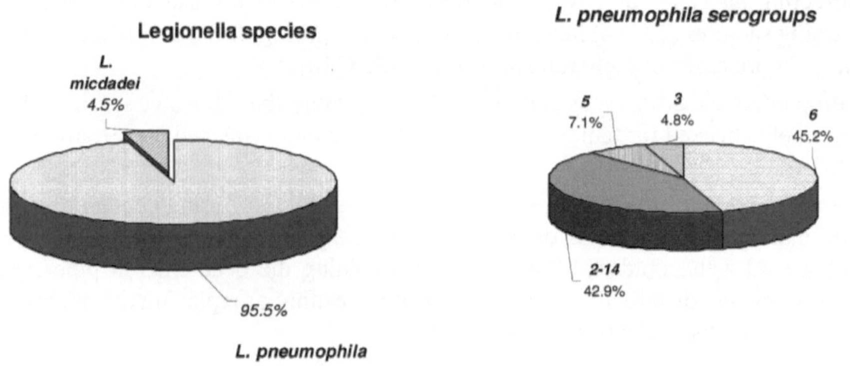

Figure 1. *Legionella* identification: species and serogroups.

Detection of microbial indicators of faecal contamination and total microbial counts at 22°C and 37°C were performed (25); bacterial load was variable ranging from 0 to 1,000 CFU/ml and from 0 to 784 CFU/ml at 37°C and 22°C, respectively, independently of *Legionella* spp. growth; it was demonstrated no link between microbial count and the presence of *Legionella* spp. in water samples. In only one sample microbial counts were 230 and 768 CFU/100 ml at 37°C and 22°C, respectively, in which total and fecal coliforms were isolated (30 and 8 CFU/100 ml, respectively) but not *Legionella* spp.

We examined the relation between residual free chlorine and *Legionella* spp.: 0–0.2 mg/l residual free chlorine concentration was associated to a contamination of the 50% of the water samples, 0.81–2 mg/l to 5.4%; *Legionella* spp. did not significantly decrease in association to a residual free chlorine concentration of 0.21–0.80 mg/l (Figure 2).

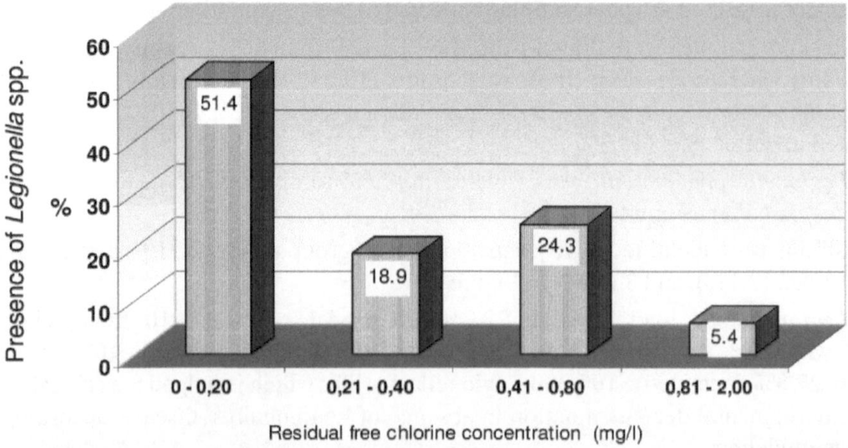

Figure 2. Relation between residual free chlorine concentration and presence of *Legionella* spp. in water samples.

Water temperature of *Legionella* spp. positive samples ranged from 20°C to 40°C (50% ranging from 20°C to 30°C and 50% ranging from 31°C to 40°C); *Legionella* spp. was not identified in water samples whose temperature ranged from 41°C to 60°C.

Of the 90 water samples, six (6.6%), collected in a single cruise-ship, had temperature ranging from 42.4 to 56.6°C. Negative cultures of these water samples might be due to their residual free and total chlorine, ranging from 1.80 to 1.95 and from 1.90 to > 2, respectively.

CONCLUSION

The absence of a correct prevention of *Legionella* infections onboard ship might cause a lot of medical—sanitary, legal, and economic problems (deaths, negative impact on tourism, possible removal of the ship from the service and suspension of activity of its crew for many days, etc.) [8, 13, 17].

Furthermore, environmental decontamination is useful as punctual action but does not lead to a definitive solution to the problem.

Therefore, it is important to identify a person responsible for supervision and health safety in order to prevent or to control the risk from exposure, according to EWGLI and Italian guidelines; the person has to conduct an assessment of the sites at risk in the water systems present in the premises and to implement precautions for controlling any identified risk from *Legionella* bacteria. He has to be competent to assess the risks of exposure to *Legionella* bacteria in the water systems present in the premises and the control measures (e.g. a microbiologist, environmental health officer or water engineer with is specific expertise).

This aspect might be fundamental in Sardinia, an island devoted to tourism, where prevention of infectious disease acquisition from environmental sources and healthcare have to be associated to elevated level of quality of dwelling places.

Shipping companies have a keen interest in effects of our epidemiological study, showing willingness to proceed with investigation targeted to *Legionella* bacterium and to verify the efficacy of decontamination performed after the survey.

KEYWORDS

- **Aerosolization**
- ***Legionella* spp.**
- **Legionellosis**
- **Respiratory therapy**

AUTHORS' CONTRIBUTIONS

All of the authors participated in planning and design of the study, and all read and approved the manuscript. Marco Dettori and Maria Grazia Deriu participated to the waters analysis. Antonio Azara, Andrea Piana, Giovanni Sotgiu, Maria Dolores Masia, Bianca Maria Are and Elena Muresu conceived the study, participated in its design and wrote the manuscript.

ACKNOWLEDGMENTS

The authors would like to thank the public health medical doctors and technical staff of Maritime and Airline Health Office (Porto Torres, Sardinia, Italy) of Italian Ministry of Health.

COMPETING INTERESTS

The author(s) declares that he has no competing interests.

Chapter 2

Risk of Malaria for Travelers with Stable Malaria Transmission

Eduardo Massad, Ronald H. Behrens, Marcelo N. Burattini, and Francisco A. B. Coutinho

INTRODUCTION

Malaria is an important threat to travelers visiting endemic regions. The risk of acquiring malaria is complex and a number of factors including transmission intensity, duration of exposure, season of the year, and use of chemoprophylaxis have to be taken into account estimating risk.

A mathematical model was developed to estimate the risk of non-immune individual acquiring *falciparum* malaria when traveling to the Amazon region of Brazil. The risk of malaria infection to travelers was calculated as a function of duration of exposure and season of arrival.

The results suggest significant variation of risk for non-immune travelers depending on arrival season, duration of the visit and transmission intensity. The calculated risk for visitors staying longer than 4 months during peak transmission was 0.5% per visit.

Risk estimates based on mathematical modeling based on accurate data can be a valuable tool in assessing risk/benefits and cost/benefits when deciding on the value of interventions for travelers to malaria endemic regions.

The risk of malaria for visitors to the nine Brazilian states of the Legal Amazon region—Acre, Amapá, Amazonas, Maranhão (western part), Mato Grosso (northern part), Pará (except Belém City), Rondônia, Roraima, and Tocantins (western part)—is predominantly *P. vivax* (75%) with *P. falciparum* making up the remainder one quarter of surveillance reports. In addition, it should be noted that multidrug-resistant *P. falciparum* has been reported [1] in the same region. Transmission occurs in most forested areas below 900 m though there is some urban transmission around settlements and small cities in the region. Transmission intensity varies according to the season and municipality. It is higher in jungle areas where recent (<5 years) mining, lumbering and agricultural settlements than in urban areas, such as larger cities like Boa Vista, Macapá, Manaus, Maraba, Pôrto Velho, Rio Branco, and Santarém, where transmission occurs on their outskirts. However, in the central areas of these cities transmission is negligible or non-existent.

In 2007 Brazil reported approximately 50% of the total number of the malaria cases in the Americas. Ninety-nine percent of those cases were from the Legal Amazon, where 10% to 15% of the population of Brazil population live [2]. Case numbers fell between 1992 and 2002 from 572,000 to 349,873, with around 16.5% of all the slides examined resulted positive for malaria. A rebound occurred between 2003 to 2007 with number of cases peaking at 607,000 in 2005 and 458,041 cases in 2007. All reported malaria cases were confirmed by laboratory analysis, and 19% in 2007 were *P. falciparum*. These cases were predominantly associated with population movement to the periphery of large cities in the Legal Amazon Region [2]. Therefore, the average burden of malaria over the last decade has been approximately 600,000 cases per year, with the proportion of *falciparum* around 20% of total [3]. WHO estimated the total numbers of malaria cases in 2006 as approximately 1.4 million [2]. The difference between the two figures reflects either an underestimation (Brazilian official data) or an overestimation of the actual number of cases (WHO estimates). The true values probably lies between the two.

Brazil has the second largest number of foreign visitors in Latin America after Mexico [4]. In 2005, Brazil recorded 5.4 million international arrivals with 57% of these traveling coming from North America and Europe [5]. Of the total, 44% were leisure tourists. Preliminary analysis of tourism arrivals for 2004/2005 by Embratur [5], reveal that 39% of tourists cite Brazil's natural beauty as their reason for travel. However, 7% of leisure tourists (3% of total tourists) state they visited the Brazilian Amazon. Therefore, estimated visits to the malaria endemic areas of Brazil are of the order of 160,000 per year. Embratur [5] identifies that tourists from the domestic market is much larger. The latest study indicates that of the annual 11 million domestic Brazilian travelers, around 300,000 visit the Amazon region. Therefore an estimated half a million non-resident visitors are exposed to malaria per year in this region [4].

Malaria prevention in non-immune travelers is based on chemoprophylaxis, recommended for all visitors to the region where there is active malaria transmission. However, all regimens have well recognized and not infrequent side effects, including severe events that interfere with routine daily activity. Therefore, risk-management requires the balance of risk of infection and risk of toxicity when prescribing chemoprophylaxis. This balance is particularly important when the risk of malaria is low and the numbers exposed are significant [6].

This study was designed to use a mathematical model to estimate the risk of acquiring *falciparum* malaria for travelers to the endemic regions of Brazil.

The Model

The model assumes that the population of humans is subdivided into three classes and the population of mosquitoes is similarly divided into three compartments. It was separated from the human general population (individuals that are in the area) a cohort [7], denoted by primes and named "probe", which represent a cohort of travelers, followed through their entire exposure in the region, to calculate the risk of malaria acquisition.

A deterministic version (precisely determined through a known relationship) of the model was used to describe the malaria dynamics in the resident population level and a stochastic version (using a ranges of variable values providing a probability). On the equations analyzing the probes to describe the risk (probability of contracting malaria) of a single individual traveler visiting the region. This is based on the assumption that, since the probe is a small number of individual, the biting rate will randomly fluctuate and the probability of infection is unpredictable.

The model's parameters are: α is the mosquitoes daily biting rate; α' is the mosquitoes daily biting rate in the probe; *b* is the proportion of infected bites that are actually infective to humans; *b'* is the proportion of infected bites that are infective to humans in the probe; *c* is the proportion of bites that are infective for mosquitoes; μ_H is the humans mortality rate; γ_H is the humans recovery rate from parasitaemia; r_H is the humans birth rate; α_H is the malaria-induced mortality rate of humans; σ_H is the lost of immunity due to malaria; μ_M is the mosquitoes daily mortality rate, τ is the extrinsic incubation period; r_M is the mosquitoes fertility rate; κ_H is the humans carrying capacity and κ_M is the mosquitoes carrying capacity. We introduced the term $[c_S\text{-}d_S\sin(2ft)]$ in the susceptible mosquitoes population in order to simulate seasonality in the mosquitoes population [8, 9]. The parameters c_S and d_S ($c_S > d_S$) vary the intensity by seasonality, mimicking severe or mild winters, through adjusting these parameters' values.

The seasonality parameters c_S and d_S where chosen to represent the observed seasonal variation in the Amazon region described by Tadei [10], who described a 30 fold difference in mosquito number between summer and winter.

Around 250,000, *falciparum* malaria cases will occur annually, a number similar to WHO estimates for Brazil in 2006 [2].

Estimating the Risk of Malaria

In order to calculate the probability of an individual acquiring malaria infection, π_{mal} after the introduction of a single case in an entirely susceptible population it was considered the probe (travelers within the region) followed through an entire outbreak. The probability of infection in this self-limiting outbreak is then given by the following expression:

$$\pi_{mal} = \frac{\int_0^\infty S'_H(t) h_{mal}(t)dt}{N'_H(0)} \tag{1}$$

In the above equation, $S¢_H(t)$ and $N¢_H(t)$ are respectively the number of susceptible hosts and the total population of the cohort used as a probe, and $h_{mal}(t)$ is the force of infection of malaria, defined as the per capita number of new cases per time unit [7] and expressed as

$$h_{mal}(t) = a' b'_{mal} \frac{I_M(t)}{N_H(t)} \tag{2}$$

where $I_M(t)$ is the number of infected mosquitoes.

One can also calculate the average risk (probability) of infection for a traveler who arrives in the affected region at week Ω after the outbreak is triggered and remains there for ω weeks, $\pi_{mal}^{travelers}$. This is done by setting the limits of integration in equation (1) as:

$$\pi_{mal}^{travelers} = \frac{\int_{\Omega}^{\Omega+\omega} S'_H(t) h_{mal}(t) dt}{N'_H(\Omega)} \tag{3}$$

The average risk for a traveler who arrived in the Amazonian region at four different time periods was calculated, namely, in the dry season (winter) in the spring, in the wet season (summer) and in the fall. The model produces a result of 250,000 cases *falciparum* malaria per year. This number is very dependent on a number of other variables and parameters. In the sensitivity analysis below all the parameters are varied and as a consequence the yearly number of cases varies. The result for the risk calculation is shown in Figure 1.

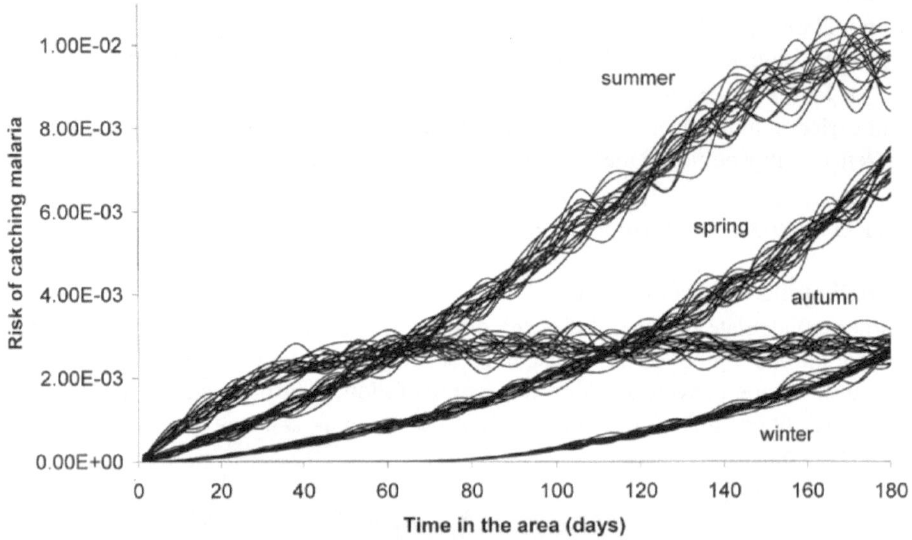

Figure 1. Stochastic risk of catching *falciparum* malaria for travelers as a function of the period of the year they arrive and the time remaining in the area (the figure shows 20 iterations of the 1000 simulated).

Sensitivity Analysis

In this section we analyze the sensitivity of the model to the parameters. This is done in two steps: a deterministic analysis at the populational level, which describes the sensitivity of the model to measurement variance in the parameters; and a stochastic analysis at the individual level, which determines the variation in the model's outcomes due to intrinsic stochasticity in some of the parameters.

Sensitivity of the Model to Variance in the Parameters Measures

The risk of malaria acquisition π as given by equation (3) is a function of a number of parameters collectively denoted by Pari. For a small variation of Pari, ΔPari, the variation in the risk π, $\Delta\pi$, is given by the well-known error-propagation formula [11]:

$$\Delta\pi = \sum_i \frac{\partial\pi}{\partial Par_i} \times \Delta Par_i \tag{4}$$

The relative variation in the risk π, Δπ/π, as a function of the relative variation in the parameters $\Delta Par_i/Par_i$, is therefore:

$$\frac{\Delta\pi}{\pi} = \sum_i Par_i \frac{\partial\pi}{\partial Par_i} \times \frac{\Delta Par_i}{Par_i} \times \frac{1}{\pi} \tag{5}$$

The sensitivity of the model is significantly influenced by with the season of the year. The two parameters that are most influential in the model *i* are the biting rate a and the mosquitoes mortality rate μm. Biting rate and mosquito mortality are well recognized by entomologists as important parameters as they describe vectorial capacity (a quadratic component) and mortality expressed exponentially in the equation.

Variation in the Model's Outcomes Due to Intrinsic Stochasticity in Some of the Parameters

The biting rate a single individual is subject, a', and the probability that an infectious biting is infective to the individual, *b'*, for an occasional traveler are obviously stochastic variables. As mentioned above, it was assumed a Poisson distribution for the parameter a' and a Gamma distribution for the parameter *b'* with a small variance.

The highest risk of malaria acquisition occurs for individuals arriving in autumn (around one case for every 500 visitors) as the infected mosquitoes population is close to its peak and the proportion infected high (see Figure 2).

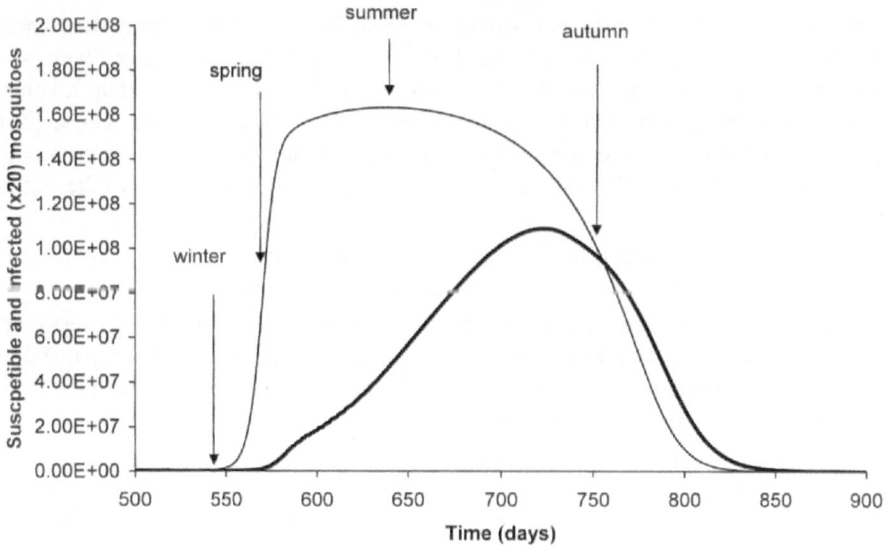

Figure 2. In the figure we show in the x-axis time in days. It starts arbitrarily at day 500 and illustrates seasonal variation of a mosquito population (susceptible and infected). The arrows define the relative season and seasonal impact on the susceptible mosquitoes populations (thin line) over the year. The figure also shows the infected mosquitoes (thick line) amplified 20 times.

Where an individual remains for a 1 year their risk is approximately $1.10 \times 10^{-2} \pm 2.75 \times 10^{-5}$, that is, a relative error of ±0.25%. This rate closely correlates with the incidence observed in Amazon residents of 1.16×10^{-2} per person-year. PAHO [12] estimates that this incidence, a maximum of 75 malaria cases per 1,000 inhabitants annually will occur. We are estimating only the cases of *falciparum* malaria, which represent about one third of the total malaria cases, hereby total predicted *P falciaprum* malaria cases for this region is of the order of 33 cases per 1,000 inhabitants per year.

DISCUSSION

Mathematical models for estimating risks, as described in this chapter, should be considered as auxiliary tools for decision-makers. Some caveats, however, are necessary; the model's outcomes are determined by assumptions in the dynamics of the system modeled and on the values given to the parameters. In our model, the most critical assumptions relate to homogeneity. For example, the Amazon region is very large and therefore, it is likely that some parameters will vary from region to region, such as the densities of vectors and human hosts (determined by the respective carrying capacities). The seasonal variations assumed in the model are simple and are only an approximation of the actual climatic variations that occur in the Amazon region. Notwithstanding the oversimplifications of our model, we believe that our results are a good approximation in the sense that the actual risk of malaria lies within the estimated confidence intervals calculated by the model.

Previous studies have attempted to determine the cumulative risk of acquiring malaria in travelers [6, 13, 14], but the estimated incidence rates were not generalizable to all travelers at all times, as malaria incidence varies greatly from year to year [15].

Mathematical modeling is well suited to adjust for seasonality and annual variations. In a previous analysis we modeled the risk of dengue and yellow fever, with similar approach to the one described here [16-18]. This is the first time that travelers' malaria risk estimates have been calculated using mathematical modeling. Our models are robust and have been tested extensively on Amazonian data [19]. Risk for malaria risk for endemic populations has also been estimated using modeling by Okell et al. [20].

The analysis presented quantifies the risk for non-immune travelers visiting the Amazonian region, adjusting by season and/or epidemic cycle.

A traveler arriving in summer (Dec–Feb) exposed for 120 days has at least a 10-fold higher risk of infection than a traveler who arrives in the winter (June–Aug) for a visit of similar duration. It is shown that the risk increases nonlinearly with time, but this again varies by season of exposure.

National and international recommendations for long term travelers; particularly those traveling through regions of varying transmission and with different malaria species have been very crude (all or nothing) and have a very limited evidence base [21].

The model can be used for highlighting the malaria risk in a way that many advisors and their clients can interpret. An individual arriving during the summer (Jan–Mar), that is, rainy season, has a probability of 0.00015 (1:6666) of being infected within a week of arrival if totally unprotected while it takes approximately 3 months for a traveler arriving during the winter months (Jun–Aug), that is, dry season, to be infected with the same likelihood, with intermediary values for arrivals during other seasons. In fact, Behrens et al. [22] estimated the incidence of malaria in UK travelers to Brazil as 1 case per 3,000 person-years exposed over the years 2000–2005. During this period, there were 394,559 visits with average visit duration of 22.5 days resulting in nine vivax cases and no *P. falciparum* cases in UK travelers. Running the model with this data the model produced a result of one case of *falciparum* malaria. Assuming that travel was predominantly during the winter months, this single case is a similar incidence (0) as observed in UK travelers, affirming the reliability of our current assumptions and values used in the model.

The model does not take account of pre-existing malaria immunity although for most naïve travelers this is not important. Another aspect that was not considered in this chapter is chemoprophylaxis, which is about 95% efficient against *falciparum* malaria. Therefore, if only 50% of the travelers are compliant, then the number of expected cases is reduced by approximately 48%, although the risk for a non-treated individual does not change.

It is important to stress what is gained in terms of risk estimation with our model. It is known that the annual incidence of malaria among Amazon residents is of the order of 50 cases per 1,000 inhabitants. This figure can be used as a proxy for the risk to travelers staying for at least one year in the region. However, the model provides estimations of the risk for travels of shorter durations and, since the risk for these short visits is dependent on the season of the year travelers arrive in the area, the model is essential for those estimations.

The model for the resident population is a modification of the classical Macdonald model [23]. The sensitivity of the model's outcome for errors in the measurements of the parameters was calculated. With exceptions of Macdonald [23] and Burattini et al. [8] who analyzed the sensitivity of the basic reproduction number to variation on the parameters, it seems to us that, this is the first time the sensitivity of other Macdonald's model outcomes is analyzed. The results of this analysis point to a model, that is very sensitive to the mosquitoes biting rate, *a*, and natural mortality rate, μm. A 1% error in the measurement of these parameters assumed but perhaps this can be improved. The travelers' population was approximately treated stochastically. By this we mean that, we considered the bites received by a single individual are Poisson distributed with average equals to the deterministic value of mosquitoes biting rate, *a*, suffered by the resident population. In fact, the number of bites suffered by each individual is the product of the mosquitoes biting rate *a* times the number of infected mosquitoes in a certain area corresponding to the mosquitoes flying range, which was considered to be approximately constant. We also considered that the probability of infection to humans, *b*, as Gamma distributed around the average value used for the resident population and with a small variance.

The basic model could be applied to other regions where local information on force of transmission, parasite rates, or similar malariometric data are available. Such risk estimates would help the travel medicine provider with a better starting point in their risk assessment and provide travelers with a feel for what their malaria risk is and balance this with the appropriateness of chemoprophylaxis.

KEYWORDS

- ***Falciparum* malaria**
- **Mosquitoes**
- **Parasitaemia**
- **Stochasticity**

ACKNOWLEDGMENTS

This work was partially supported by FAPESP, CNPq and LIM01-HCFMUSP.

It was in part undertaken at UCLH/UCL who receives a proportion of funding from the Department of Health's NIHR Biomedical Research Centres funding scheme.

Chapter 3

Alcohol Problems in Party Package Travel

Morten Hesse, Sйbastien Tutenges, Sanna Schliewe, and Tine Reinholdt

INTRODUCTION

People traveling abroad tend to increase their use of alcohol and other drugs. In the present study we describe organized party activities in connection with young tourists' drinking, and the differences between young people traveling with and without organized party activities.

We conducted ethnographic observations and a cross-sectional survey in Sunny Beach, Bulgaria.

The behavior of the guides from two travel agencies strongly promoted heavy drinking, but discouraged illicit drug use. Even after controlling for several potential confounders, young people who traveled with such "party package travel agencies" were more likely to drink 12 or more units when going out. In univariate analyses, they were also more likely to get into fights, but were not more likely to seek medical assistance or medical assistance for an accident or an alcohol-related problem. After controlling for confounders, the association between type of travel agency and getting into fights was no longer significant. Short-term consequences of drinking in the holiday resort did not differ between party package travelers and ordinary package travelers.

There may be a small impact of party package travels on young people's drinking. Strategies could be developed used to minimize the harm associated with both party package travel and other kinds of travel where heavy substance use is likely to occur.

Millions of young people travel abroad on holiday for one or two weeks each year. A large proportion of these young travelers are attracted to resorts with a wild party scene and easy access to intoxicants [1].

A number of adverse health consequences have been observed from substance use in nightlife, including fights, accidents, and a range of other negative effects [2]. Heavy drinking in particular may lead to negative consequences, such as blackouts, personal injuries, and sudden death. Heavy drinking may also contribute to accidents, violence and rape [3], and be a risk factor for sexually transmitted diseases [4], and the development of alcohol dependence [5]. On the other hand, drinking alcohol in the Nordic culture has strong links with the perception of maturity and adulthood, and with drinking heavily and losing control [6].

Substance use undertaken in a foreign country has additional risks: language and geography are generally unfamiliar and this may obstruct access to health services, and individuals far from home are not held back by the constraints of work and family that normally moderate substance use [7]. Accordingly, a range of studies have identified amplified substance use in people on holidays abroad [8-10]. Young people who come to destinations attracted by the "party reputation" of a scene consume even more drugs and alcohol than other young people [4].

As shown by Bellis et al. [11], patterns of substance use differ in travelers going on different kinds of travels. For instance, young British travelers in Ibiza have an unusually high consumption of drugs whereas young British backpackers in Australia have an increased use of alcohol rather than drugs. But how do travel agents affect the use of intoxicants among travelers? And how can travel agents improve their strategies to minimize substance use and the harms associated with substance use? In this chapter, these questions will be treated by a case study of young Danish travelers going to the Bulgarian nightlife resort Sunny Beach (SB).

During the summer 2007, approximately 5,100 young Danes in the ages 16–30 years went to SB with party package agencies, according to information from the agencies. A probably similar but unknown number of young Danes traveled with traditional travel agencies. The Centre for Alcohol and Drug Research conducted a study of the drinking behavior of young Danes in SB during this period.

MATERIALS AND METHODS

Ethnographic Fieldwork

This study draws on ethnographic fieldwork conducted by one if the authors at SB in the period from June 19–August 12, 2007. Systematic observations were made in the daytime and nighttime at bars, discotheques, hotels, the beach, and other locations where Danish tourists and guides could be found. The observations were made overtly. They were written down on paper *in situ*, for instance while sitting at a bar desk. Shortly after they were completed and typed on a computer. As a complement to the observations, semi structured tape-recorded interviews were carried out with Danish tourists and guides. One to six persons were interviewed at a time. In all, 27 interviews were tape recorded with a total of 63 people, nine of whom were guides. In addition, we have scrutinized travel agents' web pages and made systematic assessments of the health problems in a selection of venues in SB.

Cross-sectional Survey

A cross-sectional survey was undertaken at Bourgas airport between July 4th and July 21, 2007. Tourists holidaying in SB mainly use this airport. The procedure and questionnaire were highly similar to the procedure used in studies at Ibiza by Bellis and colleagues [10, 12].

Research assistants were instructed to target young people, approximately 16–30 years old, and approach them while they were waiting to check in for their return flights to Denmark.

Only individuals returning to Denmark were asked to complete the short, anonymous questionnaire. Data collected included individuals' basic demographics and levels of substance use (alcohol, tobacco, illicit drugs) in Denmark and during the current holiday in SB. Individuals were also asked whether their parents were staying at SB, and which travel agency they were traveling with.

We collected questionnaires on 13 different days at a total of 30 flights. We strived to approach as many young people as possible at each flight. Researchers approached potential participants and asked if they had time to fill in a short questionnaire for a research project conducted by Aarhus University. Gender of those who refused was recorded. Consenting participants were then informed of the nature of the questionnaire, and if they refused at this stage, their gender was recorded.

Data collected included individuals' basic demographics, and levels of substance use (alcohol, tobacco, amphetamine, ketamine, cannabis, ecstasy, LSD, cocaine, and GHB) in Denmark and during the current holiday in SB. The questionnaire was similar in layout to the questionnaire used in the Ibiza surveys, [10], but due to the different nature of the party scene in SB, specific questions about ecstasy use were replaced by questions about binge drinking.

The questionnaire also contained true false items related to getting into fights, seeking medical assistance, and number of sexual partners. After the item about medical assistance ("Have you had to go to hospital or see a doctor whilst on this holiday"), the next part was labeled "If yes, what was this for?" This was followed by four boxes. These boxes were labeled "Drug related problem or accident," "Alcohol related problem or accident," "Other accident" and "Illness." In the following, we refer to seeking medical assistance as those who said yes to the item about medical assistance, and as seeking medical assistance for an alcohol related problem those who said yes to both the medical assistance item and the alcohol related problem.

The questionnaire contained questions about frequency of drinking broken into the following categories: drinking more than 6 units per day, drinking more than 12 units per day, and drinking to intoxication. Note that due to time restrictions of youth waiting to check in on a flight, we had limited time and space to explain concepts such as "alcohol unit". Therefore, the respondents' understanding of a unit may have varied. Moreover, drink sizes and contents vary substantially in the venues of SB. Some venues serve drinks with large amounts of alcohol, others serve drinks with low amounts of alcohol—it is almost impossible to taste the difference. Therefore, there is some uncertainty about the actual amount consumed.

Analyses of the Survey Data

Analysis utilized a combination of $\chi 2$, Spearman Rank order correlations, and ordinal regression analysis. As the main indicator of drinking, we used the proportion of days in SB, where subjects reported drinking 12 or more units of alcohol (number of days/days of drinking>12 units). This variable was recoded into three levels: Never, 1–5 days per week during the vacation, and 6–7 days during the vacation. As a secondary indicator, we used getting into fights during the stay at SB.

As predictors, we considered variables that were likely to attract young people to party package travel rather than to another type of travel. For example, tourists who reported that they had felt attracted to a resort by its party reputation might also select a travel agency advertising party activities. Therefore, an apparent association between traveling with a party package travel and drinking or fighting during the vacation might in fact represent an association between traveling with the intention of partying and the outcome, rather than a causal link between the type of travel and the outcome. We did not include drinking on the vacation as a predictor of outcomes, including fights, as drinking on the vacation would likely be a mediator rather than a confounder of outcomes.

Ethical Considerations

Institutional review boards in Denmark do not review studies unless medication is manipulated, or an invasive procedure is used. We do not believe that our study is in any way in violation of the declaration of Helsinki [13].

In the survey, tourists were informed of the nature and purposes of the study. In doing ethnographic fieldwork, it is not always possible to obtain informed consent from everyone with whom the researcher has contact, but ST who did the fieldwork, openly talked about his work during his stay in SB. During data collection in Bourgas airport, SS and TR wore t-shirts with a logo indicating that they were from the University of Aarhus.

Ethnographic Fieldwork

The SB is located on the Black Sea and attracts a large number of tourists, especially from Northern Europe, with its warm weather, long beach strip, low prices, and wild nightlife. Young tourists from Denmark going to SB basically choose between two types of travel agencies: "traditional agencies" that provide airfare and perhaps hotel lodging, sightseeing in the region and one or two evening activities during the week; and "party package agencies" offering flight, hotel, and a range of party activities during the week. One of the Danish party package agencies, for instance, had a "Party Power Package" with the following party activities during the week: "Welcome party", "Pub-Crawl", "Nachos Night", "Pool Party", and "Mega Pub Crawl". The party package agencies have trained guides who participate in the festivities day and night. They entertain with risqué shows, singing, dancing, competitions, and drinking games and assist in creating a permissive atmosphere with a clear focus on sex and drunkenness. The guides repeatedly invite tourists to drink heavily and act wildly with verbal instructions such as "bottoms up", "run amok!", "What happens at Sunny Beach stays at Sunny Beach" and so on. Already at the weekly welcome meetings, guides often emphasize that the newly arrived tourists should let go of their inhibitions. As one guide put it during an interview: "We tell them at our meeting to just let go. They should do whatever they want. It's their free choice because they have paid for their vacation. Down here there are no rules. So they should take advantage of that."

It should be added, that most of the Danish tourists that we have interviewed express a strong wish to indulge in wild behavior. Indeed, as the sociologist Maffesoli has argued, it seems that contemporary western youth have a strong and unbending urge for wildness [14]. The guides assist the tourists in overcoming their inhibitions and let lose. In addition to the use of verbal instructions, guides also purposively make use of loud music to lift the mood, they gather people in big crowds to intensify the festivities, and they encourage people to drink large amounts of alcohol. All this taken together constitutes a powerful constellation that can help tourists in moving far away from the norms and rules of everyday life and into a domain of experimentation and excess. The following field-notes illustrate some of the techniques that the guides employ to make people go wild.

The beer relay race begins after dinner. Three teams are formed, and each participant is supposed to run 15 m to a waiting guide who holds a large draft beer. The participant must down the beer, run five times around the guide, roll forward, run back and give way to the next in line. Everyone must take two turns, and drink two beers. The participants are overwhelmingly male. The guide says into the microphone: "Now we're gonna play a game we learned in Spain. We're gonna dig holes, so grab a shovel." He takes a break and laughs. There are four teams, each with three players. They are told to dig for 10 minutes. The guide with the microphone tells those not participating to come close and cheer. Some of the other guides encourage others nearby to "come watch, this is cool as hell". The diggers are given small shovels, and they really get to work. Some discuss tactics while digging. Others just give it their all. A female guide runs up to the bar: "Beer, beer, lots of beer." She walks around with a tray and serves the diggers, who are laboring under the relentless sun (ST's field notes July 19, 2007).

Thus, the guides actively encourage drinking and they also tend to take part in the drinking—both when they are on duty and when they are not.

On the other hand, the Danish party package agencies arrange meetings for newly arrived tourists where they call attention to some of the main risks in the nightlife of SB. The agencies all have 24-hours services with at least two sober guides who can be called upon in case of emergency. In case of severe accidents, the guides lend first aid, escort victims to the hospital and/or contact the police.

Thus, tourists traveling with Danish party package agencies always have Danish-speaking staff close at hand. Moreover, the party package agencies give wristbands to their customers indicating whom they are traveling with and giving access to an array of privileges such as free entrance to certain discotheques. Tourists who are caught taking illicit drugs have their wristbands taken away, and guides stress that they have a zero-tolerance policy with regard to illicit drugs. Although we have never observed this threat being carried out, the threat is repeated several times to travelers from the moment they arrive in the area.

The party package travel agents cooperate with local bars and discotheques in arranging party activities, and the venues earn considerable amounts of money on the oftentimes hundreds of big spending Danes that the party package agencies bring along. Therefore, venue owners are generally less accepting of security guards' abusive or violent behavior against guests wearing the wristband. And violent guards are a real problem in SB; that is during the summer 2007, a Swedish tourist was beaten to death by local security guards.

SURVEY

Sample Description

On the 13 days, we approached a total of 1,238 subjects. A total of 87 women and 197 men refused (26%). Those who indicated that they had time were then informed of the nature of the questionnaire (n = 1068), and among these compliance was 95% (n = 1011). The respondents were 55% male, and the mean age was 19.9 years (range: 13 to 34, standard deviation [SD] = 3.1). The mean number of days spent in SB was 7.8 (range: 1–15, SD = 2.2). At total of 18.1% traveled with a long-term partner, 11.9% with their parents, 2.0% with both partner and parents, and 71.6% with neither. Due to missing data, the number of subjects included in each analysis was reduced for particular analyses, as indicated below.

A total of 55 subjects did not report what agency they were traveling with. An approximately equal number of respondents came to SB with a party package travel (n = 450) as a regular package travel agent (n = 506). Subjects going with party package travel agents were more likely to be men ($\chi2(1) = 8.90$, $p = 0.003$), and were younger than those traveling with other package travel agents (mean for party package travelers: 19.2 years, standard deviation (SD) = 1.9; others: 20.6, SD = 3.8, $t = -7.5$, $p < 0.0001$). Travelers going with party package travel agents were also much more likely to have been attracted to SB by the place's party reputation (68.0% vs. 32.1%, $\chi2(1) = 121.2$, $p < 0.0001$), and drank more frequently in Denmark (on an ordinal scale from 0 to 8, where 0 is never, and 8 is "5 or more times per week," Mann Whitney U test, $Z = 5.12$, $p < 0.00001$).

Univariate Analyses

We first analyzed whether tourists traveling with companies offering no party activities (n = 236) differed from tourists traveling with one or two weekly party activities (n = 236), and from tourists traveling with agencies with more than two parties a week (n = 388). When comparing those from companies with no party activities with those with one or two party activities, we found no statistically significant difference in drinking 12 or more units ($\chi2(2) = 2.00$, $p = 0.37$). We therefore decided to treat all those traveling with agencies offering fewer than three parties per week as one category.

Among party package travelers, 58.8% drank 12 or more units 6–7 days per week during their stay in SB, 29.4% drank 12 or more units 1–5 days per week, and 11.9% never drank 12 or more units. Among other travelers, 26.5% drank 12 or more units 6–7 days per week during their stay in SB, 29.4% drank 12 or more units 1–5 days per week, and 43.4% never drank 12 or more units. The difference was statistically significant ($\chi2(2) = 126.8$, $p < 0.0001$, $N = 860$). Very few travelers with any kind of agency used illicit drugs in SB, and the difference was not significant (3.3% of party package travelers vs. 2.1% of travelers with other agencies, $\chi2(1) = 0.73$, $p = 0.39$).

Party package travelers were also more likely to get into fights (12.4% of party package travelers, 5.5% of other travelers, $\chi2(1) = 13.9$, $p = 0.00019$).

The associations with other indicators of alcohol-related harm, including seeking medical treatment (7.8% of party package travelers vs. 5.5% of other travelers, $N = 929$, $\chi2(1) = 1.98$, $p = 0.16$), seeking medical treatment for an alcohol-related problem (1.6% of party package travelers, 0.9% of other travelers, $\chi2(1) = 1.23$, $p = 0.27$), or for another accident (3.2% of party package travelers, 2.2% of other travelers, $\chi2(1) = 0.83$, $p = 0.36$) were not significant.

Thus, there were strong indications that party package travelers were heavier drinkers than other travelers. However, to test the impact of potential confounders on drinking on the location we next decided to conduct an ordinal regression.

Ordinal Regression Analyses

The ordinal regression analyses were carried out controlling for several confounders, including gender, age, frequency of drinking in Denmark, whether young people were traveling with their parents, traveling with a partner, and whether they reported being attracted to SB by the resort's party reputation.

For drinking 12 or more units per day, both the Spearman rank order correlations and the results of the ordinal regression are shown in Table 1.

Table 1. Associations between predictors and heavy drinking (n = 760).

	Spearman rank-order correlation	Coefficient	Standard error	z	P > z	Lower 95% Conf. Interval	Higher 95% Conf. Interval
Male gender	***0.43	1.80	0.17	10.31	0.000	1.45	2.14
Age	0.02	–0.03	0.03	–1.07	0.284	–0.08	0.02
Travelling with parents	***–0.43	–2.00	0.30	–6.61	0.000	–2.60	–1.41
Staying +7 days	***–0.30	–0.09	0.20	–0.46	0.648	–0.47	0.29
Attracted by party reputation	***0.19	1.48	0.18	8.22	0.000	1.13	1.83
Frequency of drinking at home	***0.50	0.35	0.06	6.02	0.000	0.24	0.46
Travelling with party package travel	***0.38	0.38	0.19	1.98	0.048	0.00	0.75
Travelling with partner	***–0.41	–1.95	0.24	–8.28	0.000	–2.41	–1.49

The regression analysis for frequency of drinking 12 or more units could be conducted for 757 respondents. The statistics for the analysis indicated that the model added information over an intercept only (likelihood ratio $\chi2(8) = 537.90$, $p < 0.001$, pseudo $R^2 = 0.33$).

Going with a party package travel agent was significantly associated with heavy drinking (coefficient = 0.38, z = 1.98, p = 0.048). Also associated with heavy drinking was male gender ($p < 0.001$), being attracted to the area by its party reputation ($p < 0.001$), and frequency of drinking in Denmark ($p < 0.001$). Traveling with parents ($p < 0.001$) and a long-term partner ($p < 0.001$) were both associated with a decreased risk of heavy drinking.

For getting into fights, both the Spearman rank order correlations and the results of the logistic regression are shown in Table 2.

The regression analysis for frequency of getting into fights could be conducted for 815 respondents. The statistics for the analysis indicated that the model added information over an intercept only (likelihood ratio $\chi2(8) = 36.15$, $p < 0.001$, pseudo $R2 = 0.08$).

Going with a party package travel agent was not associated with getting into fights (p = 0.332), but male gender was (p = 0.002). Trends were found for lower risk of getting into fights with higher age (p = 0.050), and traveling with a partner (p = 0.051). Since we did not find that choosing a party package travel agent was associated with getting into fights after controlling for confounders, we did not attempt to analyze whether there was an indirect effect from party package travel to fights mediated through heavier drinking.

Table 2. Associations between predictors and getting into a fight: spearman rank order correlations and logistic regression (N = 819).

	Spearman rank-order correlation	Coefficient	SE	z	Probability	Lower 95% Conf. Interval	Higher 95% Conf. Interval
Male gender	–0.05	–0.12	0.06	–1.96	0.050	–0.23	0.00
Age	***0.15	0.93	0.30	3.08	0.002	0.34	1.52
Travelling with parents	–0.04	–0.22	0.54	–0.41	0.678	–1.28	0.84
Staying +7 days	–0.05	–0.30	0.38	–0.79	0.430	–1.06	0.45
Attracted by party reputation	**0.10	0.20	0.29	0.67	0.500	–0.37	0.76
Frequency of drinking at home	0.09	0.05	0.09	0.57	0.569	–0.12	0.22
Travelling with party package travel	**0.12	0.30	0.31	0.97	0.332	–0.31	0.91
Travelling with partner	–0.13	–1.23	0.63	–1.95	0.051	–2.45	0.00

DISCUSSION

The main result of this study was that going with a party package travel agency was associated with higher frequencies of heavy drinking. The majority of young people traveling with a party package agency drank 12 or more units daily or almost daily during their vacation, and the association held after controlling for several known important confounders, including gender, drinking frequency in Denmark, traveling with a partner or parent, and being attracted to SB by the party reputation of the resort. The associations with acute adverse side effects of going with a party package travel on the other hand were modest, and did not hold after controlling for potential confounders.

Those traveling with party package travels differed from those traveling with other types of agencies in terms of their behavior at home, and it seems very likely that the marketing of party package travels attracts tourists who are looking for a vacation with opportunities for drinking and going out in the nightlife. Thus, whether party package travels causally influence drinking is not established. Our data suggest that they may causally contribute, but that the influence may be small.

Strengths and Limitations

The strengths of this study include an adequate sample size, a high acceptance rate, and the use of on-site ethnographic fieldwork to aid the interpretations of the survey data.

A limitation of this study was the use of cross-sectional data to measure events retrospectively. For instance, respondents' self-reports of their drinking behavior and their motives for going on the vacation may have been influenced by their experiences during the vacation. Also, their recollection of the actual drinking behavior may have been biased in a number of ways. Respondents who have consumed more than 12 drinks in a night may have suffered a blackout and failed to remember events, such as being in a fight or having been taken to a doctor.

Also, the amount of data that was collected about each respondent was limited. It was our belief that it would be difficult to engage people who were about to board a plane after a vacation in completing a long questionnaire over several pages.

We did not find any differences between party package travelers and other travelers in terms of adverse outcomes associated with heavy drinking. While, we have previously shown that heavy drinking was associated with getting into fights and seeking medical help for an alcohol-related problem, the sensitivity of these items as indicators of heavy drinking is unknown, and potentially low.

Another limitation is that we cannot rule out that pre-existing differences other than those controlled for in the regression analyses were responsible for the differences found in drinking, rather than the party program and behavior of guides. This limitation will apply to any non-experimental design.

Also, we cannot disentangle the effects of different aspects of the "party package program", for instance pub-crawls, parties, drinking games, foam parties, and the specific weight of the guides' behavior, and the net effect of being at a party where most of the other guests also are drinking heavily.

Opportunities for Harm Reduction?

In terms of preventing drug and alcohol-related harm some interesting questions arise in connection with the role of party package travel agents and their guides. Clearly, the amount of alcohol consumed is higher among the party package travelers. This may be a result of the binge-oriented parties organized by party package agencies. Or it may be because the party package agencies attract youth with a penchant for heavy drinking. Our data give no compelling evidence of higher short-term harm associated with drinking among party package travelers. We have observed on the scene that the guides have high esteem among the young people. They have non-drinking guides with first-help equipment available, and they crack down on illicit drug use. The guides have an ambiguous role: they actively encourage heavy drinking and they try to prevent harm among the tourists.

But does the guides' behavior function as effective harm reduction to an extent that offsets the negative consequences of the increased alcohol consumption of those traveling with party package travel agents? Do they contribute to the overall very low prevalence of illicit drug use? And is there a potential way of intervening in the context of the SB party scene, to make better use of the "on the spot party guides" as harm reducing agents?

The party scene in SB differs from Denmark in specific ways. It is much more unsafe to walk around alone or in small groups while intoxicated; assaults, robberies, and rapes against tourists are reported in high numbers. Certain areas are particularly dangerous to access after dark, such as the beach. When intoxicated young people take taxies at night, drivers often demand extreme prices upon arrival at the destination, harass customers and try to sell illegal drugs. The doormen and security staff can be violent and erratic in their behavior; the police are not an authority to be trusted. All these factors mean that the things young people do at home to take care of themselves when intoxicated, like taking a taxi rather than walking home or contacting the police when in trouble, are behaviors that could be dangerous in SB [15]. Guides do inform young people of necessary security measures, and simply by being in large groups can protect tourists from many threats.

On the other hand, most of Danish guides are young and also participate in the party scene and for consecutive weeks. Even when, the guides are not intoxicated while on duty they are marked by a prolonged period of sleep deprivation and substantial alcohol consumption. In that respect, they may not be the ideal harm reduction advocates. The guides warn tourists against drug use, but they also have a clear tendency to downplay the many dangers of heavy drinking.

Another strategy to prevent harm would be to prohibit the sale of party package travels to young people under the legal drinking age. In Denmark, the legal age for drinking in bars and restaurants is 18 years, and it would seem consistent to prohibit selling pub-crawls with alcohol to young people aged less than 18 years for instance. As always, potential harm reduction should be weighted against the potential benefits of having guides available for the young people who do drink while on vacation. In general, guides could do more to warn against the negative effects of heavy drinking and give advice about how to limit some of these negative effects—for instance by emphasizing that it is vital to eat food and drink sufficient amounts of water. Guides should also avoid encouraging heavy drinking and instead shift their focus to other party activities such as dancing and non-alcoholic party games and competitions.

Obviously, travel agencies are not interested in over-stating the dangers at travel destinations or in appearing to be preaching from a "moral high ground", but with the right dialogue between authorities and agencies, agencies could be motivated to make a stronger effort. This dialogue should also involve the local Bulgarian authorities, who could do a much better job in reducing the alarming crime rates in the Bulgarian nightlife resorts.

CONCLUSION

Young people going with party package travel agencies drink more than visitors traveling with other travel package agencies, but the difference is small when controlling for other confounders. The behaviors of guides constitute a mixture of risk-inducing encouragement of drinking and harm reduction promotion. The situation at holiday resorts calls for harm reduction measures.

KEYWORDS

- **Demographics**
- **Ethnographic**
- **Illicit drugs**
- **Univariate analyses**

AUTHORS' CONTRIBUTIONS

Sébastien Tutenges and Morten Hesse planned the quantitative study and adopted the questionnaire from Mark Bellis' and Karen Hughes' original questionnaire. Sébastien Tutenges planned the ethnographic study. Sébastien Tutenges, Sanna Schliewe, and Tine Reinholdt collected the questionnaires and carried out the ethnographic observations. Morten Hesse drafted the manuscript and carried out the statistical analyses. Sébastien Tutenges drafted the sections about the ethnographic data, and all authors read and discussed the chapter and approved the final manuscript.

ACKNOWLEDGMENTS

The questionnaire used for the study was kindly provided by Karen Hughes.

COMPETING INTERESTS

The authors declare that they have no competing interests.

Chapter 4

Cumulative Incidence of Novel Influenza A/H1N1 in Foreign Travelers

Marc Lipsitch, Martin Lajous, Justin J. O'Hagan, Ted Cohen, Joel C. Miller, Edward Goldstein, Leon Danon, Jacco Wallinga, Steven Riley, Scott F. Dowell, Carrie Reed, and Meg McCarron

INTRODUCTION

An accurate estimate of the total number of cases and severity of illness of an emerging infectious disease is required both to define the burden of the epidemic and to determine the severity of disease. When a novel pathogen first appears, affected individuals with severe symptoms are more likely to be diagnosed. Accordingly, the total number of cases will be underestimated and disease severity overestimated. This problem is manifest in the current epidemic of novel influenza A/H1N1.

We used a simple approach to leverage measures of incident influenza A/H1N1 among a relatively small and well observed group of US, UK, Spanish, and Canadian travelers who had visited Mexico to estimate the incidence among a much larger and less well surveyed population of Mexican residents. We estimate that a minimum of 113,000–375,000 cases of novel influenza A/H1N1 have occurred in Mexicans during the month of April, 2009. Such an estimate serves as a lower bound because it does not account for underreporting of cases in travelers or for nonrandom mixing between Mexican residents and visitors, which together could increase the estimates by more than an order of magnitude.

We find that the number of cases in Mexican residents may exceed the number of confirmed cases by two to three orders of magnitude. While, the extent of disease spread is greater than previously appreciated, our estimate suggests that severe disease is uncommon since the total number of cases is likely to be much larger than those of confirmed cases.

A reliable estimate of the cumulative number of infections for an emerging disease, such as novel influenza A/H1N1, is critical to determine both the magnitude of the problem and the severity of disease. Cumulative incidence is the most direct estimate of the magnitude of the epidemic, while cumulative deaths and hospitalizations must be divided by cumulative incidence (with appropriate correction for reporting delays and censoring [1]) to estimate the probability of severe outcomes for individuals that become infected. While critical for situational awareness, cumulative incidence is often difficult to measure in a large epidemic, because often there is a bias toward ascertainment of severe cases.

Where underreporting of asymptomatic and mild cases, especially those that do not present for medical care, is likely, there is a need for nonstandard approaches to estimate the magnitude of the epidemic and severity of disease. Here we propose and apply such a method to estimate the number of cases of novel influenza A/H1N1 in Mexico up to approximately April 30, 2009, based on the number of cases observed in foreign travelers. Intuitively, the notion is that such travelers act as "canaries in the mine" who briefly experience the daily risk of infection prevalent in Mexico during their visit, then return home to areas where, given the elevated level of concern, they may be detected as cases of novel H1N1, even if not severe. By assuming (conservatively) that the risk of infection experienced by Mexicans is at least equal to that experienced by visitors, and using travel data to assess the amount of person-time at risk for visitors, we estimate the incidence rate in proportion to the Mexican population, and estimate a lower-bound of how many cases may have been present in Mexico at a defined time.

Here we estimate that at least 113,000–375,000 cases of novel H1N1 influenza occurred in Mexicans before the end of April, 2009. We discuss the uncertainties associated with this estimate and present our rationale for why this number represents a lower bound for the true number. Finally, we discuss the implications for estimating the case-fatality proportion of this infection in Mexico.

Baseline Estimate

We estimate that approximately 375,000 Mexicans were infected with novel H1N1 influenza with symptom onset up to approximately April 30, 2009. This estimate derives from 283 cases among US, UK, Spanish, and Canadian travelers, counting confirmed and probable cases for the US and confirmed cases only for the other two countries. Citizens of these countries together accounted for approximately 689,250 airplane passenger visits to Mexico in the period April 1–30, 2009, and international visitors to Mexico had a mean length of stay of approximately 3.5 days, for a total of 2.4 million person-days of exposure during this period (Table 1). This implies that visitors experienced an incidence rate of 191 cases per million person-days at risk. In the same period, the Mexican population of approximately 107 million persons had 30×107 million, or 3.2 billion person-days of exposure.

Table 1. Cases of novel influenza A/H1N1 among travelers to Mexico from three countries as of May 6, 2009 (Canada) or May 8, 2009 (US, UK, Spain) and associated estimates.

	US (confirmed+probable)	Canada (confirmed)	UK (confirmed)	Spain (confirmed)	Total
Cases with Mexico travel history	132	62	19	70	283
Cases with travel history known/ total cases	928/1890	86/179	37/38	93/93	
With only one case per possible cluster, and near border cases removed	85	56	17	no data to assess clusters; 70 assumed	228
Travel volume for April	526,861	119,473	22,013	20,903	668,347
Inferred incidence rate (/million person-days)*	72	148	246	957	117
Inferred cases in Mexico	229,000	475,000	789,000	3,062,000	375,000
Inferred incidence rate (/million person-days)*	18	44	55	241	35
Inferred cases in Mexico*	*59,000*	*142,000*	*178,000*	*771,000*	*113,000*

Sensitivity Analysis: Unknown Travel History

Travel history was known for 49% (929/1890) of US confirmed cases and 48% (86/179) of Canadian confirmed cases, 97% (37/38) of the UK cases and 100% (93/93) of Spanish cases. If the proportion of cases with travel history to Mexico is assumed to be the same for those with missing data in this field, the imputed number of total cases with travel history would rise to 418, and the implied number of cases in Mexicans would rise to 554,000. We strongly suspect that travel history is more likely to be known in those who did travel to Mexico than in those who did not, which would suggest that the correction for missing travel history should be somewhat less than assumed here. We therefore do not include this large estimate in our overall range of estimates.

Sensitivity analysis: possible clusters among travelers, and border state cases

Several cases among travelers may have resulted from clusters of exposure and/or from transmission within the traveling group. In order to exclude the effects of transmission among travelers or cases of disease imported by means other than air travel, we provide a revised estimate calculated from a subset of 228 cases. This reduced number of cases excludes both secondary cases within putative clusters of travelers (these data were available for travelers from each country except Spain) and excludes US cases residing in or south of the closest major city to the Mexican border who may have visited by means other than air travel. This approach yields an estimate of 302,000 cases in Mexicans; additional correction for clustering in Spanish cases, if the required data were available, would further reduce this figure.

Sensitivity Analysis: Length of Stay

For reasons discussed below, we believe that 3.5 days is an appropriate estimate for the mean duration of stay in Mexico for all visitors, which heavily weights US visitors because the US is the largest source of visitors. However, given that one study suggests a considerably longer length of stay [2], and that non-US visitors likely stay longer given the longer trip involved, we performed a sensitivity analysis assuming that visitors from the US, Canada, and European countries have lengths of stay of 8.7, 10.5, and 13.9 days respectively, using numbers from an unpublished 2008 update of the 2001–05 survey (Gerardo Vazquez, Mexico Ministry of Tourism, personal communication). Using the data with possible clusters and near-border cases removed, produces a low estimate of 113,000 cases in Mexican residents.

Sensitivity Analysis: Non-homogeneous Disease Across Mexico

This analysis assumes that incidence during April was homogeneous across 107 million Mexicans. If the rates of disease among Mexicans in travel destinations was higher or lower than elsewhere, this might substantially alter these estimates. The national cumulative incidence of suspect cases as of May 9 was 17.32/100,000, which was 16x higher than that in Puebla, the state with the lowest incidence, and 4x lower than that in Distrito Federal, the capital, with the highest reported incidence. Quintana Roo, the state containing Cancun, which is the most popular single destination for travelers from these countries, reported incidence of 12.10/100,000. If these incidence numbers reflect true incidence variation in the country (which is unlikely to be the only source of variation), then total Mexican incidence should be 1.4 times higher than that estimated from Cancun travelers, or 4x lower than that estimated for Mexico City travelers. Unfortunately, destination data are not available for the majority of travel-associated cases in any of the four countries we considered.

DISCUSSION

We have estimated that there are likely to have been at least 113,000–375,000 cases of novel H1N1 influenza among Mexicans with onset during the month of April, 2009. Taking into account what we consider to be extreme sensitivity analyses, this estimate could change by approximately 2-fold in either direction. This exceeds the number of confirmed cases reported to WHO, 1204 as of May 8, 2009 (http://www.who.int/csr/don/GlobalSubnationalMaster_20090508_1815.jpg), by a factor of approximately 100 or more.

It is unsurprising that we estimate a larger number than the number of cases confirmed in Mexico, since ascertainment there has been particularly focused on severe cases. Nevertheless, we regard this estimate as likely a lower bound on the actual number of cases in Mexico, for two principal reasons. First, the analytic approach assumes that the incidence rate in Mexicans in Mexico is equal to that in travelers. If indeed the infection has been transmitting extensively within Mexico, one would expect that the exposure of travelers to the virus would be somewhat less than that of residents, due to nonrandom mixing between residents and travelers; travelers should be less exposed to residents than other residents are. Prior models of influenza transmission (set in the US) have assumed that 36–51% of influenza transmission takes place outside of home or school [3]. One might roughly estimate that this is the proportion of transmission to which both visitors and residents would be exposed, suggesting that incidence in residents might be 2–3x as high as that in visitors; however, this approach has obvious limitations given the uncertainty of those estimates and the fact that they were made for a different country.

Second, while most cases ascertained in the traveler population to date have been mild, one nonetheless expects that many mild cases (as well as probable but unconfirmed cases) in travelers are absent from our calculations. A survey in New York City, where case ascertainment was aggressive surrounding the St. Francis School outbreak, indicated that over 1,000 persons associated with the school experienced influenza-like illness, in a period where only 74 confirmed or probable cases were ascertained. If these figures reflect the typical rate of under-reporting in the US, then the inferred figures from Mexico should increase by >1000/74 = 14-fold. Likewise, any foreign residents who became ill in Mexico (rather than in their home country) may have been missed in our counts of travelers. In essence, the method used here is a way to estimate cases in a population where they are likely being undercounted, based on travelers to countries in which undercounting, though present, is less severe. Since the inferred number of cases in Mexican residents scales linearly with the number observed in travelers, the number in Mexican residents is likely to be considerably higher than we have estimated.

Forty-eight deaths were observed up to May 9 among laboratory-confirmed cases in Mexico [4]. While it might be tempting to calculate a case-fatality proportion by dividing this number by the estimated number of cases in Mexico, such a calculation would likely be misleading, for several reasons. In a growing epidemic, given a significant delay from illness onset to death [5], one expects to underestimate the case-fatality proportion as the deaths reflect cases from an earlier, smaller phase of the epidemic [6]. Also, counting only laboratory confirmed deaths is likely to result in a significant underestimation of the true number of deaths, because of insensitivity depending on the timing and adequacy of the specimen, the fact that many severe pneumonia patients were not tested (approximately 1,000–2,000 such cases typically occur in Mexico in April [7]), and the fact that a majority of influenza deaths are attributed to circulatory causes rather than identified as pneumonia or influenza [8]. Nonetheless, as the number of deaths accumulates, especially if illness onset dates are available for fatal cases, our estimates may provide an appropriate denominator for revised estimates of the case-fatality proportion. The number of hospitalizations associated with suspect cases was 6,754 as of May 9 [4], which combines with our denominator to give a hospitalization proportion of about 2%, closer to figures observed elsewhere.

We have shown in Table 1 the estimates obtained using only travelers from each country individually. Here, the US-based estimates are the lowest, with greater estimates from those based on Canadians and still greater estimates based on Europeans. In part this may reflect a longer duration of trips for travelers from more distant destinations, but even using the destination-specific duration data does not remove this effect. As we note below, we cannot rule out the possibility that some transmission occurred on airplanes; such transmission might be more likely in travelers flying longer distances. Differences in patterns of exposure within Mexico, chance variation and other factors must account for the remaining differences.

This simple model has several principal limitations. First, we do not incorporate exposure of travelers who arrive by ship or overland, only by air. While we have excluded from the numerator the one traveler case with a known cruise ship exposure, we may have slightly overestimated the incidence in travelers by neglecting such exposures. Second, our calculations make the assumption that incidence is uniform geographically throughout Mexico and across age group. All but one state in Mexico have now reported cases (http://portal.salud.gob.mx/sites/salud/descargas/pdf/influenza/situacion_actual070511.pdf), and all have at least suspect cases [3], so it is likely reasonable to assume that persons throughout Mexico were exposed to some extent. However, the exposure may not have been uniform. This may be a further reason to consider our estimate as a lower bound, since the detected cases are heavily concentrated in the State of Mexico and the Distrito Federal, the destination of <18% of visitors from these countries, while the most popular airport of entry for visitors from the US, UK, and Canada in April, 2009 was Cancun, which accounted for 47.5%–74.5% of visitors for each nationality but had relatively low reported incidence. As the pandemic has evolved, it has become clear that different age groups experience different risks of confirmed and probable infection with the pandemic virus, with the highest rates of confirmed and probable infection among persons under 25 years old (http://www.cdc.gov/h1n1flu/surveillanceqa.htm). Finally, we assume that transmission to travelers occurred in Mexico, not on an aircraft. An influenza outbreak on an aircraft has been documented [9], and if a cluster of such infections were included in our numbers, it would result in an overestimate of incidence in Mexico. Notably, 36% of travel-associated cases in Spain for whom data were available were symptomatic during the inbound flight; given the incubation period of influenza, these travelers, at least, could not plausibly have become infected during the flight [10].

Our estimates of cases are larger, by about 10-fold, than those reported by Fraser et al. [11]. Importantly, this reflects the fact that we base ascertainment on numbers available on May 6–8, while Fraser et al. base ascertainment on numbers available on April 30. With rapid epidemic growth, the difference of one week is likely to account for a difference of perhaps 2-8-fold. Also, Fraser et al. use a longer mean length of stay (9 days) and a larger travel volume. Estimates of the length of stay cited by Fraser et al. [11] were close to 9 days in 2001–05 [2], and we have considered a sensitivity analysis based on an updated version of that survey, using numbers specific to origin of the travelers. For our primary analysis, however, we used figures from the Ministry of Tourism indicating a mean length of stay of 3.4 days (see Materials and Methods), while an independent study conducted by the National Association of Hotels and Motels finds a similar value of 3.6 days for the mean length of hotel stay by foreign visitors, and a very recent survey found that the majority of US leisure travelers interested in visiting Mexico take vacations for 4 nights or less (personal communication). Our travel volumes are lower in part because we have used citizenship rather than first destination outside Mexico (to better reflect likely final destination) and have used data on number of incoming passengers (corrected to estimate outgoing passengers) rather than flight data, which may perhaps reflect capacities rather than actual numbers. Altogether, these differences in data sources could account for approximately a 3-fold variation in estimates, apart from the variation due to different time periods considered.

Accurate estimation of the magnitude of an emerging epidemic is essential for maintaining situational awareness and determining a rational public health response. The simple approach applied here indicates that the likely number of cases of H1N1 influenza among Mexican residents during the month of April, 2009 was at least two orders of magnitude larger than that detected. While such calculations should not be interpreted as precise estimates of cumulative incidence, they provide important perspective in interpreting data from detected cases in situations where extensive surveillance is unlikely to occur.

MATERIALS AND METHODS

Data Sources

Cases in Travelers

Cases ascertained in the US in travelers were obtained from the US CDC (Centers for Disease Control) line list dated May 8 at 0100 EDT (Eastern Daylight Time), reflecting cases reported up to May 7. Possible clusters of traveler cases were detected by manual scan of the line list for cases with common county of report, closely related onset dates, and no indication that they lived in different households. Cases ascertained in

Canada in travelers were obtained from a copy of the Canadian line list dated May 6 residing at the US CDC. Possible clusters of traveler cases were noted on the line list itself. Cases ascertained in the UK in travelers were obtained from a comprehensive scan of press reports cross-checked with UK Health Protection Agency daily updates to ensure consistency of numbers, and possible clusters were ascertained the same way. One case from the United States known to be in a woman visiting Mexico on a cruise ship was excluded since cruise ship visitors were not included in our travel estimates. The number of cases in travelers was denoted U. Use of line lists from 6–8 days after our period of interest was selected because for those entering the US CDC line list, the mean delay from symptom onset was 7 days. Hence, the US data, which represented the majority of cases, should be representative of cases with onset in the period up to April 30. The number of cases from Spain was taken from the recent report produced by the Surveillance Group in Spain [10].

Person-time at Risk

The Mexican population was assumed to be P_M = 106,682,518 persons as estimated by the National Council for Population of Mexico (http://www.conapo.gob.mx/index.php?option=com_content&view=article&id=125&Itemid=193). Estimates of the number of travelers returning from Mexico during the period April 1–30 were obtained using data from Mexican immigration records deposited in the Sistema Integral de Operación Migratoria (SIOM). This database contains information on the citizenship of all travelers arriving into Mexican airports. Assuming that the populations of inbound and outbound travelers from Mexico are in near-steady state the number of inbound travelers should give a reliable estimate of the number of outbound travelers. Records were abstracted for the period April 1–30. Note that our method is not strongly sensitive to the exact period considered, since additional days would proportionately increase the person-time for Mexican residents and approximately proportionately increase the person-time for visitors. We did not decrement the person-time to account for time no longer at risk once a Mexican resident was infected.

The number of Canadian, British, and Spanish travelers arriving into Mexico began to drop off on April 27th, likely in response to the media coverage of the outbreak, while the number of US travelers to Mexico began to decrease on April 26th. As it is unlikely that the number of outbound travelers decreased over this period we calculated the average number of travelers arriving into Mexico for each day of the week using data for the first three weeks of April. These estimates were used instead of the actual daily numbers of travelers for the latter days of April. The total number of travelers into Mexico was denoted P_t. The mean duration of stay was assumed to be D = 3.5 days. This was based on a mean stay of 3.6 days from survey data for hotel stays in April, 2009 from the National Association of Hotels and Motels of Mexico (personal communication) and on a mean stay of 3.4 days from survey data posted by the Mexican Tourism Ministry (http://www.sectur.gob.mx/wb/secturing/sect_8978_study_of__tourist_pr). In addition, a survey of a representative sample of US leisure travelers interested in visiting Mexico conducted in February and March of 2009 found that 74% of all vacations taken by this group were 4 nights or less (P. Yesawich, National Leisure Travel Monitor, personal communication).

Alternative estimates obtained from a 2008 Bank of Mexico tourism survey (Gerardo Vazquez, Mexico Ministry of Tourism, personal communication) an earlier version of which was used by Fraser et al. [11] give longer durations of stay overall and indicate heterogeneity by nationality in length of stay: 8.7 nights for US citizens, 10.5 nights for Canadians and 13.9 nights for others. These estimates were used in a sensitivity analysis. We note that with a typical incubation period of about 1–2 days for influenza A [13], individuals infected early on in a stay of two weeks would have been sick for a week or more before returning home, at which point they might have stopped shedding detectable virus. Our estimates are based on infections confirmed in the country to which a traveler returned, and would therefore tend to miss many such infections, suggesting that only a fraction of such a long stay would be "at risk" for the event of infection detected upon return.

ANALYSIS

If the incidence rate in Mexicans were times that in visitors, then the following equality should hold, relating the incidence rate in each population:

$$x\frac{U}{DP_t} = \frac{M}{30P_M},$$

where in the month of April each Mexican had 30 days at risk, and each visitor had D days at risk on average. Estimates for each quantity except for M, the unknown number of incident cases in Mexican residents, were provided from data, under the conservative assumption that $x = 1$, and the equation was solved for M. The major statistical uncertainty in our estimates comes from the number of visitors who were infected, which as a count with a value of 283 should have a coefficient of variation of 6%, negligible compared to the uncertainties of underreporting and differences in exposure of the visitor and resident populations. For this reason, statistical uncertainty was not explicitly quantified in our estimates.

KEYWORDS

- **Incubation period**
- **Novel influenza**
- **Pneumonia**
- **Putative clusters**
- **Symptomatic**

AUTHORS' CONTRIBUTIONS

Conceived and designed the experiments: Marc Lipsitch, Joel C. Miller, Steven Riley, and Scott F. Dowell. Performed the experiments: Marc Lipsitch. Analyzed the data: Marc Lipsitch, Justin J. O'Hagan, Ted Cohen, Joel C. Miller, Edward Goldstein, Leon Danon, Jacco Wallinga, Carrie Reed, and Meg McCarron. Wrote the chapter: Marc

Lipsitch. Obtained the data: Martin Lajous, Justin J. O'Hagan, Carrie Reed, and Meg McCarron.

ACKNOWLEDGMENTS

We thank Lyn Finelli, Martin Cetron, and David Shay for assistance in initiating this project, and Neil Ferguson for helpful comments. We also thank Gerardo Vazquez from the Ministry of Tourism, Mexico, Luis Barrios from City Express Hotels, Alejandro Vazquez from Posadas Hotels and Peter Yesawich from Ypartnership for providing length of stay data.

Chapter 5

Health, Parks, Recreation, and Tourism

Kelly S. Bricker, Jessica Leahy, Dave Smaldone, Andrew Mowen, and Chad Pierskalla

INTRODUCTION

Presented by Kelly S. Bricker

Over the past few years, there has been increased awareness of the connection between health and outdoor recreation and a proliferation of alliances, partnerships, and statewide efforts to promote the health benefits of outdoor recreation (Memorandum of Understanding (MOU)) [1, 2]. The alliances formed underscore the relevance of outdoor recreation in promoting healthy lifestyles, healthy environments, and healthy communities. As a result, many initiatives are underway to connect the outdoors to a healthier lifestyle. This progressive movement is exemplified by the following cooperative efforts.

In 2002, several federal agencies created a MOU to promote public health and recreation: the Department of Health and Human Services, including the Centers for Disease Control and Prevention (CDC), Indian Health Services, and the Office of Public Health and Science; the Department of Agriculture, including the U.S. Forest Service and the Center for Nutrition Policy and Promotion; the Department of Interior, including the Bureau of Indian Affairs, Bureau of Land Management, Bureau of Reclamation, Fish and Wildlife Service, and National Park Service; and the Department of the Army, Army Corps of Engineers. The purpose of the MOU was to establish a general framework for cooperation among these agencies. Through the MOU, they agreed to work together to promote the uses and benefits of the Nation's public lands and water resources to enhance the physical and psychological health and well-being of the American people.

Progress to date includes a range of initiatives and findings:

- The CDC has collaborated with the American Hiking Society to promote trails and health, and to publicize National Trails Day in June 2008;
- A growing body of research has demonstrated that people in activity-friendly environments are more likely to be physically active in their leisure time;
- The National Recreation and Park Association and the Sajai Foundation have joined forces to develop a science-based curriculum called Sajai Wise Kids that teaches children about making healthy nutrition and activity choices.

The roundtable discussion summarized current initiatives related to health, parks, and recreation. The following are examples of other initiatives and programs and how they are transcending boundaries in the formation of new and exciting partnerships.

HEALTH, RECREATION, AND OUR NATIONAL PARKS

Co-presented by Dave Smaldone and Jessica Leahy

As part of the increasing focus on improving individual health, the Healthier U.S. initiative proposed in 2002 by President Bush promoted the use of public lands to improve personal health by encouraging the use of these lands for physical activity. In 2006, each National Park partnered with a university researcher and a variety of stakeholder organizations to design and implement interventions with one or more of the following three broad goals: (1) to increase park users' awareness of the health benefits derived from recreation in National Parks; (2) to increase healthful recreation/physical activity behaviors in National Parks; and (3) to increase healthful recreation/regular physical activity behavior as a lifestyle at home.

Based on the recommendations of the National Park System Advisory Board Subcommittee on Health and Recreation (2006), seven diverse National Park Service sites (one per region) were chosen for a study on the relationship between health benefits and National Parks. These seven parks were: Cuyahoga Valley National Park (Ohio), C&O Canal National Historical Park (Washington, D.C., area), Acadia National Park (Maine), Point Reyes National Seashore (California), Sitka National Historical Park (Alaska), Timucuan Ecological and Historical Preserve (Florida), and Zion National Park (Utah). The pilot projects are intended to lead to service-wide health and recreation initiatives that are evidence-based and grounded in science. Dr. Ross Brownson of St. Louis University, a leading expert in public health and physical activity, was the National Coordinating Principal Investigator for the seven pilot studies. Funding came from the Fee Demonstration Program for federal agencies.

In 2006 and 2007, each pilot project site designed a specific intervention plan based on the resources and visitors at that site. All sites have completed individual reports, and a comprehensive final report is in progress. Details will be released when the final report is completed sometime in 2008.

Update on Four of the National Park Service Pilot Projects

Presented by Jessica Leahy, University of Maine

Four of the seven pilot projects evaluated their pre- and post-intervention designs with the same visitor intercept survey, allowing for cross-site comparisons. A summary follows:

- "Take a Walk in your Park" was the slogan utilized in Sitka National Historic Park, in cooperation with the University of Alaska Southeast. The intervention strategy was a walking tour for cruise ship passengers. To promote the campaign, rangers stood on the dock handing out brochures as cruise ship passengers unloaded.
- Point Reyes National Seashore, in partnership with Dominican University, adopted the slogan, "Take a Walk on the Wild Side." Their campaign promoted walking and cycling among both visitors and local residents. They used television ads, newspaper ads, brochures, and posters to reach their audiences.
- Zion National Park was evaluated by the University of Utah. Their campaign slogan was "Take a Walk in Zion". In this locale, the goal was to encourage

walking among park bus riders. In particular, the campaign encouraged visitors to walk back to the visitor center after taking the bus one-way into the park. The intervention strategies included posters, maps, brochures, and scripts for bus drivers to read.

- Acadia National Park was evaluated by the University of Maine. The campaign slogan for this park was "Walk the Great Meadow Loop to Health: Pathways to the Park". The physical activity targeted was walking, and both visitors and residents were target audiences. The intervention strategies included newspaper ads, newspaper articles, brochures, posters, bus placards, events, emails, websites, and television public service announcements.

Increasing Walking at the C&O Canal National Historical Park: An Intervention Focused on Local Employees

Presented by Dave Smaldone

The C&O Canal National Historical Park project focused on the Washington, D.C., area of the Park and investigated the effects of social support and targeted messages on participants' beliefs, attitudes, and behaviors. The Park partnered with Georgetown University, George Washington University, and the Georgetown Business Improvement District to target the employees of businesses near the Park. This study was very similar to a multi-worksite employee wellness research program. Volunteer participants formed teams and competed in a 7-week walking challenge. Pre- and post-challenge surveys were used to measure the effects of the interventions, and were distributed to all participants (N=183) online and through the mail. The program "interventions" consisted of: 1) message "flyers" delivered via email to half the participants (chosen randomly) every other week; and 2) social support development through team formation and the use of a website to track and compare participants' progress. Comparisons between these two groups—social support only and social support plus flyers—assessed the impacts from the interventions. Results indicated that overall walking behavior did not change; most participants were already active walkers, and overall walking rates did not increase. However, those participants receiving the flyers increased their walking rates by 1 day per week. Awareness levels also did not change, most likely because participants had a high level of awareness regarding the health benefits of walking and of using National Parks for health reasons at the start of the Challenge.

THE PARKS FOR PHYSICAL ACTIVITY RESEARCH CONSORTIUM (PPARC) INITIATIVE

Presented by Andrew Mowen

Parks and open spaces are increasingly being acknowledged as a potential asset in promoting public health. A growing body of evidence suggests that parks may play a role in enhancing physical activity levels, but little is known about the nature and extent of this role. There are limited data on the demographics of people who use parks for physically active recreation and the extent of physical activity that occurs in park settings. In addition, park-based physical activity data collection and measurement efforts have been inconsistent and have made it difficult for park managers and policy makers to understand the relative importance of parks and open spaces in promoting physical activity across multiple settings. As such, consistent data collection methods and measures are necessary for comparing physical activity across different types of settings and will help to identify contextual factors that correspond with higher levels of park-based physical activity.

The PPARC was formed in early 2007. Initiated by the National Recreation and Park Association, the PPARC working group comprises scholars and park, recreation, and health professionals who collaborated to create and pilot-test a survey instrument. Questions from this instrument are designed to measure park-based physical activity and barriers to physical activity in park settings, and can be adopted for use in visitor surveys, master planning efforts, and Statewide Comprehensive Outdoor Recreation Plans. Adding these questions into ongoing survey efforts will allow comparisons of findings with the national and state health prevalence data (e.g., Behavioral Risk Factor Surveillance System, National Health and Nutrition Survey).

MEASURING THE RESTORATIVE CHARACTER OF NATURE-BASED ACTIVITY

Presented by Chad Pierskalla

"[I]n the interest which natural scenery inspires there is the strongest contrast to [the mental fatigue caused by thinking about the future]. It is for itself and at the moment it is enjoyed. The attention is aroused and the mind occupied without purpose" [3].

Human-environment interactions have been defined in terms of perceptual intake of information (attention to external stimuli or events over time). As more attention is directed toward the environment, more burden is placed on information processing, contributing to mental fatigue. Ulrich et al. [4] found that the behavioral responses to this type of taxing situation may include avoidance, alcohol use, and cigarette use. The linkage between stress and drug use was further supported in a 2003 study conducted by the National Center on Addiction and Substance Abuse. It found that high-stress teens (26% of all US teens) are twice as likely to smoke, drink, get drunk, and use illegal drugs. Perhaps the most important research linking child performance with the physical environment has been conducted by the Landscape and Human Health Laboratory at the University of Illinois, Urbana-Champaign. The researchers recommend adding trees and greenery near homes and schools to supplement established treatments and improve the functioning of youngsters with chronic attention-deficit hyperactivity disorder (ADHD) symptoms [5, 6]. ADHD symptoms, including difficulty paying attention or focusing on tasks, affect up to 7% of children, yet current treatments, drugs, and therapy may not work in all cases. Although the focus of this presentation is drug-use prevention, it is important to note that many other personal, social, economic, and environmental benefits have been attributed to human-nature interaction studied at the Laboratory.

Many argue that human-nature interaction can help reduce stress, and thus reduce the likelihood of drug use by young people. Providing background support for this proposition, more than 100 studies of recreation experiences in wilderness and urban nature areas indicate that restoration (or stress mitigation) is one of the most important benefit opportunities offered by nature [4]. According to the Attention Restoration

Theory proposed by Kaplan [7], involuntary attention to events that are non-threatening and interesting—and thus automatically hold our attention—offer a reprieve from the burden of directed attention (allowing the neurons to restore). That is, recreation is metaphorically similar to sharpening a dull pencil (i.e., drug abuse and addiction prevention through recovery from directed attention fatigue) rather than destroying the pencil and creating a new one (i.e., crisis management). Despite the growing body of knowledge in this area of research, we still do not know what "dose" of restorative nature (quality and quantity) should be recommended for highly stressed young people to minimize their risk of substance abuse. Similar research questions have been addressed for physical activity requirements (e.g., children and adolescents should participate in at least 60 min of moderate-intensity physical activity most days of the week, preferably daily). We propose several challenges that must be addressed before fully developing national guidelines for nature exposure as it relates to drug-use prevention. Selected findings from the authors' own line of research is provided.

Challenge 1

Indicators of restorative benefits must incorporate the measurement of time. As noted by Aiken and his colleagues, "The position taken by transactionalism in the social sciences is that of understanding person-in-environment contexts as a function of particular ongoing transactions between persons and environments...The focus is on change as an integral part of people's experience. Change is initiated by an event which creates imbalance and transformation" [8]. Therefore, measurements such as duration (e.g., 60 min), intensity (e.g., moderate intensity), and frequency (e.g., most days of the week) of nature exposure are necessary components of a well written restorative guideline.

We conducted a review of three texts containing 58 research studies on aesthetics or restorative character of the natural environment between 1973 and 2001 that used 60 different methodologies. Seventy-three percent of those studies used photographs or slides and relied heavily on researcher inference to capture the actual content of participants' experiences over time [9-12]. Comparatively, process-based research is better able to incorporate time into the analysis of perception. A frequently used approach for measuring human experience over time is the experience sampling method [13]. This approach has been used extensively to measure the quality of the real-time experience by collecting assessments of the present moment. This method is useful because real-time assessment may capture satisfaction as it varies during the experience [11]. For example, Jarman [14] used a continuous response system (real-time assessment involving hand-held dials) that provided feedback in 1-second intervals to identify the strongest and weakest arguments made by candidates during a 2004 Presidential debate. This Perception Analyzer technology (MSinteractive) has also been employed to measure audience reaction to simulated hiking events on wilderness trail [15]. In that study, researchers demonstrated that perceived video events (patterns of change) can be counted: the average number of total dial turns (quantity of events) ranged from 19 to 31 per video clip (or approximately 13–21 perceived changes per minute of video) in their study of three wilderness trails (8 trail segments). One-second sampling intervals seem warranted in future studies of nature hiking.

Challenge 2

A global measure of restorative character is needed. Five components of restorative environments have been identified in the literature [7, 16-18] including:

- Novelty: "In these surroundings, I would feel I am in a different environment than usual"
- Escape: "In these surroundings, I would feel away from my obligations"
- Extent: "All of the elements of this scene go together"
- Fascination: "I would feel absorbed in these surroundings"
- Compatibility: "I feel I would be capable of meeting the challenge of these surroundings"

Chang et al. [19] found a large degree of congruency between post-hoc psychological measures of restorativeness and three real-time physiological responses (muscle tension, brainwave activity, and blood volume pulse). Despite this finding, time was not adequately incorporated into the analysis, which may lack ecological validity. In fact, it would likely be too demanding to ask subjects to respond to all five components of restorative environments at very short time intervals. A global measure of restorativeness, one that simultaneously measures all components of restorative environments in real-time, is needed to better incorporate time into the analysis.

Pierskalla et al. [15] also used Perception Analyzer to examine the construct validity of a global, real-time measure of restorative character (0=low restorative character to 100=high restorative character) of simulated hiking events. In their preliminary study, they found significant relationships between number of dial turns (real-time) and novelty (post-hoc), average restorative character (real-time) and fascination (post-hoc), average restorative character (real-time) and compatibility (post-hoc), and minimum restorative character (real-time) and extent (post-hoc). This global measure appears promising and can be used to simultaneously record psycho-physiological indicators of restoration. Packaging and cross-validation of Perception Analyzer and biofeedback equipment in laboratory studies are needed to determine the enduring restorative effect of various doses of nature.

Challenge 3

There is a need to measure the behavioral response to restoration. Psychological and physiological responses to restoration have been documented in the literature. However, more research is needed to better understand the behavioral response to restorative environments—in particular, the reduction in substance use as proposed here.

KEYWORDS

- **Flyers**
- **High-stress**
- **Interventions**
- **Prevention**

Chapter 6

Eco-medical Tourism

Robert S. Bristow

INTRODUCTION

Medical tourism has gained popularity over the past few years. While its roots may be found in the Neolithic and Bronze Ages with visits to mineral springs around the Mediterranean, current medical tourism is more likely to be driven by patients seeking less expensive medical procedures in eastern Europe, southeast Asia, and Latin America. This chapter explores the role of medical tourism in Costa Rica, a country better known as a premier ecotourism destination. In this exploratory study, the question of sustainability is raised.

An Associated Press poll in late 2007 found that the most important issues for American citizens were the economy and health care [1]. While healthcare has been usurped by increased concerns about the economy and has dropped to third in importance in more recent polls [2], health is tied to both economic and personal well-being concerns. Bargain hunters are now seeking less expensive yet high-quality medical care outside their home countries. For instance, it is estimated that as many as 500,000 Americans are seeking medical procedures overseas today [3]. "The medical tourism industry, as it's called, is only a few years old," Rahim [3] reports, "and most tourists make arrangements through special agencies or the foreign hospitals themselves. As a result, it's hard to find reliable, independent information on foreign hospitals' standards, doctors' qualifications, or patients' legal protection" [3]. This chapter explores the role of contemporary medical tourism in one Latin American country that has both an established ecotourism industry and highly acclaimed medical services. Costa Rica is becoming a world-class medical center as more and more hospitals cater to foreigners seeking high quality treatment at an affordable cost.

The origins of medical tourism may be traced back thousands of years. Visitors have sought the medicinal values of mineral springs for millennia. Cultures in Asia and northern Africa have written records of bathing in mineral and thermal springs that date as far back as 4000 BC when the Sumerians built the earliest health spas. Artifacts from the Bronze Age (2000 BC) provide evidence of well established spas in present-day France and Germany [4].

Health spas became popular in the United States during the 19th century. In the northeast, Saratoga Springs, NY, became a popular destination for people escaping the urban centers found along the coast. As early as the 14th century, the sacred springs of Saratoga were visited by indigenous Native Americans for their healing powers. In the late 1700s, Sir William Johnson was the first foreign visitor to the region [5]. The waters became popular for therapeutic consumption and even today are considered an upscale equivalent of European mineral water [6].

Contemporary medical tourism has roots in the need to go to a foreign country for services unavailable or unaffordable at home. Fertility treatments [7] and faith healing [8] are still popularly sought treatments. But today people are more likely to be seeking affordable health care in a world where the industry has become a $3-trillion enterprise [9]. Further, even in the affluent US, some 46 million citizens are uninsured [10], making the 40–80% savings on medical procedures abroad even more attractive. Burkhart and Gentry [11] estimate that medical tourism could become a $40 billion industry as soon as 2010, while Hansen [12] suggests that in less than two decades, medical tourism could be a $190 billion industry in India alone.

Beyond the economic reasons, there are other benefits of overseas medical care. According to Forbes [13], high quality treatment, more personalized care, and the availability of procedures not yet approved by the US Food and Drug Administration are influential factors. The chief advocate for the elderly, the AARP, adds that the convenience of a short waiting time to see a doctor is another possible benefit of overseas medical care [14].

Typically, American vacationers will find significantly substandard health care facilities abroad. In some countries it is best to evacuate back home for emergency medical care. In other countries, the lax regulation of prescription drugs allows visitors to self-medicate and address some immediate health concerns. For example, in Costa Rica it is possible to ask for some medicina de la tos at a farmacia and receive codeine (Figure 1). The US Department of State [15] provides a formal assessment of health care in Costa Rica with this note of caution: "Medical care in San Jose is adequate, but is limited in areas outside of San Jose. Most prescription and over-the-counter medications are available throughout Costa Rica." By contrast, in a guide to living in Costa Rica, Borner [16] recounts that her husband suffered a heart attack while on vacation in Costa Rica and received superior local medical care.

Yet, it would be naive to believe that only Western citizens are seeking medical treatment abroad. At the Annual Health Tourism Congress, held in Spain in April 2008, 40% of the attendees were from Arab countries, including Saudi Arabia, Kuwait, United Arab Emirates, Qatar, Bahrain, and Oman [17].

The next section of the chapter summarizes the current state of eco-medical tourism in Costa Rica, where the ecotourism industry is well established and extensive. A Certification in Sustainable Tourism (CST) program is sponsored by the Costa Rican Tourism Institute to distinguish tourism businesses based on a sustainable model of natural, cultural, and social resource management. The medical equivalent to this accreditation is the Joint Commission International (JCI). The appropriateness of both accreditations for eco-medical tourism will be explored.

Figure 1. Farmicia in la Fortuna, Costa Rica.
Source: Author, 2005.

MATERIALS AND METHODS

A comprehensive review of eco-medical opportunities in Costa Rica was undertaken using primary sources, the Internet, and the popular press in the country. A review of business-to-business and business-to-consumer organizations was tabulated. This database provides an overview of the existing eco-medical tourism in a country best known as an ecotourism destination.

Located between Panama and Nicaragua, Costa Rica enjoys a relatively high standard of living. The average per capita income is US$5,000 a year, and the adult literacy rate is 95% [18]. These statistics exceed those of neighboring Latin American countries.

For the well established ecotourism industry, Costa Rica has an extensive national park system that protects natural areas along the coasts and in the interior mountains. Currently there are 20 national parks, eight biological reserves and monuments, 27 protected forest areas, and nine wildlife refuges. Collectively these lands represent 25% of the country, a larger percentage than any other country on Earth. For many, this small country is exactly what the International Ecotourism Society means by its definition of ecotourism: "responsible travel to natural areas that conserves the environment and improves the well-being of local people" [19].

How can we be sure that natural resources are protected and that the industry is sustainable? One way is to have an independent body evaluate the practices of the industry. The Costa Rican Tourist Board's CST emphasizes the need to: evaluate physical and biological interactions; assess management policies and operational systems for infrastructure and service; review management practices to encourage clients' participation in sustainable actions; and evaluate the companies' socio-economic interaction with local citizens and businesses. These four areas cover the sources of potential positive and negative impacts generated by Costa Rica hotels [20].

Costa Rica also has a comprehensive healthcare system. Foreign eco-medical tourists are attracted to the high-quality healthcare opportunities and extremely competitive pricing. American or western European eco-medical tourists may be able to save 40–90% of the cost of having the same procedures in their home countries. The extensive ecotourism industry in Costa Rica addresses the needs of recovering patients and can provide a variety of traditional ecotourism experiences. For example, every week, the White House Hotel, Restaurant, Casino, and Medical Spa advertises in the *Tico Times* [21], Central America's most popular English language newspaper; the spa's thriving eco-medical business caters to visitors seeking hormone replacement and age management treatments.

For this investigation, we use a definition of eco-medical tourism suggested by the US Senate: "the practice of patients seeking lower cost health care procedures abroad—often packaged with travel and sightseeing excursions" [22]. As with ecotourism, an independent organization can evaluate the eco-medical tourism industry.

The medical equivalent of the CST is the JCI, a nonprofit arm of the Joint Commission that accredits some 15,000 hospitals in the US. Based in Illinois, the JCI assures that medical standards are met at overseas facilities as they are in the US, but it also ensures that all medical facilities converse in the same language. This latter point is important since common language is meant to ensure safety and consistency among all providers [23].

In the evaluation of overseas eco-medical facilities, one important question is whether it is possible to link sustainable ecotourism practices with sustainable practices of medical tourism. Are the two accreditations even compatible? The next section will delve into these questions and attempt to find common ground.

DISCUSSION

The two industries, ecotourism on one hand and medical tourism on the other, have quite dissimilar motivations; yet can reap the benefits of collaboration. Ecotourism has a fairly long history in Costa Rica. Medical tourism is a more recent phenomenon. What remains unanswered in this report is how to link the two. One might argue that linking the accreditation process may help. The challenge is large, since medical accreditation has the distinct motivation to consider the patient first and foremost, much akin to the way traditional tourism caters to tourists. If service is important to the patient, and it is certainly important, how can industry cater to the interests of the local people since this extra service comes at a cost? Since Costa Rica citizens spend approximately 8.6% of their per capita income on health care and Americans spend only 5.8%, it might appear that the eco-medical tourist can afford to pay extra for the additional service at a foreign destination. Differences in the exchange rates will also contribute to the disparity.

The Costa Rican healthcare industry should continue to seek JCI accreditation, which would enhance the likelihood of insurance companies' sponsoring medical procedures in Costa Rica. The Hospital Clínica Bíblica in San Jose is Costa Rica's first hospital to gain JCI accreditation (see Figure 2). The hospital has 120 beds and employs more than 400 doctors. Two other Costa Rican hospitals are being reviewed for accreditation: CIMA Hospital (Escazí) and Catílica Hospital (Guadalupe).

Table 1. Comparison of Latin American countries' expenditures on health care.

Country	Per person health care expenditures (US$)	Population (Millions)	Percent GDP spent on health care
Cuba	326	11.30	6.2
Suriname	376	0.40	5.7
Argentina	555	38.00	5.1
Uruguay	399	3.40	5.1
Costa Rica	433	4.10	4.9
Panama	296	3.10	4.8
Barbados	657	0.30	4.3
Dominica	243	0.10	4.3
Guyana	179	0.80	4.2

Source: World Mapper 2008.

Figure 2. Hospital ClΗnica BΗblica in San Jose, round top building, upper left of photo.
Source: Author, 2005.

It appears that medical tourism in our global economy is here to stay. A Google search for "medical tourism Costa Rica" in May of 2008 found nearly 303,000 sites, 100,000 more than were available only 2 months earlier. Clearly, this is a growing field in both Costa Rica and the world.

What obstacles remain? One obvious concern is the legal uncertainty regarding medical tourism. What rights do patients have? Since there is no current international legal regulation of medical tourism, what options are left to a patient who may suffer needlessly [25].

It makes sense that the Costa Rican government should be the chief advocate for developing the country as an eco-medical destination. This step would ensure that local citizens' benefit from the influx of eco-medical tourists by taxing the revenue received from foreign currency. The government could also link the CST and JCI accreditations to provide a sustainable approach to eco-medical tourism in a country widely known for its natural attractions and excellent health care opportunities. The term "eco-medical tourism" could then in practice live up to the definition offered by the International Ecotourism Society (1990).

RESULTS

If the medical tourism industry continues to grow, and all statistics point to this future, two questions of sustainability need to be addressed:

1. Can local people living near eco-medical facilities get needed medical care? and
2. How are medical wastes being handled? This section of the chapter will explore these questions.

The growth of medical tourism is so dramatic in many countries that local citizens are unable to get adequate health care. For example, Thailand has an extensive medical tourism industry, and many of the country's doctors prefer to work for private hospitals, where they can earn a week's salary in 1 day compared to the wages offered at public facilities [26]. In this case and others like it, public or nationalized healthcare provides equal access to free or low-cost medical care, yet the market allows more affluent citizens to pay extra for better and/or faster services than are available under the managed system. It is simply a case of supply and demand.

In Costa Rica, local citizens have access to medical care, at least at Latin American standards. Table 1 provides a summary of the spending on public health services (estimated per person in US dollars) and the percent of public spending on healthcare in nine Latin American countries in 2001. It appears that Costa Rica is at least comparable to other countries in the region. By comparison, the US spends $2,217 per person on health care, has a population of more than 300 million, and spends 6.2% of its gross domestic product on health.

Second, environmental concerns need to be addressed. Medical waste is a worldwide problem. Simply defined, medical waste includes used needles, soiled dressings, blood, body parts, chemicals, pharmaceuticals, expired medicines, scalpels, medical devices, and radioactive materials. According to the World Health Organization

(WHO), approximately 20% of the waste generated from health care facilities is hazardous. Hazardous materials could be infectious, toxic, or radioactive [27].

Medical waste is a serious concern in Costa Rica. Hospitals in San Jose alone produce 17 tons of waste a day and about 2% of it is classified as biohazardous. These materials are disposed of in bright red plastic bags. The contents pose a health and safety risk to scavengers who comb landfills to gather items for recycling or financial reward in colónes, Costa Rica's currency [28].

KEYWORDS

- **Certification in sustainable tourism**
- **Eco-medical tourists**
- **Joint Commission International**
- **Medical tourism**

Chapter 7

Walking Benefits of C&O Canal National Historical Park

Dave Smaldone

INTRODUCTION

This study sought to increase walking in the C&O Canal National Historical Park (NHP). The C&O Canal NHP joined with Georgetown University, George Washington University, and the Georgetown Business Improvement District (GBID) to target the employees of these businesses. The study was very similar to a multi-worksite employee wellness research program. Volunteer participants formed teams and competed in a 7-week walking challenge. Pre- and post-challenge surveys were used to measure the effects of the interventions, and were distributed to all participants (N = 183) online and through the mail. The program "interventions" consisted of: (1) message fliers delivered via email to half the participants (chosen randomly) every other week and (2) social support development—through team formation, and the use of a website to track and compare their progress for all participants. Comparisons between these two groups—social support only and social support plus fliers—assessed the impacts from the interventions. Results indicated that the overall walking behavior did not change. Most participants were already active walkers, and overall, walking rates did not increase. However, results indicated that those participants receiving the fliers increased their walking rates by 1 day per week.

Although numerous studies have shown that physical activity is a critical component of health [1], the proportion of Americans meeting physical activity standards remains low [2]. In fact, 55% of Americans do not meet the minimum physical activity recommendations for health, and almost 25% are sedentary [3].

As part of the increasing focus on improving individual health, the Healthier US Initiative proposed in 2002 by President Bush promoted the use of public lands to improve personal health, by encouraging the use of these lands for physical activity. Based on the recommendations of the National Park System Advisory Board Subcommittee on Health and Recreation (2006), the C&O Canal NHP was chosen to participate in a pilot study (as one of seven NPS sites) to examine this link between health benefits and national parks. The purpose of this study was to use messages and social support to increase walking in the C&O Canal NHP by targeting employees who work in one specific area of the park, the Georgetown area of Washington, DC.

LITERATURE REVIEW

One avenue to address improving health focuses on the use of outdoor recreation resources, such as state and federally managed parks, forests, and other sites, to encourage physical activity. Surprisingly, information is lacking in regards to the empirical relationships between leisure behaviors, natural parks, and physical health, although more researchers have begun to explore these areas during the last decade [4-7]. While a great deal is known about the demographics of trail and park users [8-11], as well as the restorative benefits of outdoor recreation [12], less research has focused on promoting the healthy physical benefits of outdoor recreation areas and the effects of interventions to increase use [13].

Strategies to Promote Physical Activity

Nonetheless, a variety of strategies have been implemented to promote physical activity in general, and walking in particular. While numerous theories and approaches—including the health belief model, the transtheoretical model, social cognitive theory, and social marketing—have been used to address factors that predict the intention, implementation, or maintenance of a variety of health-related behaviors, one of the most widely used is the theory of planned behavior (TPB). According to the TPB, a specific behavior is based on a series of connected beliefs. Therefore, in order to attempt to modify or change a person's behavior, it is critical to understand the beliefs related to that specific behavior [14].

The TPB has been used in many studies that addressed a variety of health behaviors [15-19]. In regards to physical activity specifically, numerous studies have consistently found strong relationships between TPB constructs and physical activity [20-24]. In addition, social support has been noted as an important factor in determining physical activity [8, 25-27]. Developing and providing opportunities for social support in community settings has been recommended as an effective method to promote physical activity [28].

Study Purpose

This study sought to use theoretically derived messages and social support to increase walking behavior at the C&O Canal NHP (measured using self-report mail-back and online surveys).

MATERIALS AND METHODS

Study Area

The C&O Canal NHP is a 185-mile-long linear park running from Washington, DC to Cumberland, MD. It receives 3 million visitors every year, making it one of the most visited national park areas. With so many people working and residing near the park, the primary visitation pattern is repeated, short visits. This pattern was an important factor in selecting the audience for this project.

The geographic area of focus for the project was the trail/towpath along the Canal within and just outside the Georgetown area of Washington, DC. Walking was chosen because it is the most widespread outdoor physical activity due to its ease, accessibility, and acceptability [29, 30]. The overall goals of the project were: (1) to increase park users' awareness of the health benefits derived from recreation in the park and

(2) to increase their use of the park for walking. This study reports only the outcomes related to goal 2—increasing walking in the park.

The park worked with the GBID to target the employees of those businesses, as well as Georgetown University and George Washington University employees. The GBID has a membership of about 1,000 businesses in Georgetown, and seeks to collectively market and enhance the Georgetown area as a place for business and a destination for visitors (similar to a Chamber of Commerce). The volunteer participants were the recipients of a multi-component program—derived from using social support, TBP, and the elaboration likelihood model (ELM)—to encourage walking, both in the C&O Canal NHP and elsewhere. This project was very similar to a community or employee wellness program, but more complex because it involved numerous jobsites.

Data Collection

Onsite interviews and a focus group of GBID employees were first used to elicit beliefs of the target sample regarding walking in the C&O Canal NHP, and the results were used to develop the targeted messages used to motivate participants during the Challenge [31, 32]. The program "interventions" consisted of: (1) targeted messages delivered via email fliers to half the participants (chosen randomly) every other week and (2) social support development—through team formation, and the use of a website to track and compare their progress for all participants. Comparisons between these two groups, (1) social support only and (2) social support plus message fliers, assessed the impact from the interventions.

Focus Groups

During the focus group (held in May 2007), all participants were given a series of questions to be answered individually, followed by a group discussion of the same questions. Using the TPB [31-33] to guide this phase of the research, interviewers asked participants specific questions related to their: (1) salient personal beliefs and attitudes; (2) salient normative beliefs; and (3) salient perceived behavioral control beliefs. In this study, the specific targeted behavior addressed in the questions was "walking for at least 30 min a day, 5 days a week on the C&O Canal NHP trails."

In addition, nine onsite interviews were conducted in May 2007 with C&O Canal NHP visitors. A convenience sample of individual visitors was approached, and respondents were asked the same series of questions used in the focus groups. The interviewers wrote down the responses verbatim.

Results of the focus group and interviews were combined, analyzed for content, and coded for common themes centered on the three main types of beliefs noted above [32]. A comparison of the beliefs of both "walkers" (those currently using the C&O Canal NHP towpath to walk for exercise or health improvement) and "nonwalkers" found that the most salient beliefs that should be addressed were: (1) enjoying the view/scenery on the towpath (behavioral belief, which more walkers than nonwalkers mentioned); (2) safety on the towpath (behavioral belief, noted by both groups); (3) having a walking buddy for motivation (a control belief, which more nonwalkers than walkers stated); and (4) lack of time to walk (a control belief, which more nonwalkers mentioned). Four fliers were then developed and sent during the 7-week challenge. These message fliers targeted the positive and/or negative beliefs associated with raising awareness and encouraging walking for 30 min. a day on the C&O Canal NHP trails and elsewhere [32]. Principles from the ELM were also used to help design these targeted messages—specifically by using humor, attempting to make the messages novel and relevant, and targeting both peripheral and central routes to persuasion [34].

Description of the Challenge and Interventions

As noted, the study used social support and team competition, in conjunction with theoretically derived messages, as the two main strategies to encourage the participants to walk. Volunteer teams were organized from the groups noted above and competed against each other to complete the overall goal/challenge: to walk 185 miles (the length of the Canal) in 7 weeks as a team. (If each team member walked 5 miles per week, it would take an average of 7 weeks for the team to reach 185 miles.) Individuals were also encouraged to participate. Teams were encouraged to have five members, which would be the optimal number to ensure that each person walked at least 30 min a in order to reach 185 miles. In reality, teams formed of varying sizes, and competed by comparing average miles per team. In order to track miles, this study used 20 min of walking as a measure for 1 mile, based on findings in a variety of studies [35, 36].

A website and web-log were set up and maintained as a major source of feedback for the participants. They uploaded their miles to chart their progress and compare it against other teams (similar to the Walk Across Texas program). All teams or individuals were required to register online, and throughout the course of the study were reminded to upload their miles and track their progress on a weekly basis. The website was modeled after the President's Council on Physical Fitness and Sports site, "The President's Challenge Physical Activity and Fitness Awards Program," as well as the "Walk Across Texas" program's website [37]. As additional incentives, the three teams and individuals with the most number of average miles walked by the end of the Challenge received gift certificates, and all participants who completed the Challenge received small prizes.

Data Collection Procedures

This study used a pre- and post-intervention survey to measure changes in self-reported walking rates before and after the program. Both surveys were distributed to all participants (N = 183) online and through the mail. All registered participants were asked to fill out a survey at the start of the challenge in early September, 2007, and again at the end in early November. Modifying Dillman's method [38], reminder emails were sent approximately 1 week, and again 2 weeks, after the start of each survey. A second paper copy was sent to nonrespondents after 3 weeks. These survey instruments included questions related to respondents' demographics, awareness and knowledge of importance of health benefits related to walking, self-reported walking behaviors (using separate questions to differentiate between walking in the park and outside the park), and awareness and impact of targeted messages and social support on walking (only on post-intervention survey).

ANALYSIS

This project used a quasi-experimental research design (pre-test, post-test) to evaluate the results. No control group was feasible to use for this project, so two intervention groups were used. All participants received the social support intervention (teams, weblog, etc.), but only half the participants also received the targeted messages. The data from all online surveys were collected using a Microsoft Access database, converted to Excel, and then imported into the SPSS software package. Mailed-back surveys were entered directly into the SPSS database.

DISCUSSION

Insufficient evidence was found for the effectiveness of the C&O Canal NHP's program to increase walking in the park. However, evidence was found that the message fliers may have had a statistically significant impact on walking in general, increasing the average days walked per week from 5–6 days. Interestingly, although no significant difference was found in walking rates in the C&O Canal NHP, about 40% of the respondents reported that they thought it did increase their use of the park. Social support through the use of teams for the Challenge was reported as the primary motivator to walk. Encouraging people to join teams and engaging in friendly team competition may be an effective way to motivate, and even sustain, walking behavior.

Although this study targeted individuals working near the park, most still chose to walk elsewhere. Unfortunately, the reasons for this preference are not known. Merely providing a place to walk is clearly not enough to get participants to alter their walking behavior, and decisions to walk are generally made by considering numerous factors (e.g., time of day, time allowed/needed to walk, walking buddies, family considerations, having clean/appropriate clothing).

In addition, this challenge sought to attract and encourage nonwalkers; however, it attracted only participants who were already walking. Thus, little change would likely be noted, since the challenge was not planned for active walkers. However, it did appear to give walkers a new avenue or outlet (the social aspect of the team challenge) and to motivate them in new ways to keep walking. Many noted that just being on a team was the part of this program that motivated them the most. Finally, future research should carefully consider the recruitment methods, in order to attract the most appropriate sample (nonwalkers vs. walkers).

Several limitations were associated with this study, particularly the analysis of the paired surveys. The response rate for those completing both surveys was quite low. The small initial sample size and the low response rate on the paired surveys make it inappropriate to generalize the results to other worksites or parks. However, a brief phone survey of a random sample of nonrespondents (N = 13) was used to assess potential nonresponse bias, and no systematic bias was indicated. In addition, this project was unable to measure long-term outcomes to see whether the increase in walking due to the fliers was maintained. Future research should attempt to measure both short- and long-term outcomes. This study also encountered a number of problems due to the heavy reliance on the website, including participants' creating multiple accounts, and surveys that were incomplete due to participant confusion, computer error, or other limitations. Relying on email to contact participants was convenient, but this project may have overused that avenue of communication (i.e., frequent emails may have caused people to disregard them). One finding from the nonresponse bias check was that participants just wanted to join their team and then walk, and not be bothered with getting frequent emails, or filling out mileage logs or surveys. Similar walking challenges (e.g., "Walk Across Texas") have found that having an active and committed team captain is critical to the success of logging miles, and that addition might have helped this project as well.

RESULTS

The total number of participants was 183, with 39 teams made up of varying numbers of people, and 29 individuals. Ninety-nine participants (including individuals and those on a team) completed the challenge. Ninety-nine respondents returned the pre-challenge survey, for a 54% response rate, and 58 participants returned the post-survey, for a response rate of only 32%. Forty-one individuals (22%) returned both surveys, and most of the paired analyses were conducted on only these 41 participants (except as noted).

The majority of participants (N = 99) were female (77%) and the participants' average age was 43 years. The majority were college graduates (73%), with 38% having a graduate or professional degree. Most participants were white (65%) or African American (23%).

At the start of the Challenge, most participants were already active walkers, with 86% walking 5 or more days per week for at least 10 min (M = 5.9 days); and 85% reported they walked for at least 30 min on those days (M = 58 min). However, only 44% reported walking on the C&O Canal NHP towpath specifically (19% reported walking only 1 day per week on the towpath, while 25% reported walking 2 or more days per week in the park). Sixty-five percent of the C&O Canal NHP walkers spent at least 30 min walking (M = 52 min). At the end of the challenge (N = 58), those figures remained roughly the same (see Table 1).

Table 1. Walking results, based on all survey respondents.

Variable	Pre-Challenge (N=99, Means)	Post-Challenge (N=58; Means)
Number of days walked in general	5.9 days	5.6 days
Number of days walked at the C&O	1 day	1 day
Number of minutes walked per day in general	58 minutes	54 minutes
Number of minutes walked per day at C&O	52 minutes	56 minutes
Percentage walking for at least 30 minutes (each day they walked)	85%	86%

Analysis using paired t-tests (N = 41) found no significant differences pre- and post-challenge between: (1) the number of days walked in general; (2) the number of days walked specifically at the C&O Canal NHP; (3) the number of minutes walked per day in general; or (4) the number of minutes walked per day (Table 2). Thus, the walking challenge did not appear to increase walking rates. The critical p-value for determining significant differences in all statistical tests was $p < 0.05$.

However, analysis using independent t-tests to test for differences between the "fliers and social support" group and the "social support only" group, found that the group receiving the fliers walked approximately 1 more day per week in general, 6 days versus 5 days ($t = 2.646$, $p < 0.011$). Therefore, the fliers may have increased the number of days the participants walked in general. No differences were found in regards to the number of days walked specifically at the C&O Canal NHP, the number of minutes walked per day in general, or the number of minutes walked per day at the C&O Canal NHP.

Participants were also asked about their beliefs regarding the motivation effect of the various interventions, as well as the Challenge in general. Overall, it appears that being part of a team and being able to track their progress online provided the most motivation to walk (see Table 3).

Table 2. Walking results, paired t-tests (N = 41).

Variable	Pre-Challenge (means)	Post-Challenge (means)	*t* value, level of significance
Number of days walked in general	6 days	6 days	$t = .608, p < .547$
Number of days walked at the C&O	1.25 days	1.27 days	$t = .086, p < .932$
Number of minutes walked per day in general	64 minutes	60 minutes	$t = .396, p < .695$
Number of minutes walked per day at C&O	75 minutes	48 minutes	$t = 2.058, p < .079$

Table 3. Beliefs about motivation and the interventions.

	Means (N = 58)	% that "strongly agreed" or "agreed" *
During the past 2 months, **just knowing I was part of a team** participating in the "Your Towpath to Healthy Living Challenge" motivated me to walk.	3.87	77%
During the past 2 months, **being able to track my individual and team progress online** motivated me to walk.	3.74	72%
During the past 2 months, **actually walking with my team members** motivated me to walk.	3.37	54%
During the past 2 months, **receiving email fliers** about walking in the "Your Towpath to Healthy Living Challenge" motivated me to walk.	2.98	37%
During the past 2 months, **participating in the ranger-led walks** motivated me to walk.	2.43	9% (agreed, 4 people)
During the past 2 months, **listening to C&O Canal NHP podcasts** motivated me to walk.	2.24	2% (agreed, 2 person)

*Note: Response scale was a 5-point Likert scale, from 1 = "strongly disagree," to 5 = "strongly agree."

Two different questions specifically addressed beliefs regarding whether the challenge increased their use of the C&O Canal NHP towpath. The first asked, "In general, did participating in the 'Your Towpath to Healthy Living Challenge' increase your use of the C&O Canal NHP for walking?" and 42% responded "Yes," while 54% reported "No."

The second question asked, "In the last 2 months, has the number of times you walk/run on the C&O NHP towpath increased, and why?" The answer percentages were similar to the first question, with 37% reporting an increase, 14% reporting a decrease, 33% reporting no change, and 12% saying they "did not know." In regards to the open-ended comments (N = 22) that addressed why their walking had increased, 73% noted social support related to the team challenge as the reason.

Thus, just over one-third (between 37 and 42%) of respondents reported that the Challenge increased their use of the park for walking. Although no statistical significance was found in walking rates in the C&O Canal NHP (Table 2), the results of the two questions above show that about 40% believed it did increase their use of the park. Therefore, regardless of actual behavior change, many perceived that their behavior (walking in the park) had changed. In answer to the open-ended question that asked, "What was the most important thing that motivated you to walk…?" the two most frequently reported comments (N = 41) were social support related to the team challenge (34%), and the physical health benefits from walking (39%). Barriers to walking that were reported in response to an open-ended question (N = 49) were lack of time (39%), physical limitations or injuries (27%), and bad weather (10%).

CONCLUSIONS

In conclusion, this study did not find evidence of the effectiveness of the C&O Canal NHP's program in regards to increasing active visits to the C&O Canal NHP. However, the message flier intervention had a statistically significant impact on walking. Problems related to low response rates on the surveys limit the ability to make specific recommendations based on the findings. Interestingly, while no significant differences were found in walking rates based on the challenge, about 40% of the respondents perceived that it did increase their use of the park. Other lessons learned included: (1) the importance of social support through teams as a motivator; (2) the need to form partnerships with well established or large organizations who can aid in recruitment; and (3) recognizing participants' needs regarding the use of technology.

KEYWORDS

- **Canal national historical park**
- **Focus group**
- **Georgetown business improvement district**
- **Theory of planned behavior**
- **Volunteer participants**

Chapter 8

Travel Patterns and Imported *Plasmodium falciparum* Rates among Zanzibar Residents

Andrew J. Tatem, Youliang Qiu, David L. Smith, Oliver Sabot, Abdullah S. Ali, and Bruno Moonen

INTRODUCTION

Malaria endemicity in Zanzibar has reached historically low levels, and the epidemiology of malaria transmission is in transition. To capitalize on these gains, Zanzibar has commissioned a feasibility assessment to help inform on whether to move to an elimination campaign. Declining local transmission has refocused attention on imported malaria. Recent studies have shown that anonimized mobile phone records provide a valuable data source for characterizing human movements without compromizing the privacy of phone users. Such movement data in combination with spatial data on *P. falciparum* endemicity provide a way of characterizing the patterns of parasite carrier movements and the rates of malaria importation, which have been used as part of the malaria elimination feasibility assessment for the islands of Zanzibar.

Records encompassing 3 months of complete mobile phone usage for the period October–December 2008 were obtained from the Zanzibar Telecom (Zantel) mobile phone network company, the principal provider on the islands of Zanzibar. The data included the dates of all phone usage by 770,369 individual anonymous users. Each individual call and message was spatially referenced to one of six areas: Zanzibar and five mainland Tanzania regions. Information on the numbers of Zanzibar residents traveling to the mainland, locations visited and lengths of stay were extracted. Spatial and temporal data on *P. falciparum* transmission intensity and seasonality enabled linkage of this information to endemicity exposure and, motivated by malaria transmission models, estimates of the expected patterns of parasite importation to be made.

Over the 3-month period studied, 88% of users made calls that were routed only through masts on Zanzibar, suggesting that no long distance travel was undertaken by this group. Of those who made calls routed through mainland masts the vast majority of trips were estimated to be of less than 5 days in length, and to the Dar Es Salaam Zantel-defined region. Though this region covered a wide range of transmission intensities, data on total infection numbers in Zanzibar combined with mathematical models enabled informed estimation of transmission exposure and imported infection numbers. These showed that the majority of trips made posed a relatively low risk for parasite importation, but risk groups visiting higher transmission regions for extended periods of time could be identified.

Anonymous mobile phone records provide valuable information on human movement patterns in areas that are typically data-sparse. Estimates of human movement patterns from Zanzibar to mainland Tanzania suggest that imported malaria risk from this group is heterogeneously distributed; a few people account for most of the risk for imported malaria. In combination with spatial data on malaria endemicity and transmission models, movement patterns derived from phone records can inform on the likely sources and rates of malaria importation. Such information is important for assessing the feasibility of malaria elimination and planning an elimination campaign.

Many countries are committing to nationwide malaria elimination and global eradication is once more back on the international agenda [1-3]. Historically, the technical feasibility of achieving malaria elimination in a region has been conceptualized as being composed of "receptivity" and "vulnerability" [4, 5]. Receptivity represents the strength of transmission in an area, while vulnerability is the risk of malaria importation [6]. While both have been regularly discussed theoretically, neither have been quantified, nor methods for their quantification ever defined.

Quantifying imported malaria risk represents a central component for not only assessing the feasibility of malaria elimination from a region, but also for planning the implementation of an elimination campaign. Malaria is constantly being exported and imported around the World, and in areas of high transmission, malaria importation is generally a minor concern. As local transmission is reduced and after malaria has been eliminated from a region, however, importation becomes a primary concern.

Zanzibar, an island group of the coast of Tanzania, is one of the territories in sub-Saharan Africa that has recently expressed its willingness to move from control towards elimination. Since 2003, the introduction of artemisinin-based combination therapy (ACT) and high coverage's of long-lasting insecticide treated nets and indoor residual spraying, has reduced malaria prevalence to just 0.8% [7, 8]. These efforts have resulted in the government of Zanzibar considering an elimination campaign and undertaking an elimination feasibility assessment. Nevertheless, proximity and high connectivity to the mainland where transmission levels remain substantially higher in many places [9] implies that imported malaria will be a constant problem [10].

In general, parasites can be imported into Zanzibar in one of three ways: (i) the migration of an infected mosquito, (ii) infected humans visiting or migrating from the mainland, (iii) residents visiting the mainland and becoming infected, then returning. While mosquitoes may occasionally arrive though wind-blown or accidental aircraft or ship transport, typically they will only fly short distances. Human carriage of parasites, therefore, represents the principal risk, and is to blame in many past instances elsewhere where malaria has resurged [11-14]. Quantifying such movements both temporally and spatially, and the resulting imported infection risks, represents an important task if effective, evidence-based planning for elimination is to be undertaken.

Recent approaches to quantifying human mobility patterns point the way to novel insights from new data [15, 16], especially through the analysis of mobile phone records [17-19]. Anonimized phone call record data that has both the time each call was made and the location of the nearest mast that each call was routed through can be used to construct trajectories of the movements of individuals over time [19]. Here, the potential of such data for estimating importation risk in the malaria elimination feasibility assessment for the islands of Zanzibar is demonstrated. The low market share on the mainland for the network provider restricts the focus here to those infections brought in by residents returning from mainland travel. However, the approaches put forward are sufficiently generic to be applied to alternative regions, elimination settings and phone network provider data. Moreover, this exercise aims to present the first exploration of mobile phone based approaches to the quantification of vulnerability to inform malaria elimination decisions and planning.

MATERIALS AND METHODS

Study Area

Like other areas of sub-Saharan Africa, the islands of Zanzibar, off the coast of Tanzania in East Africa (Figure 1), have falciparum malaria and efficient vectors, including Anopheles gambiae, and at many points in the past, malaria in Zanzibar would have been called hyperendemic (PfPR in the 2–10 age group ~50–75%). Recent control efforts [8], possibly combined with socioeconomic changes, have pushed *Plasmodium falciparum* prevalences down to 0.3% for the southern island of Unguja, and 1.4% for the northern island of Pemba [7], meaning approximately 8,500 infected people at any one time; 3,000 on Unguja and 5,500 on Pemba.

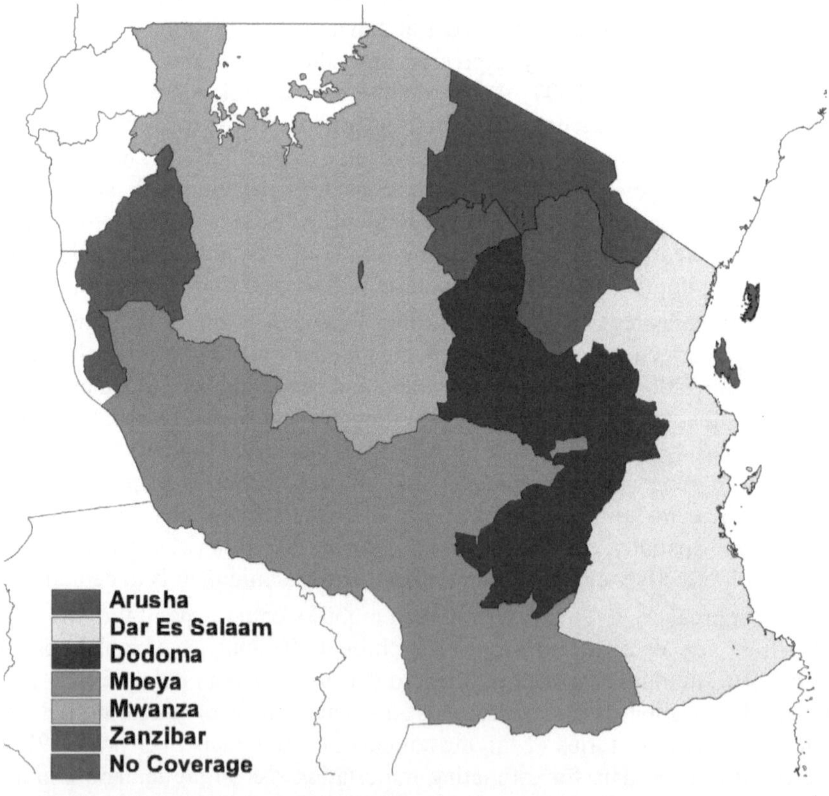

Figure 1. Zantel coverage regions in Tanzania.

Zanzibar, however, has strong transport connections to the mainland where transmission levels are higher, resulting in concerns about achieving and sustaining elimination being raised [10], and making the quantification of human movement patterns and ultimately, imported infection rates, a critical aspect of elimination feasibility. While daily flights bring in around 10,000 people a month [20], these are mainly tourists from non-endemic regions, who will likely be taking prophylaxis, and thus represent a low risk in terms of imported infections and onward transmission. Ferry services have capacity to move up to 1,800 people daily between Zanzibar and the mainland. This route, as well as informal movements such as small fishing and trading vessels, likely represent the highest risk pathways for any imported infections. Figure 2 shows the recorded total numbers of ferry passengers each month for 2007, with these numbers likely split equally between visitors from the mainland and Zanzibar residents [21].

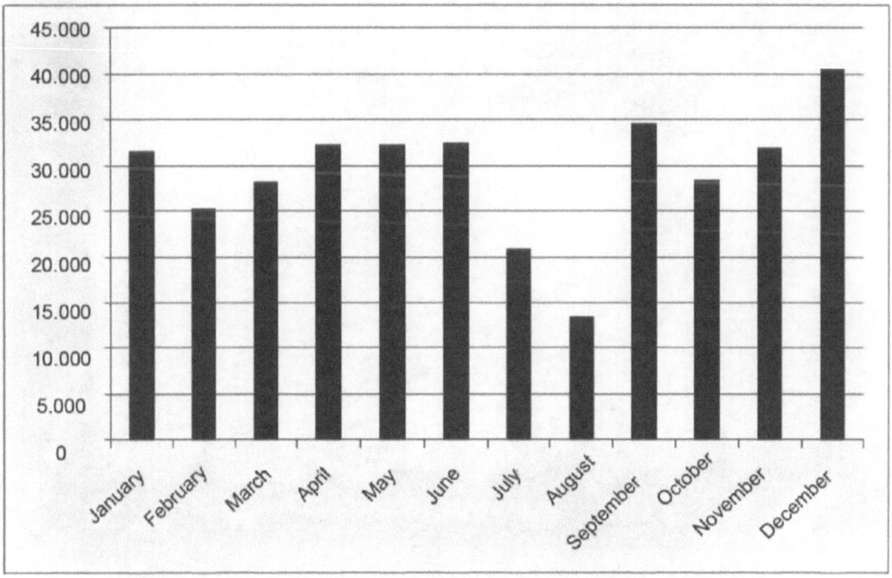

Figure 2. Total ferry passenger numbers between Dar Es Salaam and Zanzibar for 2007.

Plasmodium falciparum Malaria Endemicity Data

A new global map of *P. falciparum* malaria endemicity for 2007 has now been published [9]. This provides a continuous prediction of prevalence (*P. falciparum* parasite rate in the two up to 10 year old age group, PfPR2-10, between 0 and 100%) for every 5 × 5 km pixel within the stable limits of *P. falciparum* malaria transmission [22]. It represents a contemporary measure of global malaria endemicity, based on evidence in a huge repository of parasite rate surveys [23]. Using mathematical models described previously [24-26], the parasite rate map was converted to a map of the daily entomological inoculation rate (dEIR), a more relevant measure for assessing the risk of infection acquisition in an area. The dEIR data for the study area was extracted and is shown in Figure 3(a). Maps showing the start and end months of the principal (Figures 3c and d) and secondary *P. falciparum* transmission seasons [27] extracted for Tanzania were also obtained to enable spatial refinement of transmission levels during the study period.

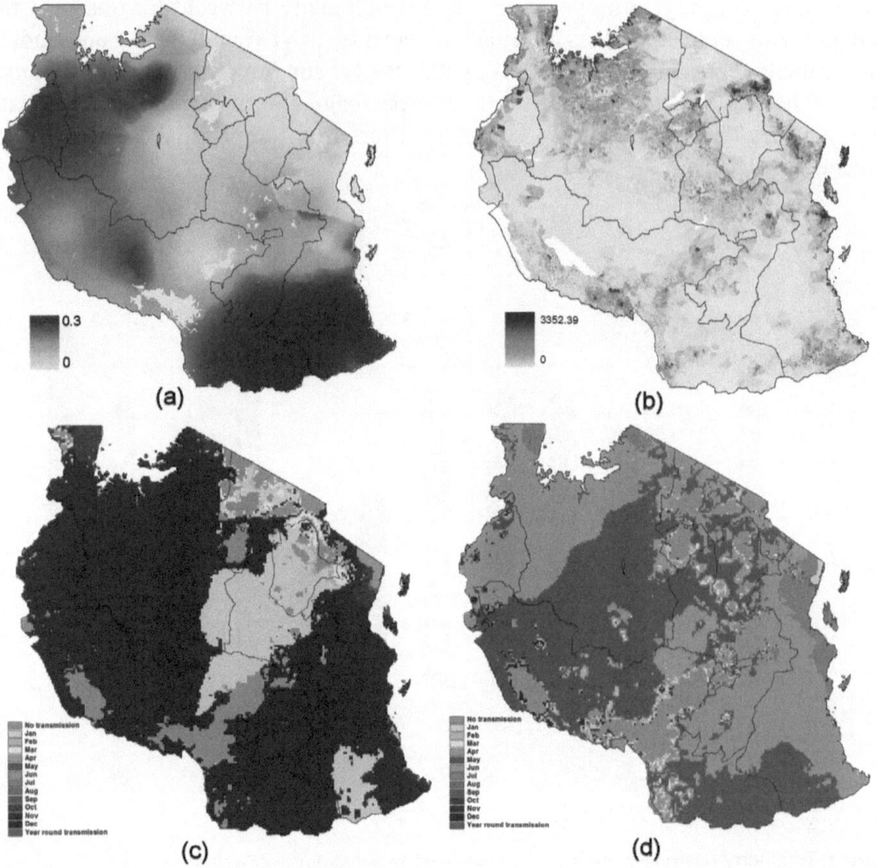

Figure 3. Zantel coverage regions for Tanzania overlaid on (a) daily entomological inoculation rate (dEIR); (b) Population distribution; (c) Month of start of principal malaria transmission season; and (d) Last month of principal malaria transmission season.

Population Distribution Data

Population distribution maps for 2002 at 100 m spatial resolution, as described in Tatem et al. [28] and available through the AfriPop project [29], were obtained for the study area. These were projected forward to 2008 to match the mobile phone data by applying national, medium variant, inter-censal growth rates [30] using methods described previously [31] and are shown in Figure 3(b).

Mobile Phone Data

The Zantel mobile phone operator has approximately a 10% share of the Tanzanian market [32]. While nine out of ten Tanzanians are reported to have "access" to a mobile phone, what these Figures mean in terms of ownership and usage are subject to debate and uncertainty [33, 34]. However, while the 10% share Zantel has likely represents an unrepresentative sample of Tanzania as a whole, Zantel does have a 99% market share on Zanzibar. With over 330,000 individual users apparently resident on Zanzibar (see later analyses) out of a total population of just over a million, this suggests that a substantial sample of Zanzibar phone users is covered by the dataset. Analyses here were, therefore, focused on Zanzibar residents only.

Records encompassing three months of complete mobile phone usage for the period October–December 2008 were obtained from Zantel. This represents the limit of available Zantel data, since the company only keeps the preceding three months of records. Nevertheless, this covers the busiest period in terms of travel to and from Zanzibar (Figure 2), and, therefore, enables a conservative upper limit on infection importation risk to be estimated. The data included the dates of all phone usage by 770,369 individual users, making a total of 21,053,198 calls and text messages. Prior to receiving the data, Zantel assigned each individual user a unique code to ensure that the anonymity of users was maintained and that the data could only be used for studying general patterns of mobility. Each individual call and message was spatially referenced to one of six areas: Arusha, Dar Es Salaam, Dodoma, Mbeya, Mwanza, and Zanzibar (Figure 1). Any individual that made just four or less calls in any one month (an average of one per week) was removed from further analyses to ensure that sufficient temporal resolution existed in the remainder of the dataset for trajectory analysis.

Estimating Exposure to Transmission Levels

For each of the 3 months in the study period, and for each Zantel region, the areas within their principal (Figures 3c and d) or secondary transmission seasons were identified and overlaid onto the dEIR map (Figure 3a), with non-transmission season areas masked out. The minimum, mean and maximum dEIR values for each Zantel region and month were then calculated, and the gridded population data and dEIR data were combined to calculate population weighted mean dEIRs for the entire regions, and their principal cities (Table 1). To examine the ranges of possible results, should for instance the unlikely case of all visitors traveling to the highest transmission part of each Zantel region be reality, analyses were undertaken with the extreme conditions of minimum and maximum possible dEIR exposure per region. With Zantel coverage principally available in the major populated areas, and travelers more likely to visit heavily populated regions than empty rural areas, it was assumed however that the population-weighted measures likely represented the more realistic range of estimates for dEIR exposure within each coverage region. Moreover, with a high percentage of travelers likely visiting just the principal cities when traveling to each region, the population weighted mean dEIR within the city limits of Arusha, Dar Es Salaam, Dodoma, Mbeya, and Mwanza, as defined by the global rural-urban mapping project urban extent map [35], were also calculated. These scenarios and assumptions were tested through comparing estimated imported infection numbers (see the quantifying imported malaria risk section) to the known numbers of infections present at any one time on the islands of Unguja and Pemba.

Quantifying Imported Malaria Risk from Returning Residents

Malaria importation risk or vulnerability have been discussed in relation to malaria elimination for decades (e.g., [4, 5, 12]), but never quantified. In simple terms, malaria importation risk as a measurable quantity in a focal country or area is the product of human immigration rates from other malaria endemic countries or areas and their corresponding level of endemicity. However, it may not be sufficient to estimate the number of people who cross the borders of a country or region infected with malaria elsewhere; it also matters how long they stayed in endemic regions, how long they remain infected and infectious in the country or area of interest, as well as where they stay. Thus, the risks deriving from visitors from the mainland and returning residents should be quantified differently.

For Zanzibar residents visiting the mainland on day t, their length of stay, L, and dEIR in the area of stay are the key factors. Recent research efforts have provided spatial quantification of *P. falciparum* endemicity [9] enabling estimation of the dEIR at the locations that Zanzibar residents are visiting. Motivated by malaria transmission models [36], the probability of obtaining an infection, P, is thus:

$$P = 1 - e^{\left(-\sum_{t=D}^{t=1} dEIR\right)}$$

The total number of imported infections, I, over all N trips made in the 3 month study period is therefore:

$$I = \sum^{N} 1 - e^{\left(-\sum_{t=D}^{t=1} dEIR\right)}$$

Given the estimates of trip length, range of estimates of dEIR and proportion of travelers captured in the dataset, the total number of infections brought into Zanzibar by returning residents were estimated, as well as the distribution of infection origins. With only around 8,500 infections on the islands at any one time, and just 3,000 on Unguja, where the majority of movements to and from the mainland derive from, this places a realistic limit on the estimates of imported infection numbers, and thus, a guide to the likely dEIR visitor exposure for each Zantel region.

DISCUSSION

Results here show that, despite data limitations, spatially and temporally referenced mobile phone usage data can provide valuable information on human movement patterns. In combination with spatial data on malaria endemicity, derived movement patterns can inform on the likely sources, risks, and case numbers of imported malaria. The estimates presented represent the first quantification of the vulnerability of an area to imported malaria, a necessary quantity in determining the feasibility of achieving and sustaining elimination.

According to the Zantel data, of the 770,369 users in the entire dataset (made up of Zanzibar and mainland residents), only just over 100,000 traveled anywhere during

Table 1. Monthly estimates of dEIR for each Zantel region.

	Minimum			Mean			Maximum			Population weighted mean			Pop weighted principal city mean		
Zantel region	Oct	Nov	Dec	Oct	Nov	Dec	Oct	Nov	Dec	Oct	Nov	Dec	Oct	Nov	Dec
Arusha	0.0	0.0	0.0	0.00005	0.00021	0.00063	0.00068	0.00154	0.00341	0.00001	0.00008	0.00014	0	0.00006	0.00006
	0.0	0.0	0.0	0.00104	0.00840	0.04049	0.00285	0.05654	0.21508	0.00082	0.00213	0.00855	0.00023	0.00023	0.00023
	0.0	0.0	0.0	0.00032	0.00099	0.00792	0.00332	0.0322	0.05258	0.00021	0.00084	0.00785	0	0.00199	0.00199
	0.0	0.0	0.0	0.00625	0.00974	0.02517	0.00995	0.06526	0.29468	0.00444	0.00848	0.03133	0	0.00512	0.00512
	0.0	0.0	0.0	0.00031	0.00066	0.00846	0.00221	0.00887	0.03671	0.00009	0.00032	0.0169	0	0.00492	0.00492

the 3-month study period. Of those Zanzibar residents that traveled, the overwhelming majority went solely to the Dar Es Salaam region (and likely to Dar Es Salaam city itself), where the population weighted average dEIR is relatively low. The majority of these trips were for just one to 2 days, thus posing a relatively low risk of acquiring an infection and again confirming that most trips could not have involved travel to much further beyond Dar Es Salaam city itself. If malaria prevalence levels continue to fall on the nearby mainland [37, 38], there is reason to believe that importation risk on Zanzibar will fall simultaneously. There do however exist small mobile groups that (i) travel for extended periods to the mainland from Zanzibar (ii) travel to higher transmission areas from Zanzibar. These represent the risk groups contributing most to the imported infection numbers brought in by residents visiting the mainland. Moreover, basic analyses on mainland resident movement patterns, suggest that similar risk groups exist among visitors to Zanzibar.

As described in the Materials and Methods section, the data used here have specific limitations that prevent more comprehensive analysis. With just a 10% share of the market on the mainland and Zantel subscribers more likely to travel to Zanzibar than non-subscribers, detailed analyses were not presented based on visitors from the mainland, since the data probably exhibits significant biases. In addition, the activities of visitors to high transmission areas are unknown—in extreme scenarios, some may sleep under bed nets in air-conditioned hotels, while others may spend the night outdoors. Further, those traveling to or from further afield than Tanzania are not captured by this dataset, nor are those who switch to an alternative network provider on the mainland, nor are trips longer than 3 months captured. Finally, information on movement patterns on Zanzibar are also lacking, preventing an understanding of the likelihood of onwards transmission, since imported cases may play a key role in sustaining local transmission in some parts of Zanzibar. Previous work has shown however, that many mobile phone companies often have the ability to provide more precise spatial locations on data (e.g., [19]), potentially improving upon conclusions made, should similar malaria-related studies be undertaken. Moreover, additional studies are planned and should be encouraged to test the approaches presented here further and help to arrive at a clear methodology for the quantification of vulnerability. The importance of preserving the anonymity of phone users should remain the utmost priority though.

The information derived from these analyses can be used to guide strategic planning for elimination, should the Ministry of Health decide to pursue such a campaign. Typically, three principal means of reducing imported infection risk are considered: (i) identify infected individuals and treat them promptly, ideally before or upon entry, before they can infect competent local vectors and lead to secondary cases and sustained foci of indigenous transmission; (ii) address the source of infection by directly reducing transmission in all regions that are primary sources of infected travelers; (iii) provide prophylaxis to residents visiting endemic areas. While the second method is being addressed indirectly through the scaling up of control on the mainland [37, 38], these analyses provide baseline data to inform on the first and third approaches. Screening with rapid diagnostic tests (RDTs) or microscopy at the ports of entry and providing follow-up treatment of infected individuals may play an important role in reducing imported case numbers and outbreaks. Such an approach is being used for all individuals entering the island of Aneityum in Vanuatu [39], while visitors from Africa were tested at the airports of Oman during its elimination campaign. Moreover, the details of all visitors to Mauritius from endemic regions are recorded and follow-up is undertaken by health surveillance officers [40]. When movement rates are high and resources are limited however, as in the case of Zanzibar, screening all visitors at the ports or providing follow-up may be prohibitively expensive and inefficient due to the large number of low-risk trips undertaken (Figure 6).

Modeling work on achieving and maintaining elimination done for the Zanzibar malaria elimination feasibility assessment suggests that as long as effective coverage with vector control measures is higher than 80%, elimination will be achieved and can be maintained. However, once transmission is reduced to very low levels, scaling down prevention without risking resurgence will only be possible if the importation levels estimated here are lowered considerably (Moonen, B., Cohen, J., Smith, D. L., Tatem, A. J., Sabot, O., Msellem, M., Le Menach, A., Randell, H., Bjorkman, A., and Ali, A. (2009). Malaria elimination feasibility assessment in Zanzibar I: Technical feasibility. *Malar Journal*, in preparation). Prophylaxis for Zanzibari travelers is unlikely to be cost-effective or even practical given the high frequency of travel to mainly low risk regions. Screening on the ferries, especially of high risk groups during high risk periods of the year, might be a simpler and more cost-effective option compared to screening at the port of entry. Passengers are on the slow and fast ferries for 6 and 2 hr, respectively; enough time to administer a short questionnaire a RDT and treatment if necessary. However, better data are necessary to determine the PfPR in ferry travelers to appreciate the operational consequences of such an approach.

Future work will aim to link the findings here to GIS data on travel networks in the region, and build these into stochastic metapopulation models of transmission, providing flexible tools for elimination planning. Moreover, retrospective analyses of health facility records at Zanzibar malaria early epidemic detection system sites are being undertaken at present, while surveys on the ferries are planned to corroborate and compliment findings here. This work also links into and is complemented by other datasets being gathered and analyzed as part of a new research agenda initiated by the Malaria Atlas Project [41] to quantify human movement patterns in relation to assessment of malaria elimination feasibility.

Malaria elimination requires a significant investment of resources and capacity and, as has been demonstrated twice before on Zanzibar, failure to achieve this ambitious target can lead to fatigue among donors and policymakers and subsequent devastating resurgence of malaria. As more countries across the world make progress toward malaria elimination, there is a need for evidence based and locally-tailored assessments of the feasibility of making the final step in initiating an elimination campaign. With mobile phone uptake continuing to grow around the world, this novel data source has the potential to play a key role in providing such valuable evidence. While "vulnerability" has been discussed in relation to malaria elimination for decades, the approaches outlined here represent a first step towards finally quantifying it. Replicating and refining these approaches in other areas will enable the development of a standardized methodology for malaria importation risk assessment to aid countries that are considering and planning elimination.

RESULTS

Identifying Travelers

Of the 770,369 individual phone users in the Zantel dataset, 24,625 (3.2%) made four calls or less per month in the 3 month study period, and were thus removed from further analysis. Of the remaining users, 335,621 made the majority of their calls on Zanzibar. From here on, we assume that these represent Zanzibar residents, since the majority of calls by a customer are most likely to be made in their home region. There will of course be exceptions to this, for instance, if a mobile phone is principally used for business use when traveling, but in the absence of further information, this represents a reasonable assumption to make. Of the 335,621 Zanzibar resident users, just 12.08% of them (40,543 users) made calls from the mainland. Thus, the vast majority of users only made calls from Zanzibar, indicating a lack of travel.

Locations Visited

Figure 4 shows, of those Zanzibar residents who traveled in the study period, the proportions that made the majority of their non-home calls at each other mast location. It is clear that of those who traveled to the mainland, a substantial proportion made the majority of their non-Zanzibar calls in the Dar Es Salaam region, with only a small proportion making the majority of their non-Zanzibar calls at the other four mast locations.

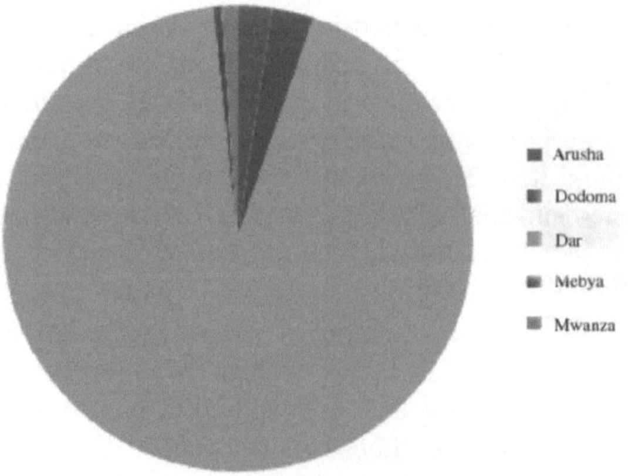

Figure 4. The proportions of Zanzibar resident users that made the majority of their non-home calls at each location.

Trip Lengths

To estimate the lengths of trips made by those making calls from more than one location, it was assumed that the date of the first mainland call made represented the start of a trip. The end of this trip was estimated as the date when the first Zanzibar-based call was made again. For each user, the start and end dates of each individual trip made were estimated in this way and the trip lengths quantified and recorded. A total of 73,095 trips were made, with 12,584 residents traveling in October making a total of 24,439 trips, 11,947 in November making 24,335 trips, and 12,882 in December making 24,321 trips. These figures correspond well with the ferry passenger numbers (Figure 1) and, assuming residents made up around half of ferry passengers [21], suggest that around 95% of all trips made by Zanzibar residents to the mainland were captured in the dataset.

Figure 5 shows the distribution of trip lengths made by Zanzibar residents. As shown in Figure 4, the vast majority of trips made were to the Dar Es Salaam region. What is clear from Figure 5 is that the majority of trips made to the mainland were of less than 5 days long. In fact, 17.4% of all trips to the Dar region were estimated to be of just 1 day in length, while 29% were of 2 days in length or less. A similar pattern is shown for the other regions, though with substantially fewer visits made, and a higher proportion of longer (10–30 days) trips made by those traveling further, for example Mbeya or Mwanza.

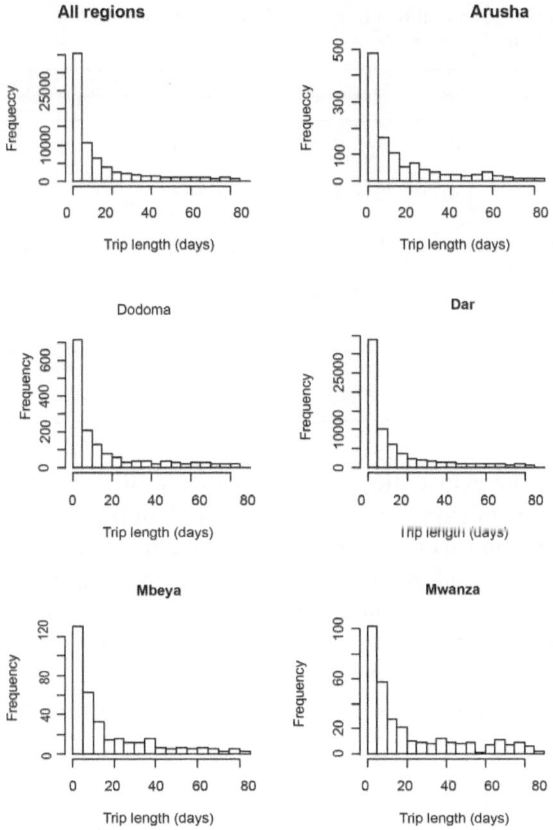

Figure 5. The distributions of trip lengths made by Zanzibar residents to the mainland, overall and by Zantel region. Note differing y-axis limits.

Estimating Imported Malaria Risk

To provide estimates of imported case numbers from returning Zanzibar residents and likely origins of infections, the data on dEIR scenarios for each Zantel region were combined with the trip length estimates using equation (2). Table 2 shows that only the results from the population weighted region and city scenarios fall under the realistic limits of total infections on the islands, given that imported infections will also be brought in by visitors from the mainland and that the majority of travel is to Unguja. Realistically, while a significant majority of visitors to each region will visit the principal cities, others will travel to alternative population centers, thus the regional population weighted mean dEIR (upper) and principal city population weighted mean dEIR (lower) scenarios represent credible limits for estimating the likely number of imported infections per month arising from returning residents. Thus, converting these to annualized measures, estimates of between one and 12 imported infections per 1,000 people per year from returning residents represent realistic limits. Given increased travel in October–December (Figure 2), these also likely represent conservative overestimates.

Table 2. Estimated average monthly numbers of imported infections under the differing dEIR scenarios outlined in Table 1.

Zantel region	Minimum	Mean	Maximum	Pop weighted mean	Pop weighted principal city mean
Arusha	0.0	1.84063	11.18779	0.47931	0.25034
Dar Es Salaam	0.0	3541.63122	8518.20389	1191.30602	81.11407
Dodoma	0.0	22.60743	127.97949	21.75056	10.77893
Mbeya	0.0	19.62360	53.46253	19.67336	6.03524
Mwanza	0.0	6.23628	22.12087	9.59984	6.88978
SUM	0.0	3591.93917	8732.95458	1242.80909	105.06836

Figure 6 shows the distribution of trips by probability of infection acquisition, P, under the scenarios of exposure to regional population weighted mean dEIR and principal city population weighted mean dEIR. Each scenario highlights that the majority of trips made entailed a probability of infection acquisition of less than 0.05. Figure 7 shows the regional composition of these distributions, illustrating that under both scenarios, the trips made by residents to Dodoma, Mbeya, and Mwanza provided greater risks of infection acquisition, due to a higher proportion of longer stays in these regions typically, combined with overall high levels of transmission.

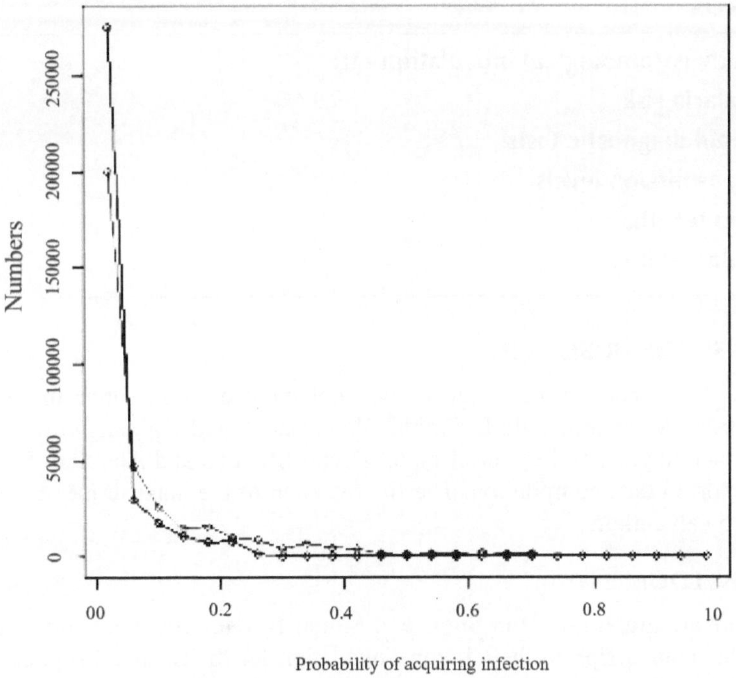

Figure 6. All trips made by Zanzibar residents plotted by probability of infection acquisition, based on region population weighted mean dEIR (red line) and population weighted principal city mean dEIR (blue line).

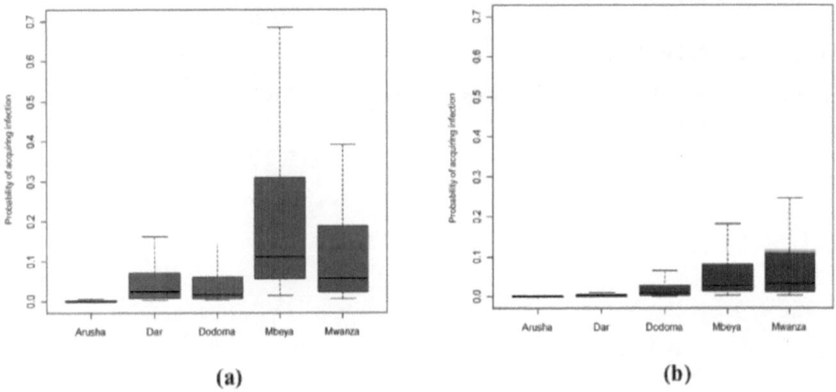

Figure 7. Boxplots of trip probabilities of infection acquisition by Zantel region under scenarios of (a) region population weighted mean dEIR; (b) population weighted principal city mean dEIR. The central dark line in each box shows the median value, the box size shows the interquartile range, while the whiskers extend to the most extreme data points that are no more than 1.5 times the interquartile range from the box.

KEYWORDS

- **Daily entomological inoculation rate**
- **Malaria risk**
- **Rapid diagnostic tests**
- **Transmission levels**
- **Trip lengths**
- **Vulnerability**

AUTHORS' CONTRIBUTIONS

Andrew J. Tatem conceived, designed and implemented the research and wrote the chapter. Bruno Moonen, David L. Smith, Oliver Sabot, and Youliang Qiu aided with ideas, methodological and editorial input. Bruno Moonen and Abdullah S. Ali provided support in data compilation. The final version of the manuscript was seen and approved by all authors.

ACKNOWLEDGMENTS

The authors are grateful to Bob Snow and Simon Hay for comments on earlier versions of this manuscript, to the Clinton Foundation for the financial support that facilitated this work, and to Noel Herrity and Shinuna Kassim at Zantel for supply of the data used in the research. Andrew J. Tatem and David L. Smith are supported by a grant from the Bill and Melinda Gates Foundation (#49446). This work forms part of the output of the Malaria Atlas Project (MAP, http://www.map.ox.ac.uk), principally funded by the Welcome Trust, UK.

COMPETING INTERESTS

The authors declare that they have no competing interests.

Chapter 9

Neglected Tropical Diseases of the Caribbean

Peter J. Hotez

INTRODUCTION

Almost 40 million people live on the islands, islets, and cays that comprise the Caribbean [1]. This is one of the most tourism-dependent regions in the world, with approximately one-quarter of the workforce involved in a business that in some way caters to tourists [2]. According to the Caribbean Tourism Organization (CTO), an association of government and private sector agencies that disseminates data on the region, almost 22 million visitors comes to the Caribbean annually, where they spend an estimated US$21.6 billion [3]. More than 80% of these visitors are people of means from the US (11.4 million), Canada (1.7 million), and Europe (5.3 million), almost all of whom come to the region for the purpose of a holiday vacation [3].

Away from the beaches, resorts, and cruise ships, however, there lies a hidden underbelly of poverty in the Caribbean, and with this poverty, endemic neglected tropical diseases (NTDs) [4]. Shown in Table 1 are four Caribbean countries—Dominican Republic (DR), Guadeloupe, Haiti, and Jamaica—that exhibit an unusually high burden of NTDs. In addition, the island nations of Antigua and Barbuda, Barbados, Saint Lucia, and Trinidad and Tobago also stand out for their high NTD disease burdens. For example, of the Western Hemisphere's 720,000 cases of lymphatic filariasis, a mosquito-transmitted disfiguring parasitic helminth infection caused by *Wuchereria bancrofti* that can result in elephantiasis, almost 90% of the cases occur in the Caribbean, including 560,000 cases in Haiti and 50,000 in DR [5]. Outside of Brazil, the second largest number of cases of the blood fluke infection, schistosomiasis (caused by *Schistosoma mansoni*), occur in the DR (258,000 cases) [6], especially in the eastern part of the island where the Biomphalaria snail vector is still present [7, 8]. Another 4,400 cases occur in Guadeloupe, and transmission still occurs in Saint Lucia and Antigua and Barbuda [6]. High prevalence of the three major intestinal helminth infections—ascariasis, trichuriasis, and hookworm infection—are also found throughout the poorest areas of the Caribbean, particularly in the DR, Haiti, and Jamaica, but also in Barbados and Trinidad and Tobago [9]. The existence of high rates of lymphatic filariasis, schistosomiasis, and hookworm infection in the region is made all the more poignant by an observation made recently in PLoS NTDs that these NTDs were most likely introduced into the Caribbean through the Atlantic slave trade [10], and even today such infections still occur almost exclusively among people living in poverty or people of African descent (P. Hotez, M. Bottazzi, C. Franco-Paredes, S. Ault, M. Roses Periago, and unpublished data).

Table 1. Estimated burden (number of cases) of selected neglected tropical diseases in the Dominican Republic, Guadeloupe, Haiti, and Jamaica.

Country (Population)	Ascariasis	Trichuriasis	Hookworm Infection	Dengue	Lymphatic Filariasis	Schistosomiasis
Dominican Republic (9.1 million)	456,643	628,962	94,775	5,540	50,000	258,000
Guadeloupe (0.4 million)	Not Determined	Not Determined	Not Determined	3,874	None	4,400
Haiti (8.1 million)	2,637,883	3,788,362	776,573	Not Determined	560,000	None
Jamaica (2.6 million)	559,852	1,205,124	81,427	52	None	None
Reference	[9]	[9]	[9]	[13]	[5]	[6]

In addition to the slavery-associated parasitic infections, there are other NTDs of great importance. Leprosy is still reported from Cuba, DR, Haiti, Jamaica, Saint Lucia, and Trinidad and Tobago [11], but because of the availability of multi-drug treatments, it is no longer considered a major public health threat to the region. However, dengue fever is now a serious problem, which is now common not only in the poorest Caribbean countries listed in Table 1, but also in Puerto Rico and other more developed areas [12]. The emergence of this mosquito-borne infection has been linked to an increase in flooding from hurricanes and other natural phenomena that may result from global warming [13]. The rat-borne zoonotic NTD leptospirosis has also emerged in Jamaica and elsewhere following flooding and hurricanes [14].

With the possible exceptions of dengue [15] and cutaneous larva migrans resulting from canine hookworm infection [16], most of the Caribbean's NTDs are not considered significant threats to the health of American, Canadian, and European tourists. The real tragedy of these conditions is that despite the enormous amount of wealth infused into the Caribbean economy every year through tourism, very little if any trickles down to the poorest people in the region who suffer daily from chronic, debilitating, disfiguring, and stigmatizing NTDs. Equally tragic is the evidence base to support the feasibility of NTD elimination and at low cost. For instance, through a demonstration project conducted in Leogane, Haiti, annual mass drug administration (MDA) with diethylcarbamazine (DEC) and albendazole has resulted in the near elimination of lymphatic filariasis after five rounds [17]. The DEC can be purchased for pennies per person, while albendazole is donated free-of-charge by GlaxoSmithKline [18]. Similarly, it is possible to eliminate schistosomiasis by MDA with the low-cost generic drug praziquantel and achieve dramatic reductions in the prevalence and intensity of the intestinal helminth infections ascariasis and trichuriasis through MDA with donated albendazole or mebendazole [19]. Given that industry is either donating the NTD drugs, or they are available as low-cost generic drugs, these last vestiges of American slavery could be controlled or eliminated for a ridiculously small amount. Indeed, if every American, Canadian, and European tourist over the course of a single year donated only US$1.00, the estimated $20 million generated should be sufficient to achieve the elimination of lymphatic filariasis and schistosomiasis from the Caribbean and achieve important reductions in morbidities from intestinal helminths [4].

Additional funds could also be set aside to develop new "antipoverty vaccines" to prevent hookworm infection, dengue, and other more intractable NTDs in the region [20].

The Global Network for NTDs has been established to mobilize resources for NTDs through MDA with donated or low-cost generic drugs [19]. I believe that there is an urgent need to identify an innovative financial mechanism for NTD control in the Caribbean through increased commitments by local governments or through external mechanisms such as a modest US$1.00 airline or cruise ship tax or a tax on tourist entry, or though more conventional donations from North American and European governments and private foundations. Such efforts would require careful coordination by organizations invested in the region, including the Caribbean Epidemiology Center, the Pan American Health Organization, the US Centers for Disease Control and Prevention, and the Global Network for NTDs, to ensure an equitable distribution of resources and universal access to essential medicines.

Given the impact of the NTDs on child development, pregnancy outcome, and worker productivity, ultimately, US$1.00 (less than the cost of a single piña colada!) per tourist in order to eliminate massive NTD health disparities in the Caribbean is a very reasonable and easy-to-digest financial mechanism, as well as a highly cost-effective means to lift the region's poorest people out of poverty.

KEYWORDS

- **Albendazole**
- **Caribbean tourism organization**
- **Dominican Republic**
- **Mass drug administration**
- **Neglected tropical diseases**

COMPETING INTERESTS

Peter J. Hotez is Executive Director of the Global Network for Neglected Tropical Disease Control and President of the Sabin Vaccine Institute. He is an inventor on US Patent 7,303,752 B2 (issued December 4, 2007), entitled "Hookworm vaccine."

Chapter 10

Small Islands and Pandemic Influenza

Martin Eichner, Markus Schwehm, Nick Wilson, and Michael G. Baker

INTRODUCTION

Some island nations have explicit components of their influenza pandemic plans for providing travel warnings and restricting incoming travelers. But the potential value of such restrictions has not been quantified.

We developed a probabilistic model and used parameters from a published model (i.e., InfluSim) and travel data from Pacific Island Countries and Territories (PICTs).

The results indicate that of the 17 PICTs with travel data, only six would be likely to escape a major pandemic with a viral strain of relatively low contagiousness (i.e., for $R_0 = 1.5$) even when imposing very tight travel volume reductions of 99% throughout the course of the pandemic. For a more contagious viral strain ($R_0 = 2.25$) only five PICTs would have a probability of over 50% to escape. The total number of travelers during the pandemic must not exceed 115 (for $R_0 = 3.0$) or 380 (for $R_0 = 1.5$) if a PICT aims to keep the probability of pandemic arrival below 50%.

These results suggest that relatively few island nations could successfully rely on intensive travel volume restrictions alone to avoid the arrival of pandemic influenza (or subsequent waves). Therefore most island nations may need to plan for multiple additional interventions (e.g., screening and quarantine) to raise the probability of remaining pandemic free or achieving substantial delay in pandemic arrival.

There were large (voluntary) reductions of travel volumes associated with the global spread of severe acute respiratory syndrome (SARS) [1]. There have also been media reports of reduced tourist flows associated with the swine-origin (influenza virus A (H1N1)) influenza pandemic during 2009 (particularly for Mexico). Such a phenomenon may reoccur with the emergence of more virulent waves of the current pandemic or if new strains of pandemic influenza emerge.

In addition to voluntary changes in travel volumes, governments may also impose legal restrictions on travel and use exit and entry screening. Indeed, some island nations have explicit components of their influenza pandemic plans for providing travel warnings and restricting incoming travelers that is, New Zealand [2] and all four PICTs with published plans that were examined in a recent review [3]. Furthermore, some modeling work suggests that international air travel restrictions may contribute to delaying the global spread of a pandemic [4].

While a World Health Organization Writing Group [5] recognized that islands have achieved border control successes with pandemic influenza in the past, a more recent review cited expert opinion against the use of mandatory travel restrictions for pandemic influenza control [6]. However this review appeared to be in the context of large countries and did not consider islands (especially low-income island nations which cannot necessarily afford some other control options). Therefore, to better guide the use of these interventions, we aimed to quantify the potential impact of travel volume reductions to prevent (or at least delay) the entry of pandemic influenza into small Pacific island nations.

MATERIALS AND METHODS

Model of a Global Pandemic and Assumptions

We considered that a global influenza pandemic would spread around the world via aircraft travel and have an average reproduction number (R_0) in the range of 1.5–3.0 (with a mid-range value of 2.25). The pandemic was assumed to be in the form of a single pandemic wave that would end within a year.

For this pandemic scenario, we developed a probabilistic mathematical model that is described in detail in the technical appendix along with a numerical example for one island nation. An interactive software application that was based on this model was also developed and is freely available online at www.influsim.info/software/escaval [7].

The key parameter calculated was the "island escape probability" which was the probability that an island nation would avoid an outbreak of pandemic influenza for the full course of the global pandemic. The values of the input parameters used in our model for the global pandemic were based on the published model InfluSim [8] (with version 2.1, April, 2008, being freely downloadable). In addition, we made the two other assumptions to increase model realism:

- Only 50% of "moderately sick" cases (as defined in [8]) were assumed to be well enough to travel.
- Only 10% of "severely sick" cases (as defined in [8]) were assumed to be well enough to travel.

Such assumptions are likely to be very conservative as they assume no exit screening by pandemic-affected nations. We also assumed that no other pandemic influenza control measures would be utilized in the island nations. That is, no entry screening; no provision of antiviral to travelers; no quarantine; and no use of pre-pandemic vaccine or of a vaccine that had been developed after the emergence of the new pandemic strain.

Assumptions on Travel Reductions

We assumed that voluntary travel reductions (averaged over the course of the pandemic) might be similar to those experienced during SARS for travel between Hong Kong and the US at 79% [9]. Much higher levels of travel volume reduction (i.e., 99%) were assumed to relate to restrictions imposed by governments of island nations and to reflect essential diplomatic and emergency travel only (or complete "official" border closure with some leakage attributable to illegal yacht movements and private plane use).

Travel Data

We collected travel volume data for all the PICTs that were: (i) members of the Secretariat of the Pacific Community (SPC); (ii) which had a population of under one million (which excluded Papua New Guinea), and (iii) which had an airport (i.e., which excluded Tokelau and Pitcairn Island). Data were from the SPC website [10] and from its links to the websites of the Statistics Departments/Ministries of the PICTs (where these existed).

Calculating the Escape Probability

Using these data, we expect that a given number of infected individuals enter the island during the global pandemic. Depending on their course of disease and on the remaining time of contagiousness, the expected number of secondary cases per index case varies, and so does the probability that the index case triggers a major outbreak on the island. We combine all possible events, taking into consideration their individual probabilities, to calculate the probability that an island will either experience a major outbreak or ultimately escape the pandemic. Our calculations assume that travel restrictions are performed from the very beginning of a pandemic until the end or until the failure to prevent introduction becomes evident.

DISCUSSION

Main Findings and Interpretation

This analysis suggests that only a few PICTs might be expected to avoid pandemic influenza by relying on extremely rigorous travel volume reductions alone. Consequently, most PICTs need to consider multiple additional options in their pandemic planning (especially for pandemics with high case fatality ratios). These measures might include: entry screening using health questionnaires and use of rapid diagnostic tests; routine facility quarantine [11] or home quarantine with intensive monitoring; possibly the routine provision of antiviral to incoming travelers; pre-pandemic vaccination of their populations (if an appropriate vaccine became available); enhanced capacity for disease surveillance in the community and for rapid outbreak control capacity. As nearly 75% of infected travelers arrive without symptoms, entry screening based on the travelers' symptom states alone only slightly improves the escape probability (e.g., it increases Tonga's escape probability from 32 to 46% for the $R_0 = 1.5$ scenario with 99% travel reduction) if all symptomatic travelers are prevented from infecting anybody.

Our calculations assume that travel reduction remains constant during the whole period of the global pandemic. Higher numbers of travelers may temporarily be admitted from regions which are not or only slightly afflicted by the pandemic, but this strategy may be too difficult to implement because it would require the travel history of each arriving traveler to be verified. An alternative to these interventions is planning for complete border closure (i.e., practically 100% travel volume reduction) at the first sign of a global pandemic—a response that some PICTs used successfully during the 1918/19 influenza pandemic [12].

Even rigorous travel volume reductions might, however, be difficult for those PICTs that partially depend on food imports and other critical imports (e.g., medical supplies). Nevertheless, some PICTs might be able to facilitate ongoing trade by aircraft and shipping while keeping the crews of these vessels entirely separated from the local population (e.g., with high security unloading facilities where the crew never actually disembark while their vessel is unloaded). Others could enhance food self-sufficiency by increasing fishing and diverting export crops (e.g., coconut oil) for use as food.

Pandemic severity varies greatly with the experience of the current swine-origin (H1N1) influenza pandemic (at least to mid-2009) indicating a severity that might even be less overall than seasonal influenza. Therefore, good data on severity at the start of a pandemic (or a new pandemic wave) will help island nations decide if mandated travel volume reduction is a worthwhile intervention. Key variables for such early decisions from affected countries (especially developing countries) are hospitalization rates and case fatality ratios.

Also of note that some actions that would assist with severe travel volume reductions during pandemic influenza might be worthwhile in their own right. One example is building infrastructure to improve access to the Internet and to allow videoconferencing. Diversifying island economies (to reduce reliance on tourism) may also cushion island economies against other natural disasters and routine fluctuations in tourism numbers.

Although travel restrictions may not be sufficient to prevent the successful importation of an infection, they should (at least on average) delay it. Scalia Tomba and Wallinga [13] demonstrated with a simple mathematical model that an overall travel reduction by 99% should delay an epidemic on an island by about 3 weeks if R_0 is approximately 2.

Limitations

This analysis made many simplifying assumptions. It could potentially be improved by developing a more complex stochastic model that used log-normal or gamma-distributed sojourn times (rather than the exponential distributions used here). Such a model would also be able to provide information on the average time of pandemic arrival. Improved modeling (including combining additional border control interventions with travel reductions) may not only facilitate pandemic planning among PICTs but also help other island nations (and sub-national island jurisdictions) in the Caribbean, Southeast Asia, and off the coast of most continents.

Although we considered a range of values of R_0, it is conceivable that in a global pandemic the effective R_0 would decline after the first few months of pandemic emergence. This decline is because many countries around the world are very likely to adopt social distancing and other control measures. Possibly after some months, relevant technologies such as a pandemic strain vaccine might also become available (and start to be used by those planning to travel). Indeed, arriving travelers might be required to show a certificate of vaccination with a new pandemic vaccine.

The missing and suboptimal nature of some of the travel data shown in Table 1 is problematic. There is a need for regional agencies to encourage improved data collection and publication by PICTs so that studies such as the one reported here can be undertaken with more realism.

Finally we note that this work has not assessed the value to policy makers of island nations in presenting "escape probabilities" in the way that we have. It could be that to use a mandated travel reduction intervention, policy makers would need to have indications of much higher rates of success than thresholds of 50% (as used in Table 1). They may also need indications of the potential number of hospitalizations prevented and lives saved before there is political and popular acceptance of the policy (e.g. as calculated from case fatality ratios in other countries).

RESULTS

The results (Table 1) indicate that for the 17 PICTs with travel data, only six would be likely to avoid introduction of pandemic influenza, even if the pandemic strain was of relatively low contagiousness (i.e., for $R_0 = 1.5$) and if very tight travel reductions of 99% were applied throughout the course of the global pandemic (Table 1). For more severe pandemics ($R_0 = 2.25$ or higher), only four to five PICTs would have more than 50% probability of escaping. Only one country (Tuvalu) was considered to have a high chance of escaping a relatively "mild" pandemic by relying on voluntary travel volume reductions alone (i.e., a 79% reduction level).

Table 1. Probability of small islands in the South Pacific escaping a global influenza pandemic (for different values of R_0 and different travel volume reductions for arriving travelers).

Country (year for traveler arrival data)	Total annual traveler arrivals	Island escape probability for global influenza pandemic					
		99% travel reduction			79% travel reduction		
		$R_0 = 1.5$	$R_0 = 2.25$	$R_0 = 3.0$	$R_0 = 1.5$	$R_0 = 2.25$	$R_0 = 3.0$
Guam (2007/08)	1,210,600†	<0.01	<0.01	<0.01	<0.01	<0.01	<0.01
Fiji (2004)	596,084	<0.01	<0.01	<0.01	<0.01	<0.01	<0.01
Northern Mariana Islands (2004)	589,244*	<0.01	<0.01	<0.01	<0.01	<0.01	<0.01
French Polynesia (2006)	221,549*	0.02	<0.01	<0.01	<0.01	<0.01	<0.01
Samoa (2007)	196,627‡	0.03	<0.01	<0.01	<0.01	<0.01	<0.01
Vanuatu (2006)	154,101§	0.06	<0.01	<0.01	<0.01	<0.01	<0.01
Cook Islands (2007)	109,115	*0.14*	<0.01	<0.01	<0.01	<0.01	<0.01
New Caledonia (2006)	100,491*	*0.16*	0.01	<0.01	<0.01	<0.01	<0.01
Palau (2006)	86,375*	*0.21*	0.02	<0.01	<0.01	<0.01	<0.01
American Samoa (2006)	72,800	*0.27*	0.04	0.01	<0.01	<0.01	<0.01
Tonga (2003)	63,451	*0.32*	0.06	0.02	<0.01	<0.01	<0.01
Federated States of Micronesia (FSM) 2005	18,958*	**0.71**	*0.43*	*0.32*	<0.01	<0.01	<0.01
Solomon Islands (2007)	13,748*	**0.78**	**0.54**	*0.44*	<0.01	<0.01	<0.01
Marshall Islands (2005)	9173*	**0.85**	**0.66**	**0.57**	0.03	<0.01	<0.01
Kiribati (2006)	4704#	**0.92**	**0.81**	**0.75**	*0.17*	0.01	<0.01
Niue (2006)	4588**	**0.92**	**0.81**	**0.76**	*0.18*	0.01	<0.01
Tuvalu (2007)	1130	**0.98**	**0.95**	**0.93**	**0.65**	*0.34*	*0.24*
Nauru	n/a	-	-	-	-	-	-
Wallis and Futuna	n/a	-	-	-	-	-	-

Two of the 19 PICTs had no travel data and for the others much of the data were suboptimal in that they did not always include numbers of returning citizens, and often only the arrivals by air (i.e., ignoring arrivals by sea; for details, see Table 1).

Figure 1 shows how the island escape probability depends on the total number of travelers arriving on a PICT during the course of the global pandemic. For $R_0 = 1.5$, the critical number of travelers must not exceed 380, if the PICT aims to have an escape probability above 50%. For $R_0 = 2.25$ and $R_0 = 3.0$, these critical values are 155 and 115 travelers respectively.

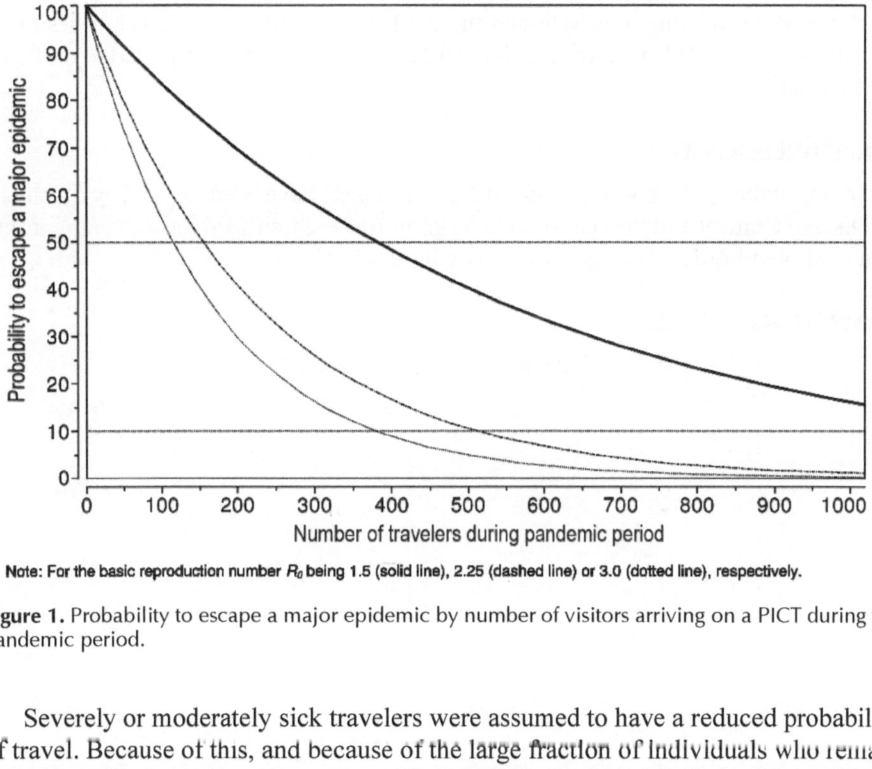

Note: For the basic reproduction number R_0 being 1.5 (solid line), 2.25 (dashed line) or 3.0 (dotted line), respectively.

Figure 1. Probability to escape a major epidemic by number of visitors arriving on a PICT during the pandemic period.

Severely or moderately sick travelers were assumed to have a reduced probability of travel. Because of this, and because of the large fraction of individuals who remain asymptomatic throughout the course of their infection, nearly 75% of infected visitors do not show any symptoms upon arrival on a PICT. This value only depends on the natural history of the disease and on the propensity of sick people to travel, but it is independent on R_0 (see the online Technical Appendix for more details).

CONCLUSION

These results suggest that relatively few island nations could successfully rely on intensive travel volume restrictions alone to avoid the arrival of pandemic influenza. Therefore most island nations will need to plan for multiple additional interventions (e.g., screening and quarantine) to raise the probability of remaining pandemic free.

KEYWORDS

- **Escape probability**
- **Global Pandemic**
- **Pacific Island Countries and Territories**
- **Travel Reductions**

AUTHORS' CONTRIBUTIONS

This study was conceived by Nick Wilson and Michael G. Baker. Martin Eichner developed the modeling approach and the mathematics. Markus Schwehm designed the software. Nick Wilson collected the input data. All authors contributed to drafts of the manuscript.

ACKNOWLEDGMENTS

Two of the authors (Nick Wilson and Michael G. Baker) have been assisted by a Centers for Disease Control and Prevention (USA) grant for research work on pandemic influenza control at borders (i.e., grant: 1 U01 CI000445-01).

COMPETING INTERESTS

The authors declare that they have no competing interests.

Chapter 11

Filariasis in Travelers and GeoSentinel Surveillance Network

Ettie M. Lipner, Melissa A. Law, Elizabeth Barnett, Jay S. Keystone, Frank von Sonnenburg, Louis Loutan, D. Rebecca Prevots, Amy D. Klion, and Thomas B. Nutman

INTRODUCTION

As international travel increases, there is rising exposure to many pathogens not traditionally encountered in the resource-rich countries of the world. Filarial infections, a great problem throughout the tropics and subtropics, are relatively rare among travelers even to filaria-endemic regions of the world. The GeoSentinel Surveillance Network, a global network of medicine/travel clinics, was established in 1995 to detect morbidity trends among travelers.

We examined data from the GeoSentinel database to determine demographic and travel characteristics associated with filaria acquisition and to understand the differences in clinical presentation between nonendemic visitors and those born in filaria-endemic regions of the world. Filarial infections comprised 0.62% (n = 271) of all medical conditions reported to the GeoSentinel Network from travelers; 37% of patients were diagnosed with *Onchocerca volvulus*, 25% were infected with *Loa loa*, and another 25% were diagnosed with *Wuchereria bancrofti*. Most infections were reported from immigrants and from those immigrants returning to their county of origin (those visiting friends and relatives); the majority of filarial infections were acquired in sub-Saharan Africa. Among the patients who were natives of filaria-nonendemic regions, 70.6% acquired their filarial infection with exposure greater than 1 month. Moreover, nonendemic visitors to filaria-endemic regions were more likely to present to GeoSentinel sites with clinically symptomatic conditions compared with those who had lifelong exposure.

Codifying the filarial infections presenting to the GeoSentinel Surveillance Network has provided insights into the clinical differences seen among filaria-infected expatriates and those from endemic regions and demonstrated that *O. volvulus* infection can be acquired with short-term travel.

As international travel increases, there is rising exposure to many pathogens not traditionally encountered in the resource-rich countries of the world. The GeoSentinel Surveillance Network, a global network of medicine/travel clinics, was established in 1995 to detect morbidity trends among travelers. Filarial infections (parasitic worm infections that cause, among others, onchocerciasis (river blindness), lymphatic filariasis (e.g., elephantiasis, lymphedema, hydrocele) and loiasis (African eyeworm)) comprised 0.62% (n = 271) of the 43,722 medical conditions reported to the GeoSentinel

Network between 1995-2004. Immigrants from filarial-endemic regions comprised the group most likely to have acquired a filarial infection; sub-Saharan Africa was the region of the world where the majority of filarial infections were acquired. Long-term travel (greater than 1 month) was more likely to be associated with acquisition of one of the filarial infections than shorter-term travel.

Parasitic diseases are widespread throughout the developing world and are associated with a heavy burden of morbidity and mortality. Human filariae, nematodes transmitted by arthropod vectors, are endemic in tropical and subtropical regions of the world. With an estimated 80 million people who travel to developing countries each year [1], exposure to filarial parasites is likely to become more common. It has been suggested that infection with filariae requires prolonged and intense exposure to the vectors that transmit them [2]. Moreover, when comparing nonendemic visitors who have acquired filarial infections with those born in endemic regions, the nonendemic visitors appear to have greater numbers of objective clinical symptoms and fewer clinically asymptomatic (or subclinical) infections [3-7].

The GeoSentinel Surveillance Network, a global network of specialized travel/tropical medicine clinics on six continents, was established in 1995 to contribute clinician-based sentinel surveillance on all travelers seen [8]. We examined data from the GeoSentinel database to identify demographic and travel characteristics associated with filaria acquisition in addition to species distribution of filarial acquisition and patient symptoms. Because there have been no comprehensive studies that have addressed the acquisition of filarial infections among nonendemic travelers, the present study was performed to understand travel-related filarial infections from a global viewpoint that could inform physicians and travelers alike.

MATERIALS AND METHODS

Data Source

Demographic, travel, and clinical data were collected from all patients seen at each GeoSentinel site. Travel information was also collected, including trip start and end dates for travel within 6 months and countries visited in the previous 5 years. Countries listed included birth country, country lived in prior to age 10, country of residence, and country of citizenship. Patient classification, the reason for recent travel, symptoms, and final diagnosis were reported by health care providers at GeoSentinel site clinics. Patient information was entered without identifiers into an Access database (Microsoft). Each individual record with a diagnosis of filarial infection was examined manually to verify that the place of exposure was in a filaria-endemic country and that the data provided were accurate and complete.

The GeoSentinel data-collection protocol was reviewed by the institutional review board officer at the National Center for Infectious Diseases at the Centers for Disease Control and Prevention and classified as public health surveillance and not as human-subjects research requiring submission to institutional review boards.

Inclusion Criteria

Data entered into the GeoSentinel database from patients seen from August 1997 through December 2004 were used. This analysis focused on data extracted from persons who were assigned codes corresponding to infection with *Onchocerca volvulus*, *Wuchereria bancrofti*, *Loa loa*, other filarial species, or unknown filarial species. Prior to analysis, a survey of all GeoSentinel sites was performed to ensure that the definition of infection was uniform among the reporting sites.

Definitions and Groupings

Patient Classifications

Patients were classified into seven categories: immigrants/refugees, foreign visitor, urban expatriate, non-urban expatriate, student, traveler, and military. These categories were based on country of origin, place of GeoSentinel site visit, and purpose of travel. An immigrant was defined as someone born and raised in a filarial-endemic region. A traveler was defined as one who crossed an international border and returned to his/her country of residence and presented to a clinic site. A foreign visitor was someone who sought medical care at a GeoSentinel site during their trip but was not a resident or citizen of that country. Persons who emigrated from one filaria-nonendemic country to another filaria-nonendemic country and classified as "immigrant" were reclassified to an appropriate category. Students from filaria-endemic regions studying in nonendemic regions were reclassified from student to immigrant for the purposes of these analyses. Persons born and raised in filarial nonendemic regions and traveling to filarial-endemic regions are collectively referred to as "nonendemic visitors".

Reason for Recent Travel

The reasons for recent travel were categorized into immigration, tourism, business, research/education, missionary/volunteer, or visiting friends or relatives (VFR) based on patient self-report to physician. The VFRs are people born and raised in a filaria-endemic region, but currently residing in a filarial nonendemic region. Students from filaria-endemic regions studying in nonendemic regions were reclassified from education to immigrant for the purposes of these analyses.

Diagnoses

Physician-reported final diagnoses were assigned a diagnosis code and entered into the GeoSentinel database. Diagnoses are defined as suspect, probable, or confirmed. Confirmed means that the diagnosis was made by an indisputable clinical finding or diagnostic test (identification of the parasite or parasite DNA), and probable indicates that the diagnosis was supported by evidence strong enough to establish presumption (classical clinical findings and positive serology, and response to definitive treatment), but not proof. All sites used the best available reference diagnostics in their own country. Some of the "filarial species unknown" diagnoses were reclassified into *O. volvulus*, *W. bancrofti*, or *L. loa* if the country of exposure had only one filarial species present. Of the 65 originally classified as unknown filarial species, 50 were reclassified.

Regions

Countries were grouped into regions: Southeast Asia, Eastern Europe, Northern Africa (including Canary Islands), Oceania, Western Europe, sub-Saharan Africa, South America, Caribbean, South Central Asia (including Tibet), Western Asia, Australia/

New Zealand, North America, Antarctica, Eastern/North Asia (including Taiwan), and Central America.

Duration of Travel, and Time to Presentation to a GeoSentinel Site
Detailed travel data were available for only a subset of patients. In those for whom this information was available, trip duration and time to presentation were divided into 1 month, 1-6 months, and over 6 months to group short, medium, and long-term exposure and incubation periods. Those without definitive travel data related to the place of exposure were excluded only from this particular type of analysis. Trip duration and time to presentation were determined only for those who did not have lifelong exposure to filarial infections. The time to presentation was the interval between the clinic visit and date of return from the most recent travel to a filarial-endemic region of the world.

Statistical Analysis
Data were managed in Microsoft Access and were analyzed using SAS v.9.1 (SAS Institute). Crude odds ratios were calculated from a bivariate analysis, and statistical significance was determined by χ^2 tests.

From a total of 43,722 individual patient encounters, filarial infections were diagnosed for 271 (0.62%) persons who presented to GeoSentinel sites from August 1997 through July 2004. The reporting of cases to GeoSentinel was lowest in 1997-1998 (3.7% and 8.9% respectively); from 1999 through 2004, filariasis as a proportion of morbidity (ill patients reporting to the clinics) fluctuated between 11% ($n = 30$) and 17.5% ($n = 47$). Of the 271 patients with filarial infections, 37% were diagnosed with *O. volvulus*, 25% were infected with *L. loa*, and another 25% were diagnosed with *W. bancrofti*. Among all filarial infections, 5.5% were identified as other filarial species, (e.g., *Mansonella*, *Brugia* spp.), and 5.5% of all filarial infections reported in the database were unspecified. Three patients were coinfected with *L. loa* and other filarial species; one patient presented with *O. volvulus* and *L. loa* coinfection (Figure 1). Overall, 122 (45%) patients were female; gender was not recorded for 17 (6.3%) patients. Patient mean age was 34.9 years (range 0–84). The region of acquisition among filaria-infected individuals was assigned when possible ($n = 230$). The majority (75%) of infections were acquired in Africa (both Northern Africa and Sub-Saharan Africa) and 10% in South America (see Table 1). The remaining individuals were exposed in, Oceania, the Caribbean, South Central Asia, and Central America. Of all, filarial infections reported to the GeoSentinel ntwork ($n = 271$), the majority were reported by the North American sites (76.4%); 18.5% were reported from European sites, and the remainder were reported from GeoSentinel sites in the Middle East, Australia/New Zealand, and South Central Asia.

Among the 271 patients diagnosed with filarial infections, the majority (62%) occurred among immigrants. Non-urban expatriates and travelers represented the second largest group of patients with filarial infections. Foreign visitors, urban expatriates, and students (Figure 2) comprised the groups in which there were relatively few filarial infections. As an overall proportion of GeoSentinel reports, filarial infections were found to occur in 1.6% of immigrants, 2.4% of non-urban expatriates, 1.5%

of students, 0.2% of foreign visitors, 0.2% of urban expatriates, and 0.2% of travelers. The "reasons for travel" were predominantly for immigration or for immigrants who were VFR in endemic regions (63%). An additional 16% of patients traveled for missionary or volunteer activities, and the remainder traveled for tourism, research/education, or business-related purposes (Figure 3). When grouped by type of parasite, immigrants, and VFR had the greatest proportion of diagnosed onchocerciasis (48%) compared with nonendemic visitors (20%). Twenty-nine percent of VFR and immigrants with filarial infections were infected with *W. bancrofti*, while only 18% of nonendemic visitors had *W. bancrofti* infection. The diagnosis of *L. loa* was greatest among nonendemic visitors (43%), compared with 15% of VFR and immigrants with loiasis (Figure 4).

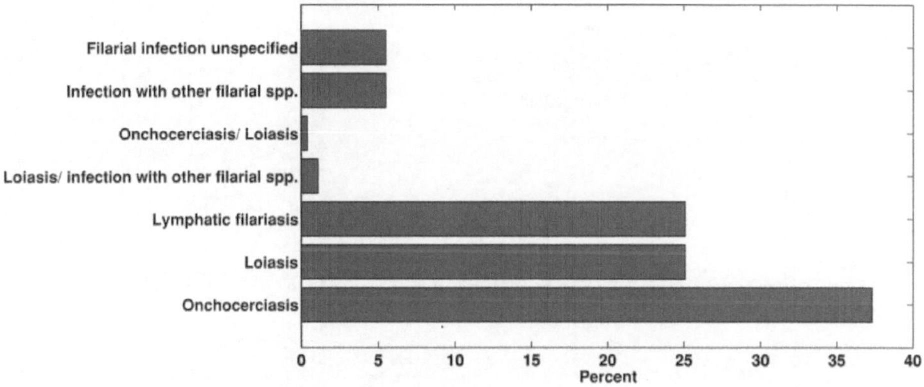

Figure 1. Distribution of filarial infections among international travelers reported in the GeoSentinel Surveillance Network.

Table 1. Region and countries of exposure to filarial parasite.

Region	Country	N (%)
Africa		172 (75.1%)
	Benin	2
	Burkina Faso	3
	Burundi	1
	Cameroon	62
	Central African Republic	6
	Comoros	1
	Congo	5
	Cote d'lvoire	3
	Egypt	1
	Ethiopia	9
	Gabon	7

Table 1. *(Continued)*

Region	Country	N (%)
	Ghana	9
	Guinea	2
	Liberia	11
	Nigeria	10
	Senegal	1
	Sierra Leone	10
	Tanzania	1
	Niger	2
	Sudan	4
	Togo	1
	Uganda	1
	Unspecified	18
	Zaire	2
South America		23 (10%)
	Brazil	1
	Guyana	22
South Central Asia		15 (6.6%)
	Bangladesh	1
	India	8
	Nepal	1
	Sri Lanka	5
Caribbean		8 (3.5%)
	Dominican Republic	2
	Haiti	6
South East Asia		5 (2.2%)
	Philippines	3
	Vietnam	2
Oceania		4 (1.7%)
	Guam	1
	Papua New Guinea	1
	Samoa	1
	South Pacific Islands	1
Central America		2 (0.9%)
	Mexico	1
	Nicaragua	1
Total		229 (100%)

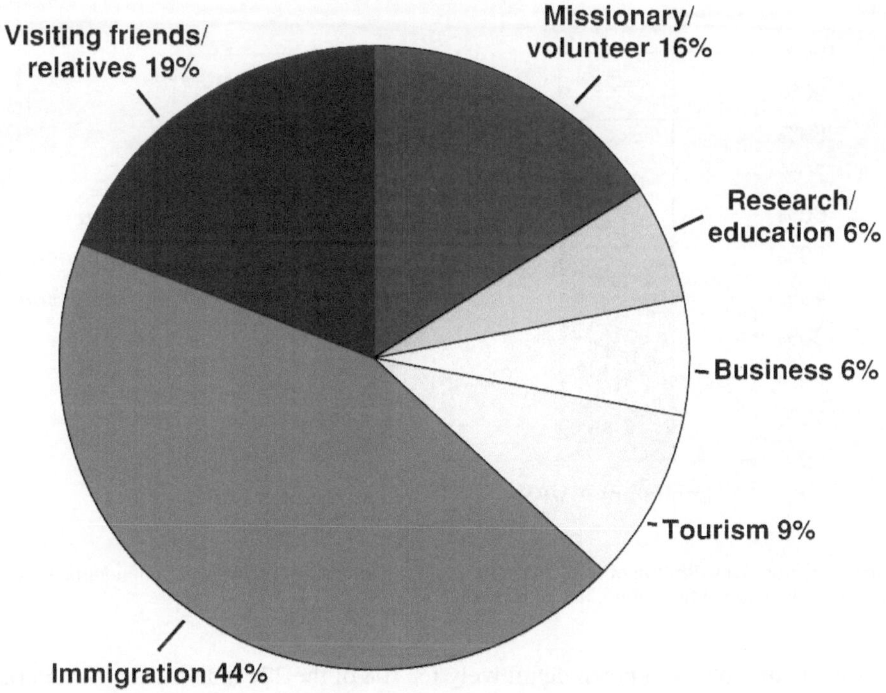

Figure 2. Patient classification among persons with filarial infections reported in the GeoSentinel Surveillance Network.

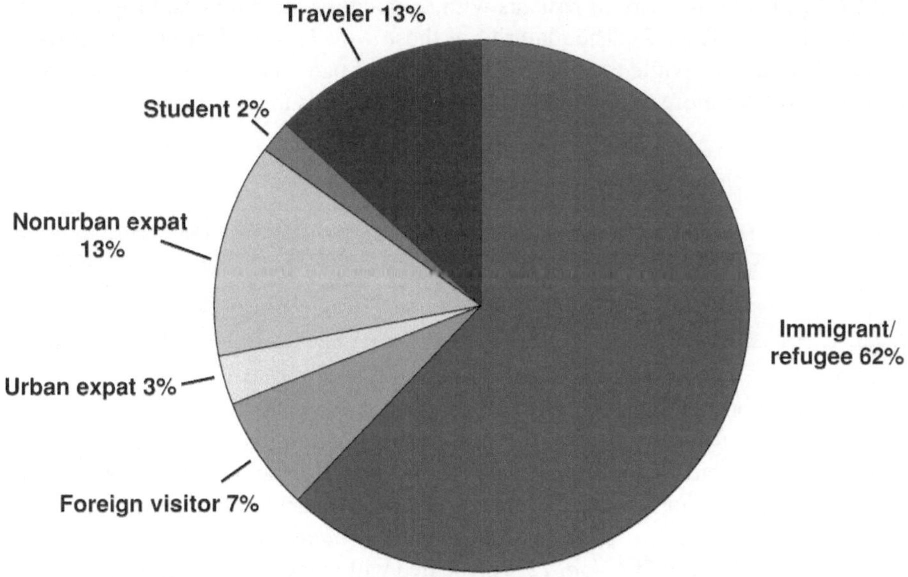

Figure 3. Reason for travel among persons with filarial infections reported in the GeoSentinel Surveillance Network.

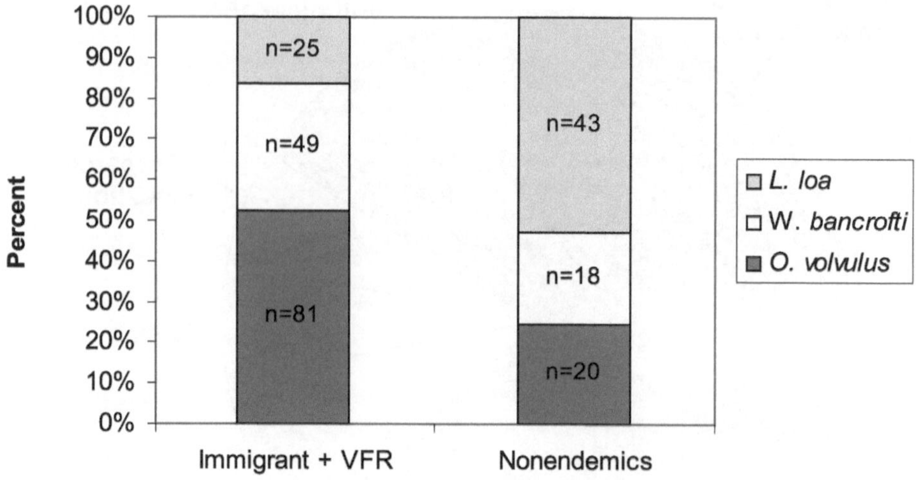

Figure 4. Regional distribution of filarial infections among immigrants, VFR, and nonendemic visitors reported in the GeoSentinel Surveillance Network.

Travel duration was known definitively for 108 of the 271 individuals with filarial infection. Among these 108, 48 persons originated from nonendemic regions but only 34 had recorded travel data definitively related to the place of exposure. Trip duration ranged from 7 days to 17.7 years (geometric mean duration: 125 days; median duration: 87 days). The majority of patients with *O. volvulus* infections had trip durations of up to 1 month (Table 2). The majority of those with *L. loa* infections had traveled between 1-6 months, while the highest percentage of patients with *W. bancrofti* infection occurred after more than 6 months of travel (and presumed exposure).

Table 2. Trip duration by filarial infection among nonendemic visitors.

# Days	O. volvulus *n* (%)	W. bancrofti *n* (%)	L. loa *n* (%)	Other filarial spp. *n* (%)
0–31	7 (77.8)	0	2 (12.5)	1 (14.3)
32–180	1 (11.1)	0	9 (56.3)	1 (14.3)
>180	1 (11.1)	2 (100)	5 (31.2)	5 (71.4)

The time to presentation to a GeoSentinel site after arrival in a filaria-nonendemic country was calculated to identify the possible incubation period between exposure and clinical presentation in only nonendemic visitors (VFR and immigrants excluded from this analysis). For *O. volvulus* infections, 67% presented to a GeoSentinel site within 1 month of return, and 100% of those with *W. bancrofti* presented between 1-6 months. Among those with *L. loa*, 12% presented within the first month of return, 77% within 1-6 months of return, and the remainder at least 6 months after return. Among patients infected with other filarial species, the majority presented within 1 month of return. These data suggest that Onchocerca infections are more likely to be symptomatic early in the infection compared to either *Loa loa* or *Wuchereria bancrofti* (data not shown).

In studies done previously in loiasis [3] and onchocerciasis [4] among limited numbers of expatriates, the data suggested that the clinical symptoms were more pronounced (and less likely to be asymptomatic) in travelers (temporary visitors) to filaria-endemic regions of the world compared with those with lifelong exposure and chronic infections [3]. To examine this issue more closely, a comparison was made between those infections that were clinically symptomatic and those that were clinically asymptomatic (Table 3). Characterization of symptoms included those associated with the following organ systems: skin, cardiac, respiratory, gastrointestinal, genitourinary, neurologic, musculoskeletal, ophthalmologic, and otolaryngologic, in addition to complaints of fatigue, fever, and psychological problems. If the patient had no complaints or symptoms or in which filarial infection was identified incidentally following evaluation for another condition, then asymptomatic was recorded. As seen, those individuals in the GeoSentinel database identified to have filarial infection who were born and raised in endemic regions were 2.5 times as likely to be clinically asymptomatic (CI 1.07, –5.93) compared with those who traveled from filaria-nonendemic to filaria-endemic regions ($P<.03$)

Table 3. Association between patient endemicity status and commonly presenting symptoms of filarial infections.

Symptomatic	Endemic	Nonendemic	Total
No	35	7	42
Yes	152	75	227
Total	187	82	269
		Missing: 2	
OR (95% CI)	2.5 (1.05, 5.81)		

DISCUSSION

While filarial infection and disease are most frequently diagnosed among native residents of endemic regions, the risk of infection acquisition among travelers from nonendemic regions is sizeable. Filarial species are found in tropical and sub-tropical regions of the world and, as travel to these regions becomes more popular, filarial infection among nonendemic visitors becomes increasingly common as well. We describe here important epidemiologic characteristics of filarial infections acquired by world travelers from nonendemic regions as reported to the GeoSentinel network. While clinical presentation of filarial disease is known to differ between visitors to and natives of endemic regions [3], our analysis also provides a quantitative assessment of filarial acquisition among travelers and helps describe the differences in clinical presentation between those native to filaria-endemic regions and those traveling to those regions.

Filarial infections comprised 271 cases (0.62%) of all medical conditions reported to the GeoSentinel network. *O. volvulus* was responsible for the greatest number of filarial infections (n = 101), followed by equal numbers (n = 68) of *L. loa* and *W. bancrofti* (Figure 1). Because the GeoSentinel database includes immigrants/refugees who undergo laboratory screening that includes filarial serologies when eosinophilia or clinical signs or symptoms of filarial disease are present, it is not surprising that the majority of filaria-infected patients in the GeoSentinel network were immigrants (62%). Due to lifelong chronic exposure, the prevalence of filarial infections among immigrants can be significant.

It has, however, typically been said that infection acquisition is low for short-term, nonendemic travelers. Although travel information was only available for a subset of the total number of filaria-nonendemic visitors, it was still unexpected to find that almost one-third (30%) of travelers from nonendemic regions acquired their filarial infections during trips of 31 days or less (the majority of *O. volvulus* infections), and only 38% of filarial infections occurred from trip durations exceeding 180 days (Table 2). There are numerous case reports and case series that describe durations of exposure as short as 10 days among filaria-infected patients from nonendemic regions [5, 9-12]. It is possible that the lack of preventive measures such as insect repellent and bednets, as well as individuals close proximity to vector habitats, played a role in infection acquisition regardless of short durations of exposure. Further, development of symptoms may also be dependent on the density of filarial larval inoculation as well as individual innate immune responses [13].

Because almost all of the major filarial infections (*O. volvulus*, *W. bancrofti*, *L. loa*, *M. perstans*, *M. streptocerca*) are endemic in sub-Saharan Africa, it is not surprising that 72% of filarial infections reported to GeoSentinel were acquired in this region: 95.5% of those with onchocerciasis were acquired in sub-Saharan Africa; three were acquired elsewhere. Thirty-two percent of the *W. bancrofti* infections were acquired in South America, compared with only 12% of *W. bancrofti* infections reported from sub-Saharan African regions, 22% from South Central Asia, and 14% from the Caribbean. As expected, 100% of loiasis cases were acquired in West and Central Africa, as the parasite is endemic only in this region.

While short-term nonendemic visitors appear less likely to acquire filarial infections, among those with relatively long-term exposure there have been many case reports of travel-related filarial infections and associated clinical symptoms [3-5, 11, 13-15]. Presentation of clinical disease among patients with *L. loa*, *O. volvulus*, and *W. bancrofti* differs considerably between expatriates (or long-term temporary residents) and those born in filaria-endemic regions of the world. Among those infected with *L. loa*, infected expatriates typically have a greater frequency of Calabar swellings, higher grade levels of filaria-specific antibody and peripheral eosinophil counts, and more nonspecific complaints, while those born and raised in endemic regions are more likely to have asymptomatic infections associated with microfilaremia. Those born in regions with endemic *O. volvulus* infection generally have higher levels of skin microfilariae and more ocular disease than do nonendemic visitors to these regions [16]. Those living in regions with endemic lymphatic filariasis most commonly have asymptomatic (or subclinical) infections, although significant proportions of infected individuals develop hydrocele, lymphedema elephantiasis, or chyluria. Nonendemic visitors (and short-term visitors) rarely have asymptomatic microfilaremic condition, but rather are more likely to develop lymphadenitis, hepatomegaly, splenomegaly, and reversible lymphedema [17].

This study corroborates many of the anecdotal reports about the differences between the clinical presentations among travelers compared with those with chronic (and often lifelong) exposure to filarial parasites. Case report findings describe the clinical manifestations of filarial disease to be greater among expatriates, while those from filaria-endemic regions present commonly without symptoms. Indeed, our results from the GeoSentinel network indicate that filaria-infected patients with long-term exposure to filariae were more commonly asymptomatic (or subclinical) compared with those expatriates with filarial infections.

With the collection of surveillance data on travel-related medical conditions by the GeoSentinel network, epidemiologic data can describe morbidity and mortality trends among travelers [18]. While these networks are generally used to follow acute infections among nonendemic visitors, we have demonstrated here the utility of surveillance for chronic infections, as well. Diagnoses of filarial infections in industrialized countries will likely continue to rise as increasing numbers of people travel to endemic regions and as increasing numbers of refugees and immigrants arrive from endemic areas. The majority of nonendemic filaria-infected visitors (64.7%) presented to a Geo Sentinel site clinic between 1 and 6 months after return of travel, underscoring the need for surveillance of chronic infections to ensure safety and treatment of returning travelers from developing regions.

In conclusion, analysis of data on filarial infections available from the GeoSentinel network enabled us to describe characteristics of patients presenting with filarial infection and to determine that filarial infections can be acquired with relatively short-term exposure. Our study not only corroborates but expands the understanding of the differences in filarial disease manifestation between those traveling to and those born in filaria-endemic regions of the world by providing a quantitative analysis of filarial acquisition among nonendemic visitors. Moreover, our data demonstrate that globally acquired travel data can be used to follow not only acute but also chronic infections and can ultimately provide a more comprehensive backdrop to pre-travel advice and to post-travel treatment for those at risk of acquiring a filarial infection.

MEMBERS OF THE GEOSENTINEL SURVEILLANCE NETWORK

In addition to the authors, members contributing data include:

Graham Brown and Joseph Torresi, Royal Melbourne Hospital, Melbourne, Australia; Giampiero Carosi and Francesco Castelli, University of Brescia, Brescia, Italy; Lin Chen, Mount Auburn Hospital, Harvard University, Cambridge, Massachusetts, USA; Bradley Connor, Cornell University, New York, New York, USA; Jean Delmont and Philippe Parola, Hôpital Nord, Marseille, France; Carlos Franco and Phyllis Kozarsky, Emory University, Atlanta, Georgia, USA; David Freedman, University of Alabama, Birmingham, Alabama, USA; Stefanie Gelman and Devon Hale, University of Utah, Salt Lake City, Utah, USA; Alejandra Gurtman, Mount Sinai Medical Center, New York City, New York, USA; Jean Haulman and Elaine Jong, University of Washington, Seattle, Washington, USA; Kevin Kain, University of Toronto, Toronto, Canada; Carmelo Licitra, Orlando Regional Health Center, Orlando, Florida, USA; Prativa Pandey, CIWEC Clinic Travel Medicine Center, Kathmandu, Nepal; Patricia Schlagenhauf and Robert Steffen, University of Zurich, Zurich, Switzerland; Eli Schwartz, Sheba Medical Center, Tel Hashomer, Israel; Marc Shaw, Travellers Health and Vaccination Centre, Auckland, New Zealand; Mary Wilson, Harvard University, Cambridge, Massachusetts, USA; Murray Wittner, Albert Einstein School of Medicine, Bronx, New York, USA.

KEYWORDS

- **Filarial infections**
- **GeoSentinel Surveillance Network**
- ***Loa loa***
- **Onchocerciasis**
- ***Onchocerca volvulus***
- ***Wuchereria bancrofti***

AUTHORS' CONTRIBUTIONS

Conceived and designed the experiments: Thomas B. Nutman, Louis Loutan, and Frank von Sonnenburg. Analyzed the data: Thomas B. Nutman, Louis Loutan, Elizabeth Barnett, Jay S. Keystone, Ettie M. Lipner, Melissa A. Law, Frank von Sonnenburg, D. Rebecca Prevots, and Amy D. Klion. Contributed reagents/materials/analysis tools: Louis Loutan, Elizabeth Barnett, Jay S. Keystone, Ettie M. Lipner, Melissa A. Law, Frank von Sonnenburg, and D. Rebecca Prevots. Wrote the chapter: Thomas B. Nutman, Louis Loutan, Elizabeth Barnett, Jay S. Keystone, Ettie M. Lipner, Melissa A. Law, Frank von Sonnenburg, D. Rebecca Prevots, and Amy D. Klion.

ACKNOWLEDGMENTS

We thank NIAID intramural editor Brenda Rae Marshall for assistance.

Chapter 12

Travel Restrictions for Moderately Contagious Diseases

Martin Camitz and Fredrik Liljeros

INTRODUCTION

Much research in epidemiology has been focused on evaluating conventional methods of control strategies in the event of an epidemic or pandemic. Travel restrictions are often suggested as an efficient way to reduce the spread of a contagious disease that threatens public health, but few chapters have studied in depth the effects of travel restrictions. In this study, we investigated what effect different levels of travel restrictions might have on the speed and geographical spread of an outbreak of a disease similar to severe acute respiratory syndrome (SARS).

We used a stochastic simulation model incorporating survey data of travel patterns between municipalities in Sweden collected over 3 years. We tested scenarios of travel restrictions in which travel over distances >50 km and 20 km would be banned, taking into account different levels of compliance.

We found that a ban on journeys >50 km would drastically reduce the speed and geographical spread of outbreaks, even when compliance is <100%. The result was found to be robust for different rates of intermunicipality transmission intensities.

This study supports travel restrictions as an effective way to mitigate the effect of a future disease outbreak.

Knowledge of the speed at which a contagious disease travels between geographical regions is vital for making decisions about the most effective intervention strategies. The actual routes a disease will take are strongly determined by how individuals travel within and between regions [1-4]. As was shown during the outbreak of SARS [5], current travel patterns enable contagious diseases to spread to far corners of the globe at alarming rates. This demonstrates the need for a new type of model that in corporates travel networks.

Several authors have responded to the call, resulting in now-classic papers. Rvachev and Longini [6], with their followers Grais et al. [7], were among the first to publish such studies, using deterministic models. Hufnagel et al. [8] have demonstrated how a simple stochastic model in conjunction with data on aviation traffic could be used to simulate the global spread of the SARS epidemic. Using a stochastic transmission model on both a city level and globally, with each city interconnected by the international aviation network, they produced results in surprising agreement with World Health Organization (WHO) reports of the actual epidemic. With some exceptions, most prominently Japan, all infected countries in the simulation were also present in the WHO reports. The orders of magnitude were also closely matched.

Our study applied a version of the Hufnagel model to Sweden in order to predict the effect that travel restrictions might have on the geographical spread of an outbreak. Instead of using only the aviation network, which connects only some 30 towns in Sweden, we used survey data on all intermunicipal travel, including all forms of travel.

Sweden is, by European standards, a large country, with a small population. Just over 9 million people share 450,000 square kilometers. The population is, however, largely urbanized, and in that respect similar to other industrialized nations with large areas.

Eubank et al. [9] estimated a travel network at community level using census data. Our data directly cover traveling over the whole nation on all scales, although we have kept only the regional data. It is sufficiently extensive that simulation or smoothing for estimating a travel network could be avoided and thus can, in some respects, be regarded as "real". Using such data in a simulation at this geographic level, is unique.

The choice of a stochastic modeling approach [10] was based on the fact that it mimics the highly random initial phase of an epidemic better than does the traditional deterministic approach [11, 12]. We first present the survey data used to estimate travel intensities between different municipalities in Sweden. We then introduce the simulation model for simulating the spread of the diseases and study the effect of travel restrictions. This introduction is to some extents a recapitulation of Hufnagel's model. Following this, we present the results of the simulations. We conclude our study with a discussion of the validity of the model and possible conclusions for future policy interventions.

MATERIALS AND METHODS

For this study, we used data from a random survey carried out by Statistics Sweden from 1999 to 2001, inclusive [13]. A total of 17,000 individuals took part in the survey, constituting 71.9% of the selection. In all, 34,816 distinct intermunicipal trips were reported. An intermunicipal journey was defined as a trip between two points where the individual lives, works, or conducts an errand. In other words, we treated a journey between home and work as several trips if the traveler made stops on the way for errands, provided that a municipal border was crossed between each stop. The data were weighted to correspond to 1 day and to the entire population for ages 6 to 84 years.

As it turned out, roughly 1% of the data was significantly erroneous and was consequently removed*. From the remaining set, we estimated a travel intensity matrix with each element corresponding to the one-way travel intensity between two municipalities. The number of non-zero elements was 11,611 (to be compared with the size of the matrix: 83,521). The matrix elements stood in direct correspondence with the underlying data, weighted for time and population. Even though the matrix gives a good picture of the traveling pattern in Sweden, we must treat any travel intensity between two specific communities with care. This is especially true for small communities with only a single or very few journeys made between them.

A total of nine scenarios, with 1,000 realizations each, was simulated to study the effects of three levels of travel restrictions as a control measure, for three different levels of the global intercommunity infectiousness parameter, γ, which was used to calibrate the model in the study of Hufnagel et al. Sixty days was chosen as the simulation period, as this gives sufficient time for a possible extinction to occur and for all stochasticity to play out its part in all but the smallest and most distant municipalities. Each scenario started with a single infectious individual in Stockholm, and treated the country as isolated from influx of disease. The traveling restrictions were divided into three levels. In the first level, we used the complete intensity matrix. In the following two, we removed data corresponding to journeys >50 km and journeys >20 km, respectively. The simulations were designated SIM, SIM50, and SIM20, respectively. In Figure 1, the datasets are displayed as geographical plots.

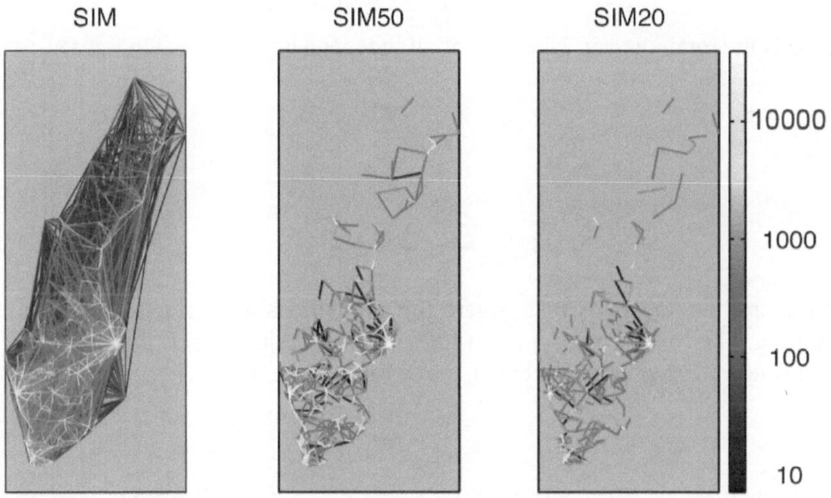

Figure 1. The intermunicipal travel network. The intermunicipal travel network with travel intensities indicated by color lines. The scale is logarithmic in trips per day. SIM shows the complete dataset. In SIM50 and SIM20, all journeys >50 km and 20 km, respectively, have been removed. The lines are drawn between the population centers of each municipality, so in many cases the trips are shorter than the lines representing them.

We also considered the case if the travel restrictions were not obeyed wholly by the public. Perhaps 5% might not heed the restrictions, resulting in a small but non-zero intensity for trips longer than the set restrictions. Full 1,000-run simulations were made at varying levels of distance restrictions and compliance, resulting in a mesh surface of the incidence.

We used a simplified version of the model suggested by Hufnagel et al. [8], and thus the following is as much a description of Hufnagel's model as our own. The individuals in both models can be in four different states:

- S: susceptible
- L: latent, meaning infected but not infectious
- I: infectious
- R: recovered and/or immune.

The rate at which individuals move from one category to the next is governed by the intensity parameters: $\alpha = 0.55^{\dagger}$; $\beta = 0.21$, which is the inverse infectious time and $\nu = 0.19$, the inverse latency time [14, 15]. Individuals become infected at a rate proportional to α and the number of infected (force of infection). They subsequently become infectious at rate β, contributing to the force of infection, and recover at rate ν. Thus far, this is a description of a regular random-mixing epidemic model. We now assume a traveling component contributing to the force of infection, a term for each of the connected municipalities proportional to the number of infectious there.

As the process is assumed to be Markovian, as in Hufnagel's model, the time between two events, Δt, is random, taken from an exponential distribution,

$$\Delta t \,\varepsilon\, \mathrm{Exp}(1/Q) \tag{1}$$

where Q is the total intensity, the sum of all independent transmission rates:

$$\begin{aligned} Q_i^L &= \alpha I_i \frac{S_i}{N_i} + \sum_{j\neq i} \gamma_{j,i} I_j \frac{S_i}{N_i}, \\ Q_i^I &= \nu L_i, \\ Q_i^R &= \beta I_i. \\ Q = \sum_i Q_i^L &+ \sum_i Q_i^L + \sum_i Q_i^L. \end{aligned} \tag{2}$$

These are the equations that govern the simulations and give us the continuous time setting. The component $\gamma_{j,i}$ in (2) (note the reversed indexes) is the intermunicipal infectiousness corresponding to the one-way route j to i. If,

$$\omega_{j,i} = M_{j,i} \Big/ \sum_i M_{j,i}$$

where $M_{j,i}$ is the travel intensity (i.e., ω_j, i is the probability that a traveler in j will choose the route j to i, then $\gamma_{j,i} = \gamma\omega_{j,i}$. In cases where restrictions are active, this expression is further scaled row-wise to match the smaller mass of the matrix. γ is the global intermunicipal infectiousness parameter mentioned above. We use the approximation given by Hufnagel et al. based on data from the actual outbreak, $\gamma = 0.27$. The parameter γ is influenced by the total travel intensity, the medium of travel, and as we have seen, the propensity for travel in different communities.

We would have liked to calibrate our model in a similar way, but as we have no outbreak data for Sweden, we needed to see whether changes in γ would drastically alter our conclusions. To get an idea of its effect, we compared Hufnagel's estimate of γ with other possible values. As γ is an infectiousness parameter playing a similar role in the governing equations above as α, we argue that $\alpha = 0.55$ is an upper bound for γ. The force of infection between two municipalities with equal population and number of infectious is unlikely to be higher than from within those municipalities. To find an appropriate lower bound we extrapolated proportionately from these, producing 0.13.

Although this is not mentioned in the original work by Hufnagel et al., the expression above means that everybody, regardless of where they live, is equally prone to travel outside their home, the uptake area of the airport or, in our case, the municipality.

This is a heavy assumption indeed, as it depends on the function of the municipality varying. The municipality may be a suburb or self-sufficient community, just as airports may be transit hubs or terminals. One of the strengths of Hufnagel's model is that it seems to be forgiving towards many simplifications, this one included, with the correct choice of γ. We investigated corrections for this assumption, such as row-wise scaling according to the known probability for travel, but found little effect on absolute incidence and none on the qualitative conclusions of the current study. As such, we were reluctant to stray from Hufnagel's model.

After the initial conditions were set up, including a single infected person in Stockholm, the simulation ran as follows. First, we moved forward in time with a random step Δt given by (1). We then selected the event that would occur with a probability proportional to the corresponding intensity. All intensities were updated according to the new state, and the process was repeated until the disease died out or the simulation period, 60 days, was passed.

The results for all nine scenarios were plotted geographically and color-coded according to the mean incidence (Figure 2).

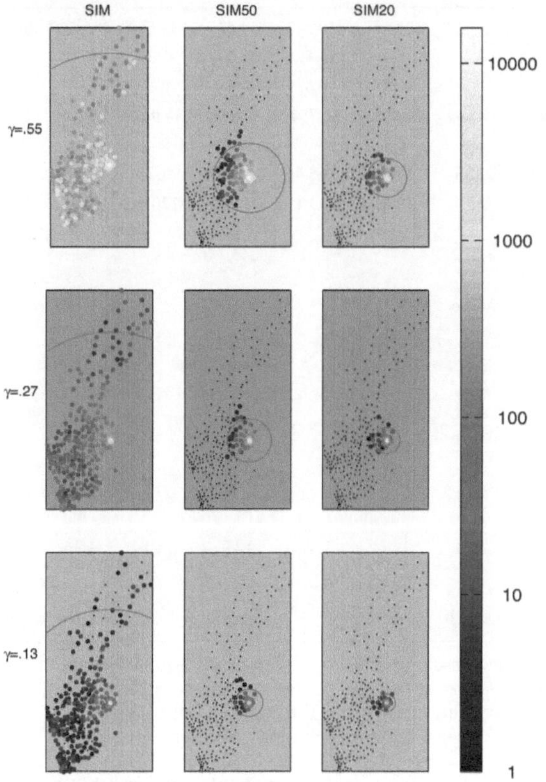

Figure 2. Epidemic spread for different restrictions and values of γ. Geographical plot of the municipalities, logarithmically color-coded according to the mean incidence after 60 days. SIM depicts the complete data set. In SIM50 and SIM20, all journeys > 50 km and 20 km, respectively, have been removed. The red circle signifies the mean extent of the epidemic from Stockholm.

A scenario with no restrictions resulted in an outbreak in which a majority of the municipalities became affected regardless of γ. Only the incidence differed. A ban on journeys >50 km stifled the dynamics of the outbreak. For the two lower values of γ, we see that the disease remained in the Stockholm area after 60 days, and for the higher value of γ, the disease did not manage to spread far from the densely populated areas around the largest Swedish cities. Prohibiting journeys >20 km would result in an even slower spread with a small number of afflicted municipalities, mainly localized around Stockholm. What is more, the total incidence after 60 days as well as the incidence in each municipality dropped as we imposed the restrictions.

Table 1 compares the country's total incidence in the three simulations for which Hufnagel's estimate of γ was used. Table 2 presents the incidence broken down into a few selected municipalities.

Table 1. Main results.

	SIM			SIM50			SIM20		
Results	**Mean**	**95% SI**		**Mean**	**95% SI**		**Mean**	**95% SI**	
Total number of infected	320 587	301 587	339 243	154 517	145 664	163 678	64 307	60 326	68 293
Percentage of population	3.6	3.4	3.8	1.7	1.6	1.8	0.72	0.67	0.76
Intermunicipal infections (n)	0.3	0.3	0.3	0.3	0.3	0.3	0.2	0.2	0.2
Incidence after 60 days (n)	77 184	72 760	81 784	37 065	34 941	39 321	15 240	14 307	16 190
Percentage of population	0.9	0.8	0.9	0.4	0.4	0.4	0.17	0.16	0.18
Afflicted municipalities (n)	262.1	258.5	265.4	47.2	46.6	47.8	34.0	33.6	34.5
Mean incidence in municipalities (n)	267.1	251.4	283.1	128.3	120.5	136.0	52.7	49.5	56.1
Mean influence distance (km)	1 222	-		245.1	-		153.8	-	
Travel intensity matrix	Value			Value			Value		
Total travel intensity (millions/day)	4.2	-		2.9	-		1.5	-	
Intermunicipal one-way routes (n)	11 611	-		1 386	-		797	-	
Summary	Value			Value			Value		
Extinction runs (n)	262	-		268	-		305	-	
Mean time for extinction (days)	3.48	2.84	4.14	3.48	2.78	4.25	3.61	2.85	4.46
Mean number of afflicted municipalities before extinction (n)	1.33	1.26	1.41	1.29	1.21	1.36	1.27	1.22	1.34
Total number of realizations	1 000	-		1 000	-		1 000	-	

The table show the main results along with miscellaneous information about the simulation.
Figures refer to simulated values at the end of the run, 60 days. The mean, where applicable, was taken over the set of runs that ran their course through the full 60 days.
The extinction runs hence did not affect the means but their numbers are of course interesting in their own right.
The 95% simulation intervals (SI) were calculated by bootstrapping 10 000 samples.
By incidence, we mean the number of infectious people.
Intermunicipal infections is the percentage of the total number of infected that caught the disease via intermunicipal infection. There are 289 municipalities in Sweden and the poulation is approximately 8.9 million.

Table 2. Municipalities of key interest.

	SIM			SIM50			SIM20		
Municipality	**Mean**	**95% SI**		**Mean**	**95% SI**		**Mean**	**95% SI**	
Stockholm	18 563	17470	19645	13 231	12437	14066	6029	5653	6412
Göteborg	730.7	654.4	813.9	-	-	-	-	-	-
Malmö	338.6	295.4	390.2	-	-	-	-	-	-
Huddinge	3473	3277	3668	26.7	2453	2761	1218	1136	1298
Upplands-Bro	537.7	537.0	610.7	362.2	337.7	388.1	84.1	76.2	92.4
Norrtälje	939.1	882.0	998.2	214.6	197.9	232.3	37.4	33.5	41.8
Södertälje	1133	1060	1205	638.2	593.5	685.1	60.7	51.4	72.3
Västerås	864.4	789.9	934.1	27.0	23.1	31.3	2.9	1.9	4.0
Eskilstuna	692.4	639.8	748.8	60.7	53.4	68.9	26.0	22.1	30.5
Umeå	118.2	98.1	144.6	-	-	-	-	-	-
Luleå	237.4	201.9	278.4	-	-	-	-	-	-
Örebro	557.0	507.7	611.1	0.3	0.1	0.4	-	-	-
Jönköping	227.6	206.4	250.9	-	-	-	-	-	-
Linköping	528.5	479.5	582.6	1.7	1.3	2.3	-	-	-
Helsingborg	143.0	128.9	158.3	-	-	-	-	-	-
Borås	140.3	127.6	154.5	-	-	-	-	-	-
Gävle	559.2	517.5	601.1	21.9	18.7	25.5	1.8	1.3	2.4
Ljungby	29.7	26.7	33.0	-	-	-	-	-	-
Hofors	72.9	66.8	79.2	2.9	2.1	3.9	-	-	-
Örkelljunga	4.9	3.8	5.0	-	-	-	-	-	-

A selection of municipalities with the mean incidence and bootstrapped 95% simulation intervals with extinction runs filtered out. This set and its ordering is the same for the individual rows in the table, which explains the zero-valued lower interval bounds and other discrepancies.
After Stockholm, Guteborg and Malmu are the largest cities in Sweden. The single most traveled route is that between Stockholm and neighboring Huddinge, traveled by approximately 37 000 people daily, each way. The decline in incidence closely follows that in Stockholm.
Upplands-Bro is representative of an outer suburb to Stockholm. SudertΔlje and NorrtΔlje are nearby towns but are not considered suburbs.
VΔsteres and Eskilstuna are more distant, but have a fair number of commuters. Llrebro through Lulee are larger towns at some distance from Stockholm with no notable commuter traffic. Finally, the last four are small towns in southern Sweden.
SI, simulation intervals

The reason for the decrease in incidence is of course the limited transmission paths available to the disease. The disease, after having spread from one municipality to another will constantly be transmitted back into the originating municipality, provided that there is a flow of travelers in the opposite direction in the travel intensity matrix. Travel restrictions limit both spread to other municipalities and reintroduction. For comparison, if traffic is removed altogether, the mean incidence in Stockholm will be 917.

The process outlined above is also responsible for the decreased number of extinction runs. For a regular continuous time branching process where the number new cases is completely independent between individuals, one would expect the probability of extinction to be I/R0 = 37% and this was confirmed in the course of testing our model.

It is also clear how travel restrictions confer increasing protection on cities that are further from the capital, the focal point of the infection. The major cities of Göteborg (Gothenburg) and Malmö would be protected even though traffic into these cities is heavy. In fact, the farthest the disease would ever make it in SIM50 is Ljungby, 1,471 km from Stockholm and still some 200 km from Malmö. For SIM20, the farthest city is Uddevalla, 441 km away and a suburb of Göteborg. The mean reach of the epidemic in those cases is only 276 and 34 km, respectively.

An objection to the applicability of this model is that in all probability, complete enforcement of the restrictions may not be achievable or even desirable, as in the case of high-priority professionals with crucial functions in society during a crisis situation. Incidence does indeed climb the more restrictions are ignored, but not to such an extent as to render the travel restrictions dubious as a means of disease control (Figure 3). A plot with unrestricted travel, duplicated from Figure 2, is given for comparison. Figure 4 shows a finer spaced mesh of incidence versus restriction distance and compliance. Bear in mind that there was no attempt to correlate the randomness between the simulation sets. Therefore, the random numbers used in each were completely independent, giving rise to considerable simulation noise. Even though the landscape is rough, the trend in both dimensions was clearly visible. Looser travel restrictions and lower compliance means higher incidence.

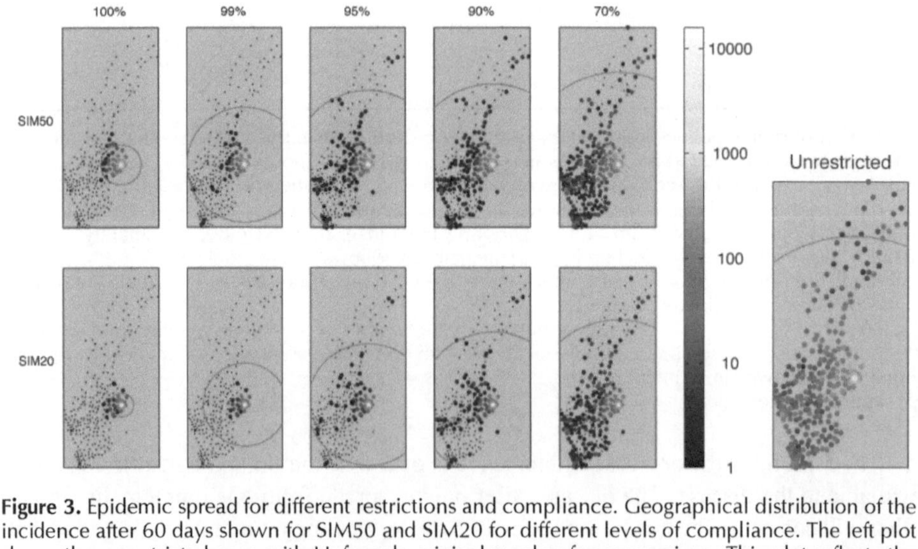

Figure 3. Epidemic spread for different restrictions and compliance. Geographical distribution of the incidence after 60 days shown for SIM50 and SIM20 for different levels of compliance. The left plot shows the unrestricted case with Hufnagels original γ galue for comparison. This plot reflects the same data as that on the middle row, right column of Figure 2 but with scale to match the current figure.

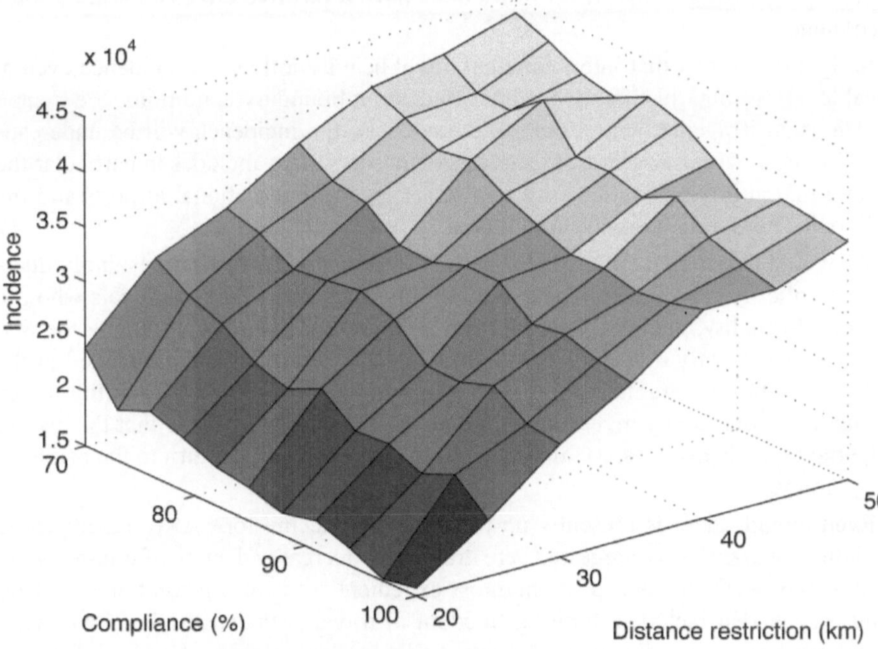

Figure 4. Total incidence for varying compliance and restrictions. A surface plot showing incidence after 60 days with the parameters of compliance and distance restrictions on the data axes. 1,000 realizations were made for each point. The surface has its highest values at high set distance limit and low compliance. Its low values are found at opposite corner.

DISCUSSION

Our results show clearly that traveling restrictions would have a significant beneficial effect, reducing both the geographical spread and the total and local incidence. This holds true for all three levels of intercommunity infectiousness, γ, simulated, γ is influenced by many factors, most notably by total travel intensity, but also by the medium of travel, the behavior of the traveler, the model of dispersal by travel, and the infectiousness of the disease. Hufnagel et al. calibrated γ using data from the actual outbreak. As mentioned, no attempt was made on our part to find the "true" value of γ in the new settings, as no such outbreak data are available for Sweden. This would be considered a flaw for a quantitative study on a SARS outbreak in Sweden. By simulating for different values of the parameter, however, we can be confident in the qualitative conclusion, namely, that the same general behavior can be expected in the unrestricted scenario and in response to the control measures, regardless of γ.

The same reasoning supports generalization of the results to other countries or regions. The survey travel data give a fairly accurate picture of travel patterns in Sweden and mirror many western countries. Some countries, for example, the USA, are more dependent on motor vehicles for commuter traffic, and infectiousness would therefore be anticipated to be lower. Such effects are, again, included in calibration of γ. Keep in mind that the used value of γ was taken from a model including only global air traffic. Figure 2 shows that travel restrictions have a positive effect for γ in the proposed range.

In light of the fact that intermunicipal travel heavily influences incidence even at a local level, we may justifiably be concerned about boundary conditions. We treated Sweden as an isolated country, but quite obviously, the incidence will be underestimated for areas with frequent traffic across the borders. This includes in particular the Öresund region around Malmö, and to a lesser extent, international airports and the small towns bordering Norway and Finland.

We would like to point out that, as in most epidemiologic simulations, individuals are not explicitly represented in the model. This is also true for individuals who are traveling. In reality, people who travel run an increased risk of contracting the disease. This is correctly modeled, as individuals who are traveling are included in the travel influx into the municipalities. The influx in turn affects the probability of additional infections at any given time. Of course, it is highly probable that this would be the travelers themselves, as, almost without exception, they return to the origin of their journey.

Even though there is presently no treatment or vaccine for SARS, results show that limited quarantine as suggested here drastically decreases the risk of transmission, and this may well turn out to be the most expedient form of intervention. In many countries, Sweden included, limiting freedom of travel is unconstitutional and must take the form of general recommendations. Additionally, certain professions of crucial importance to society during a crisis situation must be exempt from travel restrictions. The study shows that even if a substantial fraction of the population breaks the restrictions, this strategy is still viable. For other types of disease for which preventive treatment (pandemic flu) or vaccine (smallpox) are available, our results show that long-distance travelers are an important group for targeted control measures.

It is worth noting on the travel intensity matrix, where the elements directly reflect the underlying survey data, that there are several proposed alternatives, using smoothing techniques or data-generating simulation. Completing the matrix in such a way would correctly introduce many connections that are missing from our data, but a substantial number would be falsely represented, and could endanger the validity of the model due to unforeseen stochastic mechanisms. The methods all have inherent imprecisions and flaws, which unfortunately in this context would be difficult to estimate. The choice of one in preference over another would certainly be contended. Our scheme of direct extrapolation from the raw data is certainly no better but does have the benefit of transparency and reasonable control over errors. As is explained in further detail in the appendix, this means that certain connections between municipalities that are used in reality, however infrequently, are missing, while on the other hand some will be heavily overestimated. This is especially true for certain unusual municipalities. The routes between the more populated communities and other heavy connections are much better estimated, as crude statistical analysis will indicate. Also close to the true value is the travel intensity as a whole, as well as the summed influx and outflux of any municipality.

CONCLUSION

Our methods show that restricting travel between municipalities in such a way that travel above a certain distance is banned, would indeed have a beneficial effect on the speed of transmission of a highly contagious disease, geographically and in absolute numbers. This conclusion is true for a range of plausible values of the intermunicipal infectiousness. Even in scenarios of compliance as low as 70%, travel restrictions are effective. Thus, the effectiveness of travel restrictions as a means of mitigating a future epidemic is supported. The model and results are robust and there is no reason to believe that the results are not generally applicable to any country or region.

KEYWORDS

- **Hufnagel model**
- **Intermunicipal travel network**
- **Matrix elements**
- **Parameters**

AUTHORS' CONTRIBUTIONS

Martin Camitz performed all coding and simulations, carried out analyses and is the main author of the manuscript. Fredrik Liljeros conceived the project and design, and initiated the work. He participated in analyses and drafting of the chapter. Fredrik Liljeros approved the final version of the chapter.

NOTES

* The erroneous records were long-distance journeys, mostly between individual communities in an unreasonably short time. Had they not been removed, their influence would have been significant, accelerating the spread across the country. The correct data were irretrievable but the effect of their absence was deemed within the margin of error for long-distance journeys.

† Some authors refer to this as the "attack rate" although this is not the commonest definition.

ACKNOWLEDGMENTS

This study was supported by The Swedish Institute for Infectious Diseases Control, Swedish Council for Working Life and Social Research, and the European Union Research NEST Project (DYSONET 012911). The authors would like to express their gratitude to Tom Britton and Åke Svensson, Department of Mathematics, Stockhholm University, Monica Nordvik, Department of Sociology, Stockholm University and Alden Klovdahl, Social Sciences, Australian National University and the members of S-GEM, Stockholm Group of Epidemic Modeling http://www.s-gem.se for their kind support.

COMPETING INTERESTS

The author(s) have received financial support from the organizations mentioned in acknowledgments.

Chapter 13

New *Salmonella enteritidis* Phage Types in Europe

Karin Nygerd, Birgitta de Jong, Philippe J Guerin, Yvonne Andersson, Agneta Olsson, and Johan Giesecke

INTRODUCTION

Among human *Salmonella enteritidis* infections, phage type 4 has been the dominant phage type in most countries in Western Europe during the last years. This is reflected in *Salmonella* infections among Swedish travelers returning from abroad. However, there are differences in phage type distribution between the countries, and this has also changed over time.

We used data from the Swedish infectious disease register and the national reference laboratory to describe phage type distribution of *Salmonella enteritidis* infections in Swedish travelers from 1997 to 2002, and have compared this with national studies conducted in the countries visited.

Infections among Swedish travelers correlate well with national studies conducted in the countries visited. In 2001 a change in phage type distribution in *S. enteritidis* infections among Swedish travelers returning from some countries in southern Europe was observed, and a previously rare phage type (PT 14b) became one of the most commonly diagnosed that year, continuing into 2002 and 2003.

Surveillance of infections among returning travelers can be helpful in detecting emerging infections and outbreaks in tourist destinations. The information needs to be communicated rapidly to all affected countries in order to expedite the implementation of appropriate investigations and preventive measures.

Salmonella enteritidis is the most common serovar causing food-borne salmonellosis in humans, causing approximately 80% of salmonellosis cases reported in Europe [1]. During the 80s and early 90s, a steady increase in *S. enteritidis* infections was reported in Europe and North America [2-4]. The most common phage types of *S. enteritidis* varies between countries; while phage type (PT) 4 is reported to be dominant in most countries in Western Europe, PT 8 is common in North America and also a few European countries [5-7]. Epidemiological and environmental studies have implicated eggs and poultry products as primary risk factors for infection [3, 8]. Approximately 70% of outbreaks caused by *S. enteritidis* in Europe during the 90s, were related to eggs and egg products [1]. Based on these findings, prevention and control measures in the egg, and poultry industry have been implemented in the European Union and in the US [9, 10]. These measures seem to have been effective in reducing *S. enteritidis* contamination of eggs [11] and are believed to have lead to a decrease in human incidence of *S. enteritidis* in recent years [1, 9, 12].

In Sweden, about 85% of the reported *Salmonella* infections are acquired during travel abroad and the levels in domestic animals and food products is low [13].

Therefore, trends in human salmonellosis in Sweden have mainly reflected trends in foreign travel and countries with popular package tour resorts account for the majority of infections.

In this study, we investigate trends in travel related *S. enteritidis* infections, describe the phage type distribution of *S. enteritidis* isolated from Swedish travelers returning from abroad related to country of infection, and discuss possible reasons for the emergence of a new phage type of *S. enteritidis* in 2001. A preliminary analysis of a subset of these data was published as a short letter in the Lancet in 2002 [14].

MATERIAL AND METHODS

In Sweden, salmonellosis is a mandatory notifiable disease. Both clinicians and laboratories are required to report a case to the infectious disease register at the Swedish Institute for Infectious Disease Control (SMI). Based on the patient's travel history, information on probable country of infection is collected on the notification forms. Diagnosis of *Salmonella* infections is made at regional microbiology laboratories, and all isolates are submitted to the national reference laboratory at SMI for serotyping and phage typing. In this study we have included all cases of *S. enteritidis* notified to SMI from January 1, 1997 through December 31, 2002.

To investigate trends in travel-related infections, we collected information on air travel from the Swedish Civil Aviation Administration (CAA) [15]. The figures include all passengers carried on flights from any CAA airport to their first foreign destination, without indicating whether this destination is for transfer or the final destination. Using these figures as denominators, we calculated annual incidence rates (IR) for countries reported as place of infection for the three most popular countries for charter tourism among Swedes—Spain, Greece, and Turkey. The IR were calculated by dividing the number of cases reported as infected in the respective countries by number of flight passengers to that country.

For the geographical description of dominant phage types in the different countries the analysis was restricted to infections acquired in countries in Europe during 1997–2002, and to countries from which more than ten cases were reported during this period. A phage type was considered dominant if it represented >30% of the isolates and was at least twice as common as the second most common phage type. If none of the phage types fulfilled these criteria, the two most common phage types that together represented >50% of the cases were defined as the dominant types. The pattern for 1997–2000 was compared with the pattern for 2001.

Of 13,271 cases of *S.enteritidis* infections notified during 1997–2002, 11,570 cases (87%) were reported as infected abroad, 1,032 (8%) were reported as infected in Sweden, and information of probable country of infection was not available for 669 (5%). The total number of cases reported each year varied from 1,598 to 2,629 cases, with the highest being reported in 1999 and the lowest in 2002. Imported cases varied between 1,404 and 2,164. The most common countries of infection during the 6-year period were Spain, Greece, and Turkey, accounting for 34%, 8%, and 4% of all cases, respectively.

For six countries—"Spain, Greece, Turkey, Poland, Thailand, and Portugal—>50 cases of infection with *S. enteritidis* among Swedish travelers were reported each year during 1997–2002." These are all popular destinations for leisure travel among Swedes. Figure 1 presents IR for the three most popular countries for charter tourism, Spain, Greece, and Turkey, using the number of flight passengers from Sweden to the first foreign destination as the denominator. The figure shows that the incidence rate among travellers to Spain and Turkey seemed to decrease during the six-year period, while for Greece the incidence peaked in 2001.

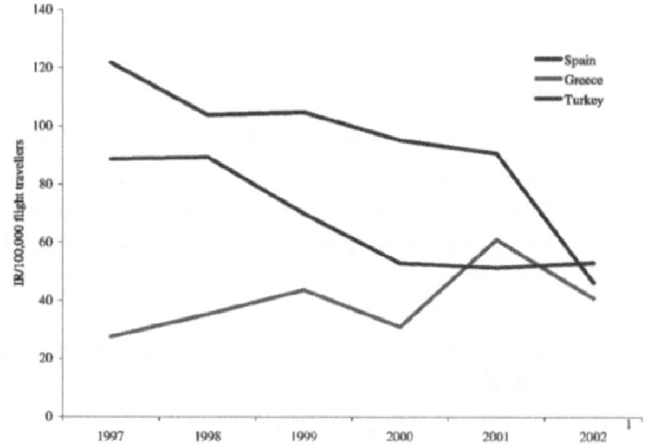

Figure 1. Incidence rates (IR) of *Salmonella enteritidis* infections among Swedish travelers to Spain, Greece and Turkey. Country specific annual incidence rate of *Salmonella enteritidis* per 100,000 air travelers from Sweden. The IR are calculated based on the number of cases notified to the Swedish infectious Disease register using the number of flight passengers from Sweden to the first foreign destination as the denominator.

Eighty-six percent (10,049) of the isolates from 1997 to 2001 were phage-typed, increasing from 75% in 1997 to 95% in 2001. The most common phage types over the period were PT 4 and PT 1 (Figure 2), accounting for 35% and 16% of all cases, respectively. In travellers returning from most countries in Western Europe, PT 4 was the dominant phage type. In Eastern Europe, PT 1 was dominant, and this phage type was also common among travellers returning from the Iberian Peninsula. PT 8 seemed to be more common among travellers returning from central European countries.

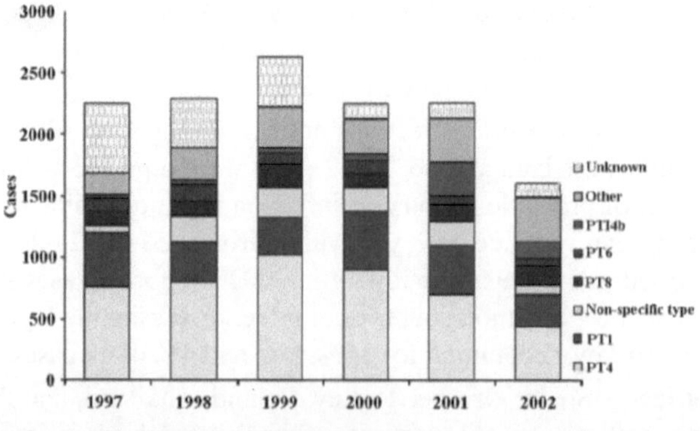

Figure 2. Distribution of phage types of *Salmonella enteritidis* cases notified in Sweden, 1997 to 2002.

In 2001 this pattern changed when PT 14b increased among travelers from several countries in Southern Europe (Figure 3b). PT 14b was the third most common phage type among returning travelers in 2001, accounting for 13% of all isolates that were phage-typed that year (272/2,132), compared with 2% of all that were phage-typed in the previous four years (154/7,917). This trend continued into 2002 when PT14b accounted for 9% (134/1,489) of all typed isolates. The majority of the PT 14b cases in 2001 and 2002 were reported among travellers returning from Greece (Figure 4), and this phage type accounted for 54%(157/293), 47%(83/176), and 42%(50/117) of all cases of *S. enteritidis* from Greece in 2001, 2002, and 2003, respectively.

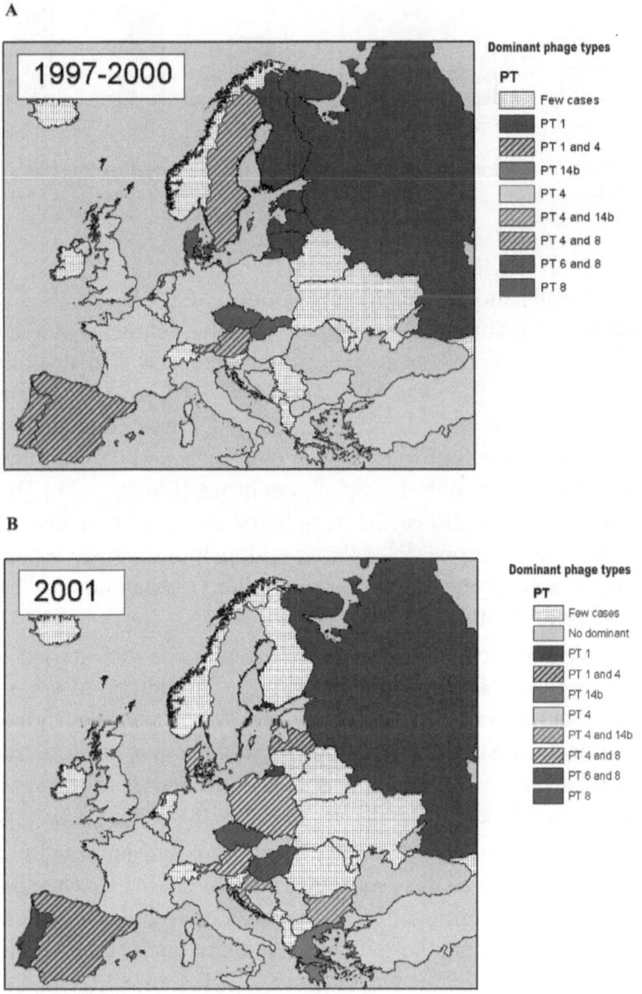

Figure 3. Dominant phage types of *Salmonella enteritidis* infections among Swedish travellers according to country visited. Only countries with more than 10 reported cases and phage types accounting for > 25 % of all cases are shown. (a) 1997—2000 (b) 2001.

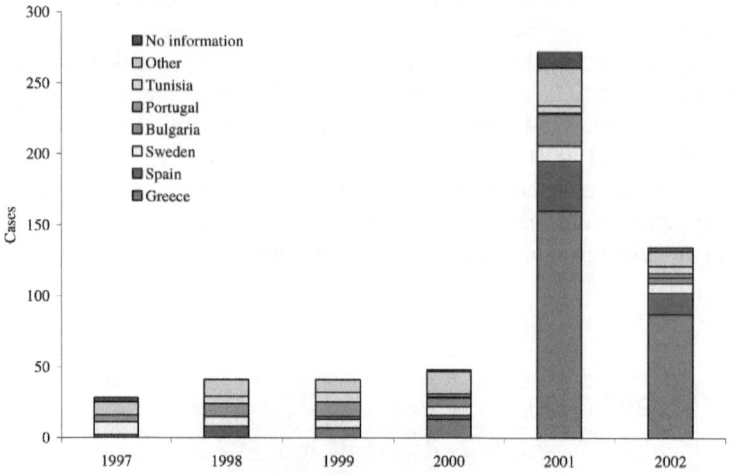

Figure 4. Notified cases of *Salmonella enteritidis* PT 14b among Swedish travellers by country of infection, 1997—2002.

DISCUSSION

We have described trends and phage type distribution of *S. enteritidis* isolates among Swedish travelers infected abroad. Phage type 4 was the dominant phage type among returning travelers. There were, however, some differences in distribution between the countries and with time. Between 1997 and 2000, PT 1 dominated among travelers returning from Russia and the Baltic countries, PT 8 was commonly seen among travelers returning from some central European countries, and PT 4 dominated among travelers returning from most other European countries (Figure 3). In 2001 a change in phage type distribution was observed among Swedish travelers returning from some countries in South-Eastern Europe. PT 14b, a previously rare phage type, appeared to become predominant among travelers returning from Greece and also became more common among travelers from some other countries.

During the six-year period, the *S. enteritidis* incidence rate among travellers to Spain and Turkey appeared to decline. This trend is in contrast to surveillance data from Spain, which seem to show an increasing incidence over the same period [16]. The reason for this declining trend among tourists was not investigated, but may be related to an increased awareness among tourists concerning the prevention of traveler's diarrhoea or to improved food control efforts in some of the popular tourist resorts.

There are some uncertainties when calculating IR based on number of travelers. The number of travelers used as the denominator in the incidence rate calculations is based on the statistics of the airport of first landing after leaving Sweden. If the first airport is not the final destination, these travelers will not be included in the denominator for the destination country. Thus the calculated IR for transit countries will be too low, while the IR for the final destination countries will be too high.

When comparing *S. enteritidis* phage types isolated from Swedish travelers with studies conducted in the countries visited, isolates found in travelers were generally consistent with the dominant strains reported among inhabitants in the respective countries. Table 1 summarizes the results of published studies on salmonellosis from a number of countries. The percentages of PT 4 and PT 6 among human *S. enteritidis* infections in Austria and Denmark, respectively, have been reported to be decreasing in the last years [6]. These same trends were reflected among returning Swedish travelers.

Table 1. Dominant *Salmonella enteritidis* phage types by country*. Comparison between findings among Swedish travelers and studies conducted in the countries visited.

Country	Number of S. Enteritidis-infections notified among Swedish travellers 1997–2001	Most common S. Enteritidis phage types among returning Swedish travellers 1997–2001 (%*)	Predominant phage type described in studies from the country visited	Year of study	Reference
Spain	4125	1 (33%), 4 (36%)	1, 4, 6	1990s	[29]
Greece 1997–2000	916	4 (44%)			
		14b (59%)			
Turkey	496	4 (65%)	4	Not mentioned	[30]
Poland	354	4 (40%)	4, 8	1986–95	[31]
Portugal	344	1 (43%)			
Morocco	310	4 (50%)			
Germany	235	4 (59%)	4	1998	[32]
Denmark 1997–1998	223	6 (42%), 8 (43%)	6, 8	1997–98	[33]
1999		34 (73%)	PT34 outbreak in DK	1999	
2000–2001		4 (30%), 8 (30%)	4, 8	2000–2001	
Czech Republic	194	8 (68%)	8	1989–98	[34]
Bulgaria	180	4 (55%)			
Cyprus	166	1 (36%), 4 (45%)			
Tunisia	152	4 (75%)	4	1990–93	[29,35]
Italy	152	4 (47%)	4	1997–2000	[36]
United Kingdom	133	4 (76%)	4	1992–94	[37]
Hungary	120	4 (50%)			
France	110	4 (56%)			
Austria 1997–2000	81	4 (52%), 8 (38%)	4	1995–2001	[6]
2001		4 (33%), 8 (42%)			
Latvia 1997–2000	76	1 (63%)			
2001		1 (60%), 4 (40%)			
Egypt	63	4 (55%)			
Croatia	53	4 (63%)			

Table 1. D

Country	Number of S. Enteritidis-infections notified among Swedish travellers 1997–2001	Most common S. Enteritidis phage types among returning Swedish travellers 1997–2001 (%*)	Predominant phage type described in studies from the country visited	Year of study	Reference
Belgium	45	4 (72%)			
Russia	42	1 (62%)	1	1980–93	[38]
Estonia 1997–2000	37	1 (58%)			
2001		1 (25%), 4 (75%)**			
Bosnia and Herzegovina	26	4 (64%)			
The Netherlands	20	4 (75%)	4	1997–2001	[6]
Slovakia	14	8 (62%)	8	1995	[39]
Lithuania	12	1 (50%)			

* Calculated as a percentage of all isolates that were phage-typed during 1997–2001.
** Based on less than 10 cases.

People returning from travel abroad may have a higher tendency to seek medical care and have a stool sample taken if an imported infection is suspected. In addition, visitors may be more susceptible to pathogens circulating in the community than the local inhabitants. The detection of new, emerging strains in travelers after returning to their home countries may therefore be helpful in detecting changes in the pathogen reservoir occurring in the countries visited, especially in tourist destinations. However, tourists have a tendency to aggregate in some smaller resorts that may have a different pathogen reservoir and rely on food supplies that are different from the rest of the country. This may lead to differences in risks and pathogens between the inhabitants and the tourists visiting the country that needs to be taken into consideration.

The change in phage type distribution observed among Swedish travelers returning from some countries in Southern Europe in 2001 was not observed among inhabitants in the countries visited. In total, the two most common phage types among Swedish travelers were, as in previous years, PT 4 and PT 1. However, the third most common was PT 14b, a phage type hitherto uncommon in Sweden with only 20 to 40 cases reported annually prior to 2001. The majority of the cases were among travelers returning from Greece (90%). More cases were also reported among travelers returning from Spain and Bulgaria than in previous years. During the same time period, an increase in the same phage type had also been registered among Norwegian and Finnish travelers returning from Greece [17]. A request on Enter-Net (European network for the surveillance of enteric infections—*Salmonella* and VTEC O157) sent by the Norwegian Public Health Institute gave no response on increases of PT 14b in other countries. Spain reported an outbreak of the same phage in a school in January (unpublished data). But after this event, no further increase was noted. The UK later reported an increased number of the same phage type, both among travelers and among people who had been infected in the UK. However, there the 14b isolates of domestic origin were aerogenic, while isolates associated with travel to Greece were predominantly anaerogenic [18]. The isolates among Swedish travelers returning from Greece were also predominantly anaerogenic.

No explanation for the sudden increase in this phage type among Nordic travelers to different countries in Southern Europe has been found. PT 14b is not a new phage type and outbreaks reported previously have been mainly related to eggs and egg-products (ice-cream, tiramisu [19, 20]) or improper hygiene practices [21, 22]. However, these outbreaks were localized, of limited duration, and the incriminated food products found and the outbreaks contained. The cause of the increase of this phage type among Nordic travelers in 2001 is still unclear. It may represent a geographically more widespread outbreak than previously described, possibly due to increased trade in food products, animals, or animal feed across the borders. Another possible explanation for this increase may be that changes in PT 14b could have contributed to increased resistance or virulence factors, thereby facilitating the spread of this phage type in the environment. Alternatively, acquisition or loss of a plasmid or spontaneous mutations may have resulted in a conversion from another phage type to PT 14b. Such change has been described for other phage types [23-25] and a conversion from PT 8 to PT 14b has been described after inoculation into pathogen-free chicken [26].

Our data presented are limited by the small numbers of cases from each country investigated on an annual basis. It is therefore difficult to evaluate trends with any certainty. However, the possibility of using surveillance data of infections among returning travelers to detect emerging pathogens should be further investigated. In addition, data from countries that routinely collect information on travel could be pooled in order to increase the numbers of travel-related infections. In several countries outside Europe, laboratory capacity is limited and it may take a long time to detect the emergence of new pathogens or subtypes. Not all countries in Europe collect information on the probable place of infection and phage typing of *Salmonella* isolates is not routinely performed in some countries. However, if available, this information will be included in the data reported to Enter-Net. Data from this network has previously been useful in detecting travel-related outbreaks [27, 28], and may also be useful in describing pathogen patterns in countries where laboratory capacities are limited or routine typing is not performed. Importantly, Enter-Net may expedite the dissemination of information concerning emerging pathogens.

CONCLUSIONS

This study demonstrates that surveillance of infections among returning travelers may be helpful in detecting emerging infections and outbreaks in tourist destinations, and provides some useful supplementary data about infectious diseases and trends in other geographical regions. Characterization of isolates from travelers can detect changes in the pathogen and antimicrobial resistance patterns in the destination country. This information may be an important supplement in countries where surveillance systems are deficient or lacking, or where the laboratories have limited capacity to do detailed sub-typing and resistance testing. In addition, infections and outbreaks among tourists may not always affect the local residents and therefore may not be detected by the local public health authorities. If proper investigations, and appropriate prevention and control measures are to be implemented in the countries visited, it is important that the surveillance information compiled from the traveler's home countries is rapidly communicated to the affected countries.

KEYWORDS

- **Incidence rates**
- ***Salmonella enteritidis***
- ***Salmonella* infections**
- **Salmonellosis**
- **Swedish travelers**

AUTHORS' CONTRIBUTIONS

Karin Nygård performed the data analysis and drafted the manuscript. Philippe J Guerin, Yvonne Andersson, and Birgitta de Jong participated in the design and coordination of the study. Agneta Olsson conducted typing and provided advice regarding laboratory issues. Johan Giesecke participated in the design and discussion, and provided advice on data analysis. All authors read and approved the final manuscript.

ACKNOWLEDGMENTS

We thank Dr Rebecca Grais-Freeman for her valuable comments on the manuscript.

COMPETING INTERESTS

None declared.

Chapter 14

HIV-related Restrictions on Entry in the WHO European Region

Jeffrey V. Lazarus, Nadja Curth, Matthew Weait, and Srdan Matic

INTRODUCTION

Back in 1987, the World Health Organization (WHO) concluded that the screening of international travelers was an ineffective way to prevent the spread of human immunodeficiency virus (HIV). However, some countries still restrict the entrance and/or residency of foreigners with an HIV infection. HIV-related travel restrictions have serious implications for individual and public health, and violate internationally recognized human rights. In this study, we reviewed the current situation regarding HIV-related travel restrictions in the 53 countries of the WHO European Region.

We retrieved the country-specific information chiefly from the Global Database on HIV Related Travel Restrictions at hivtravel.org. We simplified and standardized the database information to enable us to create an overview and compare countries. Where data was outdated, unclear, or contradictory, we contacted WHO HIV focal points in the countries or appropriate non-governmental organizations. The United States Bureau of Consular Affairs website was also used to confirm and complement these data.

Our review revealed that there are no entry restrictions for people living with HIV (PLHIV) in 51 countries in the WHO European Region. In 11 countries, foreigners living with HIV applying for long-term stays will not be granted a visa. These countries are: Andorra, Armenia, Cyprus (denies access for non-European Union citizens), Hungary, Kazakhstan, Moldova, the Russian Federation, Tajikistan, Turkmenistan, Ukraine, and Uzbekistan. In Uzbekistan, an HIV-positive foreigner cannot even enter the country, and in Georgia, we were not able to determine whether there were any HIV-related travel restrictions due to a lack of information.

In 32% of the countries in the European Region, either there are some kind of HIV-related travel restrictions or we were unable to determine if such restrictions are in force. Most of these countries defend restrictions as being justified by public health concerns. However, there is no evidence that denying HIV-positive foreigners access to a country is effective in protecting public health. Governments should revise legislation on HIV-related travel restrictions. In the meantime, a joint effort is needed to draw attention to the continuing discrimination and stigmatization of PLHIV that takes place in those European Region countries where such laws and policies are still in force.

We read the article, "Fear of foreigners: HIV-related restrictions on entry, stay and residence" [1], in this journal with great interest. In their contribution to the debate over HIV-related travel restrictions, Amon and Todrys stress the urgency on this issue, which affects not only the lives of PLHIV all over the world, but also the wellbeing of the communities in which they live. HIV-related travel restrictions not only violate the fundamental rights of PLHIV, but they also impede HIV prevention, care, and treatment efforts among all people.

The United Nations Human Rights Committee has stated, "Liberty of movement is an indispensable condition for the free development of a person" [2]. Earlier, the Office of the High Commissioner for Human Rights stated that:

The (International) Covenant (on Civil and Political Rights) does not recognize the right of aliens to enter or reside in the territory of a State party. It is in principle a matter for the State to decide who it will admit to its territory. However, in certain circumstances an alien may enjoy the protection of the Covenant even in relation to entry or residence, for example, when considerations of non-discrimination, prohibition of inhuman treatment, and respect for family life arise [3].

Governments do, of course, have the right to control entry to their borders and have a certain margin of appreciation to justify differential treatment compatible with international human rights law. But the measures must pursue a legitimate aim and need to be proportional to the achievement of this aim [4].

Back in 1987, the WHO concluded that the screening of international travelers was an ineffective way to prevent the spread of HIV [5]. In 2002, Member States of the WHO European Region resolved "to develop a supportive social and legal environment for groups at risk, especially sex workers, and for PLHIV/AIDS and to fight social and legal exclusion, including travel restrictions" [6].

Since then, travel restrictions connected with communicable diseases in general and HIV in particular have often been discussed [7-9], including recently in conjunction with the 2009 outbreak of influenza virus A (H1N1). Together with international organizations, such as the International AIDS Society (IAS) [10], the International Organization for Migration and the Joint United Nations Programme on HIV/AIDS (UNAIDS) [11], Amon and Todrys emphasize how HIV-related travel restrictions have serious implications for individual and public health and violate internationally recognized human rights.

This important discussion prompted us to review the current situation in the 53 countries of the WHO European Region, given that restrictions on entry, residence, and stay affect a wide range of PLHIV, including not only students and employees, but also members of vulnerable groups, such as refugees, asylum seekers, and other migrants.

MATERIALS AND METHODS

In this study, which we carried out in April and May, 2009, our concern was to map formal entry and residence restrictions that required an HIV test or a medical certificate of HIV status. It should be noted that in practice, however, some of the countries did not apply the rules that were legally valid at this time. We also reviewed whether people can be denied entry when applying for long-term stay (but not residence) or be deported if authorities obtain evidence of HIV infection.

To obtain a valid, up-to-date overview of HIV-related travel restrictions in the European Region, we collected data from a variety of sources. We retrieved the information chiefly from the Global Database on HIV Related Travel Restrictions at hivtravel.org[12], an initiative of the German AIDS Federation, the European AIDS Treatment Group (EATG) and the IAS. The information in this database is based on replies to a structured self-administered questionnaire from German embassies abroad and foreign embassies in Germany between November 2007 and June 2008.

We simplified and standardized the database information to enable us to create an overview and compare countries. Where data was outdated, unclear or contradictory, we searched the websites of foreign ministries in the countries and contacted WHO HIV focal points in the countries or appropriate non-governmental organizations (NGOs), such as the Eurasian Harm Reduction Network and the Hungarian Civil Liberties Union.

We also used the United States Bureau of Consular Affairs website [13] to confirm and complement these data. Most of the information provided by the focal points and NGOs was clear, sufficient and based on national laws and regulations. However, in some instances, the information was vague, and several communications were sometimes necessary to clarify unresolved questions.

For 11 of the 53 countries (Armenia, Belarus, Bulgaria, Cyprus, Georgia, Hungary, Israel, Moldova, Tajikistan, Ukraine, and Uzbekistan), publicly available information did not provide a sufficient or clear picture of HIV-related travel restrictions. In these cases, we contacted focal points and NGOs, receiving replies from every country except Israel.

The resulting information and our initial review of the hivtravel.org database revealed that there are no entry restrictions for PLHIV in 51 countries (see Figure 1). In Uzbekistan, however, the law mandates that visitors carry a certificate attesting that they are not infected with HIV. Foreigners from countries requiring visas to enter or stay in Uzbekistan will not be issued a visa to enter the country if they are found to be HIV positive. In Georgia, the situation for PLHIV wishing to enter the country is uncertain due to unclear information.

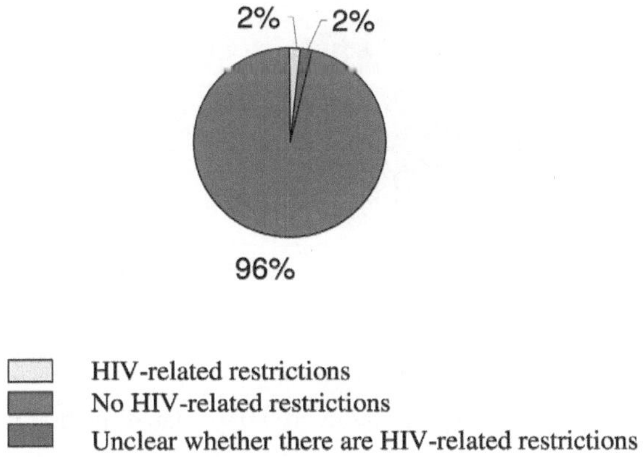

Figure 1. Percentage of European Region countries with HIV-related entry restrictions.

In 36 countries, there are also no HIV-related restrictions for long-term visits (see Figure 2). In Georgia, the policy on long-term visits is unclear. In eight countries (Belarus, Moldova, Poland, the Russian Federation, Tajikistan, Turkmenistan, Ukraine, and Uzbekistan), an HIV test is required for all foreigners wishing to stay for more than 3 months. In three of these countries (Republic of Moldova, the Russian Federation, and Turkmenistan), this requirement also applies to students and employees. In the Russian Federation, an HIV test is not required for citizens of countries in the Commonwealth of Independent States, who do not need visas for long-term stays.

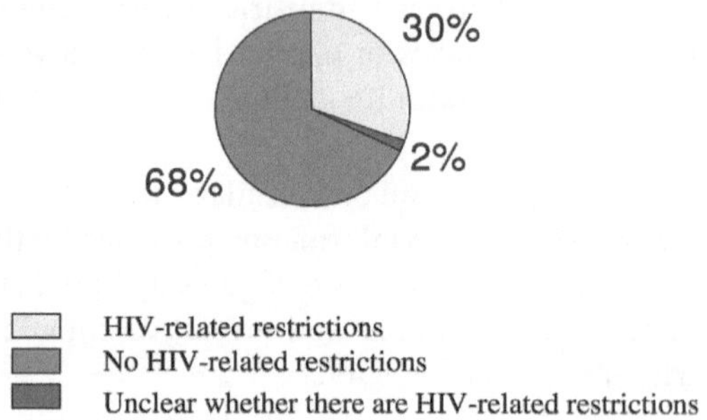

Figure 2. Percentage of European Region countries with HIV-related residence restrictions.

Andorra will not grant residency or work permits to PLHIV (See Figure 3). In Hungary, an HIV test is required of all foreigners wishing to stay for more than 1year. In Kazakhstan, an HIV test is required for foreigners staying for more than 30 days. In Cyprus, people who are not citizens of the European Union must present an HIV test to apply for a work or study permit, which will be denied if the test is positive. In Slovakia, an HIV test is also required for foreigners applying for residence or a work permit. In the German state of Bavaria, an HIV test can be required for people staying for more than 180 days, while in the states of Saxony and New Brandenburg, there is mandatory HIV testing for asylum seekers.

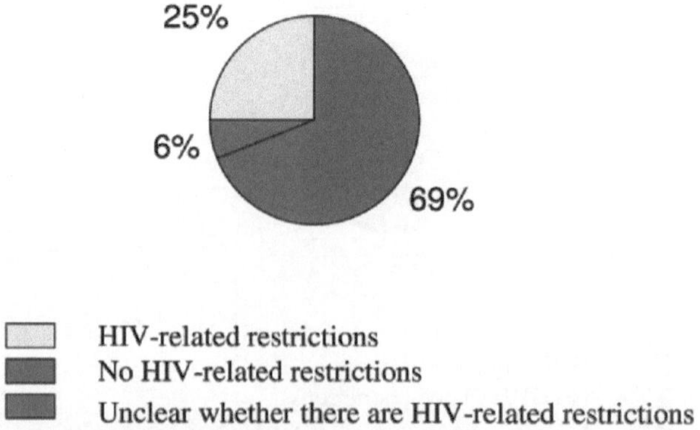

Figure 3. Percentage of European Region countries with residence restrictions where a foreigner will not be granted a visa if found to be HIV positive.

In Armenia, the situation for long-term visitors is complex. A negative HIV certificate is required from all foreigners applying for visas. Until July 14, 2009, foreign PLHIV already in the country were subject to deportation. On that date, a new law came into force, specifying that foreigners would not be deported if found to be HIV positive. Yet a foreigner applying for a visa still has to present a negative HIV test. Armenia is working to change these regulations.

And finally, while we did not find sufficient information on requirements for long-term stays in Israel, there are indications that foreigners in general do not need to present a certificate of HIV status, although an HIV test is required for all migrant workers and for migrants from regions where HIV is endemic. However, it is not clear if a migrant can be denied access based on a positive HIV test.

Of the 17 countries requiring an HIV test or certificate for applying for long-term stays, 11 countries (69%) will deny a foreigner holding a positive HIV test entry into the country. In addition to Cyprus, which denies access to non-EU citizens, these countries are Andorra, Armenia, Hungary, Kazakhstan, Moldova, the Russian Federation (for citizens outside the Commonwealth of Independent States), Tajikistan, Turkmenistan, Ukraine, and Uzbekistan.

DISCUSSION

Our research shows that only 36 out of 53 countries have no travel restrictions of any kind for PLHIV. This means that in 32% of the countries in the European Region, either there are some kind of HIV-related travel restrictions (as defined in this chapter) or we were unable to determine if such restrictions are in force.

Although most countries with HIV-related travel restrictions defend them as being justified by public health concerns, the WHO Regional Office for Europe has explicitly rejected this claim [6]. Not only do HIV-related travel restrictions tend to be ineffective and lead to a false sense of protectiona country's nationals can just as easily contract the virus abroad and spread it at home, for example—but they also contribute to and reinforce the discrimination and stigmatization to which PLHIV are subjected. Further, people facing restrictive measures at entry may hide their status and avoid HIV testing and even health care services in general. Further, the European Union HIV/AIDS Civil Society Forum has called for the elimination of all HIV-related travel restrictions in Europe by 2010 [14].

The Office of the United Nations High Commissioner for Human Rights and UNAIDS, for example, have unequivocally stated that "any restrictions on these rights (to liberty of movement and choice of residence) based on suspected or real HIV status alone, including HIV screening of international travelers, are discriminatory and cannot be justified by public health concerns" [15] because while HIV is infectious, it cannot be transmitted through casual contact [16]. Those countries without HIV-related entry, stay, and residence restrictions have not reported any negative public health consequences [17].

Additional considerations arise with respect to travel within the 27 countries of the European Union because free movement of people within the EU is one of its founding principles, a principle acknowledged not only in its founding and subsequent treaties, but also in the European Convention of Human Rights. For example, Council Directive 2004/38/EC [18] states that:

Without prejudice to the provisions on travel documents applicable to national border controls, all Union citizens with a valid identity card or passport ... shall have the right to leave the territory of a Member State to travel to another Member State [Article 4.1].

And similarly:

Without prejudice to the provisions on travel documents applicable to national border controls, Member States shall grant Union citizens leave to enter their territory with a valid identity card or passport .... [Article 5.1].

The directive later notes that:

Subject to the provisions of this Chapter, Member States may restrict the freedom of movement and residence of Union citizens ... on grounds of public policy, public security, or public health. These grounds shall not be invoked to serve economic ends [Article 27.1].

However, it goes on to place narrow limits on public health arguments for such restrictions:

The only diseases justifying measures restricting freedom of movement shall be the diseases with epidemic potential as defined by the relevant instruments of the WHO and other infectious diseases or contagious parasitic diseases if they are the subject of protection provisions applying to nationals of the host Member State [Article 29.1].

For example, travel restrictions can be used to limit the spread of highly contagious diseases, such as cholera or acute respiratory syndrome (SARS), but such measures tend to be short-term and are most likely not very effective. Even in these cases, authorities must still consider human rights and the broad social, economic, and public health consequences of initiating travel restrictions of any kind.

In general, WHO does not support travel restrictions in relation to communicable diseases, and the recent case of influenza A (H1N1) was no exception [19]. According to the International Health Regulations [20], a binding document signed by all WHO Member States, national health measures for travelers must not be more restrictive of international traffic, or more invasive or intrusive to the individual, than available alternatives that provide an appropriate level of health protection. If such measures are implemented, they should be justified by scientific principles, available scientific evidence, or WHO advice. In the case of HIV, there is no evidence that denying HIV-positive foreigners access to a country is effective in protecting public health.

CONCLUSION

In contrast to HIV, the highly contagious diseases that we have mentioned have short incubation periods and are transmitted through casual contact. While HIV transmission is mostly due to risk behaviors like sharing needles or unsafe sex, these diseases are transmitted much more readily, through droplets in the air or contaminated food, or water. In the light of these differences, as well as the potential for discrimination and stigmatization, the public health justification for HIV-related travel restrictions is inadequate and even irrational.

KEYWORDS

- **Human immunodeficiency virus**
- **HIV-related travel restrictions**
- **Influenza A**
- **People living with HIV**
- **World Health Organization**

AUTHORS' CONTRIBUTIONS

Nadja Curth drafted the chapter based on an idea from Jeffrey V. Lazarus andSrdan Matic . Jeffrey V. Lazarus fully revised the first draft and Matthew Weait reviewed and added additional material. Nadja Curth fact checked the changes. Srdan Matic fully reviewed and edited the next draft. Jeffrey V. Lazarus and Matthew Weait addressed the reviewer's comments. All authors read and approved the final manuscript.

COMPETING INTERESTS

The authors declare that they have no competing interests.

Chapter 15

Seasonal Impact on Orthopedic Health Services in Switzerland

Klazien Matter-Walstra, Marcel Widmer, and Andrй Busato

INTRODUCTION

Climate- or holiday-related seasonality in hospital admission rates (hosp ar) is well known for many diseases. However, little research has addressed the impact of tourism on seasonality in admission rates. We therefore investigated the influence of tourism on emergency admission rates in Switzerland, where winter and summer leisure sport activities in large mountain regions can generate orthopedic injuries.

Using small area analysis, orthopedic hospital service areas (HSAo) were evaluated for seasonality in emergency admission rates. Winter sport areas (WSA) were defined using guest bed accommodation rate patterns of guest houses and hotels located above 1,000 m altitude that show clear winter and summer peak seasons. Emergency admissions (years 2000–2002, n = 135'460) of local and nonlocal HSAo residents were evaluated. HSAo were grouped according to their area type (regular or winter sport area) and monthly analyses of admission rates were performed.

Of HSAo within the defined WSA 70.8% show a seasonal, summer-winter peak hospital admission rate pattern, and only 1 HSAo outside the defined WSA shows such a pattern. Seasonal hosp ar in HSAo in WSA can be up to four times higher in winter than the intermediate seasons, and they are almost entirely due to admissions of nonlocal residents (nl-res). These nl-res are in general -and especially in winter- younger than local residents (l-res), and nl-res have a shorter length of stay in winter sport than in regular areas (RegA). The overall geographic distribution of nl-res admitted for emergencies shows highest rates during the winter as well as the summer in the WSA.

Small area analysis using HSAo is a reliable method for the evaluation of seasonality in hosp ar. In Switzerland, HSAo defined as WSA show a clear seasonal fluctuation in admission rates of onlynl-res, whereas HSAo defined as regular, non-winter sport areas do not show such seasonality. We conclude that leisure sport, and especially ski/snowboard tourism demands great flexibility in hospital beds, staff, and resource planning in these areas.

Seasonal variation of hospital bed usage is a well known phenomenon [1-4]. On one hand, seasonal increases in hospital admissions may be weather dependent [3, 5-13]. On the other hand, in certain areas tourism may cause seasonal variation in health service utilization by temporarily increasing a population at risk during holiday seasons [14]. Whereas climate-dependent variations involve the local population of an area, vacation-induced increases in hosp ar may largely derive from nl-res.

Switzerland can be divided into tourist and nontourist regions. Most of the tourist areas are located in the mountains, which afford ski and snowboard activities in winter, and mountaineering and sports such as mountain biking during the summer. In general these mountain regions have a lower local population density than nontourist areas, although their population fluctuates greatly during holiday seasons. The provision of sufficient numbers of hospital beds in such areas is of key importance for resource allocation in health care, and making efficient and effective use of those available cannot rely only on local population size. Resorts providing seasonal leisure sport activities such as skiing or mountaineering may be expected to have high emergency admissions of nonlocals during peak seasons, whereas nontourist areas usually do not show seasonal effects. The estimation of emergency service treatment beds in tourist areas therefore presents a planning challenge that can be addressed only through careful analysis of admission patterns over time [15]. One method for such analysis is small area analysis based upon hospital service areas [16-19]. Using orthopedic discharge data and following the method described by Klauss et al. [16], Switzerland can be divided into 85 HSAo. In short, each discharge is labeled with a residence code called medstat (Switzerland is divided into 612 medstat regions), these medstat regions are then aggregated into HSAo according to hospital usage patterns. HSAo contain at least 1 and a maximum of 27 hospitals, with a high hospital density seen in HSAo including large major cities such as Zürich or Geneva to only one hospital in most rural HSAo. These HSAo were analyzed for seasonal effects in order to evaluate seasonal variations in emergency admissions due to tourism in mountain sport resort areas. The aim of this evaluation is to provide healthcare planners with detailed information on seasonal variations in admission rates in different area types.

MATERIALS AND METHODS

Federal discharge data for orthopedic procedures (according to CHOP [18]- and/or ICD10 codes[19]) from the Swiss hospital discharge master file from 2000–2002 were used (Swiss Federal Office of Statistics). Commercial GIS-compatible vector files for medstat regions (an aggregate of several postal code regions, built-up according to socio-economic, and geographic coherence criteria) were obtained from MicroGIS (MicroGIS Ltd, Baar, Switzerland).

The inclusion criteria for the total orthopedic dataset were: Primary or additional procedure CHOP codes 77.00–84.90 and/or primary diagnosis ICD10 M00.0-M25.9, M40-M43.9, M45-M51.9, M53-M54.9, M60-M63.8, M65-M68.8, M70-M73.8, M75-M77.9, M75-M77.9, M79-M96.9, M99-M99.9.

The inclusion criteria for the analysis of seasonal emergency admissions were:

- Swiss and foreign residents admitted during the years 2000–2002 and emergency admission type (needing treatment within 24 hr after admission).
- HSAo population counts were calculated from the 2,000 census (Swiss Federal Statistical Office, Section Geoinformation, Espace de l'Europe 10, 2010 Neuchâtel)

- Swiss HSAo were constructed according to the method described by Klauss et al. [16] and Goodman and Green [17] using all admission types and only data of Swiss residents.

A basic data set per HSAo contains five indicators that permit the calculation of further indices (numbers or ratios). The five basic indicators per HSAo are number of l-res) admitted in HSAo hospital(s), number of nl-res admitted in HSAo hospital, total number of admissions in HSAo hospital(s), length of stay, and age. On the HSAo level the following indicators per month/year can be calculated:

- l-res admission rate per 10,000 HSAo residents (loc_ar)
- nl-res admission rate per 10,000 HSAo residents (nloc_ar)
- Total admission rate per 10,000 HSAo residents (hosp_ar)
- Percentage of admitted nl-res
- Length of stay per patient (los), for l-res and nl-res
- Average age of admitted patients, for l-res and nl-res

A monthly admission index for l-res, nl-res, and total hospital admissions for each HSAo was calculated [15] by dividing each month's total number of admissions into the average monthly number of admissions for a year (total number of admissions for a year divided by 12). An overall pattern of demand is calculated by averaging month indices over years. This index removes the effect of overall population growth and compensates for the statistics of small population sizes, especially in mountain area HSAo.

For geographic presentations of the data, indicators were grouped and averaged for two seasons:

1. Winter season: December, January, February, and March
2. Summer season: June, July, August, and September

Winter sport HSAo were defined using guest house accommodation nights during the year 2003, provided by the Swiss Federal Statistical Office (UNT Division—Business, Espace de L'Europe 10;CH-2010 Neuchâtel). Switzerland offers ski slopes between 1,500 and approximately 3,500 m altitude, and corresponding lodging opportunities are found from 1,000 m altitude upwards. Therefore, HSAo offering guest beds at or above 1,000 m, showing a seasonal accommodation rate (number of accommodations per 10,000 HSAo residents) according to a winter-summer pattern -steep increase during the winter months starting in December, followed by a steep decrease in April and May, an increase during the summer months, and a decrease in October and November- were defined as WSA. HSAo not offering guest beds above 1,000 m altitude, or HSAo with guest beds above 1,000 m only showing increases in accommodation rates during the summer (HSAo with summer pattern), were defined as RegA. Additionally, every HSAo was evaluated for seasonal hosp_ar.

A Wilcoxon rank sum test was used to analyze differences of rates and indices between WSA and RegA HSAo because variables for several months were skewed. These analyses were performed for each month; the year of admission was an additional cofactor in the model. Statistical analyses where performed with SAS 9.1® (SAS

Institute Inc., Cary, NC, USA). The significance level was set at $p < 0.05$ throughout the study.

For geographic presentations ArcGis, ArcView8.2®, ESRI, Redlands CA, USA was used.

HSAo type

For the 3 years 2000–2002, in total 484,913 orthopedic admissions were registered, of which 135,460 (27.9%) were emergencies. In the Northwest of Switzerland, the 2 HSAo JU02 and JU05 have no data for emergency admissions and therefore were excluded from all analysis.

Of the 83 analyzed HSAo, 45 (54%) have guest beds above 1,000 m altitude, 24 of which (29%) show a winter-summer (WSA) pattern and were defined as winter sport HSAo. A strong correlation between the guest beds accommodation and hospital admission index ($r = 0.622$, $p < 0.001$), or nl-res hospital admission index ($r = 0.71454$, $p < 0.001$) of the 45 HSAo offering beds above 1,000 m can be observed.

The evaluation of hosp ar in all HSAo resulted in the identification of two HSAo types.

1. HSAo showing seasonal fluctuations according to the pattern: steep increase in admission rates during the winter months starting in December, followed by a steep decrease in April and May, a moderate increase during the summer months and a decrease in October and November (seasonal HSAo = SeH).
2. HSAo showing minimal to moderate fluctuations during the year without any specific pattern (constant regions = CoH).

In total 18 HSAo show a SeH pattern (21.7%), 17 of these SeH HSAo are HSAo defined as WSA (70.8%) and 1 outside the WSA (see Figure 1). 7 HSAo (29.2%) within the WSA do not show seasonal admission patterns.

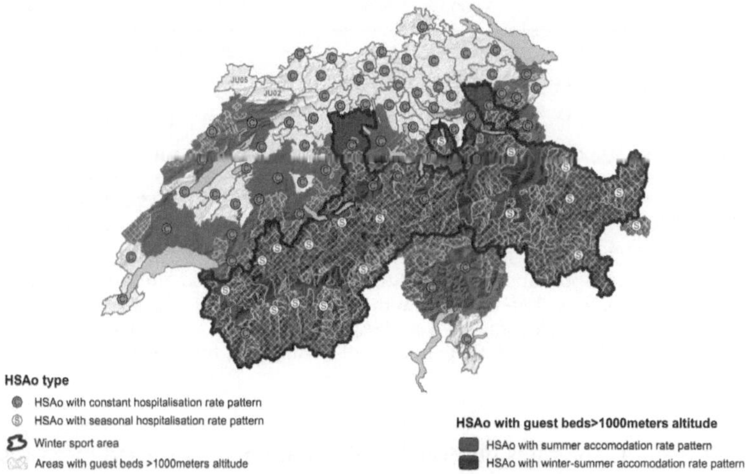

Figure 1. Seasonal and constant HSAo in Switzerland. 83 HSAo in Switzerland of which 24 lay within the winter sport area and of which 18 show a seasonal pattern in hospital emergency admission rates(S).

The SeH within the WSA correspond well with nationally and internationally known winter sport resorts such as Davos, St. Moritz and Lenzerheide in Graubünden, Crans-Montana and Zermatt in Valais, and Grindelwald, Mürren, and Gstaad in the Bernese Alps. CoH within the WSA correspond more with only locally or nationally known winter sport resorts.

Hospital Admissions, Nonlocal Versus Local Residents in Winter Sport and Regular HSAo

As shown in Table 1, HSAo defined as WSA show up to 4 times higher hosp ar than RegA HSAo (February) and a clear seasonal pattern with two mean peaks, a higher peak in winter and a moderate peak in summer. While orthopedic emergency admissions in WSA can comprise up to 55.6% of all orthopedic admissions (February) and show a seasonal pattern, the percentage of emergency admissions in RegA are mostly constant over the year with a minor increase during the summer (July 35%). Overall the yearly emergency rate in WSA is higher (42.3%) than in RegA (29.7%). Throughout the year the difference between WSA and RegA HSAo hosp ar is statistically significant.

Table 1. Emergency admission rates in winter sport and regular HSAo over the year.

		hosp-ar		% of all admissions[1])		nloc-ar		loc-ar		%nl	
		WSA	RegA	WSA	RegA	WSA	RegA	WSA	RegA	WSA	RegA
Winter	**Dec**	11.10	4.62	51.99	31.55	6.07	1.10*	5.03	3.52*	43.44	22.27
	Jan	16.32	5.15	51.65	28.60	10.78*	1.21*	5.54*	3.94*	54.14	21.02
	Feb	17.56	4.55	55.62	29.03	12.60*	1.36*	4.96*	3.19*	58.36	24.24
	Mar	13.30	4.64	48.61	27.40	8.69*	1.07*	4.61*	3.56*	51.07	22.46
	Apr	7.50	4.62	36.49	29.40	3.45	1.16*	4.05	3.45*	37.77	23.41
	Mai	5.77	4.94	31.90	29.07	1.57*	1.19*	4.20*	3.75*	24.93	22.62
Summer	**Jun**	7.21	4.97	39.65	30.88	2.75*	1.29*	4.45*	3.68*	34.54	24.34
	Jul	7.89	5.12	45.89	34.92	3.73	1.46*	4.17	3.66*	41.75	25.32
	Aug	8.86	5.14	46.39	33.36	4.15	1.42*	4.72	3.71*	40.78	25.77
	Sep	6.90	4.78	38.97	30.51	2.71*	1.28*	4.19*	3.50*	34.46	24.76
	Oct	6.39	4.56	33.53	27.66	2.08*	1.09*	4.31*	3.46*	29.64	22.72
	Nov	4.98	4.14	27.32	24.06	1.23*	0.98*	3.75*	3.16*	21.83	22.08

Average values for winter sport and regular HSAo over 3 years. Hosp-ar=hospital admission rate, nloc-ar = nl-res admission rate, loc-ar = l-res admission rate, nl% = percentage of admitted nl-res, WSA = HSAo within winter sport area, RegA = HSAo within regular area. Bold = $p < 0.05$ between WSA and RegA for a variable, *= $p < 0.05$ betweeen nl-res and l-res for an area type, [1)] = no statistical analysis done.

The higher admission rates observed in WSA are mainly caused by nl-res admitted during the winter months. HSAo within RegA present a constant low percentage

(23%) of admitted nl-res (nloc-ar) during the year. In contrast, WSA HSAo show a great fluctuation in percentage of admitted nl-res with a minimum nl% of almost 22% in November and a maximum of 58% in February. Except for the months of May and November, a significantly higher nloc-ar -in a seasonal pattern- in WSA than in RegA HSAo can be observed. Admission rates of l-res (loc-ar) differ significantly between WSA and RegA over the year as well, but the rate differences are much lower and lack a seasonal pattern. The nloc-ar in HSAo within WSA is higher than the loc-ar in the months January, February, and March, and lower in the months May, June, and September–November. For RegA HSAo the nloc-ar is lower than the loc-ar throughout the year.

Seasonal fluctuations in emergency admissions are observed only for nl-res admitted in HSAo defined as WSA. The l-res in all HSAo and nl-res in RegA HSAo show no seasonal patterns in the admission index and monthly indices are close to 1 throughout the year (see Figure 2). In WSA HSAo the highest average nloc-ar is seen in the winter season (February, 12.60 admissions per 10,000 HSAo residents), which is over 3 × higher than the maximum observed in summer (August, 4.15 admissions per 10'000 HSAo residents).

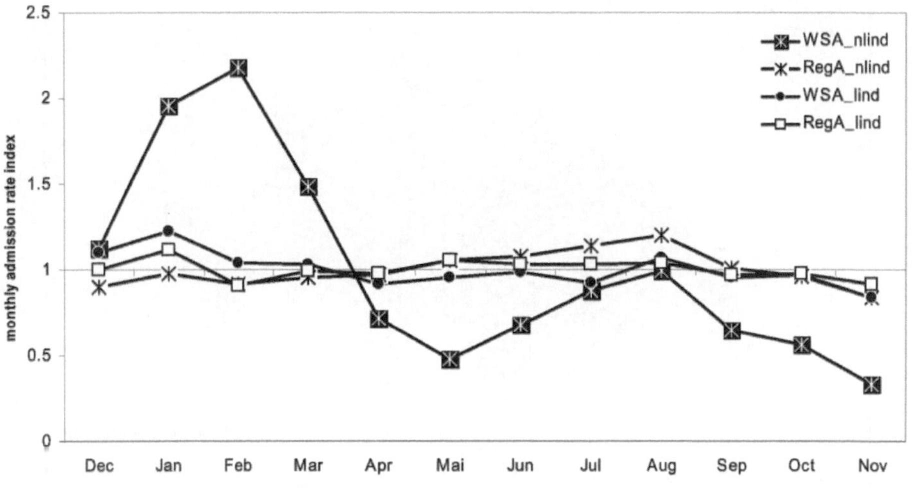

Figure 2. Monthly admission index of nonlocal and local residents in WSA and RegA HSAo. Monthly admission index of nl-res and l-res in winter sport (WSA) and regular (RegA) HSAo; 2000–2002. Nlind = nl-res admission index, lind = l-res admission index.

The geographic distribution of admitted nl-res does not differ greatly between winter and summer, as can be seen in Figure 3, with most nl-res being admitted within the WSA in winter and to a lesser degree in summer.

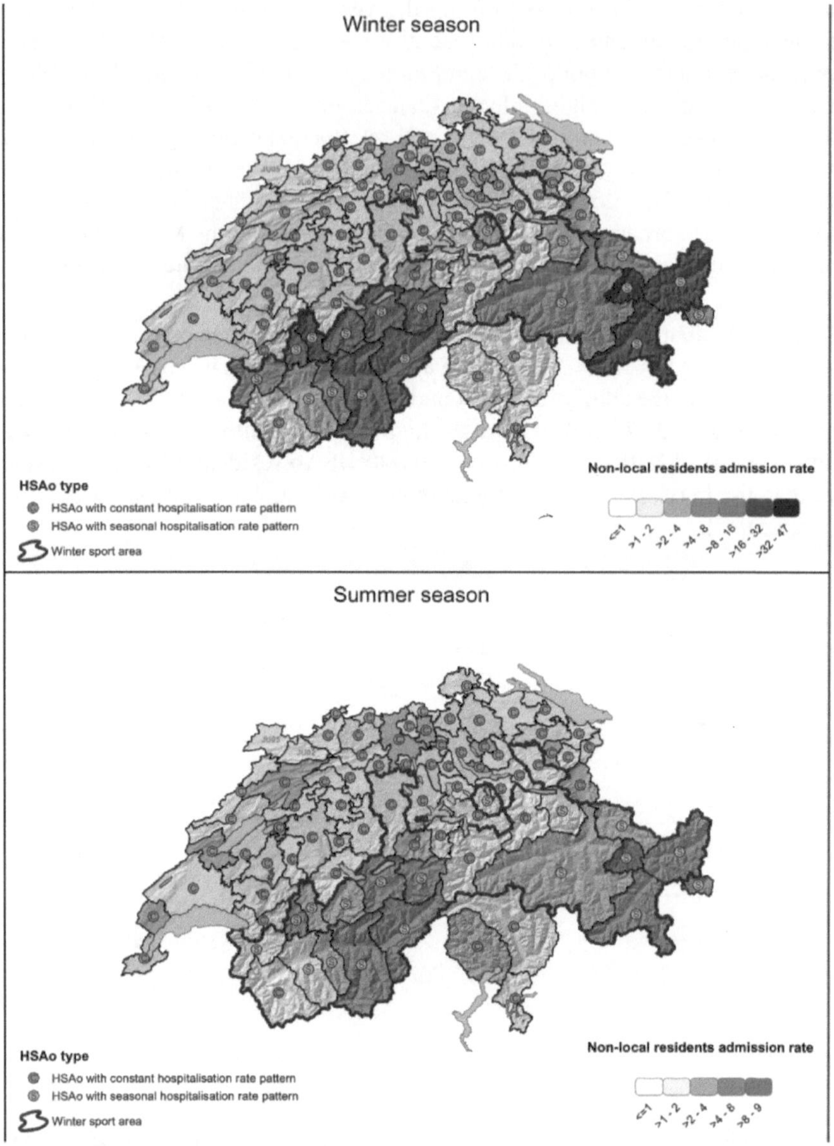

Figure 3. Nonlocal residents admission rates in winter and summer. Average monthly admission rates for nl-res in winter (December, January, February, and March) and summer (June, July, August, September) month.

Age and Length of Stay

The average age of admitted nl-res (48.2) is 8 years younger than admitted l-res (56.4). A seasonal pattern for age can be observed for nl-res in WSA HSAo, with the lowest average age observed during the winter season (see Figure 4). However, the seasonal nl-res age pattern differs from the pattern seen for admission rates. Whereas three seasons with two peaks can be seen for admission rates (mean peak in winter, secondary peak in summer), the annual variation of patient age only shows two seasons with younger persons from December until April (mean 42.5 years old) and older persons (mean 50.5 years old) from May until November. The average age of nl-res in WSA HSAo is lower than in HSAo within RegA from December-March ($p < 0.05$). The l-res are younger in WSA than in RegA HSAo in the months January, February, and April. Whereas the mean monthly age of nl-res is lower than the mean age of l-res in WSA HSAo throughout the months July-April, in RegA HSAo it differs significantly throughout the year.

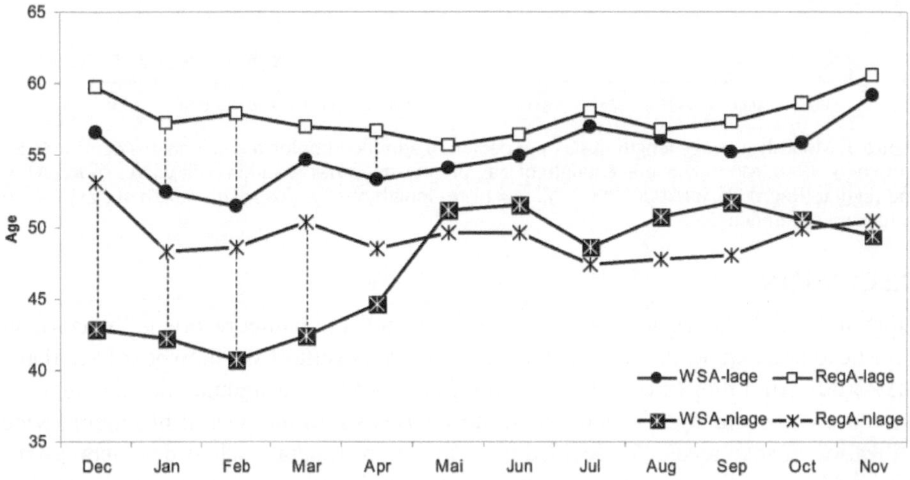

Figure 4. Monthly average age of admitted nonlocal and local residents in WSA and RegA HSAo. Monthly average age of nl-res and l-res in winter sport (WSA) and regular (RegA) HSAo; 2000–2002. nlage = nl-res age, lage = l-res age, ------ = significant difference.

The average yearly length of stay per person is the lowest for nl-res (7.4 days) and the highest for l-res within WSA HSAo (11.9 days). No seasonal pattern can be observed for length of stay. While in HSAo within WSA the monthly average length of stay per person for nl-res shows a continuous increase from December to November, length of stay for nl-res and l-res in RegA HSAo, and l-res in WSA HSAo do not show any particular pattern (see Figure 5). One steep increase in length of stay for l-res in WSA HSAo is observed for the month November. The length of stay of nl-res in WSA HSAo is lower during December-May than in RegA HSAo. There is no significant difference throughout the year between the length of stay of l-res in WSA and RegA HSAo. Except for September and November, the length of stay of nl-res is lower than for l-res in WSA HSAo. Apart from the month of February, the length of stay of nl-res in RegA HSAo is lower than for l-res.

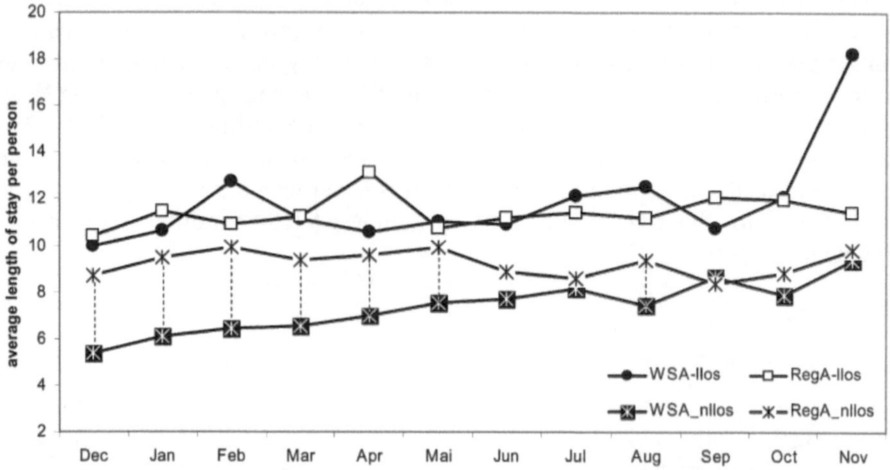

Figure 5. Monthly average length of stay per person of admitted nonlocal and local residents in WSA and RegA HSAo. Monthly average length of stay per person of nl-res and l-res in winter sport (WSA) and regular (RegA) HSAo; 2000–2002. nllos = nl-res length of stay, llos = l-res length of stay, ------ = significant difference.

DISCUSSION

Most of the ambulatory and stationary treated patients in winter resorts in Switzerland have head and extremity injuries that are mostly the result of ski/snowboard accidents (85%)[20]. An orthopedic dataset including trauma and non-trauma related diagnoses were used to evaluate to which extent these cases stress the overall hospital service utilization in such areas. We decided to include non-trauma (such as degenerative diagnosis) related diagnosis because the tourist population may as well contain (older) people with degenerative conditions. These tourists possibly will be at higher risk of having a winter condition related accident in winter sport than in flat land areas. An even better dataset would have included all hospitalized patients, but a dataset including all necessary variables was not available at the time of analysis.

Using the method of small area analysis, Switzerland can be divided into 85 HSAo, of which 24 can be defined as a WSA based upon an accommodation pattern of the guest beds above 1,000 m altitude. Seventeen of the HSAo defined as WSA show a seasonal winter-summer pattern (SeH) in hosp ar, with single HSAo showing up to 7–9 times higher admission rates in the winter season than in the intermediate season. The remaining 7 WSA HSAo do not show a seasonal hospitalization pattern. Whereas WSA HSAo showing a seasonal admission pattern all contain large nationally and internationally recognized winter sport resorts, resorts in WSA HSAo without a seasonal hospitalization pattern are, with one exception, only nationally known. None of the HSAo with guest beds above 1,000 m that have a summer season accommodation pattern show a seasonal pattern in hosp ar.

The HSAo defined as WSA differ in several ways: Injuries of nl-res can be treated locally, resulting in a seasonal pattern of hospital admissions; or, nl-res can be treated outside their HSAo of injury because, for example, the necessary health service is not available there, thus leaving too few nl-res treated locally to produce a seasonal pattern. In addition, more geographically isolated areas, such as found in Graubünden or Valais, have to treat their patients locally, whereas WSA HSAo adjacent to RegA HSAo may transfer emergency cases to those regular HSAo, where they dissolve in the mass. Also, larger, international ski resorts may produce more emergencies (when compared to smaller, more local resorts) that involve foreigners, who may be less easily transferred elsewhere.

As an alternative hypothesis, one may postulate that WSA HSAo that do not show a seasonal hospitalization pattern provide better injury prevention measures, resulting in fewer injuries during the winter than in SeH. Although this hypothesis cannot be verified with our data, it would be of great interest to investigate the link between admission rates and the number of people practicing leisure sports during a given period.

Nonlocal resident admissions in WSA, especially during the winter months, are significantly younger than admitted l-res and their average length of stay is shorter. This supports the hypothesis that winter leisure sport tourism causes the mean observed seasonal peak in hosp ar.

In general, emergency cases stress the health care system more in WSA than in RegA. With large admission fluctuations over the year, these cases require tremendous flexibility in resource planning in WSA (especially in SeH within WSA). As nl-res are the main originators of the emergency admissions, in order to avoid an imbalance between demand and supply hospital bed and staff planning cannot be based on the local population size alone. The provision of enough beds in winter may mean a half empty hospital and suspension of staff during the intermediate season, which could have substantial financial and employment consequences for mountain regions with mostly lower than average population densities and job opportunities.

Limitations

This study has some limitations. The definition of WSA is based on accommodation nights in beds above 1,000 m altitude offered by hotels or guest houses for only 1 year (2003); no data for other years are available. In addition, accommodation in private condos and chalets was not taken into account. An alternative definition criterion could have been the number of ski lifts or length of downhill slopes. A database containing the exact number of ski lifts could not be compiled that suits this study, and the length of slopes was not taken into consideration because slopes may cross HSAo borders. As the correlation between guest bed accommodation and hospitalization rates is substantial and significant, and the defined area corresponds well with the location of known winter sport resorts, the definition of the WSA is considered appropriate.

We chose to analyze and average values of HSAo according to an external definition of winter sport and RegA in order to prevent biases. Alternatively, HSAo could have been grouped and analyzed by individual hospitalization rate patterns (SeH and CoH). This would have increased the magnitude of the observed seasonal patterns in hospitalization rates, but would have excluded areas with known winter sport resorts from being analyzed as WSA. The chosen option allows the observation that not all WSA HSAo have hospitalization rates that show "winter sport" seasonality.

Calculated admission rates relate to the local HSAo population size, not the effective, temporary population size that varies by season. This might distort the results as HSAo with a low population size may have a greater relative tourist load than HSAo with higher population numbers (and vice versa), which would inflate the observed admission rates. To overcome this problem the admission index was calculated. However, this index becomes skewed when the monthly average is driven up by some extreme values for 1or 2 (winter) months, as seen for some WSA HSAo. As Table 1 and Figure 2 show, the hospital admission index for nl-res is below 1 during the summer in WSA and above 1 in RegA HSAo, although the admission rate numbers in WSA are still higher than in Reg HSAo. While these considerations are of great importance when it comes to hospital planning or injury prevention, the given evaluation does not resolve the debate on bed utilization and bed pressures.

Finally, no sex and age adjustments could be made for admission rates or length of stay because the necessary reference population for the corresponding months cannot be estimated.

Implications

The display of local and nonlocal resident admission rates in a geographic information system can be used to assist hospital planning and policymaking by highlighting areas where public health interventions can be applied. In emergency orthopedics, greater variability in bed use over the year is observed only in HSAo defined as WSA. This variability is mainly caused by nl-res and therefore high likely derives from tourism. The implications of our evaluation for hospital planning and health care resource allocation may be considerable. With its cantonally organized health care system [21], Switzerland shows great geographic and terrain-related utilization variations that make different demands upon health care not just between but within single cantons. To supply adequate hospital beds and staff throughout the year and at the same time operate cost-effectively, hospitals in HSAo located in WSA may need larger subsidies.

The observation that most of the patients treated in winter resorts in Switzerland have ski/snowboard accidents [20] emphasizes the conclusion that ski/snowboard tourism places a high burden on the hospital organization of WSA. Reducing the risk of ski/snowboard related injuries through adequate prevention programs therefore might be of great importance not only to the individual guest, but also to these regions as a whole.

CONCLUSION

Small area analysis is an appropriate method to study seasonal effects in hospitalization rates. Concerning orthopedic emergency admissions, Switzerland can clearly be separated into areas with a seasonal and constant admission rate patterns. HSAo showing a seasonal admission pattern all lie within regions containing winter sport resorts. Because the seasonality in admission rates is caused only by nl-res , it can be concluded that seasonality for orthopedic emergency admissions in Switzerland is largely due to leisure sports injuries deriving from tourism. Large variability in admission rates over the year in such areas demands great flexibility in resource planning. Further analysis of types of injuries (leisure sport related or not) and financial implications of seasonality should refine these conclusions.

KEYWORDS

- **Hospital admission rates**
- **Orthopedic hospital service areas**
- **Regular areas**
- **Winter sport areas**

AUTHORS' CONTRIBUTIONS

Klazien Matter-Walstra is responsible for drafting the manuscript. She defined the HSAo, performed GIS operations, and calculated and analyzed variables. André Busato carried out the statistics and contributed to the final version of the manuscript. All authors read and approved the final manuscript.

ACKNOWLEDGMENTS

We would like to thank the staff of the section santé and GEOSTAT of the Swiss Federal Statistical Office for providing data, MicroGIS™ for providing vector data and information on spatial area models, and the institute of geography of the University of Bern for support with GIS software. We also thank Chris Ritter for the English revision.

COMPETING INTERESTS

The authors declare that they have no competing interests. This project was supported by the National Research Program NRP 53 "Musculoskeletal Health—Chronic Pain" of the Swiss National Science Foundation (Project 405340–104607)

Chapter 16

Risk of Malaria in Travelers to Latin America

Ron H. Behrens, Bernadette Carroll, Jiri Beran, Olivier Bouchaud, Urban Hellgren, Christoph Hatz, Tomas Jelinek, Fabrice Legros, Nikolai Mühlberger, Bjφrn Myrvang, Heli Siikamäki, and Leo Visser

INTRODUCTION

A comparison was made between local malaria transmission and malaria imported by travelers to identify the utility of national and regional annual parasite index (API) in predicting malaria risk and its value in generating recommendations on malaria prophylaxis for travelers.

Regional malaria transmission data was correlated with malaria acquired in Latin America and imported into the USA and nine European countries. Between 2000 and 2004, most countries reported declining malaria transmission. Highest API's in 2003/2004 were in Surinam (287.4), Guyana (209.2), and French Guiana (147.4). The major source of travel associated malaria was Honduras, French Guiana, Guatemala, Mexico, and Ecuador. During 2004 there were 6.3 million visits from the 10 study countries and in 2005, 209 cases of malaria of which 22 (11%) were *Plasmodium falciparum*. The risk of adverse events are high and the benefit of avoided benign vivax malaria is very low under current policy, which may be causing more harm than benefit.

Many public health bodies base their recommendations for the prevention of malaria in travelers on national surveillance data, which provides information on the intensity and risk of malaria in local populations, expressed as the API, which may reflect regional risks. While this approach appears rational, there is no evidence that patterns of travel-acquired malaria correlate with transmission intensity among indigenous populations. Recommendations on prophylaxis for travelers need to balance the threat of malaria, including falciparum malaria, and the risk of a fatal outcome, against the potential toxicity of chemoprophylaxis, a risk which is not relevant to populations living in endemic regions. Rombo called into question the use of API to estimate the risk of travelers acquiring malaria [1]. Highlighting the disparity between native and traveler's vulnerability and exposure to infection he has emphasized the need to consider prophylaxis toxicity when prescribing for travel to low risk malaria regions.

Providing appropriate malaria prophylaxis advice for travelers visiting countries in Central and South America can be complex and challenging, particularly when the journey involves many regions or countries where multiple parasite species are present.

This study was set up to review rates of malaria transmission within Central and South American countries and to compare these with patterns of imported malaria among European and US travelers returned from endemic countries. The aim of the study was to try and identify whether transmission within a country reflects malaria transmission among travelers and to examine the usefulness of API in predicting travelers' risk and its value as a basis for recommendations of malaria prophylaxis.

MATERIALS AND METHODS

The local population risk is based on reports from the Pan American Health Organization (PAHO) Regional Office of the World Health Organization with information on API provided by countries within the region [2, 3]. The change in the API over the period 1998 and 2004 has been included to reflect changing trends of malaria transmission. All countries provide regional and district API data, and for this study the highest API in each country is used to represent the maximum risk likely to be faced by travelers. The malaria risk associated with travel is identified through reports from National malaria surveillance bodies, describing malaria imported in returned travelers from Central and South America (Table 1) between the years 2000 and 2005 (data for 2005 was not available for France) from nine European countries and the USA (Table 1). Most of this data was provided through and from members of TropNetEurop, a network of clinical sites, which have access to national malaria surveillance reports, and from the literature. Most reports do not contain details on region of travel within countries, and where several countries have been visited, reports do not necessarily reflect the country of acquisition. Cases provided by TropNetEurop were not included in the country malaria analysis as they would duplicate case reports. Malaria imported from Mexico was analyzed separately from the Central America region.

Table 1. Regions and countries from Central and South America included in the destination analysis and countries reporting imported malaria.

Central America	South America
Belize	Argentina
Costa Rica	Bolivia
El Salvador	Brazil
Guatemala	Colombia
Honduras	Ecuador
Nicaragua	French Guiana
Panama	Guyana
	Paraguay
	Peru
	Surinam
	Venezuela
	S America unspecified
Reported imported Malaria	
Czech Republic	Finland
France	Germany
Holland	Norway
Sweden	Switzerland
United Kingdom	United States of America

The volume of travel will have a significant bearing on the number of cases of imported malaria and therefore rates, where possible, were calculated. The World Tourism Organization collects data on international arrivals and this data provides an estimate of the number of tourist departures and arrivals by country. This data was used where no national statistics were available to estimate the numbers of visits made from the study countries [4, 5] (Figure 1). Malaria cases recorded in UK travelers were analyzed using a denominator, the number of visits made by UK citizens to the countries of malaria acquisition. Data provided by the International Passenger Survey (IPS) is collected through face-to-face interviews of passengers at all major ports within the UK. A quarter of a million passengers are interviewed throughout the year and this sample provides an estimate of the total annual visits to each country, the duration of stay and reason for travel. Malaria cases occurring in US travelers were extracted from data published by the Centers for Disease Control [6-11] and visits made by US citizens to the region were collected by the USA International Air Travel Statistics (or I-92) program. This provides data on outbound numbers of US citizens traveling, using point-to-point air traffic totals from the USA, on departing flights. Visits to, and malaria from Mexico were analyzed separately due to the large traveling population from the USA [12]. Malaria data from France was provided through a reporting network of 120 selected hospital laboratories covering approximately half of annual estimates of malaria cases to the Malaria National Reference Centre (CNRPalu). French and Dutch denominators were captured using a methodology similar to that of the USA International Air Travel Statistics (I-92) program, which reflects aircraft coupons capturing passengers departing to specific destinations between 2000 and 2004. The data on denominators were provided by the French Aviation Authority and Statistics Netherlands, but capture methods vary. In the analysis, malaria acquired in Mexico and visits to Mexico were excluded from the Central America groupings.

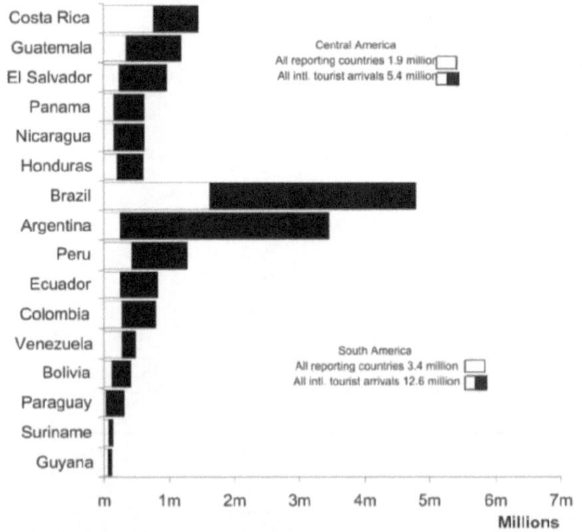

Figure 1. Total visits made by international tourists to the study countries adjusted to visits from the reporting countries.

Malaria Risk in Central and South America

Within the region, 21 countries reported malaria transmission [13, 3]. An estimated 264 million out of the 867 million inhabitants were at risk of malaria, 11 million of these at high risk [3]. Between 1998 and 2004 in countries popular with travelers, Brazil, Peru, Ecuador, and Colombia in South America, and Guatemala and Honduras in Central America, there was a decline in both annual positive slides and API in high risk regions in all but Colombia and Honduras (Table 2), and a decline in the absolute number of cases in all countries except for Peru and Colombia [14]. The most recent API's ranged from 0.07 to 287 in the highest risk regions. Mexico reported low transmission in two provinces only [3].

Imported Malaria

Case reports from Central and South America constitute a small proportion of total imported malaria. In the USA, they accounted for 10% of the total imported malaria in 2005, while in Europe, in the same year, the proportion ranged from 1.1% in the UK, 2% (2004) in France, 3.4% in Switzerland, and 2.4% in the Netherlands. By species, *Plasmodium falciparum* infections ranged between 3 and 17% of all malaria reports annually from Central America and between 17 and 24% of cases acquired in South America. The total number of imported malaria cases reported to surveillance bodies annually for the years 2000–2005 inclusive, fell from 395 to 209 cases of which 69% were non-falciparum in 2005. The bulk of cases were reported in American travelers, with Guatemala and Honduras being the main sources of infection. Total USA reports fell from 242 to 153 in 2005 of which 84% were non-falciparum, where the species was known. Six countries reported 10 or less imported malaria cases from Central and South America in 2005 (Figure 2).

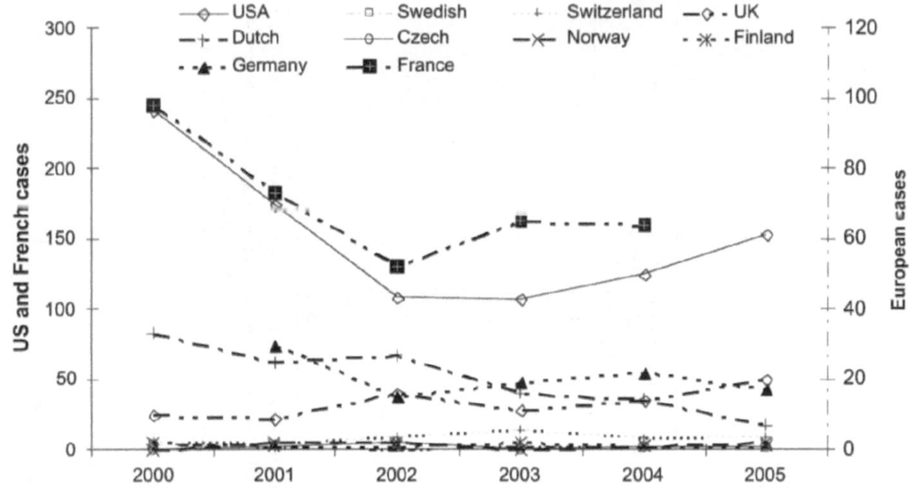

Figure 2. Imported cases by reporting countries 2000–2005. The Y axis 1 reflects US and French cases, all other countries are shown against Y axis 2.

Table 2. Numbers of malaria risk regions in popular tourist destinations, reflecting changing incidence, highest risk regions, and species diagnosed during surveillance.

		Average API's in Moderate and High risk regions				2004§			
Country	**Highest risk regions with total provinces/ departments‡**	**2004#**	**1998**	**%change API 1998–2004**	**Highest regional API 2004¥**	**P.F.**	**P.V.**	**Totals**	**P.V.%**
Guatemala	4/26	9.6	15.8	–39%	53.68 (Peten Sur Occidente)	1,300	28,983	30,283	96%
Honduras	5/9	12.6	9.2	36%	26.55 (Islas de la Bahia)	283	9,033	9,316	97%
Brazil	66/5561	28.0	64.0	–56%	242.05 (Tocantins)	75,685	276,021	351,706	78%
Colombia	18/33	26.2	12.1	116%	233.92 (Cordoba)	42,633	69,272	111,905	62%
Ecuador	12/22	12.0	15.2	–21%	64.43 (Quininde)	5,891	22,839	28,730	79%
French Guiana	5/5	147.4	216.4	–32%	231.27 (Maripasuola)	1,901	752	2,653	28%
Peru	12/34	11.7	21.6	–46%	112.60 (Tumbes)	14,740	74,720	89,460	84%
Surinam	6/10	287.39	263.96	9%	686.07 (Upper Saramacca)	12,078	1,494	13,572	11%
Mexico	2/32	0.07	0.44	–84%	0.30 (Oaxaca)	49	3,357	3,406	99%

‡Data for Colombia, Ecuador, French Guiana, Suriname, & Honduras is taken from PAHO Malaria programs in the America (based on 2002 data), the remaining data is taken from Malaria programs in the Americas (based on 2004 data).
#Data for Brazil, French Guiana & Surinam is 2003 data.
¥ Data for Colombia & Suriname is taken from PAHO Malaria programs in the America (based on 2002 data), the remaining data is taken from Malaria programs in the Americas (based on 2004 data).
§Data from 2003.

Guatemala, French Guiana, and Honduras provided half (55%) of all imported malaria over the 5 years. French Guiana was an important source of malaria for French travelers and Surinam for Dutch travelers. Surinam is a popular destination for Dutch travelers, (60% of all international arrivals in 2004 were from the Netherlands [15] and it is the source of 60% (37% *P. falciparum*) of all malaria cases in Dutch travelers from Latin America. Eighty nine percent of all malaria in French travelers was acquired in French Guiana, where they make up approximately two thirds of all tourist arrivals. Seventy percent were *Plasmodium vivax* infections and twice as many cases occurred in civil as in military personnel, although a high incidence has been reported in the military [16]. The rate in French residents returned from French Guiana averaged 6.2 per 10,000 visits (*P. falciparum* 1.3/10,000 and *P. vivax* 4.3/10,000). Honduras accounted for the largest source of infection, most were in US travelers (Figure 3) who made up over a quarter (178,285) of all tourists arrivals in 2004. Cases from Honduras, predominantly in US travelers have declined by 20% between 2000 and 2005, despite the API having increased by 36% in indigenous populations (Table 2). The rate in Honduras was the highest for all countries visited by UK travelers (5.6/10,000). There were five countries (Honduras, Nicaragua, Surinam, French Guiana, and Guatemala) where the rate of malaria was >1/10,000 visits for UK travelers. Data on the duration of visit was available for visits by UK travelers, a case per years traveling (proxy of exposure) was calculated, based on total nights away, visitors and numbers of cases of malaria. The average duration of visit by UK travelers to the South American continent (2005) was 18 days. Mexico had the lowest risk where one case occurred for very 22,664 years exposed. The risks for Peru, Columbia, and Brazil were similar, around one case for every 3,000 years exposed, and similar to the risks of UK residents visiting India [17]. Honduras and Guatemala were the highest risk countries with one case for every 103 and 513 years exposed respectively.

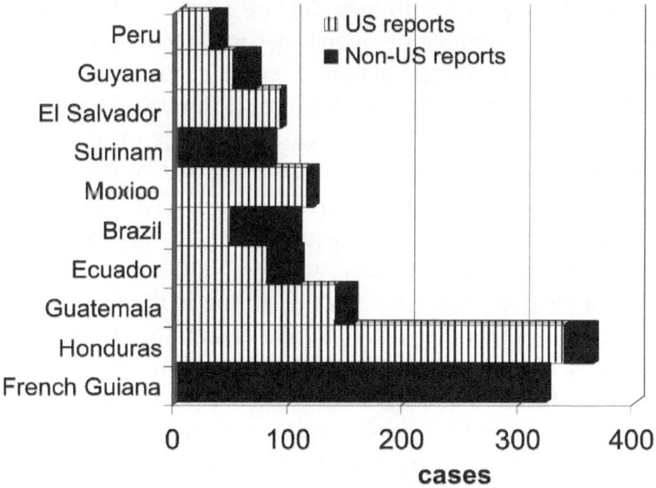

Figure 3. Total imported malaria from nine countries stratified by US and Non US reporting countries 2000–2005.

Low malaria rates were also noted in UK, French, and Dutch visitors to Venezuela, Colombia, Peru, and Brazil during 2004. These four countries received a total 2.6 million visitors from the study countries (Figure 1) and had a maximum incidence of malaria of 2.2 (UK travelers to Colombia, 2004) per 10,000 visits.

DISCUSSION

This study was designed to identify whether local transmission of malaria within countries of Latin America reflected the pattern and trends of malaria acquired by travelers from 10 developed countries. During 2004, 21 PAHO countries with active malaria programs examined 6.7 million slides, of which 13% were positive for malaria, three quarters of them were speciated as *P. vivax* infections in an "at risk" population of 262 million [3]. The detailed information collected in Central and South American countries and presented by PAHO [3, 2, 13] provides evidence of a clear trend of declining transmission across most of the countries, most notably in Brazil, which reported a 56% decrease in the high incidence regions, attributed to malaria control programs initiated in 2000. The total number of tourists visiting Latin America is not known precisely, but the World Tourism Organization [4] estimates there were 16 million international tourist arrivals to South America, with a 16% increase from 2003. Central America, during 2004, received 5.7 million inbound visitors, a 17% growth in arrivals over the previous year. The main country sources of imported malaria were Honduras, French Guiana, Guatemala, Mexico, and Ecuador, from where there were 1,066 imported cases over 5 years, accounting for 64% of all imported cases from Latin America, 75% were non-falciparum malaria. There are a number of important limitations that need to be understood when reflecting on the findings. Local transmission reported to PAHO may be inconsistent and regions not reporting or not diagnosing cases may be interpreted as no malaria transmission. The imported malaria cases collected nationally use different reporting methods and are of varied quality. The denominators used in the analysis are again of different capture methods. The USA, France and the Netherlands record the number of citizens departing to a destination while in the UK samples of departing passengers are interviewed, capturing destination, duration of travel, and reason for travel. The pattern of travel through the regions by western travelers is not recorded in the denominator data or through the malaria case reports, and therefore the proportion visiting high transmission regions are unknown.

Although a number of regions within Peru and Brazil have an API above 50/1,000 cases/year the actual numbers of malaria cases in returning travelers is low, a total of 145 cases over 5 years, and in 2005, there were only 30 cases of which three were *P. falciparum*. Asymptomatic carriage in natives living in the Peruvian Amazon near Iquitos is estimated to be less than 10% and the entomological inoculation rate for the Amazonas region reported as 10–20 annually [18]. The small numbers of travel associated cases from Peru are unlikely to be a result of widespread use of chemoprophylaxis. Currie and colleagues [19] examined prophylaxis use in tourists departing Lima, Peru. Of the 1226 travelers interviewed, 43% were from the USA. Nearly three quarters had visited only Peru and 54% had visited a malarious region (as defined by CDC). Of these around half had taken regular chemoprophylaxis (42% atovaquone/

proguanil). During that year (2003) there were 10 (six *P. vivax*) imported malaria cases from Peru. The highest numbers of imported malaria cases, over the 5-year study period, were of *P. vivax* from Honduras, Guatemala, Ecuador, and French Guiana. Despite an increase in local transmission in Honduras, total travel associated cases declined by 20% suggesting that there is no correlation between the two trends. The rates in US and UK travelers to the whole region (excluding Mexico) reveal a similar incidence of 0.3 and 0.8 per 10,000 visits despite an increasing volume of travel over the study (237,526 UK and 4.5 million US travelers in 2005).

Mexico had an estimated 20 million visits by US citizens in 2004. Visits to malaria endemic regions of Mexico are unknown, but are likely to be small. There was a fall in imported malaria to the US from Mexico, from 30 case reports in 2000 to 14 in 2005.

Current chemoprophylaxis policies recommend prophylaxis for high risk regions [20-22], but many of these regions (as shown in Table 2 have a declining risk for indigenous populations). The inconsistency between focal high transmission areas in countries popular with western travelers and small numbers of travel associated malaria is worth exploring. Significant numbers of travelers may not be using prophylaxis during their travel and the departure lounge suggests approximately 50% of visitors will be using chemoprophylaxis. Other countries visited by significant numbers of tourists as reported by WTO in 2005—Peru, (1.5 million), Brazil (5.4 million), Guatemala (1.3 million) had small numbers of cases and low rates of malaria. Although these countries have areas of high transmission, the major parts of these countries have no malaria transmission. It would appear that most visitors to these countries are at low or no risk of acquiring infection, whatever their journey and destination within the country.

Protection against *P. vivax*, disease despite using the most widely available regimens is marginal [23-25], as only the primary attack [23] is aborted. Most clinical episodes develop some months after infection when travelers have returned home and are unlikely to be missed through routine reporting systems. Severe adverse events leading to stopping medication during chemoprophylactic drug use were reported in 3–8% of users while mild to moderate adverse events were reported by 32–45% of users [26]. In the 423,416 visitors from reporting countries to Peru in 2003 [4] approximately 25% (105,000 or 50% of those visiting a malarious region) visitors were using chemoprophylaxis as identified by the airport departure lounge study [19]. During that year, 10 (two *P. falciparum*) cases of malaria were reported in nine study countries after visiting Peru. Using the minimal proportion of users encountering adverse events from the popular prophylaxis regimens [26] an estimated 34,000 travelers would have suffered an adverse event related to chemoprophylaxis use. The risk of adverse events for visitors to Peru and other regions are likely to be significantly higher than avoided infections particularly of benign *P. vivax* malaria under current policy recommendations. Unless chemoprophylaxis prescribing is significantly reduced, current recommendations are likely to be causing more harm than benefit.

Policy Change

Despite its limitations, this study suggests that the risk of adverse events from chemoprophylaxis is likely to be significantly higher than the risk of acquiring malaria in the most popular tourist destinations in Central and South America. Although current national and international policy focuses on chemoprophylaxis for focal, highly endemic malaria transmission regions in countries which have overall low API's, this strategy appears to provide limited benefit as travelers appear to have a low malaria attack rate and will acquire *P. vivax* rather than *P. falciparum* infection. The benefit of chemoprophylaxis in preventing the former is unclear. An alternate strategy adopted by a number of European countries, for example Switzerland [27], is to provide travelers with emergency standby treatment in case of malaria symptoms during travel. This has the benefit of dealing with a life threatening attack of falciparum malaria, but avoiding adverse events associated with excessive chemoprophylaxis. It has the disadvantage of cost, as all travelers will have to purchase therapy. Two of the highest risk countries reported by PAHO—French Guiana and Surinam, correlated to countries where visitors were at high risk of malaria and chemoprophylaxis would be appropriate for travel to risk areas in these countries. There appears to be no clear benefit and significant potential for toxicity in recommending chemoprophylaxis for visitors to Mexico, where the highest API is less than 0.07 for local residents and 20 imported cases annually. Despite the low or falling risk of malaria, the continued use of bite prevention measures remains important as these are effective, safe, and have the added benefit of reducing other vector borne diseases.

KEYWORDS

- **Annual parasite index**
- **Malaria rates**
- **Malarious region**
- ***Plasmodium falciparum***
- ***Plasmodium vivax***
- **Regional malaria transmission**

DATA SOURCES

USA denominator data: In flight survey ITA Office of Travel & Tourism Industries.

UK cases: Malaria Reference Laboratory, Health Protection Agency UK (Peter Chiodini).

UK denominator data: IPS Office for National Statistics.

France: Centre National de Référence du Paludisme.

TropNetEurop http://www.tropnet.net

Finland: National Public Health Institute, Finland.

Jorge Atouguia, Instituto de Higiene e Medicina Tropical, Lisboa.

Czech Republic National Institute of Public Health in Prague: C. Benes.

Switzerland: Simone Graf (Swiss Federal Office of Public Health).

Netherlands: National Center of Disease Control Institute for Public Health and the Environment Norway: Section of Infectious Disease Prevention and Control, the Norwegian Institute of Public Health (Hans Blystad).

AUTHORS' CONTRIBUTIONS

Ron H. Behrens and Bernadette Carroll designed the study, collated the data, and prepared the first draft.

Jiri Beran, Olivier Bouchaud, Urban Hellgren, Christoph Hatz, Tomas Jelinek, Fabrice Legros, Nikolai Mühlberger, Bjørn Myrvang, Heli Siikamäki, and Leo Visser obtained and analyzed national data. All authors contributed to the interpretation of the data and agreed the final draft.

ACKNOWLEDGMENTS

Jorge Atouguia for translation on information from Brazil and Joaquim Gascon and Rogelio Lopez Velez for information on malaria in Spain. We thank the institutes and persons listed below for providing data for this study.

Chapter 17

Tourism Implications of *Cryptococcus gattii* in the Southeastern USA

Edmond J. Byrnes III, Wenjun Li, Yonathan Lewit, John R. Perfect, Dee A. Carter, Gary M. Cox, and Joseph Heitman

INTRODUCTION

In 2007, the first confirmed case of *Cryptococcus gattii* was reported in the state of North Carolina, USA. An otherwise healthy human immunodeficiency virus (HIV) negative male patient presented with a large upper thigh cryptococcoma in February, which was surgically removed and the patient was started on long-term high-dose fluconazole treatment. In May of 2007, the patient presented to the Duke University hospital emergency room with seizures. Magnetic resonance imaging (MRI) revealed two large central nervous system (CNS) lesions found to be cryptococcomas based on brain biopsy. Prior chest computed tomography (CT) imaging had revealed small lung nodules indicating that *C. gattii* spores or desiccated yeast were likely inhaled into the lungs and dissemination occurred to both the leg and CNS. The patient's travel history included a visit throughout the San Francisco, CA region in September through October of 2006, consistent with acquisition during this time period. Cultures from both the leg and brain biopsies were subjected to analysis. Based on phenotypic and molecular methods, both isolates were *C. gattii*, VGI molecular type, and distinct from the Vancouver Island outbreak isolates. Based on multilocus sequence typing (MLST) of coding and non-coding regions and virulence in a heterologous host model, the leg and brain isolates are identical, but the two differed in mating fertility. Two clinical isolates, one from a transplant recipient in San Francisco and the other from Australia, were identical to the North Carolina clinical isolate at all markers tested. Closely related isolates that differ at only one or a few non-coding markers are present in the Australian environment. Taken together, these findings support a model in which *C. gattii* VGI was transferred from Australia to California, possibly though an association with its common host plant *E. camaldulensis*, and the patient was exposed in San Francisco and returned to present with disease in North Carolina.

Significant medical advances have been achieved in the fields of antimicrobial agents and vaccine development, yet both newly emerging and re-emerging infectious diseases in humans, livestock, and plants remain serious global health and economic burdens [1, 2]. Several factors influence the emergence and re-emergence of infectious diseases, and two are globalization and an increasing population of immunocompromised hosts [3, 4]. These have significantly impacted the emergence of systemic fungal infections over the past 2 decades, largely due to widespread use of broad-spectrum antibiotics, advances in healthcare, and the HIV pandemic [5].

An essential component for tracking emergence and epidemiology of bacterial, parasitic, and fungal infections is molecular strain typing. In the genomic era, whole genome sequences have allowed comprehensive typing though sequence-based methods, including multilocus sequence (MLS) and variable number of tandem repeat (VNTR) typing approaches [6, 7]. Each method has distinct benefits for increasing typing resolution, and can be used concomitantly to increase the overall power of molecular typing. The MLST has been widely applied to the fungal kingdom, and in particular for the Cryptococcus species complex [8-11]. Fewer studies have applied VNTR analysis to fungal pathogens, which was developed and is widely used in studies of bacterial pathogens [7, 12-14]. We present here the first application of a combined MLST/VNTR approach to establish relationships among a group of emerging *Cryptococcus gattii* clinical and environmental isolates.

Cryptococcu gattii is a basidiomycetous yeast closely related to other members of the *Cryptococcus pathogenic* species complex, including *C. neoformans* var. grubii and var. neoformans [15-17]. *Cryptococcu gattii* has often been associated with tropical and subtropical climates including Australia and South America [15], and has emerged as a fungal pathogen of humans and animals in temperate climates including Vancouver Island, mainland British Columbia, Canada, and the US Pacific Northwest, including Washington and Oregon [10, 18-23]. The species *C. gattii* can be subdivided into serotypes B and C based on unique capsular antigenic determinants [24, 25]. In addition, the species can be divided into four molecular types (VGI, VGII, VGIII, VGIV) based on evidence from amplified fragment length polymorphisms (AFLPs), Random Amplification of Polymorphic DNA (RAPD), and MLST [10, 11, 26]. Genetic exchange between the four VG molecular types is rare, indicating that these likely represent cryptic species [10, 11].

Cryptococcosis is the disease caused by the pathogenic Cryptococcus species complex and usually results in pulmonary infection/pneumonia, CNS dissemination, and in some cases cryptococcoma formation [17, 27]. *Cryptococcus neoformans* and *C. gattii* share some common virulence attributes but are also distinct. *Cryptococcus neoformans* has a global distribution and predominantly infects immunosuppressed hosts, while *C. gattii* is more geographically restricted and commonly infects immunocompetent individuals [28]. Incidence in immunocompetent individuals is particularly high within the VGI and VGII molecular types. Molecular type VGI commonly causes infections in Australia, whereas the VGII molecular type is responsible for the vast majority of cases related to the Vancouver Island outbreak, and its expansion into the North American Pacific NW [17, 19, 29]. The VGIII and VGIV molecular types have been reported to infect immunocompromised patients, including HIV/AIDS patients and organ transplant recipients [30-32].

In the US and Canada, a major focus of *C. gattii* research has been on molecular type VGII due to the high percentage (~95%) of clinical cases caused by this molecular type in otherwise healthy individuals, while only ~5% of cases result from VGI infection [8, 19, 20]. While VGI is the most common infectious molecular type globally and has been reported in cryptococcosis cases from the Americas including Canada, Mexico, and South America, the overall number of isolates from the US has been low [10,

17]. In the US there have been two confirmed cases of *C. gattii* molecular type VGI, both in California. One case occurred in a male Atlantic bottlenose dolphin (*Tursiops truncatus*) in San Diego; the other was in a liver transplant recipient in San Francisco [32, 33]. The isolates from these cases differed based on MLST analysis, but both are closely related or identical to isolates from Australia, indicating that an environmental source in California may have originated from the large number of Eucalyptus trees imported from Australia to California, particularly due to the strong environmental association between the VGI molecular type and Eucalyptus trees [10, 34].

Cryptococcu gattii has never been isolated from environmental sources in the Eastern US [35], and until the present study no cases in the region have been reported in humans or animals. In this study, we present the first reported clinical case of *C. gattii* in the Southeastern US, which occurred in an immunocompetent individual residing in central North Carolina. We show that this case, which resulted in large cryptococcomal granulomas in the leg and brain, resulted from infection with a *C. gattii* VGI type isolate that is distinct from both the common VGII and rarer VGI isolates associated with the Vancouver Island/Pacific NW *C. gattii* outbreak. The molecular genotype of the isolates from both leg and brain biopsies show that the molecular profile based on MLS analysis of both coding (MLST) and more variable non-coding (VNTR) markers is shared with only two clinical isolates (one from Australia, and the other from an organ transplant recipient in San Francisco, California) out of 85 VGI strains typed [10, 32]. While this is the first reported case in the Eastern US, the suspected ecological niche is in the Western US, and the patient's travel history is consistent with acquisition in the San Francisco metropolitan area. Travel to endemic areas is known to increase risk for *C. gattii* exposure and disease, and leads to acquisition in one region with presentation in a distant location [36, 37]. The Australian case, California transplant patient, and North Carolina patient isolates are closely related to, but not identical at all non-coding genomic markers (VNTR) with Australian environmental isolates. Therefore, the Australian environment is the most likely source of the original isolates, and additional sampling may be necessary, as subtle genetic changes may have occurred during expansion or infection. Our results further support the well documented emergence of *C. gattii* in temperate climates in the Western US, and put forth a model in which an emergence from Australia to California has resulted in travel-associated disease presentation in the Southeastern US.

MATERIALS AND METHODS

Isolate Identification

Melanin production was assayed by growth and the production of dark pigmentation on Staib niger seed agar medium, and urease activity was detected by growth and alkaline pH change on Christensen's Agar. These tests established that isolates were either *C. neoformans* or *C. gattii*. Isolates were then examined for resistance to canavanine and utilization of glycine on L-canavanine, glycine, 2-bromothymol blue (CGB) agar. Growth on CGB agar indicates that isolates are canavanine resistant, and able to use glycine as a sole carbon source, triggering a bromothymol blue color reaction indicative of *C. gattii*, whereas *C. neoformans* is sensitive to canavanine, and cannot use glycine as a sole carbon source, resulting in no growth or coloration on this selective indicator medium. Capsule identification was conducted though India ink analysis and microscopy after growth on Dulbecco's Modified Eagle's Medium (DMEM) for 72 hr at 37°C.

Molecular Typing

For MLST analysis, each isolate was analyzed with a minimum of eight and in some cases 11 unlinked loci [6, 9, 10]. For each isolate, genomic DNA was extracted using the MasterPure™ yeast DNA purification kit (Epicentre Biotechnologies), polymerase chain reaction (PCR) amplified, purified, and sequenced. All primers used for the analysis were designed specifically to amplify open reading frame (ORF) gene sequence regions including those with non-coding DNA regions to maximize discriminatory power. All PCR products were sequenced, and novel sequences were re-amplified and sequenced for confirmation. Sequences from both forward and reverse strands were assembled, and manually edited using Sequencher version 4.8 (Gene Codes Corporations). Based on BLAST analysis of the GenBank database (NCBI), each allele was assigned a number [10]. GenBank accession numbers with corresponding allele numbers are listed in the supplementary information. For the microsatellite analysis two software packages were used: Magellan, a freely available software package developed by Dee Carter's laboratory at the University of Sydney (http://www.medfac.usyd.edu.au/people/academics/profiles/dcarter.php) [38], and the tandem repeat finder (TRF) software package developed at Boston University [39]. Sequences were assembled and edited using Sequencher version 4.8 (Gene Codes Corporations) and aligned using the Clustal X version 2.0 software package [40].

Fertility Analysis

Mating analysis was conducted on Murashige and Skoog (MS) media, which contains myo-inositol that stimulates mating [41]. Isolates were incubated at room temperature (24°C) in the dark for 10–14 days under dry conditions. Fertility was assessed by microscopic examination for hyphae, fused clamp cells, basidia, and basidiospore formation.

Virulence

Infection assays in the heterologous host *Galleria mellonella* (greater wax moth) were conducted with a method similar to previous studies [42]. All animals were purchased in bulk and a single shipment used for each replicate virulence test (Van der Horst Wholesale, St. Marys, Ohio). The infectious inoculum was injected directly into the hemolymph via the penultimate or ultimate pseudo-pods using a Hamilton syringe (Hamilton USA). All experiments were conducted in duplicate with an infectious dose of 1.0 × 105 cells, and larvae were maintained in a 37°C controlled environment. For each replicate virulence assay, 12–19 larvae were infected for each strain analyzed. Animals were monitored at 24-hr intervals, and mortality was defined as the cessation of movement upon probing and development of a distinctive dark colorization.

Clinical Presentation of an Unusual *Cryptococcus* Infection

The patient is a 46-year-old male with an unremarkable past medical history who noticed a hard mass on his medial right thigh. The mass enlarged over the course of 3 weeks, but was not painful, and the patient had no other symptoms. His primary care physician evaluated the mass with a MRI scan, which showed a 5 × 4 × 4 centimeter mass in the inner mid right thigh involving the adductor magnus muscle. The mass had mild heterogeneous enhancement on T2 imaging (Figure 1A) and some changes consistent with limited surrounding edema. The radiographic appearance was most consistent with a malignancy, and he underwent further radiographic investigation with chest, abdominal, and pelvic CT scans.

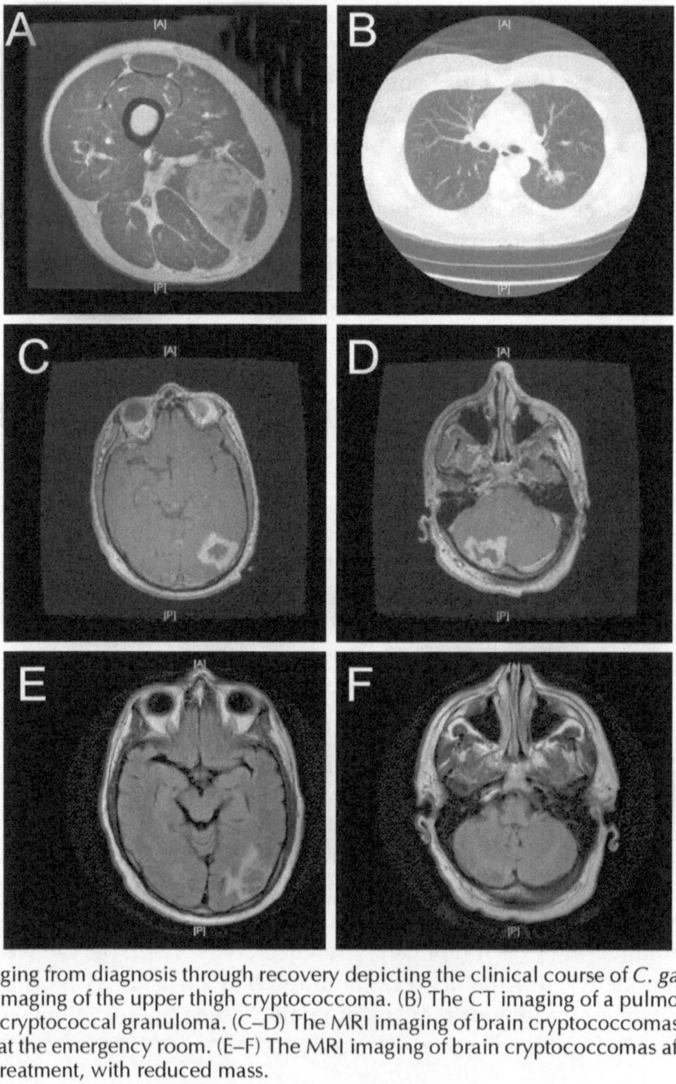

Figure 1. Imaging from diagnosis through recovery depicting the clinical course of *C. gattii* infection. (A) The MRI imaging of the upper thigh cryptococcoma. (B) The CT imaging of a pulmonary nodule, likely to be a cryptococcal granuloma. (C–D) The MRI imaging of brain cryptococcomas after seizure presentation at the emergency room. (E–F) The MRI imaging of brain cryptococcomas after long-term fluconazole treatment, with reduced mass.

The chest CT scan revealed a spiculated 1.6 × 2 centimeter left lower lobe lung mass with multiple, bilateral sub-centimeter pulmonary nodules (Figure 1B). The patient underwent a percutaneous biopsy of the thigh mass, and pathology demonstrated soft tissue necrosis and thick walled, encapsulated organisms that stained with gomori methenamine silver (GMS) and mucicarmine. The entire mass was surgically resected, and cultures from the mass grew Cryptococcus. Further evaluation demonstrated a serum cryptococcal antigen of 1:32, negative HIV serologies, and a normal CD4 lymphocyte count.

No other symptoms were revealed by a detailed medical history, but the patient was regularly exposed to birds in the workplace. However, extensive local sampling of the workplace environment and birdcages failed to reveal a local source of infection. The patient was placed on 400 mg fluconazole a day, and did well until 3 months later when he presented with a tonic-clonic seizure. An MRI scan showed a large, enhancing mass in the left parietal lobe and a similar appearing mass in the right cerebellar hemisphere (Figure 1C–D). A biopsy of the parietal mass showed numerous yeast cells, and cultures grew Cryptococcus.

After diagnosis, the patient was initially treated with amphotericin B and flucytosine, but due to renal toxicity/nephropathy was changed to oral high-dose fluconazole (800 mg daily). The large size of the mass lesions despite antifungal therapy prompted consideration that the infection might be due to *Cryptococcus gattii*, and serotyping with commercial monoclonal antibodies (Iatron, Tokyo, Japan) revealed the isolate to be serotype B, consistent with *C. gattii* (T. Mitchell, A. Litvintseva, personal communication). The patient had traveled to San Francisco 5 months prior to his original presentation. He had never been to the Pacific Northwest, Australia, South America or other *C. gattii* endemic regions and his only foreign travel had been to Western Europe.

Sixteen months after the seizure he was completely asymptomatic on fluconazole 400 mg a day, and showed a significant decrease in the cerebral cryptococcomas upon reevaluation with MRI (Figure 1E–F). The patient is currently asymptomatic and continuing fluconazole treatment as of February 2009 with a cryptococcal antigen titer testing positive at 1:4. The patient will continue treatment, and be re-scanned in the spring of 2009.

Phenotypic Analysis Reveals Isolates are *C. gattii*

Initial identification and confirmation that the leg (EJB1-L) and brain (EJB2-B) isolates were *C. gattii* was completed using several phenotypic and molecular tests. Isolates were confirmed to be *C. gattii* based on melanin production on Staib niger seed agar, production of urease on Christensen's agar, and resistance to canavanine with glycine utilization on CGB agar. Capsule production was assayed through India ink exclusion of cells grown at 37°C for 72 hr in DMEM, resulting in high levels of polysaccharide capsule indicative of pathogenic *Cryptococcus* species. Isolates were determined to be mating type α based on controlled mating assays with *C. gattii* VGIII isolates NIH312α and B4546α. Although both isolates ultimately were able to complete the sexual cycle with the a mating tester, and are therefore α mating type, there was a severe and reproducible defect in hyphae and basidiospore formation in mating assays with isolate EJB2-B when compared with EJB1-L (Figure 2), with similar results obtained using a mating type a crg1 tester strain (data not shown). Differences in mating ability were also observed in other similar or identical genotype isolates (B4496 and E296 (high fertility) versus PAT12ISO1 and E310 (low fertility)). There were no other significant differences between the isolates when comparing melanin production, growth at 37°C, growth on CGB agar, and urease and capsule production.

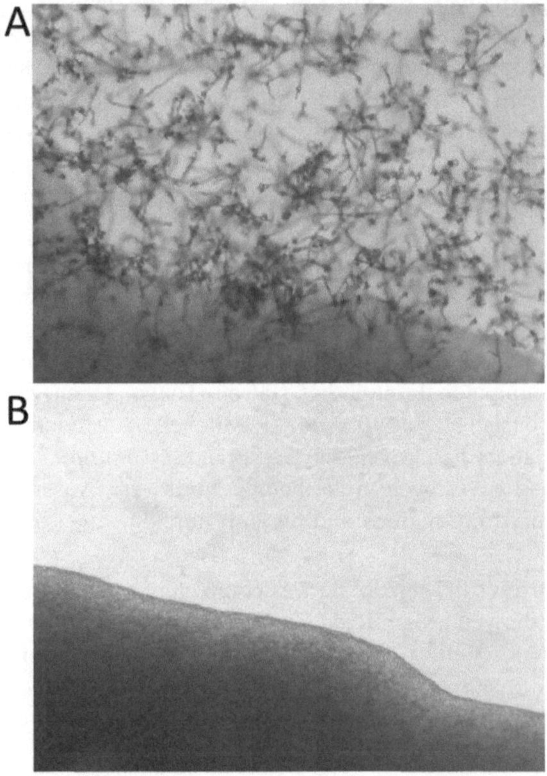

Figure 2. Clinical isolates exhibit mating differences. All mating cultures were incubated at room temperature in the dark, for 10–14 days in dry conditions using the mating type a tester isolate B4546 as a partner on Mirashige and Skoog Media. The brain biopsy isolate exhibits reduced fertility as evidenced by a marked delay and paucity in hyphal growth (A) whereas hyphal growth, basidia, and basidiospore formation indicative of sexual reproduction is evident in matings with the leg biopsy isolate (B). All mating experiments were repeated and representative images are shown here.

Molecular Analysis Reveals Isolates are VGI Molecular Type

Molecular studies were conducted to determine if this clinical case was in any way related to the outbreak of *C. gattii* on Vancouver Island that has now expanded to mainland British Columbia, Washington, and Oregon. Genomic DNA of each isolate was analyzed by MLST at a minimum of eight loci (Figure 3). In addition to the mating analysis to determine the mating type of each isolate, PCR and sequence analysis were used to detect either of the two mating type-specific idiomorphs of the SXI genes. Amplification and sequence analysis of the sex specific SXI1α mating type gene, as well as the absence of the mating type specific SXI2α gene, confirmed that both isolates had the α mating type allele (MATα). The MLST analysis also showed that all MLST alleles were identical between both the leg biopsy (EJB1-L) and brain biopsy (EJB2-B) isolates, and each typed as *C. gattii* molecular type VGI (Figure 3).

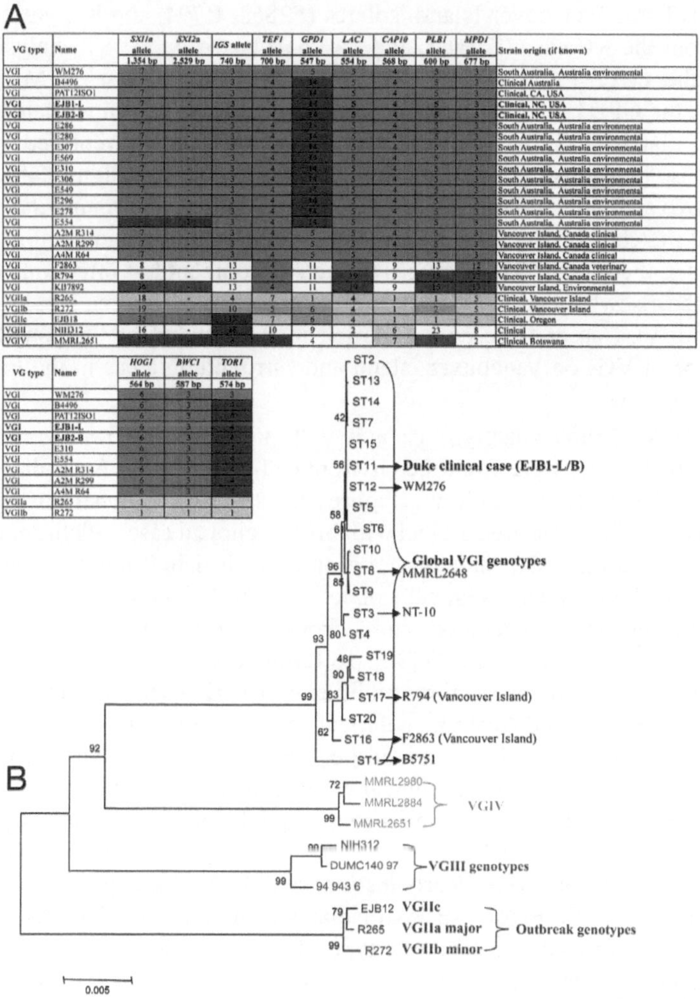

VG type	Name	*SXI1α* allele 1,354 bp	*SXI2a* allele 2,529 bp	*IGS* allele 740 bp	*TEF1* allele 700 bp	*GPD1* allele 547 bp	*LAC1* allele 554 bp	*CAP10* allele 568 bp	*PLB1* allele 600 bp	*MPD1* allele 677 bp	Strain origin (if known)
VGI	WM276	7	-	3	4	5	5	4	5	3	South Australia, Australia environmental
VGI	B4496	7	-	3	4	14	5	4	5	3	Clinical Australia
VGI	PAT12ISO1	7	-	3	4	14	5	4	5	3	Clinical, CA, USA
VGI	**EJB1-L**	7	-	3	4	14	5	4	5	3	**Clinical, NC, USA**
VGI	**EJB2-B**	7	-	3	4	14	5	4	5	3	**Clinical, NC, USA**
VGI	E286	7	-	3	4	15	5	4	5	3	South Australia, Australia environmental
VGI	E280	7	-	3	4	14	5	4	5	3	South Australia, Australia environmental
VGI	E307	7	-	3	4	14	5	4	5	3	South Australia, Australia environmental
VGI	E569	7	-	3	4	15	5	4	5	3	South Australia, Australia environmental
VGI	E310	7	-	3	4	14	5	4	5	3	South Australia, Australia environmental
VGI	E306	7	-	3	4	14	5	4	5	3	South Australia, Australia environmental
VGI	E549	7	-	3	4	15	5	4	3	2	South Australia, Australia environmental
VGI	E296	7	-	3	4	14	5	4	5	3	South Australia, Australia environmental
VGI	E278	7	-	3	4	14	5	4	5	3	South Australia, Australia environmental
VGI	E554	[illegible]	2	3	4	15	5	4	5	3	South Australia, Australia environmental
VGI	A2M R314	7	-	3	4	5	5	4	5	3	Vancouver Island, Canada clinical
VGI	A2M R299	7	-	3	4	5	5	4	5	3	Vancouver Island, Canada clinical
VGI	A4M R64	7	-	3	4	5	5	4	5	3	Vancouver Island, Canada clinical
VGI	F2863	8	-	13	4	11	5	9	13	12	Vancouver Island, Canada veterinary
VGI	R794	8	-	13	4	11	19	9	15	12	Vancouver Island, Canada clinical
VGI	KB7892	36	-	13	4	11	19	9	15	13	Vancouver Island, Environmental
VGIIa	R265	18	-	4	7	1	4	1	1	5	Clinical, Vancouver Island
VGIIb	R272	19	-	10	5	6	4	1	2	5	Clinical, Vancouver Island
VGIIc	EJB18	35	-	[illegible]	7	6	4	1	1	5	Clinical, Oregon
VGIII	NIH312	16	-	[illegible]	10	9	2	6	23	8	Clinical
VGIV	MMRL2651	[illegible]	[illegible]	[illegible]	2	4	1	7	3	2	Clinical, Botswana

VG type	Name	*HOG1* allele 564 bp	*BWC1* allele 587 bp	*TOR1* allele 574 bp
VGI	WM276	6	3	3
VGI	B4496	6	3	[illegible]
VGI	PAT12ISO1	6	3	[illegible]
VGI	**EJB1-L**	6	3	4
VGI	**EJB2-B**	6	3	4
VGI	E310	6	3	[illegible]
VGI	E554	6	3	[illegible]
VGI	A2M R314	6	3	[illegible]
VGI	A2M R299	6	3	[illegible]
VGI	A4M R64	6	3	[illegible]
VGIIa	R265	1	1	1
VGIIb	R272	1	1	1

Figure 3. Molecular typing and phylogeny of the North Carolina clinical isolates with global isolates. (A) The MLST reveals the leg and brain isolates are identical with each other, and also identical with a distinct genotype predominantly from Australia, and in a single clinical case from California, USA. (B) Neighbor joining phylogenetic analysis based on sequences from seven MLST loci in panel A (SXI idiomorphs not included) illustrates discrimination between four molecular types (VGI-VGIV), and displays the relationship of the clinical case presented in this study to global genotypes observed, including all VGI genotypes thus far reported (including the Vancouver Island VGI genotypes), and the Vancouver Island/Pacific NW outbreak genotypes VGIIa/major, VGIIb/minor, and VGIIc. Note that not all sequence types and strains in (B) are represented in (A).

Detailed analysis of the molecular profile, and comparison with >280 global isolates including 85 VGI isolates indicated that while the isolates were highly similar to the most common molecular type (VGI), they were identical to only a unique subset in the collection. To examine if these isolates were at all related to the ongoing *C gattii* outbreak on Vancouver Island, Canada, and the Pacific NW, we examined all VGI isolates from this region in detail. A total of six VGI isolates have been reported from Vancouver Island, and none of these matched the NC clinical case based on MLST analysis [8]. Three Vancouver Island isolates (F2863, R794, and KB7892) are quite diverged from the NC case (EJB1-L and EJB2-B) based on MLST analysis (Figure 3). Three others (A2M R314, A2M R299, and A4M R64) share seven MLST alleles but differ at the GPD1 allele (Figure 3). Thus, none of the Vancouver Island isolates are a direct match to the NC clinical case isolates. Of the six reported Vancouver Island VGI isolates, there are four different MLST genotypes (Figure 3A). Of these genotypes two are clinical (human), one veterinary, and one environmental. There are no identical matches between the Vancouver Island VGI environmental and clinical isolates. Thus, there are VGI genotypes in the environment but infections may have been acquired elsewhere, although wild animal cases are most often locally acquired. Currently, no VGI cases have been reported in Washington or Oregon states, and the incidence of VGI on Vancouver Island and surrounding areas in the Pacific NW region remains low.

Of the 11 VGI molecular type isolates with an identical MLST genetic profile to the NC isolate, nine were from the environment in Renmark, Australia, and were isolated from Eucalyptus tree hollows (Figure 3A) [43]. An additional Australian environmental isolate (E554) shared all loci with the NC clinical case with the exception of the mating type specific SXI idiomorph, because this isolate is mating type a (Figure 3A). The two MLST matched clinical isolates were both from human infections, one from Australia and one from a blood sample from a liver transplant recipient treated in San Francisco, California (Figure 3) [32]. To further discriminate isolates, the MLST analysis was extended to include three additional loci. This analysis included the NC, CA, Vancouver Island, and Australian clinical cases as well as representative Australian environmental isolates. However, no polymorphisms were detected in the three clinical isolates harboring the NC clinical case genotype using the additional coding markers (Figure 3A). Based on neighbor joining phylogenetic analysis [40], in which seven MLST loci were concatenated into 5.7 kb of contiguous sequence, the four discrete VG molecular types were clearly distinct, and the VGI group was separated into 20 sequence types (ST) (Figure 3B). All isolates with an identical MLST type to the NC clinical case grouped into sequence type 11 (ST-11), and were closely related to the more common sequence type 12 (ST-12), which harbors the VGI molecular type genomic reference strain WM276.

The MLST is a powerful approach to discriminate isolates in a sequence-based method, but also relies almost exclusively on the genomic coding sequences of conserved genes. For the analysis of highly clonal populations such as the VGI molecular type, variable non-coding and intergenic sequences, particularly tandem repeats, can enable more detailed characterizations of populations by allowing closely related isolates to be distinguished. Using microsatellite markers developed with the Magellan Software suite, and VNTR analysis with the TRF software, strains harboring identical MLST profiles to the isolates from the patient in this study were analyzed (Figure 3). Analysis of three independent VNTR markers showed that two of the markers were identical in all ST-11 isolates, while marker VNTR-15 was able to discriminate five of the Australian environmental isolates from all clinical isolates (NC-clinical, CA-clinical, Australia-Clinical) and the other five environmental isolates from Australia with this molecular genotype, due to a 40 base pair deletion within the tandem repeat region (Figure 4). In addition, analysis of microsatellite marker MS1 clearly distinguished the Renmark environmental isolates, which produced a smaller PCR product (~380 bp) than the three clinical isolates and VGI control isolate WM276 (~480 bp) (Figure 5A). A high GA content and repetitive nature of this locus impeded sequence analysis, as polymerase slippage resulted in low-quality sequence results. However, partial sequence affirmed that the products were specific (data not shown). Isolate WM276 was distinguished from the three clinical isolates based on a SNP in the GPD1 MLST allele locus, a 4 bp deletion in the TOR1 MLST allele, a SNP in VNTR3, and a SNP in VNTR15. In addition, the VNTR3 analysis further differentiated the NC, SF, and Australia ST-11 clinical isolates of interest from the Vancouver Island VGI ST-12 isolate A4MR64. Overall, the analysis of variable sequences further discriminated the three clinical isolates with this unique MLST type from the environmental isolates from Renmark, Australia with the same 8-loci MLST genotype (Figure 5B). These data indicate that while MLST is informative, it lacks sufficient resolution to discriminate isolates with highly similar albeit distinguishable genotypes.

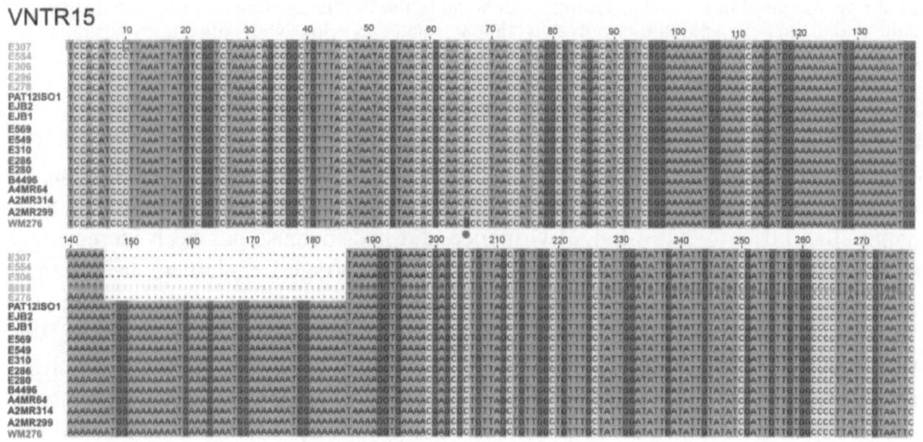

Figure 4. The DNA sequence alignment of VNTR15 among 18 VGI isolates of *C. gattii*. The non-coding VNTR marker divides the isolates with an identical MLST profile into two groups: one group contains two NC clinical isolates which are identical to one another, the other clinical isolates, and five of the 10 Renmark isolates, and the second group includes the remaining five Renmark isolates. A 40 bp deletion was observed in the following isolates: E307, E554, E360, E296, and E278. In addition, a single nucleotide polymorphism (SNP) (66A → 66G) discriminated the VGI type strain isolate WM276 from the other 17 VGI isolates (see red circle).

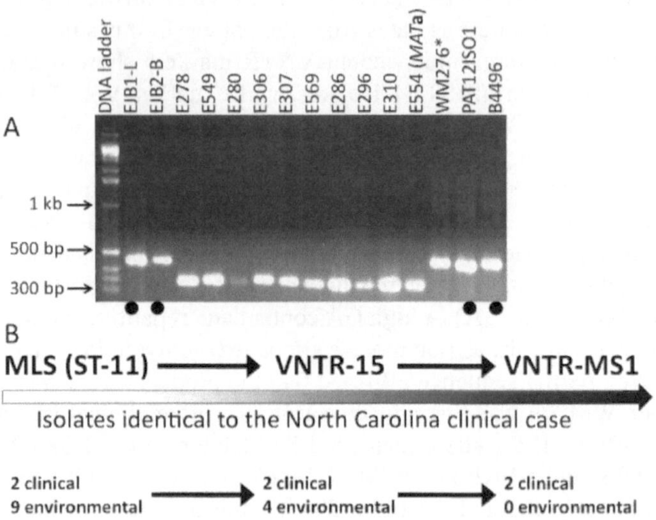

Figure 5. Molecular typing reveals that the Australian environmental isolates are distinct from clinical isolates. (A) PCR product size differences at locus VNTR-MS1 reveals that environmental isolates from Renmark harbor a deletion compared to the clinical isolates with the same MLST genotype. Agarose gel electrophoresis of the VNTR-MS1 marker, illustrating an ~100 bp difference between the larger (EJB1-L, EJB2-B, PAT12ISO1, B4496, WM276*), and smaller (E278, E549, E280, E306, E307, E569, E286, E296, E310, E554) PCR products. * Denotes that the sequenced type strain WM276 is not identical to the other clinical isolates. The bold circles represent four clinical isolates (from three cases) that type as identical through all genotypic tests conducted. (B) A linear representation of the progressive genotypic analysis. As the number of markers increased, along with the genetic variability, the number of isolates typing as identical to the North Carolina clinical case decreased. At the end of the genotypic studies only two clinical isolates, previously identified from Australia and California, typed as identical with the present NC clinical case.

Cryptococcus gattii VGI Isolates are Virulent in a Heterologous Host

To determine the relative virulence between environmental and clinical isolates of the same MLST type as the North Carolina clinical case, infection assays were conducted in the heterologous host, *Galleria mellonella* (greater wax moth). The use of non-mammalian hosts to study fungal virulence and host defense has been increasingly applied and is now well established [42, 44, 45]. Although Lepidoptera are distantly related to mammals, results in the wax moth larval model have been highly correlated with results using murine infection models [42, 46, 47]. In the virulence assay, isolates were injected at an infectious inoculum of 1 × 105 cells, using 12–19 larvae per strain per replicate at 37°C. The selected isolates analyzed were all significantly pathogenic compared to PBS control infections ($p < 0.005$) (Figure 6). There was no marked difference between ST-11 environmental and clinical isolates ($p > 0.2$). In addition, the VGI type strain control isolate (WM276) showed no difference in virulence to the tested isolates ($p > 0.2$). This uniformity in virulence between environmental and clinical isolates is consistent with direct acquisition of infections from an environmental source.

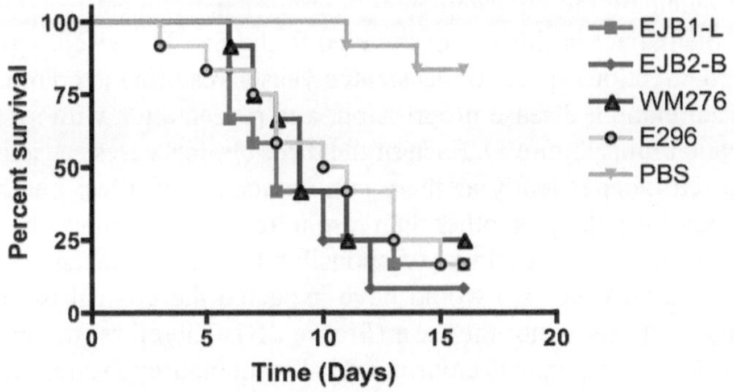

Figure 6. North Carolina clinical isolates are pathogenic in a heterologous host. Groups of 12–19 larvae of *Galleria mellonella* were each infected with an infectious inoculum of 1.0 x 105 cells of isolates EJB1-L, EJB2-B, WM276, and E296. Survival was monitored and plotted daily for 16 days. All isolates were significantly virulent ($p < 0.005$) in comparison with the mock control (sterile PBS) infection. The experiment was replicated in duplicate with similar results in each replicate, and representative results are shown here.

DISCUSSION

Our findings document the first *C. gattii* case reported in the Eastern region of the US. The most parsimonious explanation is that an otherwise healthy patient was exposed in California, resulting in disease presentation in North Carolina approximately 4–6 months after travel to an endemic region. This case highlights an overall increase in *C. gattii* infections in apparently immunocompetent individuals in temperate climates. The patient had no recent travel history to the Pacific Northwest or to other *C. gattii* endemic regions, and based on molecular typing the infectious isolate is not related to any of the VGII or VGI isolates causing the ongoing Vancouver Island outbreak, and its emergence into mainland British Columbia, Washington, and Oregon [18, 20, 22, 23, 48]. These VGI clinical isolates are also distinct from molecular types VGIII and VGIV (Figure 3B). *Cryptococcus gattii* molecular type VGI has never been reported from the environment in California, but it seems likely to be present there based on successful environmental isolation of *C. gattii* molecular types VGII and VGIII in regions of California, including San Francisco and San Diego, and the abundant presence of the host Eucalyptus trees throughout the state [34, 49].

Our current model suggests that this unique MLST VGI genotype is located in the environment and clinical setting in Australia, with probable environmental colonization in California, resulting in human infections (Figure 7). These conclusions are based on broad MLST analysis as well as analysis of four hyper-variable tandem repeats located throughout the *C. gattii* genome. The VNTR analysis showed that environmental isolates all differ at one or two rapidly evolving genomic regions, but clinical and environmental isolates that are identical at eight MLST loci are quite closely related. All environmental isolates from Australia were collected from a single location, and slight diversity in geographic regions is expected [50]. In October 2007, 70 samples were collected from Eucalyptus trees in San Francisco. No isolates of *C. neoformans* or *C. gattii* were obtained. Therefore, expanded sampling will be necessary to definitively elucidate the environmental source of the clinical isolates. We therefore posit that the patient in this report traveled to the San Francisco region, and was there exposed to infectious spores or desiccated yeasts, resulting in colonization of the lungs, and dissemination, disease progression, and presentation with systemic infection of the leg and brain (Figure 7). Each of the three clinical cases caused by this VGI genotype occurred independently as there is no evidence of direct human-to-human transmission with this pathogen, other than rare introgenic transmissions. In addition, if *in vivo* changes during infection were responsible for the clinical and environmental isolate molecular differences we would have expected the clinical isolates to differ from each other, and this is not the case (Figure 5B). Therefore, the most parsimonious explanation is independent environmental-to-human exposure, with the exact source yet to be identified in Australia and in California. These studies demonstrate that increased typing resolution can be achieved by combining coding and non-coding genomic markers, which are abundantly available for fungal pathogens with publicly available genome sequences.

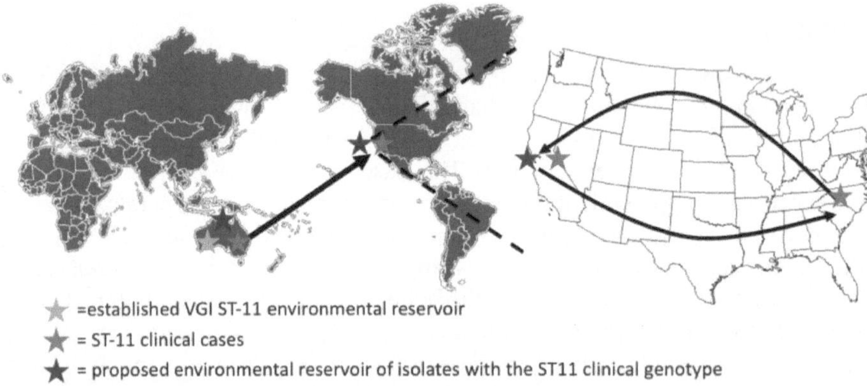

Figure 7. Proposed model for the emergence of *C. gattii* in the US. The original source is postulated to be Australia, where identical clinical and closely related environmental isolates have been reported. Given that human-human transmission other than introgenic is unknown, the most parsimonious model for geographically dispersed clinical isolates is that isolates identical to the clinical cases are present in the environments in Australia and California, USA. In this model, the patient from the Southeastern US traveled to the endemic area of CA, was exposed to the pathogen by inhalation, and ultimately returned to present with disseminated disease in North Carolina, USA.

Other clinical cases of *C. gattii* due to travel in endemic areas have been recently reported. In 2007, a 51-year-old HIV negative male from Denmark presented with *C. gattii* disease in Europe after traveling to Vancouver Island, Canada [37]. Molecular analysis established that the isolate was identical to the VGIIa/major genotype responsible for the Vancouver Island outbreak [37]. Additionally, a study from the British Columbia Centre for Disease Control indicated that intra-island travel or tourism on Vancouver Island to highly endemic areas increases the likelihood of contracting cryptococcosis [36]. These studies demonstrate the importance of human travel to endemic areas as it relates to the acquisition and presentation of cryptococcal disease. Many clinical laboratories in non-endemic regions do not differentiate *C. neoformans* infections from *C. gattii* infections; therefore, the incidence of travel associated *C. gattii* infections may be more common than currently appreciated.

While many of the studies related to *C. gattii* infections in the US and Canada have focused on the Vancouver Island outbreak, it has been known for several decades that *C. gattii* is also endemic to the environment in regions of California, causing infections in both animals and humans. In 1991, an isolate of *C. gattii* VGIIa/major outbreak genotype was sampled from a *Eucalyptus camaldulensis* tree at Fort Point Park, in San Francisco, indicating a natural occurrence in the same host tree that *C. gattii* is most commonly associated with in Australia [10, 34]. Several studies have also documented a likely endemic zone in Southern California. A large cohort of HIV positive patients with cryptococcal infections from Los Angeles hospitals revealed that the infections were principally the result of *C. gattii* serotype C infections [31]. In addition, *C. gattii* VGI has been isolated from a marine mammal case (bottlenose dolphin) near San Diego, and *C. gattii* VGIII has been isolated from the natural environment in the San Diego, California area [33, 51]. These studies provide strong evidence that multiple molecular types (VGI, VGII, VGIII) have been reported in California indicative of a likely reservoir, possibly in Eucalyptus and other tree species.

Hypotheses regarding the spread of global fungal pathogens from common associations with plants have been previously reported. It was recently shown that a basidiomycete, the sugarcane fungal pathogen *Ustilago scitaminea*, was dispersed from Asia to America and Africa due to its association with infected plant material [52]. *Cryptococcus gattii* has been isolated from *E. camaldulensis* trees in San Francisco, a common host tree species, and *C. gattii* was recently found to complete its natural sexual cycle during co-culture with this plant under laboratory conditions [34, 41, 53]. Population genetics studies of individual trees of *E. camaldulensis* have also shown that both same-sex and opposite-sex mating is likely occurring in this environmental niche [54]. These reports demonstrate the likelihood that this unique VGI genotype migrated due to plant association, and also leaves open the possibility of sexual reproduction occurring in natural populations of this genotype in the environment.

Sexual reproduction among closely related genotypes has the potential to increase pathogenicity of fungi and parasites [55, 56]. In *C. gattii* it has been postulated that same-sex mating among closely related isolates could have both contributed to the formation of the hyper-virulent VGIIa/major genotype responsible for the Vancouver Island outbreak and to the ongoing production of infectious propagules [10, 57, 58]. Another well-studied system is the eukaryotic parasite *Toxoplasma gondii*, where limited mating among clonal lineages is hypothesized to have resulted in increased virulence, and may also have enabled this pathogenic microbe to be orally transmitted from animals to humans [59, 60]. The reasons for mating differences among the isolates from the leg and brain of the North Carolina *C. gattii* case may be genetic, or epigenetic, as all other analysis indicates that these isolates are from a single rather than mixed infection. Although the exact roles of *C. gattii* sexual reproduction as it relates to virulence remain to be elucidated, the ability of virulent isolates to retain mating ability suggest this process may play a significant role in virulence and possibly also in the production of infectious propagules.

As *C. gattii* continues to emerge in the US and elsewhere it is clear that the standardization of clinical testing to identify species (*C. neoformans*/*C. gattii*) and cryptic species (VGI/VGII/VGIII/VGIV) is essential. As illustrated by this case, *C. gattii* infections may be particularly complicated to treat due to their predilection to form cryptococcomas, especially in the brain, which are difficult to manage and risk to surgical resection is considerable. Although clinical laboratory testing at Duke University confirmed that the leg and brain biopsy isolates were both fluconazole sensitive, because of disease progression and the occurrence of cryptococcomas, in which drug access is limited, clinical management was difficult. Although the overall incidence of *C. gattii* disease in the US remains low, an increasing number of cases in California, Oregon, Washington, and now North Carolina among immunocompetent and immunocompromised individuals raise the possibility that these represent the onset of an emergence in the temperate climate of the Western US.

KEYWORDS

- **Cryptococcosis**
- ***Cryptococcus gattii***
- **Multilocus sequence typing**
- **Staib niger seed agar**
- **VGI isolates**

AUTHORS' CONTRIBUTIONS

Conceived and designed the experiments: Edmond J. Byrnes III, John R. Perfect, Dee A. Carter, Gary M. Cox, and Joseph Heitman. Performed the experiments: Edmond J. Byrnes III, Wenjun Li, Yonathan Lewit, and Gary M. Cox. Analyzed the data: Edmond J. Byrnes III, Wenjun Li, Yonathan Lewit, Gary M. Cox, and Joseph Heitman. Contributed reagents/materials/analysis tools: John R. Perfect, Dee A. Carter, Gary M. Cox, and Joseph Heitman. Wrote the chapter: Edmond J. Byrnes III, Gary M. Cox, and Joseph Heitman.

ACKNOWLEDGMENTS

We thank the patient for releasing results for publication, Wiley Schell for assistance in environmental sampling of the patient's workplace and birdcages, Jim Kronstad and Karen Bartlett for isolates, and Anastasia P. Litvintseva and Thomas G. Mitchell for providing serotyping data.

Chapter 18

Risk Areas for *Cryptococcus gattii*, Vancouver Island, Canada

Catharine Chambers, Laura MacDougall, Min Li, and Eleni Galanis

INTRODUCTION

We compared travel histories of case-patients with *Cryptococcus gattii* infection during 1999–2006 to travel destinations of the general public on Vancouver Island (VI), British Columbia (BC), Canada. Findings validated and refined estimates of risk on the basis of place of residence and showed no spatial progression of risk areas on this island over time.

Cryptococcus gattii is a fungus that infects the lungs and central nervous system of mostly immunocompetent humans and animals [1]. In 1999, *C. gattii* emerged on the east coast of VI, BC, Canada [2], and is now considered endemic in the environment [3, 4], affecting human [5] and animal populations [6]. Travel histories of patients have been used to monitor fungal spread [5] and to estimate the incubation period of this disease [7, 8].

Intra-island travel on VI is common, and fungal exposure may not occur near residences of case-patients. Incidence rates calculated by using patient residence have suggested areas along the east coast of the island that may pose increased risk for infection (Figure 1) [9]. Environmental sampling has provided evidence of the fungus over a large part of eastern VI. However, this sampling was not performed randomly and may not accurately identify areas of highest risk [3, 4].

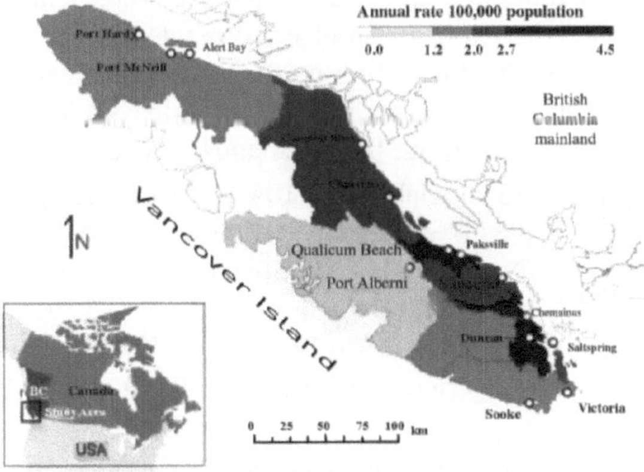

Figure 1. Annual rate of infection with *Cryptococcus gattii* by local administrative area, 1999–2006 [9], and distribution of visitor center cities on Vancouver Island, British Columbia (BC), Canada. Only visitor centers that were included in the analysis are shown.

THE STUDY

This study compared travel histories of *C. gattii*—infected case-patients with travel patterns of the general public to validate and refine these risk areas on VI. We also examined spatial progression of these areas over time to assess whether *C. gattii* spread from a single focal point since its emergence in 1999.

Cryptococcus gattii—infected case-patients were defined as BC residents with culture-confirmed *C. gattii* infection or HIV-negative residents of BC with *Cryptococcus sp.* infection diagnosed by antigen detection or histopathologic analysis. Analysis included all cases diagnosed from January 1999 through December 2006 in which the patient had documented travel history on VI. Case-patients were interviewed by using a standard questionnaire and asked about travel to any city outside their city of residence in the 12 months before symptom onset or diagnosis [8].

Tourism BC (www.hellobc.com/en-CA/default.htm) provided aggregated monthly visitor volume to 14 visitor centers in major tourist destinations (Figure 1) on VI during 2000–2006. Visitors were counted if they spoke with visitor center counselors. Only visitors classified as BC residents were included in these analyses; additional personal attributes of visitors were not collected (C. Jenkins, personal communication). Seasonal visitor centers that had only partial data available for certain months were excluded.

Proportion of visits to each visitor center city was defined as number of visits to a visitor center city divided by total number of visits to all visitor center cities. For case-patients, the proportion was similarly defined. In both instances, visits to multiple cities by the same person were counted multiple times. Differences between proportion of case-patient visits and Tourism BC visits were evaluated by Fisher exact test and StatXact software (Cytel Inc., Cambridge, MA, USA). Analysis was conducted for all years combined and in 2 4-year increments (1999–2002 and 2003–2006) to assess potential spread of *C. gattii* on VI over time. Because Tourism BC visitor data were unavailable for 1999, case data for 1999–2002 were compared with aggregated Tourism BC visitor data from 2000 to 2002. Analysis was also conducted for a subset of case-patients who resided on the mainland because they represented travel exposures uncontaminated by potential exposure in place of residence. The α value for significance was adjusted to account for testing multiple visitor center cities ($p = 0.05/14$ visitor center cities $= 0.0036$). Maps were created by using ArcMap version 8.2 (Environmental Systems Research Institute Inc., Redlands, CA, USA).

Travel history data were available for 104 (60.1%) case-patients. Eighty-two (78.8%) had traveled to >1 visitor center city. Of these, 62 (75.6%) resided on VI and 20 (24.4%) lived on the BC mainland. A significantly greater proportion of visits to Parksville (18.7% vs. 7.2%; $p < 0.0001$) and Nanaimo (21.4% vs. 7.4%; $p < 0.0001$) were reported for patients than for Tourism BC visitors (Table 1). Similar results were obtained when analysis was restricted to earlier (1999–2002) and later (2003–2006) periods (Table 1).

When analysis was restricted to data concerning mainland residents (patients with travel-associated exposure but no residential exposure to the fungus), a greater proportion of mainland case-patients visited Courtenay (19.4% vs. 7.6%; $p = 0.017$),

Parksville (30.6% vs. 8.3%; p = 0.0001), Nanaimo (11.1% vs. 6.9%; p = 0.313), and Qualicum Beach (8.3% vs. 4.7%; p = 0.239) than did Tourism BC visitors during 1999–2006; however, only Parksville reached statistical significance. Because of the small number of patients who resided on the mainland (n = 20), we could not further restrict this subset analysis to earlier (1999–2002) and later (2003–2006) periods.

Residents of VI may be exposed in their place of residence, in addition to their travel destination. However, we could not accurately weight patient exposure in the home environment to exposure at the travel destination. Minor differences in results obtained for all case-patients compared with only mainland patients may be caused by this limitation or by differences in travel preferences between these groups.

Although travel history data were unavailable for 39.9% of the case-patients, they were not significantly different in terms of mean age (p = 0.303, by F test) or sex (p = 0.574, by $\chi 2$ test). A higher proportion of included patients resided in central VI. However, travel patterns of central VI residents did not differ from travel patterns of other VI residents (data not shown). Our analysis assumes that travel patterns of Tourism BC visitors represent those of the general BC public. However, characteristics and activities of persons who use Tourism BC visitor centers may differ from those of persons who do not. Therefore, caution is necessary when generalizing results to the entire BC population. Our interpretation is limited by its inability to account for duration of time spent in each visitor center city and specific activities of persons while there, factors that may contribute to exposure risk.

Table 1. Proportion of cases of *Cryptococcus gattii* infection compared with proportion of BC residents who visited Tourism BC visitor centers, by location, Vancouver Island, British Columbia, Canada, 1999–2006*.

	1999–2002			2003–2006			All years		
Location	No. (%) cases	No. (%) visits	% Difference	No. (%) cases	No. (%) visits	% Difference	No. (%) cases	No. (%) visits	% Difference
Nanaimo	26 (20.3)	20,160 (6.5)	13.8†	14 (23.7)	35, 169 (8.0)	15.7†	40 (21.4)	55,329 (7.4)	14.0†
Parksville	25 (19.5)	24,095 (7.8)	11.8†	10 (16.9)	30,070 (6.9)	10.1	35 (18.7)	54,165 (7.2)	11.5†
Duncan	12 (9.4)	20,484 (6.6)	2.8	4 (6.8)	25,973 (5.9)	0.9	16 (8.6)	46,457 (6.2)	2.3
Victoria	24 (18.8)	58,092 (18.8)	0	16 (27.1)	94,452 (21.6)	5.6	40 (21.4)	152,544 (20.4)	1.0
Qualicum Beach	8 (6.3)	14, 197 (4.6)	1.7	3 (5.1)	26,429 (6.0)	–0.9	11 (5.9)	40,626 (5.4)	0.4
Port McNeill	1 (0.8)	5,985 (1.9)	–1.2	0	6,378 (1.5)	–1.5	1 (0.5)	12,363 (1.7)	–1.1
Courtenay	8 (6.3)	35,051	–5.1	4 (6.8)	30,859	–0.3	12 (6.4)	65,910	–2.4

Table 1. *(Continued)*

Location	1999–2002 No. (%) cases	1999–2002 No. (%) visits	1999–2002 % Difference	2003–2006 No. (%) cases	2003–2006 No. (%) visits	2003–2006 % Difference	All years No. (%) cases	All years No. (%) visits	All years % Difference
		(11.3)			(7.0)			(8.8)	
Saltspring Island	4 (3.1)	19,093 (6.2)	–3.0	1 (1.7)	20,744 (4.7)	–3.0	5 (2.7)	39,837 (5.3)	–2.7
Che-mainus	3 (2.3)	13,374 (4.3)	–2.0	1(1.7)	23,273 (5.3)	–3.6	4 (2.1)	36,647 (4.9)	–2.8
Port Alberni	4 (3.1)	23,466 (7.6)	–4.5	4 (6.8)	30,760 (7.0)	–0.2	8 (4.3)	54,226 (7.3)	–3.0
Sooke	3 (2.3)	15,450 (5.0)	–2.6	0	19,485 (4.4)	–4.4	3 (1.6)	34,935 (4.7)	–3.1
Alert Bay	0	7,891 (2.5)	–2.5	0	18,107 (4.1)	–4.1	0	25,998 (3.5)	–3.5†
Campbell River	8 (6.3)	29,219 (9.4)	–3.2	2 (3.4)	49,830 (11.4)	–8.0	10 (5.3)	79,049 (10.6)	–5.2
Port Hardy	2 (1.6)	23,106 (7.5)	–5.9	0	26,616 (6.1)	–6.1	2 (1.1)	49,722 (6.6)	–5.6†
All centers	128	309,663	–	59	438,145	–	187	747,808	–

*Visitor centers that were only opened seasonally were not included in the analysis. BC, British Columbia.

†Significant differences after adjustment for multiple comparisons according to Fisher exact test ($p \leq 0.0036$).

CONCLUSIONS

Our findings suggest that the opportunity for *C. gattii* exposure in the areas studied has existed since the beginning of its emergence and that minimal spatial progression of risk areas has occurred over time. Areas of higher risk near Parksville and Nanaimo are consistent with distribution of environmental samples, which shows a high number of *C. gattii*—positive samples in these areas [3]. Results are also consistent with annual incidence rates for *C. gattii* infection based on place of residence, which are highest along the central eastern coast (Figure 1) [9].

When compared with areas on the basis of place of residence, more refined geographic risk areas associated with our analysis may result from potential reporting bias that produced reported percentage differences that are larger than expected. The BC residents may be more likely to visit or travel through Nanaimo, a commercial center on VI and transportation gateway to the rest of the island [10], than shown in Tourism BC data. Case-patients may be more likely to report traveling to Parksville, a popular tourist destination, because it was often mentioned in media reports of the initial *C. gattii* outbreak. Alternatively, results may indicate a true increase in travel-associated risk in areas near Parksville and Nanaimo. Some case-patients who resided in areas with high incidence rates may have acquired their infections by travel to these two areas. Although Parksville and Nanaimo may represent areas of higher risk, environmental sampling suggests fungal colonization in southern and central eastern VI, and travelers can be exposed to *C. gattii* in these regions [3].

To determine travel-related risk for malaria [11] and gastrointestinal illness [12-14], travel patterns of case-patients have been compared with those of the general public. Use of visitor center information and tourism surveys is a cost-effective solution to derive comparison data during a retrospective investigation. This approach shows promise in assessing risk for environmental pathogens where location of exposure is unclear.

KEYWORDS

- **Case-patients**
- ***Cryptococcus gattii***
- **Histopathologic analysis**
- **Parksville**
- **Travel history data**

ACKNOWLEDGMENTS

We thank Carol Jenkins and the corporate division of Tourism BC for providing tourism data and prompt and valuable assistance; the BC Laboratory and Health Authority staff for analyzing and collecting *C. gattii* surveillance data; Sunny Mak for assisting with geographic information system mapping; Mei Chong for performing statistical analysis; and the BC Cryptococcal Working Group for their interest in this study.

Ms Chambers is a master of science student at the University of British Columbia School of Population and Public Health. Her research interests include communicable disease epidemiology and outbreak control investigations.

Chapter 19

Dogs as Carriers of Canine Vector-borne Pathogens

Brigitte Menn, Susanne Lorentz, and Torsten J. Naucke

INTRODUCTION

With the import of pets and pets taken abroad, arthropod-borne diseases have increased in frequency in German veterinary practices. This is reflected by 4,681 dogs that have been either traveled to or relocated from endemic areas to Germany. The case history of these dogs and the laboratory findings have been compared with samples collected from 331 dogs living in an endemic area in Portugal. The various pathogens and the seroprevalences were examined to determine the occurrence of, and thus infection risk, for vector-borne pathogens in popular travel destinations.

The 4,681 dogs were examined serological for *Leishmania infantum*, *Babesia canis*, and *Ehrlichia canis*. Buffy coats (BCs) were detected for *Hepatozoon canis* and blood samples were examined for microfilariae via the Knott's test. The samples were sent in from animal welfare organizations or private persons via veterinary clinics. Upon individual requests, dogs were additionally examined serological for *Anaplasma phagocytophilum*, *Borrelia burgdorferi,* and *Rickettsia conorii*. Overall *B. canis* was the most prevalent pathogen detected by antibody titers (23.4%), followed by *L. infantum* (12.2%) and *E. canis* (10.1%). Microfilariae were detected in 7.7% and *H. canis* in 2.7% of the examined dogs. In 332/1862 dogs *A. phagocytophilum*, in 64/212 *B. burgdorferi,* and in 20/58 *R. conorii* was detected. Of the 4,681 dogs, in total 4,226 were imported to Germany from endemic areas. Eighty-seven dogs joined their owners for a vacation abroad. In comparison to the laboratory data from Germany, we examined 331 dogs from Portugal. The prevalence of antibodies/pathogens we detected was: 62.8% to *R. conorii*, 58% to *B. canis*, 30.5% to *A. phagocytophilum*, 24.8% to *E. canis*, 21.1% to *H. canis* (via polymerase chain reaction (PCR)), 9.1% to *L. infantum*, and 5.3% to microfilariae.

The examination of 4,681 dogs living in Germany showed pathogens like *L. infantum* that are non-endemic in Germany. Furthermore, the German data are similar in terms of multiple pathogen infection to the data recorded for dogs from Portugal. Based on these findings the importation of dogs from endemic predominantly Mediterranean regions to Germany as well as traveling with dogs to these regions carries a significant risk of acquiring an infection. Thus we would conclude that pet owners seek advice of the veterinarians prior to importing a dog from an endemic area or travel to such areas. In general, it might be advisable to have a European recording system for transloca-tion of dogs.

The zoogeographical range of pathogens of arthropod-borne diseases is restricted by the distribution areas of their vectors and hosts [1]. Dogs are competent reservoir hosts of several zoonotic pathogens and can serve as a readily available source of nutrition for many blood-feeding arthropods [2]. Increasing pet tourism and importation of animals from endemic areas present German veterinary practitioners increasingly with exotic diseases, like leishmaniosis, babesiosis, ehrlichiosis, and dirofilariosis [3-7]. The frequency of dog-tourism and -import was first reported in the study of Glaser and Gothe, who analyzed 5,340 questionnaires in the years 1985–1995 [4]. The results revealed a steady increase of dogs taken abroad, rising from 31.1% in 1990 to 40.8% in 1994. Also in the UK an increasingly mobility of pets is conspicuous. Since February 2000 every pet entering the UK is registered in conjunction with the Pet Travel Scheme (PETS) and the released data show a steadily increase from 14,695 pets in the year 2000 up to 82,674 pets in the year 2006 [8, 1]. Besides the registration of departure and entry, pets have to run through a serology and ecto- and endoparasiticidal treatment 24–48 hr before re-entry to the UK [1]. This is important, because pets traveling abroad are exposed to various arthropod-borne diseases, especially in the popular destinations of the Mediterranean area and Portugal [4, 7, 9]. In addition to the pets joining their owners for a vacation, a large number of dogs, is imported to Germany by tourists or animal protection societies [3, 4, 10, 11]. While born and raised in the endemic area—their country of origin—imported dogs have an increased risk of contracting a canine vector-borne disease (CVBD) [5].

National and international investigations are necessary to be able to estimate topical risks, both in endemic and in currently non-endemic regions. This information would suggest how to avoid an import of pathogens, for example with the help of preventive measures. The increased mobility of pets is an important matter in the extension of the zoogeographical ranges for many arthropod-borne pathogens [1]. A previously non-endemic region may become endemic tomorrow. This risk is supported by the first autochthonous cases in Germany published for infections with *H. canis* [12], *L. infantum* [13], *E. canis* [14], and *D. repens* [15, 16]. These are pathogens of traditional so called travel-related diseases.

To obtain an overview of the situation of traveling, and particularly imported dogs, the results of the diagnosed 4,681 dog samples between July 2004 and December 2009 are analyzed epidemiologically including information of origin countries and length of vacation. To compare the data from non-endemic diseases in Germany a randomly selected endemic area in Portugal was selected. Blood samples of 331 dogs from Portugal were examined during the years 2007 and 2008 for examination of CVBD pathogens and their seroprevalences.

MATERIALS AND METHODS

During the period of July 2004–December 2009 blood samples of 4,681 dogs were sent in mostly for random examinations by welfare organizations and private persons via veterinary practitioners. The samples were not accompanied by a case history of the dogs, nor is any information available on the health status. The dog samples examined serological for the following pathogens: *L. infantum*, *B. canis*, and *E. canis*. All samples were examined for microfilariae using the Knott's test and BCs were detected for gamonts of *H. canis*. 1,862 of the sample were examined serological additional for *A. phagocytophilum*, 212 samples for *B. burgdorferi* and 58 samples for *R. conorii*.

In the autumn of 2007 and 2008, altogether blood samples of 331 dogs from kennels and shelters from the western part of Algarve/Portugal were collected. Blood samples were collected from brachial veins, 1 ml kept for the Knott's test and centrifuged at 1000 × g for 5 min. The BC smears were exposed, sera separated and stored at –20°C. The dog samples examined serological for the following pathogens: *L. infantum*, *B. canis*, *E. canis*, *A. phagocytophilum*, and *R. conorii*. The samples were examined for microfilariae using the Knott's test and for *H. canis* via PCR and screening the BCs.

All examinations were conducted in the same laboratory with the same methods, except the *H. canis* PCR.

Direct Pathogen Evidence—Knott's Test, Buffy coat, (BCs) PCR

All EDTA samples were screened for the presence of microfilariae using a modified Knott's test [28]. For the modified Knott's test, 1 ml EDTA blood is mixed with 5 ml of 2% formaldehyde solution in a 15 ml centrifuge tube and centrifuged at 400 × g for 5 min. The supernatant is discarded. The sediment is transferred to glass slides, covered with coverslips and examined by light microscopy at ×10 and ×40 magnifications. Positive Knott's tests were evaluated with the help of the acid phosphatase staining (1.16304.0002. LEUCOGNOST® SP, Merck, Darmstadt, Germany) following the manufacturer's instructions.

For creation of the BCs, the blood was centrifuged (1000 × g for 5 min), BC was removed and exposed on glass slides. The BCs were stained with May Grünwald's Giemsa (Merck, Darmstadt, Germany) and examined by light microscopy at ×40 magnification.

Samples of the 331 Portuguese dogs were examined additionally via a PCR on *H. canis* at the laboratory Laboklin GmbH & Co. KG (Bad Kissingen, Germany) according to their established method.

Indirect Pathogen Evidence—IFAT

Immunofluorescence antibody test (IFAT) was performed by using commercial kits for *L. infantum*, *B. canis*, *E. canis*, *A. phagocytophilum*, *R. conorii*, and *B. burgdorferi* (MegaScreen FLUOLEISH®, d4170-L, MegaScreen FLUOBABESIA canis®, 19017-Q, MegaScreen FLUOEHRLICHIA canis®, d0640-S, MegaScreen FLUOANAPLASMA ph.®, 11211-N, MegaScreen FLOURICKETTSIA con.® 10447-I, MegaScreen FLUOBORRELIA dog®, d1560-L—Mega Cor Diagnostik GmbH, Hörbranz, Austria). The slides were exposed to sera diluted (1:50) in phosphate buffer solution (PBS, pH 7.2) in a moist chamber and, after washing, to fluorescence labeled anti-dog IgG conjugate (anti-dog IgG, MegaCor, Diagnostik GmbH, Hörbranz, Austria); both incubations were at 37°C for 30 min. Slides were observed under a fluorescence microscope at ×40 magnifications and samples were scored positive when they produced cytoplasmatic inclusion bodies fluorescence. The positive cut-off adopted was at a dilution of 1:50 and all positive sera were tired.

DISCUSSION

The study reported here was conducted to evaluate the health status of dogs living in Germany that had either traveled to or were imported from CVBD endemic regions and a comparison was made with an autochthonous Portuguese group of dogs. The results of the 4,681 German dogs clearly indicates that the importation of dogs to Germany is still an explosive topic. Altogether 4,226 dogs were imported to Germany, 2,906 from the Mediterranean area including Portugal. These areas have a considerable prevalence of canine arthropod-borne diseases [5, 9, 17-24]. Serological testing detects basically chronic and inconspicuous infections and is limited by reduced ability to identify acute infections. In the present study we choose the IFAT to detect antibodies to *L. infantum*, *B. canis*, *E. canis*, *A. phagocytophilum*, *R. conorii*, and *B. burgdorferi*. Many dogs appear to be able to support chronic infection with vector-borne pathogens for months or even years without displaying obvious deleterious effects [25]. In most cases, dogs without clinical signs and without acute infections are imported to Germany mostly by animal welfare organizations. With the IFAT, we were aiming to detect clinically inconspicuous infections, in dogs that can be infected with one or even more pathogens. These asymptomatic carriers play a very important role in the epidemiology of zoonotic infection as they are still infectious to the vectors.

Babesia canis was with 1,158 dogs (24.3%) the most diagnosed for German dogs followed by *L. infantum* (12.2%), *E. canis* (10.1%), and infections with microfilariae (7.7%) and *H. canis* (2.2%). In contrast *R. conorii* is the most detected antigen in the Portuguese dogs (68.2%) followed by *B. canis* (58%), A. *phagocytophilum* (30.5%), *E. canis* (24.8%), *H. canis* (21.1%), *L. infantum* (9.1%), and microfilariae (5.3%). Differences between the German and Portuguese dogs can cause by the wide spectrum of countries of origin and destinations dogs traveled to. The spectrum of pathogens and vectors differs in different countries. For example Hepatozoon is detected just in 0.7% of 153 examined dogs from Greece [9] but in 48% of 301 examined foxes in Portugal [23]. These data are similar to the number of *H. canis* detected in the 331 Portuguese dogs. Rickettsia and Anaplasma data are only available for 58 and 1862 German dogs. They could be more similar to the Portuguese results if more samples were detected.

The DNA of *H. canis* was examined in 70/331 dogs from Portugal but only in 62 of the examined 331 BC smears gamonts of *H. canis* could be detected. Infections with a low rate of gametocyte-containing leucocytes are difficult to detect, that could be a reason why in 28 samples *H. canis* DNA is found via PCR but no gamont in the BCs. But there are 20 cases with definitive diagnosis of *H. canis* gamonts in the blood smears and no findings of DNA via PCR. So it is advisable to employ various diagnostic techniques to achieve a definitive etiological diagnosis of CVBDs, whenever available and economically feasible [26].

Altogether, in 10.2% of the German dogs and in 26.9% of the Portuguese dogs, an infection with two pathogens could be detected. In 4.3% of the dogs from Germany and in 35.6% of the dogs from Portugal multiple infections were found. This indicates that multiple infections are frequent within imported pets—and probably also within pets taken abroad. Clinical signs of dogs infected with more than one pathogen are often non-specific and very variable, such as wasting, weight loss, fever and poor appetite or anorexia, making a definite diagnosis difficult [27].

All in all, dog-tourism and -import confront practicing veterinarians increasingly with rare or still unknown arthropod-borne diseases. In addition, the expanding import and the traveling of dogs can lead to a spread of pathogens and vectors in Germany. These dogs may act as a source of infection for local and still pathogen-free vector populations. Also there is a risk that imported dogs infested with infected vectors might contribute to the further spread of travel related diseases in Germany [3].

RESULTS

In the present study we included the findings from 4,681 dog blood samples collected between July 2004 and December 2009 and additional 331 samples from Portuguese dogs on the occurrence of single and multiple infections of the following CVBD's: *L. infantum*, *E. canis*, *B. canis*, microfilariae, and *H. canis*. *Leishmania infantum*, *E. canis*, and *B. canis* were detected serological using the IFAT. All samples were examined for microfilariae using the Knott's test and BCs were detected for gamonts of *H. canis*. The 331 Portuguese samples were additionally examined for *H. canis* via PCR. *Anaplasma phagocytophilum* and *R. conorii* were detected serological in the Portuguese and in 1862 and 58 samples of the laboratory diagnosed data. Additional 212 samples of the laboratory diagnosed data were examined serological for *B. burgdorferi*.

Results of the 4,681 Samples Diagnosed from July, 2004 to December, 2009

The 4,226 of the 4,681 were imported dogs from various endemic regions (90.3%). Eighty-seven dogs were of German origin and accompanied their owners for vacation to endemic areas (1.8%). For 368 dogs, or 7.9% of the sample, the documentation sheet was incomplete, thus these dogs could not be allocated to either other group.

From the total of 4,226 imported dogs, 2,906 (68.8%) were born either in Portugal (n = 928) or in countries bordering the Mediterranean, especially Spain (n = 1,162), Italy (n = 367), Greece (n = 267), and Turkey (n = 106), but also in France (n = 37), Malta (n = 18), Croatia (n = 17), and Slovenia (n = 4).

A total of 1,320 (31.2%) of the 4,226 imported dogs were born in European countries beyond the Mediterranean region, mostly in Hungary (n = 1,013) and Romania (n = 279). Twenty-eight other dogs were born in Bulgaria (n = 14), Poland (n = 8), Switzerland (n = 2), Denmark (n = 1), Austria (n = 1), Holland (n = 1), and Czech Republic (n = 1).

The 78.2% of 87 dogs which had accompanied their owners abroad, traveled to Mediterranean countries: Spain (n = 22), Italy (n = 21), France (n = 10), Turkey (n = 8), Croatia (n = 3), Greece (n = 3), and Portugal (n = 1). Less than a quarter of the dogs (21.8%) traveled to Hungary (n = 7), Austria (n = 3), Denmark (n = 3), Switzerland (n = 2), Belgium (n = 1), Czech Republic (n = 1), Great Britain (n = 1), and Holland (n = 1).

The prevalence of antibodies was: 24.3% to *B. canis* (n = 1,138), 12.2% to *L. infantum* (n = 569), and 10.1% to *E. canis* (n = 492). Microfilariae and *H. canis* were detected in 372 (7.7%) and 133 dogs (2.2%), respectively. Antibodies to *A. phagocytophilum* were detected in 17.8% (n = 334) out of 1862 tested dogs, *B. burgdorferi* in 30.2% (n = 64) of 212 dogs and *R. conorii* in 34.5% (n = 20) of 58 dogs. The results are illustrated in Figure 1.

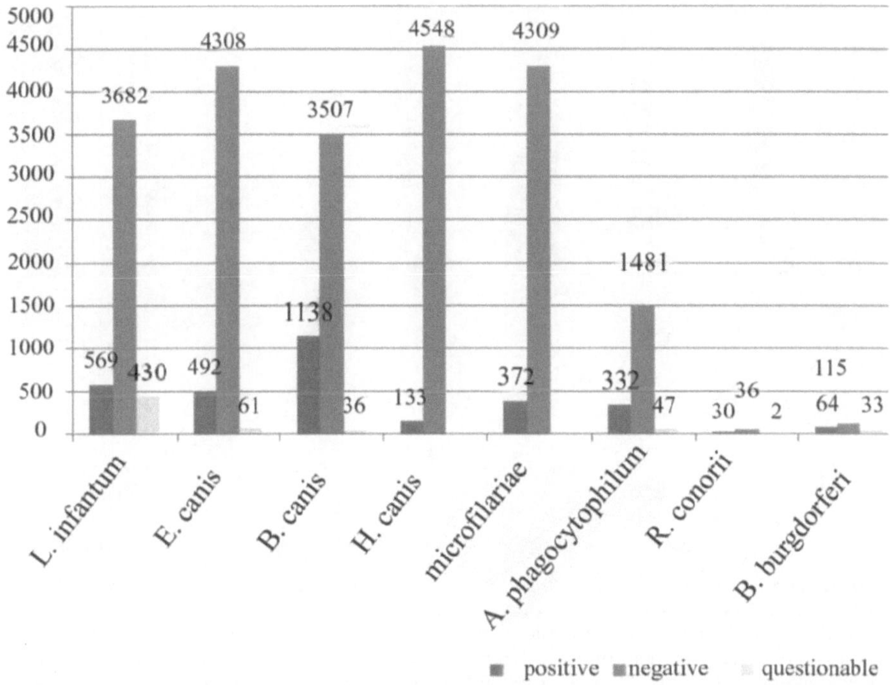

Figure 1. Number of pathogens detected by IFAT, BC, and Knott's test in 4,681 German dogs send in from animal welfare organizations and private persons between July 2004 and December 2009. Numbers of positive, negative, and questionable test results of a total of 4,681 dogs sent in from animal welfare organizations and private persons. Blood samples were examined by means of Knott's test for microfilariae. The samples were tested on *H. canis* with the help of the examination of the butty coats (BC). The seroprevalences of *B. canis*, *E. canis*, and *L. infantum* were determined by means of Immunofluorescence Antibody Test (IFAT). In 1,862 cases the seroprevalence of *A. phagocytophilum*, in 212 cases of *B. burgdorferi*, and in 58 cases of *R. conorii* were examined.

Results of the 331 Examined Dog Samples from Portugal

From the total of 331 autochthonous Portuguese dogs tested, 208 showed antibodies to *R. conorii* (68.2%). The prevalence of the other antibodies detected was: 58% to *B. canis* (n = 192), 30.5% to *A. phagocytophilum* (n = 101), 24.8% to *E. canis* (n = 82), and 9.1% to *L. infantum* (n = 30). Using PCR to detect DNA for *H. canis*, 70 dogs had a positive result (21.1%). Screening the BCs, we detected gamonts of *H. canis* in 62 of the samples (18.7%). With the help of the Knott's test we found microfilariae in 21 samples (5.3%). The results are summarized in Figure 2. With help of the acid phosphatase staining and morphological surveys, eight microfilariae of the species *Acanthocheilonema* (Dipetalonema) *dracunculoides*, seven of *Dirofilaria immitis* and six of *Acanthocheilonema* (Dipetalonema) *reconditumm* were detected in the dog samples.

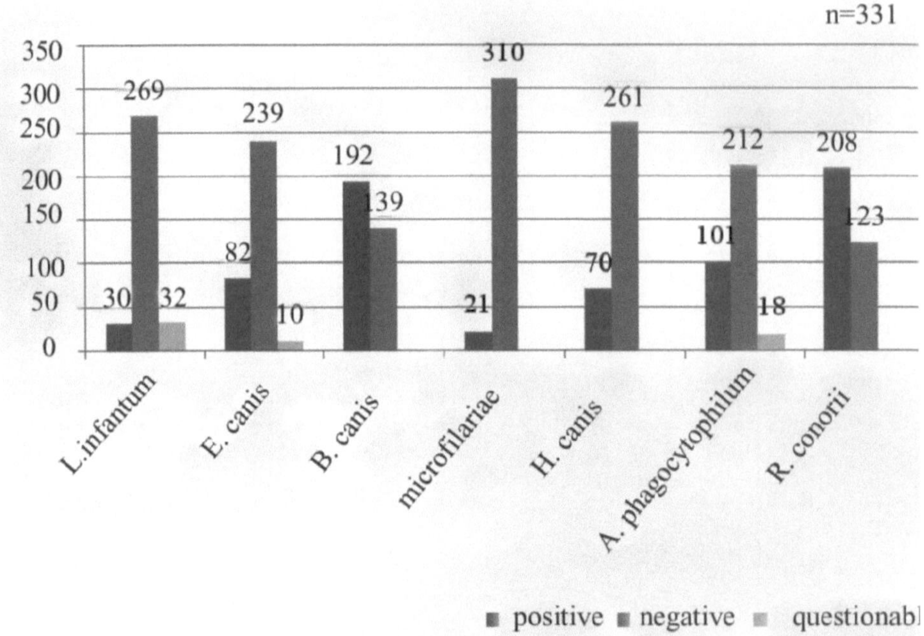

Figure 2. Number of pathogens detected by IFAT, PCR, and Knott's test in 331 autochthonous dogs from kennels/shelters in Portugal. Number of positive, negative, and questionable test results of a total of 331 dogs from Portugal. Blood samples were examined by means of Knott's test for microfilariae and on *H. canis* with the help of the Polymerase chain reaction (PCR). The seroprevalences of *A. phagocytophilum*, *B. canis*, *E. canis*, *L. infantum*, and *R. conorii* were determined by means of Immunofluorescence Antibody Test (IFAT).

Single and Multiple Infections in German and Portuguese Dogs

In both the German and Portuguese dogs double and even multiple CVBD infections were detected. In 56.3% of the German dogs investigated (n = 2,637) no antibodies or pathogens were found. In 28.7% of the dogs, antibodies or one pathogen could be detected (n = 1,341). Altogether in 10.7% an infection with two pathogens (n = 502) was found. In 4.3% of the dogs, an infection with more than two pathogens (n = 201) was determined. In contrast to the data from the German dogs, 26.9% of the Portuguese dogs had an infection with two pathogens (n = 89) and in 35.6% of the dogs (n = 118) multiple infections could be detected. Only in 43 dogs (13%) no antibodies or pathogens could be detected. These data are shown in Figure 3.

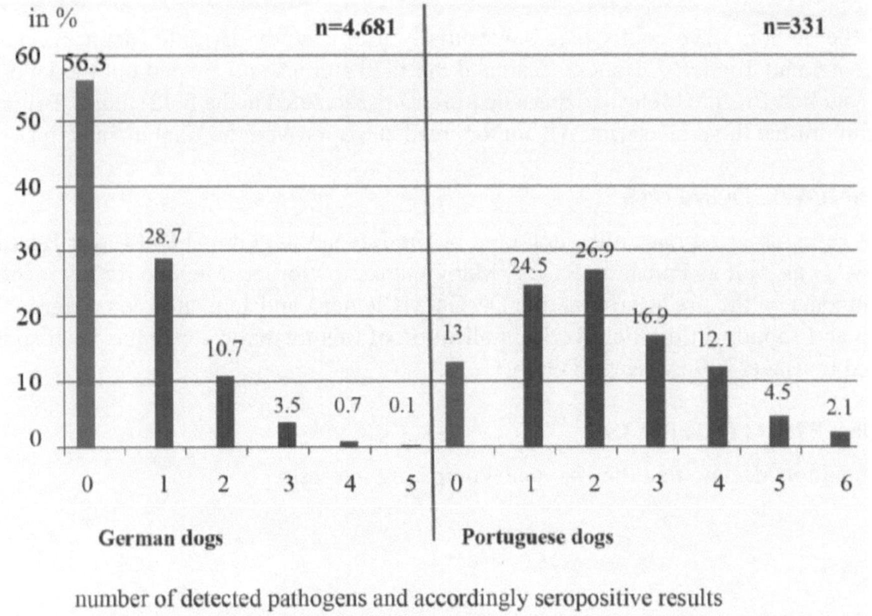

Figure 3. Single and multiple infections detected by IFAT, PCR, BC, and Knott's test in 4,681 German and 331 Portuguese dogs. Percentage of single, double, and multiple infections left from altogether 4,681 German dogs and right from 331 Portuguese dogs.

CONCLUSIONS

Frequent investigations—particularly in popular holiday destinations—are important to estimate the local risk. For the corresponding countries, specific methods in prophylaxis, diagnostics, and therapy must be elaborated.

The consultation of pet-owners with a veterinarian prior to importation of a dog or a journey with their pets to endemic regions is important to either limit importation or establish preventative measures prior to traveling. Prophylactic measures must be in place against vectors, to reduce the likelihood of transmission of vector-borne pathogens, like ectoparasiticides with repellent properties. It would be advisable to create a European recording system for translocation of dogs that register every departure and entry of pets. Standardized serology and ecto- and endoparasiticidal treatments before a re-entry to a non-endemic area should be regularized, like in the UK [1].

KEYWORDS

- **Arthropod-borne diseases**
- **Buffy coats**
- **Canine vector-borne disease**
- **Knott's test**
- **Microfilariae**

AUTHORS' CONTRIBUTIONS

All the authors have contributed substantially to this study. Brigitte Menn, Susanne Lorentz, and Torsten J. Naucke designed the field studies and carried out the laboratory studies. Brigitte Menn and Susanne Lorentz participated in the field studies. Brigitte Menn drafted the manuscript. All authors read and approved the final manuscript.

ACKNOWLEDGMENTS

This research was financially supported by the Bayer Vital GmbH and Bayer Healthcare AG as well as Parasitus Ex e.V. Many thanks to Norbert Mencke for his helpful comments on the manuscript and to Dr. Gaby Clemens and Johannes von Magnis for help and support in the fieldwork. Publication of this thematic series has been sponsored by Bayer Animal Health GmbH.

COMPETING INTERESTS

The authors declare that they have no competing interests.

Chapter 20

Healthcare Services in Mediterranean Resort Regions

Emilio Perea-Milla, Sergi Mari Pons, Francisco Rivas-Ruiz, Anna Gallofre, Enrique Navarro Jurado, Marco A. Navarro Ales, Alberto Jimenez-Puente, Fidel Fernandez-Nieto, Joan C. March Cerda, Manuel Carrasco, Lydia Martin, Damian Lopez Cano, Gonzalo E. Gutierrez, Rafael Cortes Macнas, and Jose A. Garcia-Ruiz

INTRODUCTION

The demographic structure has a significant influence on the use of healthcare services, as does the size of the population denominators. Very few studies have been published on methods for estimating the real population such as tourist resorts. The objectives of the study were: (a) To determine the municipal solid waste (MSW) ratio, per person per day, among populations of known size; (b) to estimate, by means of this ratio, the real population in an area where tourist numbers are very significant; and (c) to determine the impact on the utilization of hospital emergency healthcare services of the registered population, in comparison to the non-resident population, in two areas where tourist numbers are very significant.

An ecological study design was employed. We analyzed the Healthcare Districts of the Costa del Sol and the island of Menorca. Both are Spanish territories in the Mediterranean region.

In the two areas analyzed, the correlation coefficient between the MSW ratio and admissions to hospital emergency departments exceeded 0.9, with $p < 0.001$. On the basis of MSW generation ratios, obtained for a control zone (CZ) and also measured in neighboring countries, we estimated the real population. For the summer months, when tourist activity is greatest and demand for emergency healthcare at hospitals is highest, this value was found to be double that of the registered population.

The MSW indicator, which is both ecological and indirect, can be used to estimate the real population in areas where population levels vary significantly during the year. This parameter is of interest in planning and dimensioning the provision of healthcare services.

The demographic structure has a significant influence on the use of healthcare services, as does the size of the population denominators [1]. However, the vast majority of the studies published on the issue concentrate on factors referring to permanent populations. In areas such as tourist resorts, where large structural changes and annual fluctuations occur, the biggest problem lies in estimating the size of the population, before going on to consider its structure.

In the final decades of the 20th century, the coastal areas of developed countries in temperate climate zones advanced dramatically in both social and economic terms. In 1994, it was estimated that two-thirds of the world's population lived within 150 km of the coast, and this value was expected to increase to three quarters by the year 2025 [2]. Beyond all doubt, current levels of economic globalization have favored the increased mobility of populations [3].

In Europe, the clearest manifestation of coastal development is to be found along the Mediterranean shores from Spain to Greece, a space in which an authentic urban continuum has been created everywhere physically possible [4]. In addition to concentration in terms of land occupation, tourism also presents a high degree of variability in time, with a marked increase in activity during the summer months; this fact heightens the impact on the environment and tends to produce a model that is economically fragile.

Very few studies have been published on methods for estimating the real population [5]. The earliest studies of the mobility of patients within developed countries highlighted disparities in health-influencing factors, among both the host and the incoming populations, together with variability in the treatment offered to the latter and increasing concern among their respective governments about healthcare costs [6-8]. The lack of information about these problems means there is a corresponding lack of information about the behavior of populational denominators (the floating population or tourist load) and the effect of this on the use of healthcare services, leading to the seriously inadequate planning of healthcare resources. Indeed, this fact has been reported as impeding the estimation of rates of morbidity-mortality [9-12].

The goals of the present study are: (a) To determine the real population in a popular tourist area and (b) to evaluate the impact on the utilization of hospital emergency services by the permanent, registered population and by that of non-residents, in two popular tourist areas.

MATERIALS AND METHODS

Design: An ecological study was designed.

Location: The geographic areas analyzed were the Costa del Sol Healthcare District (CSHD) and the island of Menorca, both of which are part of Spain and in the Mediterranean region. In the years 2001–2002, Menorca had an inter-censal population of 77,036 [13]; public healthcare resources consisted of three primary-attention clinics and one hospital (the Verge de Toro Hospital) in the capital, Mahon. During the inter-censal period of 2001–2002, the CSHD served a population of 271,257 and included a public hospital in the town of Marbella (the Hospital Costa del Sol) and seven primary attention clinics.

Instrumentation: The main variable analyzed was the monthly generation of MSW in the two study areas during 2001, these data being supplied by the Association of Municipalities of the Western Costa del Sol (Mancomunidad de Municipios de la Costa del Sol Occidental) and by the Socio-Environmental Observatory (Observatorio Socio-Ambiental) of Menorca [14]. In estimating the kg of MSW generated per inhabitant per day in the CSHD, the CZ was taken as all the inland municipalities in the province of Malaga (thus excluding the coastal municipalities, the city of Malaga and a nearby dormitory town); for these areas, the demographic structure was assumed to be stable, presenting no significant changes throughout the year. In the case of Menorca, the direct estimator used was the variable known as human pressure (HP), this variable being applicable thanks to Menorca's island identity, and to the fact that all entries and exits of travelers, by sea or air, are recorded daily. Thus, the total population of the island, including the permanent and the "floating" elements, is always known. The HP variable enables us to obtain the value of the kg of MSW generated per inhabitant per day for every month of the year, rather than having to use a single annual value.

An additional variable included was the maximum accommodation capacity, or the maximum number of beds available, estimated from the total recorded population plus the number of beds in registered accommodation facilities plus the number of second homes and unoccupied residential buildings (corrected by a factor of 10% to allow for speculative housing, this being defined as the flats and houses sold within a year of their purchase) multiplied by the mean number of occupants (3.1) [15].

Statistical Analysis: The ratios calculated were applied to the production of MSW in the two study areas in order to estimate the tourist load and its range; a statistical description was achieved by means of measures of central trend and of dispersion. We estimated the Pearson correlation coefficient (after testing for normality with the Kolmogorov–Smirnov test), the coefficient of determination and the 95% confidence intervals for the estimates of the real population and the use of hospital emergency services during the year in which the study was carried out. For Menorca, these values were calculated for the relation between the MSW ratios and HP. The impact on the demand for healthcare services is described by the relative distribution of patients treated by hospital emergency services and by the patients' mean age, calculated monthly, the patients being differentiated by their place of residence within the reference healthcare district. The healthcare utilization rate was calculated from the estimated real population (assuming a MSW production of 1.4 kg per inhabitant per day). The level of significance was taken as $p < 0.05$.

The ratio of kg of MSW produced per registered inhabitant per day varied between 2.45 for the CSHD and 1.23 for the CZ. When the real population of the CSHD was estimated, based on three different ratios for the generation of MSW per inhabitant (1.2, 1.4, and 1.6 kg/person/day), the real population thus estimated exceeded the official values in every case. The estimated monthly population ranged from the 341,000 inhabitants calculated for the month of February, with a ratio of 1.6, to a maximum of 743,000 inhabitants in August, calculated using a MSW ratio of 1.2. The number of estimated inhabitants did not exceed the maximum accommodation capacity except the value calculated for the summer period with a MSW ratio of 1.2. (Table 1) Similar results were obtained for the estimated real population of Menorca using the HP parameter; during May–October, this value was double that of the official figure, while for the remaining months of the year the official value and the HP estimate coincided. The population level was minimum in January, with 70,000 inhabitants, and maximum in August with 177,000. During the months of January–March and in November and December, the estimated real population was less than the official recorded value.

Table 1. Estimate of the real population (1000s inhabitants) of the Costa del Sol health district based on MSW in 2001 and Menorca based on human pressure during 2001.

	Costa del Sol HD					Menorca		
	Registered Population	Max. Accomm. Capacity	Real population estimated with MSW ratio (kg/hab/day)			Registered Population	Max. Accomm. Capacity	Human Pressure
			1.2	1.4	1.6			
January	264	631	455	390	341	75	190	70
February	266	633	455	390	341	76	191	71
March	267	634	486	416	364	76	191	72
April	268	635	532	456	399	76	191	83
May	269	636	519	445	389	76	191	118
June	271	638	551	472	413	77	192	141
July	272	639	653	560	490	77	192	160
August	273	640	743	637	557	77	192	177
September	274	641	576	494	432	77	192	141
October	276	643	537	460	403	78	193	107
November	277	644	487	417	365	78	193	73
December	278	645	469	402	352	78	193	71

The correlation coefficient between MSW and HP in Menorca was 0.99 (Table 2). The MSW/HP ratios obtained ranged between 1.38 kg/person/day in December and 1.55 kg/person/day in January. In both Menorca and the CSHD, the degree of correlation between the MSW and the monthly number of cases treated at the emergency department of the hospital in the study areas exceeded 0.90 ($p < 0.001$).

Table 2. Bivariate correlation between the generation of municipal solid waste (in tons) and Admissions to Emergency Healthcare Hospital Department for Healthcare Districts of the Costa del Sol and Menorca during 2001, and Bivariate correlation between MSW and human pressure with MSW ratios for Menorca during 2001.

	Costa del Sol HD		Menorca				
	MSW	Admissions	MSW	Admissions	MSW	HP	Ratio
January	16935	8094	3377	1714	3377	70088	1,55
February	15275	7756	2915	1523	2915	71297	1,46
March	18069	8534	3515	1837	3515	72096	1,57
April	19141	8859	3969	1777	3969	83065	1,59
May	19312	8919	5439	2019	5439	118345	1,48
June	19845	9047	6128	2179	6128	141212	1,45
July	24308	10190	7097	2400	7097	160269	1,43
August	27628	11652	7726	2686	7726	177344	1,41
September	20743	8206	6450	1981	6450	141383	1,52
October	19982	8293	5274	1894	5274	106975	1,59
November	17520	7479	3470	1532	3470	72591	1,59
December	17437	7722	3030	1644	3030	70911	1,38
C. Corrrelation	0,93	p <0,001	0,93	p < 0,001	0,99	p < 0,001	
C.1. 95% lower upper	0,81	0,98	0,82	0,98	0,97	1,00	
C. Determination	0,86		0,87		0,98		

With respect to the impact on health care services, the unregistered population constituted up to 34.9% of all urgent admissions during the month of August in the Costa del Sol Health District, and up to 26.1% in Menorca in the same period. The mean age of non-residents decreased during the summer months in both areas, in comparison with that of the resident population, for whom the corresponding values remained stable (Table 3).

Table 3. Relative distribution and mean age of patients and percentage on the total of monthly admissions treated at hospital emergency departments in the Costa del Sol Health District and in Menorca, during 2001.

	Costa del Sol HD				Menorca			
	Emergency Admission of Unregistered		Mean Age		Emergency Admission of Unregistered		Mean Age	
	n	%	Resident	Non-Resident	n	%	Resident	Non-Resident
January	952	11,7	37,6	41,4	41	2,6	41,6	57,0
February	980	12,7	37,0	41,0	42	2,8	39,2	52,6
March	1195	14,0	37,3	41,4	98	4,7	39,3	54,3
April	1674	18,9	36,9	35,6	94	5,7	41,2	34,9
May	1316	14,8	37,3	40,4	120	6,7	40,0	36,5
June	1563	17,3	36,9	36,1	231	9,2	38,3	35,2
July	2757	27,1	38,2	32,0	375	17,5	39,5	33,5
August	4076	34,9	37,9	31,3	787	26,1	38,9	29,3
September	1578	19,3	38,2	38,0	235	12,8	39,6	37,7
October	1260	15,2	37,5	42,3	122	7,1	39,3	38,2
November	948	12,7	38,4	41,0	62	3,4	39,7	51,9
December	965	12,6	37,5	40,7	43	2,8	43,7	49,0
Average	19264	18,4	37,5	36,6	2250	9,7	39,9	35,7

In the year 2001 for the CSHD, hospital emergency service facilities were used by 25.9 per 1000 of the recorded, permanent population, with a difference of 4.3 points between the months of maximum and minimum frequency (Table 4). The permanent population utilized hospital emergency service facilities about 3–4 times more frequently than the non-resident population, this proportion remaining basically constant during the year, although with a slight decrease during the months of July and August, coinciding with the changing ratio of the non-recorded to the official population (exceeding 1.0).

Table 4. Population of the Costa del Sol estimated using MSW ratio (1.4 kg/person/day) compared with the registered population and the utilization of hospital emergency healthcare facilities per 1000 inhabitants per year in both geographic areas during 2001.

	Real Population Estimated	Registered Population (RP)	Unregistered Population (URP)	Population URP/RP	Emergency Admissions per 1000 RP	Emergency Admissions per 1000 RP	Admissions URP/RP
January	390.216	264.231	125.985	0,48	26,3	7,3	0,28
February	389.678	265.508	124.170	0,47	27,3	8,5	0,31
March	416.340	266.786	149.554	0,56	26,7	7,7	0,29
April	455.732	268.063	187.669	0,70	26,9	8,9	0,33

Table 4. *(Continued)*

	Real Population Estimated	Registered Population (RP)	Unregistered Population (URP)	Population URP/RP	Emergency Admissions per 1000 RP	Emergency Admissions per 1000 RP	Admissions URP/RP
May	444.976	269.340	175.636	0,65	27,3	7,3	0,27
June	472.493	270.618	201.875	0,75	27,7	7,7	0,28
July	560.096	271.895	288.201	1,06	26,5	9,3	0,35
August	636.588	273.173	363.415	1,33	27,0	10,9	0,40
September	493.873	274.450	219.423	0,80	24,1	7,2	0,30
October	460.405	275.727	184.678	0,67	24,6	6,6	0,27
November	417.146	277.005	140.141	0,51	23,6	6,8	0,29
December	401.777	278.282	123.495	0,44	24,4	7,6	0,32
Average	462.221	271.257	190.964	0,70	25,9	8,3	0,32

DISCUSSION

The production of MSW and the population estimates based on this parameter are positively related to the utilization of emergency healthcare services at hospitals in two geographic areas where tourist activity is significant. The frequency of use of hospital emergency service facilities varies during the year, as does the user profile.

Prior to obtaining the above correlations, we examined indirect indicators that might be used to establish the real population, such as the consumption of electricity, water, cement or hydrocarbon fuels, or the intensity of road traffic, but only the generation of MSW correlated strongly with variations in population and with the use of emergency healthcare facilities.

The choice of standard ratios for the generation of MSW to estimate population levels might introduce a degree of bias, as the areas analyzed present different demographic and economic patterns. However, the ratios obtained in the Malaga CZ match the ratio calculated under the National Plan for Urban Waste 2000–2006 (1.23 vs. 1.20 kg/person/day, respectively) [16], while in the coastal area of the same province this ratio was doubled. This phenomenon does not seem to be explained by a corresponding difference in income levels (in the province of Malaga, the weighted mean annual income in the CZ in 2002 exceeded 7,500 Euros, while in the CSHD municipalities it exceeded 10,500 Euros, only 40% higher). Neither do we observe a systematic increase in the generation of MSW in different countries as income increases [17]. The ranges of ratios applied in this study are close to those measured in European Union countries in 2001, varying between 1.2 kg/person/day (in Belgium, Portugal, and Greece) and 1.6 kg/person/day (in Germany, the UK, and Holland). The mean value for the 25 countries of the EU is 1.4 kg/person/day [18].

The estimates of real population based on the generation of MSW reveal a seasonal pattern: in the summer months, the estimated population doubles the official value. In the island of Menorca, seasonality is even greater, as in the first and fourth quarters of the year, the estimated and the officially recorded population values converge, while in the CSHD there exists an unrecorded population that remains stable during the winter months. This latter fact is consistent with the existence of different policies for tourism. On the island of Menorca, the traditional way of life, land and nature have not been displaced by mass tourism, while on the Costa del Sol there is a predominant service industry that is gradually becoming less seasonal by the integration of new areas of leisure activity.

Comparison of estimates of the real population with the utilization of healthcare resources enables us to evaluate the consistency of these findings, as the greater the population to be attended, the greater the demand for healthcare. Nevertheless, it should be taken into account that the non-resident population normally suffers fewer health problems than the permanent population. The unrecorded population that is resident in winter is usually older, being mainly European pensioners. Among hospital activities, that of the emergency departments presents the highest degree of association with MSW production, as the variability of outpatient treatment and hospital admissions is influenced by non-populational factors that are difficult to control, such as variations in healthcare personnel or changes in programmed activities. On the other hand, either of these populations (registered or unregistered) might seek other sources of care; the use of other health care facilities in primary care or the private sector might be alternative routes to care by these populations.

The correlation coefficients between the number of emergency admissions and MSW production (exceeding 0.90) indicates a strong degree of association and explains the high percentage of variability in the use of emergency healthcare facilities. It should be stressed that the correlation coefficient was identical in the two study areas. This finding is consistent with the association found between MSW production and overnight stays at winter sports resorts in France [5].

The non-resident population of the Costa del Sol is basically made up of three groups: (1) European pensioners, especially from the UK, Germany, and Scandinavia, who stay in the area for several months a year; (2) tourists, both from other areas of Spain and from many foreign countries, who visit the area mainly in summer, but also during other periods, taking advantage of the mild climate; and (3) the population living in neighboring municipalities who work in the area, mainly in the catering and construction industries. Rates of utilization of the emergency department at the Hospital Costa del Sol are stable throughout the year, both among the recorded and the unrecorded populations.

The European pensioners make a similar use of healthcare facilities to that of the permanent local population in the same age group, although many of them are not officially registered as resident in Spain. Thus there is an added demand for healthcare and other services (municipal services, infrastructure, and communications), the funding for which is provided on the basis of the officially recorded population. The relative increase in the rate of utilization of healthcare facilities during the months of greatest tourist activity (July and August), together with the fall in the mean age of patients attended, reflect the profile of a younger non-resident population with a higher level of open-air leisure activities, associated with a different morbidity profile. No analysis of healthcare facility utilization is given for the island of Menorca because the estimation method was influenced by the seasonal economic cycle characterizing the island (i.e., the fact that a greater population decrease occurs during the winter), which resulted in negative values being obtained for certain months.

The satisfactory results of the correlation analysis between MSW and HP underline the consistency of MSW as an indirect indicator of the real population, given the reliability of the HP variable in Menorca. This is of great importance, as in the case of the island no physical access is possible except that included in evaluating the HP variable.

CONCLUSION

Indicators such as the generation of MSW, which are ecological and indirect, are useful for estimating the total population in areas in which there occur significant changes during the year, if other types of indicators are not available. Annual variations in MSW generation are closely linked to the utilization of healthcare services, and particularly of emergency hospital services. Such an estimation method is of interest for the planning and dimensioning of the supply of healthcare services, and could be used in other countries in the UE, given the availability of UE MSW data within the EUROSTAT system. Future studies are required to further investigate the structural characterization of the tourist load and of the needs for healthcare services, broken down by age and sex, among other categories.

KEYWORDS

- **Control zone**
- **Correlation coefficients**
- **Human pressure**
- **Municipal solid waste**
- **Non-resident population**

AUTHORS' CONTRIBUTIONS

All authors contributed to the design of the study. Revision of the different versions of the study protocol: Emilio Perea-Milla, Sergi Mari Pons, Fidel Fernandez-Nieto, and Jose A. Garcia-Ruiz. Substantial contributions to the conception and design of the digital data record: Emilio Perea-Milla, Francisco Rivas-Ruiz, and Anna Gallofre. Acquisition of data and quality control: Francisco Rivas-Ruiz, Anna Gallofre, Gonzalo E. Gutierrez, Marco A. Navarro Ales, Fidel Fernandez-Nieto, and Joan C. March Cerda. Analysis and interpretation of data: Emilio Perea-Milla, Francisco Rivas-Ruiz, Manuel Carrasco, and Lydia Martin. All authors have read and approved the final manuscript.

ACKNOWLEDGMENTS

This study was funded by Fondo de Investigación Sanitaria (FIS) PI021084. The study forms part of the IRYSS Network investigating the operations of healthcare services, which is funded by FIS G03/202.

COMPETING INTERESTS

The author(s) declare that they have no competing interests.

Chapter 21

Backpacking Holidays and Alcohol, Tobacco, and Drug Use

Mark A. Bellis, Karen E. Hughes, Paul Dillon, Jan Copeland, and Peter Gates

INTRODUCTION

While alcohol and drug use among young people is known to escalate during short holidays and working breaks in international nightlife resorts, little empirical data are available on the impact of longer backpacking holidays on substance use. Here we examine changes in alcohol, tobacco, and drug use when UK residents go backpacking in Australia.

Matched information on alcohol and drug use in Australia and the UK was collected through a cross sectional cohort study of 1008 UK nationals aged 18–35 years, holidaying in Sydney or Cairns, Australia, during 2005.

The use of alcohol and other drugs by UK backpackers visiting Australia was common with use of illicit drugs being substantially higher than in peers of the same age in their home country. Individuals showed a significant increase in frequency of alcohol consumption in Australia compared to their behavior in the UK with the proportion drinking five or more times per week rising from 20.7% (UK) to 40.3% (Australia). Relatively few individuals were recruited into drug use in Australia (3.0%, cannabis; 2.7% ecstasy; 0.7%, methamphetamine). However, over half of the sample (55.0%) used at least one illicit drug when backpacking. Risk factors for illicit drug use while backpacking were being regular club goers, being male, Sydney based, traveling without a partner or spouse, having been in Australia more than 4 weeks, Australia being the only destination on their vacation, and drinking or smoking 5 or more days a week.

As countries actively seek to attract more international backpacker tourists, interventions must be developed that target this population's risk behaviors. Developing messages on drunkenness and other drug use specifically for backpackers could help minimize their health risks directly (e.g., adverse drug reactions) and indirectly (e.g., accidents and violence) as well as negative impacts on the host country.

Young people's behavior changes when holidaying away from their usual residence [1-3]. Typically on short 1 or 2 week holidays, risk taking behaviors (in particular alcohol and drug use) escalate as constraints from education or work commitments reduce, social mores relax, and opportunities to consume substances (through for example lower cost and increased availability) increase [2-5]. Such escalation is linked to increases in unsafe sex [6], accidents (including road traffic accidents [7, 8]) and possible damage to mental health through excessive consumption of alcohol and drugs [9-11]. Furthermore, the holiday environment of indulgence and excess can lead to social norms and peer pressure encouraging individuals who have never used illicit drugs to begin consumption [1, 2, 12]. While use of drugs anywhere can have adverse reactions including overdose, anxiety, panic attack, and dehydration, use abroad is often more dangerous because of unknown supplies, lack of knowledge of local health services, and often isolation from usual community support [13].

Increasingly, for the young residents of many countries such international travel is no longer the exception [14] but almost an expectation on an annual basis. From the UK alone over four million young people aged 18–30 are estimated to travel abroad every year [15, 16]. Most such journeys are holidays taken to European destinations with each vacation lasting 1 or 2 weeks [15, 17]. However, a large and increasing proportion of young people also set aside time for longer journeys (frequently a year) often including stays in multiple countries before returning home[18, 19]. Typically backpacking describes tourists on such protracted holidays who carry their necessary belongings in a backpack [20]. In contrast to shorter international holidays, backpacking often includes living on a low budget with less indulgent expenditure and can also involve individuals seeking employment while abroad, especially in distant countries such as Australia and New Zealand [19-21]. During the 5 year period from 1999 to 2003 the number of domestic and international backpackers traveling in Australia grew 25% (753,000–943,000); accounting for 11% of overseas visitors [22]. The largest single source of backpackers visiting Australia was the UK, accounting for 27% of individuals (121,500 [23]).

To date, studies on risk behavior and youth travel have focused largely on short-term vacations. In particular those on substance use among backpackers have been predominantly qualitative [24, 25], providing some evidence of experimentation with drugs abroad yet little epidemiological information on this type of youth travel and its relationship with substance use[12]. However, there are many reasons why behavior changes associated with backpacking might differ from those during shorter trips to holiday resorts (e.g., Ibiza [2]). Popular backpacker destinations, such as Sydney, Australia, are general tourist destinations not specifically designed for youth tourism but catering for a wider holidaying and endemic population. Consequently, regulations regarding drug use or drunkenness may be more stringently enforced [26] and opportunities to purchase illicit substances more restricted. Further, with money often more limited on such longer vacations, finance may also be a restrictive factor and the necessity to work while traveling may require individuals to avoid late nights, drug use and excessive alcohol consumption for working parts of each week [27]. Equally however, participating in employment may increase opportunities to meet local people and obtain access to local illicit drug markets.

With levels of young people backpacking increasing, health professionals (in travelers' home countries and those they visit) require information on how backpacking may alter patterns of substance use, what health risks such changes represent [11] and what interventions should be targeted at these populations. To address such issues, here we compare the alcohol, tobacco, and drug using behavior of 1008 UK residents in the last 12 months before they leave the UK and when backpacking in Australia.

MATERIALS AND METHODS

As one of the most popular international destinations for backpackers from the UK [23, 28], Australia was chosen as the country in which to conduct the survey. A cross sectional cohort study design was chosen which utilized a single questionnaire to measure individuals' backpacking experience (e.g., length of trip, destinations visited), behavior in Australia and, for within individual comparisons, their behavior in the UK prior to their trip [29]. Questions addressed alcohol, tobacco, illicit drug use, and sexual behavior and had been previously validated and utilized in studies of short holidays within Europe [2, 3]. However, some questions were adapted to examine the longer lengths of stay routinely experienced by backpackers in Australia and to include substances more commonly used in that country (e.g., methamphetamine [30]). Consequently, the range of illicit drugs examined included cannabis, ecstasy, amphetamine (i.e., amphetamine sulphate), methamphetamine, crystal meth or ice (methamphetamine in crystalline form), cocaine, crack, lysergic acid diethylamide (LSD), ketamine, gammahydroxybutrate (GHB), heroin, and steroids.

Given the diversity of nightlife and other tourist environments in Australia, two contrasting locations were identified in which to sample backpackers. The first, Sydney (population approximately 4.2 million [31]), is a major international metropolis with a flourishing nightlife, busy international transport connections and consequently often the point of arrival and departure for backpackers visiting the country [21]. In contrast, around 2,700 km north is Cairns (population approximately 120,000 [31]); the third most common tourist destination in the country after Sydney and Brisbane. Popular with overseas tourists and particularly international backpackers, the city has a less well developed nightlife but one that is very much designed for young travelers.

Ethics approval was received from the University of New South Wales Human Ethics Committee, the auspicing body for the study, and research methods complied with the Helsinki Declaration. Questionnaires were administered in Sydney (28th April–22nd November 2005) and Cairns (August 1–6, 2005). In both locations backpacking hostels were utilized as the sites for sampling potential respondents and within each hostel researchers approached individuals on a convenience basis. Inclusion criteria for the survey were being age 18–35 years, having already been in Australia for at least 2 weeks and being a UK national. In all cases researchers explained to potential respondents the content of the survey and its anonymous nature. Informed consent was recorded and participants were reimbursed $AUS10 for their time. All individuals meeting the inclusion criteria and agreeing to participate (n = 1012 of 1114 approached; participation rate 90.8%) were given a questionnaire, pen and plain envelope in which to seal the completed questionnaire and return it to the researcher. Completed questionnaires were entered into Statistical Package for Social Sciences (SPSS) for analysis [32]. At this stage a further four questionnaires were excluded as responses did not meet survey inclusion criteria for age or period of stay (n = 3) and one questionnaire was spoilt (i.e., no effort had been made to complete questions and the questionnaire had been defaced).

Analysis utilized a combination of Chi Square, Mann Whitney U, McNemar, and Wilcoxon signed rank tests with logistic regression being used to control for confounding relationships between variables when examining predictors of drug use. For logistic regression analyses, amphetamine, methamphetamine, and crystal meth were combined into a single category of "used amphetamine type" and a category of "used any illicit drug" was also created.

DISCUSSION

Here, we compared substance use of UK backpackers while traveling in Australia with their behavior in the UK. As sampling was on a convenience basis we could not identify how representative participants were of all UK backpackers traveling in Australia. However to minimize bias, participants were approached by researchers and refusal to participate occurred on only 9.2% of occasions. A second methodological concern was bias in recall of behavior in the UK. However, the periods over which individuals were asked to recall substance use were not dissimilar to established surveys which routinely evaluate individuals' substance use in the past 12 months [33]. Finally, backpackers self assessed the types of drugs they used. This again is a not an unusual methodology for large drug surveys. However, while in Australia backpackers may have thought they used amphetamine (i.e., amphetamine sulfate or "speed" in the UK) but may actually have used methamphetamine powder (also called "speed" in Australia); which can look like amphetamine and can be used in the same way. Similarly, those reporting use of Ecstasy may again have unwittingly used methamphetamine, which is frequently found in "pills" sold in Australia [34].

Across the general population of England and Wales ecstasy use in 16–34 year olds in the last year (2004/05 [33]) was 3.9% compared with 33.9% among our respondents (age 18–35) in the 12 months before leaving the UK. Consequently, we conclude that UK backpackers are more likely to be drug users than average members of the British population of comparable age. As such, those choosing to go on backpacking holidays are a risk group for drug-related harms and consequently a target group for harm minimization and prevention measures whether at home or abroad. Currently, although some information and advice on alcohol and drug use abroad is available to those intending to backpack abroad (e.g., through a gap year website [35]), once abroad interventions to address substance use among backpackers are limited.

While in Australia, cannabis was by far the most commonly used illicit drug by backpackers. There, around 10% used ≥ 5 days a week, 30 individuals used for their first time and those who used in both countries used more frequently in Australia (Table 2). Qualitative studies of backpackers suggest that cannabis is seen as a "safe" drug that allows the user to stay in control [25]. When traveling, sometimes alone, safety can be paramount [36] and taking tablets of unknown quality or other drugs with immediate and dramatic disorientating effects may be less attractive. Further, cannabis also plays a specific social role when it (usually in cigarette form) is shared between friends and to make new acquaintances [25]. Tobacco, another substance that can occupy a similar niche, also increased in both numbers using and frequency of use in Australia (Table 2). For most other drugs however backpackers were less likely to use in Australia. Thus, despite studies suggesting some uptake by travelers of local drug patterns [24], reported prevalence of methamphetamine use (the second most popular illicit drug among Australians [37]) by backpackers was actually lower than in the UK.

For all drugs, individuals who used in both countries were most likely to use at the same frequency in each (Table 2). However, for all drugs except cannabis and steroids, those changing frequency of use were significantly more likely to use at a lower frequency in Australia (Table 3). These are very different changes in drug using behavior from those seen on short holidays to nightlife resorts (e.g., Ibiza [2]) where changes in drug use are typified by drug bingeing with significant increases in frequency of use. The length of time spent overseas, financial resources and even having to work are all likely to play a part in limiting drug use on backpacking vacations. However, access to drugs may also be a major factor. Here, use in Australia of "any illicit drug" and specifically cannabis, ecstasy and cocaine were all related to length of stay to date. This is consistent with individuals requiring time to source drugs and develop confidence to buy and consume them in a country where drug laws are routinely enforced [38]. The same constraints appear to have also limited initiation of individuals into drug use or of existing drug users into the use of drugs more commonly found in Australia. Thus, cocaine use among backpackers in Australia was more prevalent than methamphetamine despite this being more commonly used in Australian nightlife and cheaper to purchase than cocaine [39]. In fact, only seven individuals who had never tried methamphetamine in the UK reported having done so in Australia with the same number also trying crystal meth in Australia for the first time. However, backpackers may have inadvertently used methamphetamine assuming, for example, it was amphetamine. Although we cannot measure the size of this effect, here 7.6% of backpackers reported using amphetamine during their stay despite, in Australia, most amphetamine being forms of methamphetamine [40]. Importantly however, methamphetamine has stronger stimulant effects, is linked to physical and mental health problems (e.g., seizures, paranoia, depression), violence and risky sexual behavior [41, 42] and should individuals later realize what they have used they may seek this stronger drug for future use.

Overall despite relatively low levels of recruitment into drug use, there were still a substantial number of individuals who used illicit drugs in Australia (55.0% used an illicit drug at least once when backpacking). Such individuals are more likely to visit nightclubs more than once a week, be male, Sydney based, traveling without their partner or spouse, have been in Australia over 4 weeks, be visiting Australia only, and also be daily or near daily ($\geq$5 days a week) drinkers and smokers. Such profiling should help information to be specifically developed for, and then directed at, those leaving the UK to backpack while also allowing services in Australia to target further information and advice at these groups. Tailored approaches to prevention and harm minimization have been shown to be more effective than general information provision that ignores the specific characteristics of the target groups [43]. Thus, information linking drugs with alcohol and tobacco would be highly applicable to this group. However, frequent alcohol use by backpackers is not only a predictor of drug use in Australia but may also be a substantial concern in its own right. Backpackers show significant increases in frequency of alcohol use when in Australia which contrasts strongly with the protective role backpacking plays against use of most illicit drugs. Numbers drinking $\geq$5 days a week nearly doubled from 20.7% in the UK to 40.3%

in Australia. While this study did not measure the amount of alcohol consumed each night, this increase in use over the long time periods associated with backpacking is a cause for concern and intervention. Alcohol is not only associated with direct acute (e.g., poisoning) and long term (e.g., liver disease) effects on health but also plays a major role in accidents (including deaths of drunk pedestrians), violence and engagement in unprotected sex [6, 44]. In hot climates it can also play a role in over exposure to the sun (e.g., through sleeping on the beach and sitting outside bars [45]), thus increasing risks of skin cancer [46]. Further, drunkenness as well as drug use and dealing can adversely affect host populations while related events such as a fatality among visitors can devastate a tourist industry [47]. Consequently, health interventions targeting backpackers in Australia are likely to be of benefit not only to travelers but also to local populations.

RESULTS

Table 1 provides the basic demographics of respondents, details of their travel plans, whether they had to visit a doctor or hospital in Australia and how frequently they went to nightclubs in Australia. Overall the median age of the sample was 23 years with significantly more males being aged 25–35 years (Table 1). Most (79.3%) individuals were not traveling with a long-term partner or spouse. For almost 40% of individuals Australia was their first destination since leaving the UK and for a similar proportion it was to be their last destination before returning to the UK (Table 1). The median planned stay was 25 weeks but males planned to stay significantly longer than females (Table 1) with over a third expecting to stay more than 40 weeks. However, length of stay at time of interview was not significantly different between sexes (Table 1). The vast majority (97.3%) of backpackers went to nightclubs (i.e., clubbing) at least once a week (Table 1). Further, during their stay approximately one-fifth of all backpackers had required hospital treatment or a visit to a doctor at least once. Over one in 10 (10.9%) of those who required such attention stated it was alcohol-related and 6.5% that it was drug-related.

Table 1. General sample characteristics and comparison between sexes of UK backpackers in Australia.

		All		Male		Female			
Survey area		n	%	n	%	n	%	X2	P
	Cairns	259	25.7	156	23.4	103	30.3		
	Sydney	749	74.3	511	76.6	237	69.7	5.62	<0.05
Age									
	18 to 20	198	19.6	138	20.7	60	17.6		
	21 to 24	457	45.3	283	42.4	174	51.2		
	25 to 35	353	35.0	246	36.9	106	31.2	6.96	<0.05
Abroad with partner/spouse		205	20.7	122	18.6	83	24.9	5.44	<0.05
Australia first destination from UK		396	39.3	268	40.2	128	37.6	0.61	0.436
Australia final destination before UK		368	36.7	247	37.3	121	35.8	0.20	0.651
Australia only destination[1]		232	23.0	155	23.2	77	22.6	0.05	0.833

Table 1. *(Continued)*

		All		Male		Female			
Stay to date (weeks)									
	2 to 4	339	33.6	215	32.2	124	36.5		
	>4 to 12	316	31.3	210	31.5	105	30.9		
	>12	353	35.0	242	36.3	111	32.6	2.08	0.354
Stay remaining (weeks)									
	2 to 4	278	28.3	155	23.9	123	36.9		
	>12 to 40	273	27.8	182	28.1	91	27.3		
	>40	431	43.9	311	48.0	119	35.7	20.74	<0.001
Total stay (weeks)									
	2 to 12	302	30.8	178	27.5	124	37.2		
	>2 to 40	359	36.6	239	36.9	120	36.0		
	>40	321	32.7	231	35.6	89	26.7	12.23	<0.005
		202	20.3	122	18.5	80	23.8	3.86	<0.05
Visited hospital/doctor in Australis									
Nights clubbing per week									
	Non	26	2.7	15	2.4	11	3.5		
	1	161	17.0	89	14.1	72	22.7		
	2 to 4	635	67.1	435	69.2	199	62.8		
	5 or more	125	13.2	90	14.3	35	11.0	12.97	<0.01

Use of both licit and illicit substances by backpackers in Australia was common (Table 2). There was no significant change in proportions of individuals who drank in Australia compared with proportions who drank in the UK (Table 2). However, there was a significant change in frequency of consumption with 35% of alcohol-using backpackers increasing frequency of drinking in Australia, and the proportion drinking 5 or more days a week rising from 20.7% (UK) to 40.3% (Australia; $X^2 = 91.31$; $P < 0.001$).

Cannabis was the most commonly used illicit drug both in the UK and in Australia. Over 40% of individuals used it in both the UK and Australia with a small but significant tendency for those who used in just one country to have used only in the UK (Table 2). However, over a quarter of those using in both countries used cannabis at higher frequencies in Australia while only 16.2% reduced frequency of consumption when backpacking. A quarter (24.9%) of individuals used ecstasy in both Australia and the UK, with a further 5.6% using in Australia although they had not used in the previous 12 months spent in the UK (Table 2). In fact, 2.7% (27/1005) of backpackers surveyed used ecstasy for the first time while on their current trip to Australia (cf. cannabis 3.0%; cocaine 0.6%; amphetamine 0.9%; methamphetamine 0.7%; crystal meth 0.7%). In contrast to cannabis, those using ecstasy in both countries were significantly more likely to use at a higher frequency in the UK (Table 2). Furthermore, the number of ecstasy tablets they consumed during a typical night of use was also significantly lower in Australia (median, inter quartile range; UK 2.5, 2.0–4.0, Australia 2.0, 1.0–2.0; $Z = 9.13$, $P < 0.001$). For cocaine, amphetamine, LSD, ketamine, and even methamphetamine, those using in one country but not the other were significantly more likely to have used in the UK (Table 2). Further, for those using cocaine or amphetamine

Table 2. Levels of substance use in UK backpackers while in the UK and when visiting Australia.

Frequency of use	Alcohol	Tobacco	Cannabis	Ecstasy	Cocaine	Crack	Amphetamine	Methamphetamine	Crystal Meth	LSD	GHB	Ketamine	Steroids	Heroin
UK	%	%	%	%	%	%	%	%	%	%	%	%	%	%
Never used	1.2	26.0	27.0	48.3	63.5	95.6	71.4	85.4	93.2	75.4	92.5	87.4	96.9	95.2
Used but not in last 12 months	1.1	15.1	20.1	17.8	13.9	3.3	16.4	9.6	4.6	19.0	6.0	8.9	2.2	3.5
Less than 1 day a week	6.8	7.5	25.6	23.8	18.8	0.8	8.8	3.1	1.6	5.1	1.4	3.3	0.6	0.8
1 day a week	16.8	4.1	7.9	6.1	2.0	0.2	1.8	1.1	0.2	0.2	0.0	0.1	0.1	0.0
2 to 4 days a week	53.5	9.2	9.6	3.5	1.4	0.0	1.0	0.5	0.3	0.2	0.0	0.1	0.0	0.2
5 or more days a week	20.7	38.1	9.7	0.5	0.4	0.1	0.7	0.3	0.1	0.2	0.1	0.2	0.2	0.2
Australia														
Never used in Australia	2.1	38.1	49.9	69.9	93.9	99.1	92.4	96.6	98.4	96.8	99.2	98.0	98.7	98.6
Less than 1 day a week	4.7	7.7	20.1	21.3	5.6	0.6	6.2	2.0	1.4	3.0	0.5	1.5	0.7	1.0
1 day a week	8.4	4.4	9.4	6.7	0.6	0.1	0.6	0.3	0.1	0.1	0.1	0.2	0.1	0.2
2 to 4 days a week	44.5	10.2	10.2	2.1	0.3	0.0	0.6	0.7	0.0	0.0	0.2	0.2	0.0	0.0
5 or more days a week	40.3	39.7	10.3	0.4	0.2	0.2	0.2	0.1	0.1	0.1	0.0	0.1	0.3	0.2
Countries recently used in[1]														
Neither	1.6	36.3	40.0	60.5	76.1	98.5	85.9	93.8	96.7	92.9	98.0	95.1	98.7	97.8
UK Only	0.5	1.8	9.9	9.1	17.3	0.6	6.6	3.1	1.7	3.9	1.3	2.9	0.2	0.8
Australia Only	0.7	4.9	7.1	5.6	1.3	0.4	1.9	1.2	1.1	1.4	0.5	1.2	0.4	0.9
Both	97.2	57.1	43.1	24.9	5.3	0.5	5.7	1.9	0.5	1.8	0.2	0.8	0.7	0.5
McNemars	0.77	<0.001	<0.05	<0.01	<0.001	0.75	<0.001	<0.01	0.34	<0.005	0.1	<0.05	0.69	1.00
Change in frequency of use[2]														
Australia>UK	35.0	13.2	28.4	9.2	5.7	0.0	7.0	10.5	20.0	5.6	0.0	0.0	28.6	0.0
UK>Australia	5.1	5.6	16.2	16.8	22.6	20.0	31.6	36.8	20.0	22.2	50.0	12.5	14.3	20.0
Unchanged	59.9	81.2	55.4	74.0	71.7	80.0	61.4	52.6	60.0	72.2	50.0	87.5	57.1	80.0
Wilcoxon's Signed Rank	<0.001	<0.001	<0.005	<0.01	<0.05	0.32	<0.005	0.08	0.66	0.13	0.32	0.32	0.41	0.32

[1]Users in the UK are those that consumed the drug in their last 12 months in the UK. For Australia they are those that consumed the drug at any time during their current visit.

[2]Calculated only for those individuals that have currently used (see above)[1] in both locations.

in both countries frequency of use was more likely to decrease than increase when backpacking.

Logistic regression analyses were employed to examine independent demographic and behavioral predictors of having used cannabis, ecstasy, and cocaine as well as combined categories of "any illicit drug" and "amphetamine types" in Australia (see Materials and Methods for category components). Use of drugs in the UK, although strongly related to use in Australia (Table 2), was not used as a predictive factor but variables were included that help identify groups at high risk of recreational drug use in Australia and could assist with targeting appropriate interventions. Being resident in Sydney (not Cairns) was a strong predictive factor for having used any illicit drug, cannabis and especially cocaine (adjusted odds ratio, 17.67; Table 3) and this may reflect easier access to drugs in Sydney. Being male, traveling without a long-term sexual partner and frequently visiting nightclubs all predicted any illicit drug use, and cannabis and ecstasy use. Length of stay completed at participation was positively related to these behaviors as well as use of cocaine. Further, daily (≥5 days/week) tobacco use was strongly associated with all types of other substance use including the category amphetamine types, while daily alcohol use (≥5 days/week) was associated with all categories except cocaine (Table 3).

All independent variables from the logistic regression that were significant predictors of at least two dependents were categorized as risk factors for drug use while backpacking. Each respondent was scored according to how many of these risk factors they displayed (scale 0–8). Figure 1 shows the relationship between number of risk factors and proportions using different drug types. Thus, all individuals having a score of eight used cannabis in Australia, most used ecstasy (93.8%) and nearly half used amphetamine types (43.8%) or cocaine (43.8%).

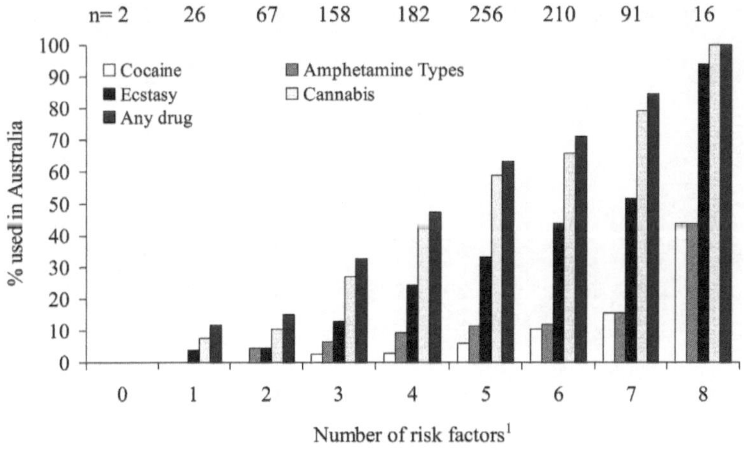

Figure 1. Relationship between number of drug use risk factors individuals display and consumption of illicit drugs in Australia. Risk factors were identified through logistic regression analysis (Table 3) and include all independent variables which were significant predictors of at least two dependents categories of drug use. Risks factors are residence in Sydney, male, only visiting Australia, traveling without a long-term partner or spouse, stay to date over 4 weeks, night clubbing more than once a week and alcohol or tobacco consumption ≥5 days per week.

Table 3. Logistic regression analysis of factors predicting use of illegal drug in Australia during their current backpacking vacation.

		Used any illegal drug[1]			Cannabis			Eccstasy			Cocaine			Amphetamine Types[2]		
		AOR	(95%Cl)	P[3]	AOR	(95%Cl)	P	AOR	(95%Cl)	P	AOR	(95%Cl)	P	AOR	(95%Cl)	P
Survey area	*Cairns*	Ref		**	Ref		**				Ref		**			
	Sydney	1.74	(1.21–2.51)		1.86	(1.27–2.72)					17.67	(2.33–134.12)				
Age	*18 to 20*				Ref		*									
	21 to 24				1.56	(1.05–2.33)	*									
	25 to 35				1.01	(0.66–1.54)	NS									
Sex	*Female*	Ref		***	Ref		***	Ref		**						
	Male	1.80	(1.31–2.46)		1.85	(1.35–2.55)		1.70	(1.2–2.41)							
Australia only destination[4]	*No*				Ref		**	Ref		*						
	Yes				1.64	(1.13–2.36)		1.49	(1.03–2.17)							
Abroad with partner/spouse	*Yes*	Ref		***	Ref		***	Ref		*						
	No	2.18	(1.5–3.16)		2.08	(1.42–3.03)		1.60	(1.05–2.42)		Ref		*			
Stay to date (weeks)	*2 to 4*	Ref		***			***	Ref		***	1.56	(0.65–3.74)	NS			
	>4 to 12	1.77	(1.23–2.55)	**	1.63	(1.13–2.36)	**	2.33	(1.55–3.5)	***	3.08	(1.29–7.4)	*			
	>12	2.34	(1.62–3.39)	***	2.42	(1.67–3.5)	***	3.10	(2.08–4.63)	***	Ref		*			
Total stay (weeks)	*2 to 12*										0.43	(0.16–1.14)	NS			
	>12 to 40										0.95	(0.37–2.46)	NS			
	>40															

Table 3. *(Continued)*

		Used any illegal drug[1]			Cannabis			Eccstasy			Cocaine			Amphetamine Types[2]		
Nights clubbing per week	*<= 1*	Ref		**	Ref		**	Ref		**						
	2 to 4	1.84	(1.24–2.72)	**	1.70	(1.14–2.54)	**	2.49	(1.51–4.11)	***						
	5 or more	2.85	(1.57–5.18)	**	2.58	(1.43–4.65)	**	2.79	(1.46–5.3)	**						
Daily alcohol-Australia[5]	*No*	Ref		*	Ref		**	Ref		*				Ref		*
	Yes	1.42	(1.01–2.01)		1.64	(1.17–2.31)		1.48	(1.05–2.1)					1.74	(1.1–2.75)	
Daily tobacco-Australia[5]	*No*	Ref		***	Ref		***	Ref		***	Ref		***	Ref		** *
	Yes	3.24	(2.35–4.47)		2.92	(2.13–4.01)		2.80	(2.03–3.86)		3.29	(1.87–5.77)		2.37	(1.5–3.77)	

Stay remaining (weeks) and whether individuals had had to visit a hospital or doctor in Australia were included in the analysis but were not significant for any types of substance use. For all other independen variables relationships that were not significant are left blank. Reference categories are identified with 'Ref' and overall levels of significance for each independent variable are presented in the same row as the reference category. AOR = Adjusted Odds Ratio; CI = Confidence Intervals.

[1]Cannabis, Ecstasy, Amphetamine, Methamphetamine, Crystal Meth, Cocaine, Crack, LSD, Ketamine, GHB, Heroin and Steroids.
[2]Includes Amphetamine, Methamphetamine and Crystal Meth.
[3]Significance is shown as *P < 0.05, **P < 0.01, ***P < 0.001, NS = not significant.
[4]Travelling from the UK to Australia and back without holiday periods in other countries on either route.
[5]Here daily is defined as anyone reporting use five or more days a week.

CONCLUSION

As increasing numbers of individuals spend more time abroad, their health protection and promotion requirements need to be more adequately understood and addressed. With a high probability of UK backpackers being illicit drug users, and many increasing their alcohol consumption while abroad, backpacking holidays represent an important opportunity to deliver drug and alcohol related messages to those most at risk. Such messages should stress that most backpackers reduce illicit drug use while traveling. Of course, health issues will always arise for some individuals as part of lengthy holidays abroad. However, the potential benefits of backpacking appear to include not only a thriving tourist industry for host countries and a growing market for travel operators but also valued personal development and reduced drug use for backpackers. Protecting such benefits is in the interest of countries, companies and travelers. However, it requires leadership for collaborative working between nations and partnerships between health and commercial companies, including airlines, holiday companies and Internet sites for backpackers. Such partnerships should deliver information not just on sun-bathing, vaccination and holiday insurance but also on the dangers of substance use. Together they can ensure that the health of backpackers is protected, access to services are adequate and opportunities to provide health information are not missed.

KEYWORDS

- **Alcohol**
- **Backpacking**
- **Illicit drug**
- **Matched information**
- **Methamphetamine**

AUTHORS' CONTRIBUTIONS

Mark A. Bellis designed and developed the research study, analyzed the data and wrote the manuscript. Karen E. Hughes developed the research study, input data and assisted in writing the manuscript. Paul Dillon developed the study, managed the research, and edited the manuscript. Jan Copeland developed the study and edited the manuscript. Peter Gates co-ordinated the research project and edited the manuscript. All authors have read and approved the final manuscript.

ACKNOWLEDGMENTS

We would like to thank Etty Matalon, Sara Edwards, Clare Lushey, Michela Morleo, Rajinder Kaur, Damien Giurco, Tara Showyin, Lucinda Wedgwood, Jennifer Siegel, Tess Fitzhardinge, and Bridget Callaghan for their assistance and support. We would also like to thank the backpackers who took part in the study. The research was supported by funds from the Higher Education Funding Council for England.

COMPETING INTERESTS

The author(s) declare that they have no competing interests.

Chapter 22

Imported Case of Marburg Hemorrhagic Fever, in the Netherlands

Aura Timen, Marion P. G. Koopmans, Ann C. T. M. Vossen, Gerard J. J. van Doornum, Stephan Günther, Franchette van den Berkmortel, Kees M. Verduin, Sabine Dittrich, Petra Emmerich, Albert D. M. E. Osterhaus, Jaap T. van Dissel, and Roel A. Coutinho

INTRODUCTION

On July 10, 2008, Marburg hemorrhagic fever (MHF) was confirmed in a Dutch patient who had vacationed recently in Uganda. Exposure most likely occurred in the Python Cave (Maramagambo Forest), which harbors bat species that elsewhere in Africa have been found positive for Marburg virus (MARV). A multidisciplinary response team was convened to perform a structured risk assessment, perform risk classification of contacts, issue guidelines for follow-up, provide information, and monitor the crisis response. In total, 130 contacts were identified (66 classified as high risk and 64 as low risk) and monitored for 21 days after their last possible exposure. The case raised questions specific to international travel, postexposure prophylaxis for MARV, and laboratory testing of contacts with fever. We present lessons learned and results of the follow-up serosurvey of contacts and focus on factors that prevented overreaction during an event with a high public health impact.

In Western countries, MHF is an imported disease with a low risk of occurrence, but it has a high profile in the public mind [1] because it can be transmitted from person to person, the course is fatal in up to 80% of cases, and the reservoir is uncertain [2, 3]. The infection is caused by the MARV, an enveloped, nonsegmented, negative-stranded RNA virus belonging, with the Ebola virus, to the family Filoviridae. Although the main transmission route is direct contact with blood or other infected body fluids, transmission by droplets and aerosols cannot be ruled out and has been demonstrated in animal models [4].

The MARV was identified in 1967 in Marburg, Germany, during a laboratory outbreak caused by handling tissues of African green monkeys [5, 6]. From 1975 through 1987, sporadic cases occurred in South Africa (1975, when the index case, a person exposed in Zimbabwe, was diagnosed in South Africa) [7] and in Kenya (1980, 1987) [8-10]. Outbreaks were reported from the Democratic Republic of Congo in 1998–2000 [11, 12], Angola in 2004–2005 [2], and Uganda in 2007 [13]. Nonhuman primates and bats are suspected as sources of infection, but their role in the natural reservoir for MARV and transmission to humans is unclear [14].

In July 2008, an imported case of MHF was diagnosed in the Netherlands. We describe the public health response involving the management of 130 contacts at risk of acquiring the disease.

THE CASE

On July 5, 2008, a 41-year-old woman was referred by her general practitioner to the Elkerliek Hospital because of fever (39°C) and chills of 3 days' duration after returning from a June 5–28 holiday in Uganda. She was placed in a hospital room with three other patients. Malaria was ruled out by three negative blood films. Routine bacteriologic tests were performed, and empiric treatment with ceftriaxone, 2 g/day, was started. On July 7, hemorrhagic fever was included among other infectious causes in the differential diagnosis because of rapid clinical deterioration and impending liver failure. An ambulance stripped of all unnecessary devices and equipped in accordance with strict isolation protocols transferred the patient to a single room with negative air pressure ventilation and anteroom in the Leiden University Medical Centre (LUMC).

After admission, rash, conjunctivitis, diarrhea, liver, and kidney failure, and finally, hemorrhaging developed in the patient. Extensive bacteriologic and virologic analyses were conducted, and plasma samples were sent to Dutch national laboratories and to the Bernhard-Nocht-Institute for Tropical Medicine (BNI) in Hamburg, Germany, for testing to detect antibodies to and RNA from filoviruses. Initial laboratory results from the Dutch national reference laboratory were ambiguous for hemorrhagic fever. On July 10, BNI reported a positive reverse transcription—PCR result for MARV [15], which was confirmed by sequence analysis of the polymerase gene. The strain was related to, but distinct from, known isolates. The MARV was confirmed by PCR by the Department of Virology at Erasmus Medical College (Rotterdam, the Netherlands). On July 11, the patient died of consequences of cerebral edema.

TRAVEL HISTORY AND HYPOTHESES FOR THE SOURCE OF INFECTION

The patient's travel group consisted of seven Dutch tourists and two guides. Three of the tourists, including the patient, and one guide visited an empty cave on June 16 in Fort Portal and the Python Cave in the Maramagambo Forest on June 19. The patient's partner recalled bats flying around in the latter cave, bumping against the visitors, and large amounts of droppings on the ground. She incurred no bite wounds, and no preexisting wounds were exposed to bats. On July 23, the travel group came within 5 m of gorillas in the wild and visited a village inhabited by pygmies, where they saw an elderly sick woman lying under a blanket.

We postulated that the most probable source of MARV infection was the visit to the Python Cave, known for its colony of Egyptian fruit-eating bats (*Rousettus aegyptiacus*). The party had photographed these bats, and this species of bat has been shown to carry filoviruses, including MARV [16, 17] in other sub-Saharan locations. We estimated the incubation period of the infection to be 13 days.

ORGANIZATION OF PUBLIC HEALTH RESPONSE

On July 8, the attending physician at the LUMC notified the Dutch public health authorities about the case. A national outbreak response team was formed of clinicians, medical microbiologists and virologists, public health specialists, staff members from the national response unit, and a press officer. This team convened a nearly daily teleconference to (1) to perform a structured assessment of the public health risks in the two hospitals and in the community, (2) perform risk classification of contacts, (3) issue guidelines for follow-up, (4) provide information to professionals and media, and (5) monitor progression of crisis response.

Immediately after the diagnosis was confirmed, on July 10, a press conference was held. Various press statements emphasizing the control measures designed to prevent secondary transmission followed the press conference. The World Health Organization was notified according to the International Health Regulations by the National Focal Point, and international warnings were issued through the Early Warning and Response System and through ProMED.

MANAGEMENT OF CONTACTS

Although MARV infectivity is highest in the last stage of the disease, when severe bleeding coincides with high viral load, we considered the onset of fever (July 2) as the starting point for contact monitoring. Follow-up measures tailored to the risk group were undertaken during the 21 days after last possible exposure [14, 18, 19]. The high-risk group comprised anyone with unprotected exposure of skin or mucosa to blood or other body fluids of the index patient. It included the other three patients in the patient's room at Elkerliek and personnel who handled her specimens without protection. The low-risk contacts were LUMC and ambulance personnel who had employed the appropriate personal protective measures while caring for the patient or diagnostic samples. Persons who had been near the patient during her holiday, the return flight, and stay in the Netherlands until Elkerliek admission but who were not exposed to her body fluids during her febrile illness and personnel from reference laboratories who worked under BioSafety Level 3 conditions were categorized as casual contacts.

A total of 130 at-risk contacts were identified, 64 at high risk and 66 at low risk (Table 1). High-risk contacts were required to record their temperature 2×/day, report to the local health authorities 1×/day, and postpone any travel abroad. The low-risk contacts were asked to record their temperature 2×/day and to report to local health authorities if it was >38°C. No limits were imposed on the casual contacts.

Because asymptomatic MARV infection is rare [20, 21] and thus unlikely to play a role in spreading the infection, we restricted further clinical and laboratory evaluation to persons with a temperature >38°C, measured at 2 points 12 hr apart. Every case of fever was to be assessed on an individual basis by the response team. Three academic hospitals provided stand-by isolation facilities for admission of contacts.

Table 1. Control measures targeting contacts with risk for exposure to Marburg virus, the Netherlands, 2008.

				Measures		
Type of contact	Date of exposure, Jul	No. persons	Risk for exposure	Temperature monitoring 2×/day	Daily temperature reporting to health authorities	Asked to limit travel and to not leave the country
Household/family contacts	2–8	4	HIGH	Yes	Yes	Yes
Persons exposed in hospital ward	5–7	6	HIGH	Yes	Yes	Yes
GP of the index case-patient	5	1	HIGH	Yes	Yes	Yes
Healthcare workers, Elkerliek Hospital	7	33	HIGH	Yes	Yes	Yes
Local laboratory workers	5–7	18	High	Yes	Yes	Yes
Ambulance staff	7	2	LOW	Yes	No	No
Health care workers, LUMC	7–11	66	LOW	Yes	No	No

*GP, general practitioner; LUMC, Leiden University Medical Centre.

On August 1, the temperature monitoring of contacts ended. Fever of at least 12 hr duration or clinical signs of MHF did not develop in any of the contacts. Fever within 21 days did not develop in any of the travel companions and local guide who joined the patient in the bat cave. Because sustained fever did not develop in any of the high-risk or low-risk contacts during the surveillance period, no clinical or laboratory follow-up for MARV was needed. The online Technical Appendix (available from www.cdc.gov/EID/content/15/8/1171-Techapp.pdf) summarizes other findings during the monitoring period, dilemmas encountered with respect to travel restrictions, postexposure options in case of a high-risk accident, and laboratory diagnosis in the early stage of infection. The online Technical Appendix also describes laboratory procedures used.

SEROLOGIC FOLLOW-UP

To identify asymptomatic seroconversion, a serosurvey was undertaken of 85/130 (65%) contact persons who participated in the study. They represented 78% (50/64) of high-risk contacts and 53% (35/66) of low-risk contacts and included the Dutch visitors to the bat cave. Blood samples were collected from December, 2008 through February, 2009, 5–7 months after possible exposure. The laboratory testing was performed at the BNI in Hamburg by using an immunofluorescent antibody (IFA) assay.

The IFA slides were prepared using the MARV strain of the index patient. Details about the laboratory testing are given in the online Technical Appendix. In two initial evaluations, all but two samples were negative for antibodies against MARV. Additional screening found that all serum samples tested negative for immunoglobulin (Ig) G and IgM to MARV.

DISCUSSION

We have described the public health response to the case of MHF in a Dutch woman returning from travel abroad, who was most likely exposed to MARV by visiting a bat cave. Outbreaks caused by filoviruses constitute a serious public health threat in sub-Saharan countries and have disruptive consequences at the individual and societal level. In countries in which these viruses are not endemic, imported cases occur only sporadically and are associated with little or no secondary transmission [22]. Our patient represents a rare case of MARV infection imported to a Western country, and her case is unusual in that her only likely exposure was visiting a bat cave while traveling in Uganda. Insectivorous bats may have been the source of sporadic cases in Zimbabwe in 1975 [23] and Kenya in 1980 and 1987 [8, 9]. Furthermore, epidemiologic evidence linked a large outbreak of MHF in Durba (Democratic Republic of Congo) to a mine containing a large population of fruit-eating bats [24]. Although the source of infection in our case is not certain, circumstantial evidence points to transmission in the Python Cave. Ecological surveys to assess the presence of infected bats in that cave are ongoing (P. Rollin, personal communication).

Our case shows that unnoticed exposure to an unknown reservoir in a country with no apparent cases of MHF can lead to infection. In countries with previous cases of MHF, entry into bat caves should certainly be avoided until we know the role of bats as reservoir for MARV. The importance of MHF for western countries may be increasing, with more persons traveling to high-risk regions and incurring exposure by intrusion into unaccustomed ecological niches. Hospital staff in low-risk countries must be alert to this possibility. In most travelers returning from tropical destinations, fevers are caused by common pathogens or by malaria. However, fever together with rapid clinical deterioration and hemorrhaging in a patient returned from a suspect region should suggest viral hemorrhagic fevers, especially if exposure to a possible reservoir could have occurred.

Inclusion of MHF in the differential diagnosis of a patient triggers an immediate public health response. This response aims primarily at reducing the chance of secondary transmission by identifying contact persons at risk. Person-to-person transmission occurs in countries to which MARV is endemic [22] but only once has been reported elsewhere [23]. In this case we identified 130 contacts with possible risk. Two hospitals, two public health departments, and three laboratories were involved. We decided to trace all people who were in contact with the index patient after her fever developed and to assess their risk for exposure on a case-by-case basis. All contacts complied with temperature monitoring and daily reporting. All but two high-risk contacts postponed further travel until the theoretical incubation period of 21 days had elapsed.

In the Netherlands, statutory power to prevent a healthy person from traveling abroad is limited, but the Public Health Law is being revised, and emergency legal provisions are being considered. Despite various recommendations [14, 18, 25-27], no evidence-based, widely accepted international protocol is available to guide contact classification and monitoring in the case of MHF. Legislation on containment of dangerous pathogens [1] and measures applied to contacts differ among countries, sometimes with extreme consequences. These differences, together with privacy issues, make international exchange of information difficult. The serosurvey of the contacts of this patient confirm that no secondary transmission took place between her and any contact who provided a blood sample. Our results are consistent with those of Borchert et al. [21], who found no serologic evidence for asymptomatic or mild MARV infection in a serosurvey of household contacts.

The present case was an exceptional situation in which visiting a tourist attraction led to MHF, a disease with a high potential for overreaction. Given this potential, a rational response must be built on a thorough and evidence-based risk assessment [1]. The response in the Netherlands was low profile and did not lead to overreacting or public alarm. Its key factors were a coordinated risk assessment and contact monitoring, together with factual updates for health professionals and the public. The MHF may be more often encountered in industrialized countries in the future due to adventure travel to regions endemic for MHF.

KEYWORDS

- **Bernhard-Nocht-Institute**
- **Marburg hemorrhagic fever**
- **Marburg virus**
- **Postexposure**
- **Serosurvey**

ACKNOWLEDGMENTS

This chapter was written on behalf of the members of the national response team, which included the authors and L. Isken, W. Ransz, A. Jacobi, B. van der Walle, P. Willemse, R. Daemen, D. van Oudheusden, A. Brouwer, C. Bleeker, and T. Schmitt. We acknowledge the invaluable support from our colleagues across the world, particularly H. Feldmann, R. Swanepoel, Matthias Niedrig, Thomas Laue, John Towner, E. Leroy, E. Gavrilin, R. Andraghetti, F. Plummer, T. Geisbert, G. Nabel, C. J. Peters, and B. Graham. We thank M. van der Lubben, H. Vennema, B. Wilbrink, G. J. Godeke, B. van der Veer, M. Timmer, B. Niemeijer, C. Burghoorn-Maas, T. Mes, G. van Willigen, E. Kuijper, M. Feltkamp, J. van Pelt, and M. Wulff for their assistance; Jim van Steenbergen for critical comments on the manuscript; and Lucy Phillips for editing.

Parts of this study were supported by a grant from the Dutch Research Foundation (ZonMw).

Dr. Timen is a senior consultant in communicable disease control at the Center for Infectious Diseases of the National Institute of Public Health and the Environment, the Netherlands. Her main research interest is the public health response to outbreaks and threats.

Chapter 23

Imported Infectious Disease and Purpose of Travel, Switzerland

Lukas Fenner, Rainer Weber, Robert Steffen, and Patricia Schlagenhauf

INTRODUCTION

We evaluated the epidemiologic factors of patients seeking treatment for travel-associated illness from January 2004 through May 2005 at the University Hospital of Zurich. When comparing persons whose purpose of travel was visiting friends and relatives (VFR travelers; n = 121) with tourists and other travelers (n = 217), VFR travelers showed a distinct infectious disease and risk spectrum. The VFR travelers were more likely to receive a diagnosis of malaria (adjusted odds ratio (OR) = 2.9, 95% confidence interval (CI) 1.2–7.3) or viral hepatitis (OR = 3.1, 95% CI 1.1–9) compared with other travelers but were less likely to seek pre-travel advice (20% vs. 67%, p = 0.0001). However, proportionate rates of acute diarrhea were lower in VFR (173 vs. 364 per 1,000 ill returnees). Travel to sub-Saharan Africa contributed most to malaria in VFR travelers. In countries with large migrant populations, improved public health strategies are needed to reach VFR travelers.

More than 800 million tourist arrivals were registered worldwide in 2005, and an estimated 2% of the world's population lives outside the country of birth [1]. Importation of infectious diseases to new countries is likely to increase among both travelers and immigrants. Approximately 80 million people from resource-rich areas worldwide travel to resource-poor countries every year [2] and are exposed to many infections that are no longer prevalent in the countries where they live. The VFR travelers—predominantly immigrants and their children returning to their home countries for vacations, to maintain family ties, or to visit sick relatives—are at particularly high risk for preventable infectious diseases, such as malaria, typhoid fever, hepatitis A, hepatitis B, and tuberculosis [3-5].

A recent review of a global surveillance network's data set showed different demographic characteristics and different types of travel-related illnesses among immigrant-VFR, traveler-VFR, and tourist travelers [5]. The population of western Europe includes ≈20 million persons living in nonnative countries; most are settled immigrants. One-third were born in a country outside of Europe [6]. In Switzerland, ≈21% (1.6 million) residents are foreign born [7]. Compared with the health of the native population of Switzerland, the health status of the immigrant population is poor [8] because of the high prevalence of infectious diseases in the home countries [9], a difficult psychosocial environment in the new country, inappropriate risk-taking behavior, [10], and social inequalities [11].

The University Hospital of Zürich serves a large proportion of the city's population, which includes a multiethnic range of patients and immigrants. The outpatient departments treat ≈120,000 patients each year, and the inpatient departments treat >35,000. We evaluated the epidemiology of imported infectious disease of patients seeking treatment for travel-associated illness at the University Hospital of Zürich from January 2004 to May 2005.

PATIENTS AND METHODS

The University Hospital of Zürich, as part of the global GeoSentinel surveillance network, contributed clinician-based surveillance data during a 17-month period, January, 2004 to June, 2005, according to demographic characteristics, risk for infectious disease while traveling, and frequency of pre-travel advice. GeoSentinel is a global sentinel surveillance network that was established in 1995 through the International Society for Travel Medicine and the US Centers for Disease Control and Prevention. The network consists of 33 globally distributed member travel/tropical medicine clinics [12] and has been widely used to document travel-related illnesses [5, 13-15].

Inclusion Criteria

To be eligible, patients must have crossed an international border ≤10 years before seeking treatment and must have sought medical advice for a presumed travel-related illness. Relevant travel details focused only on data from the 6 months before the onset of illness. Only final diagnoses were considered, and >1 diagnosis per patient was possible. Data were collected according to a standardized, anonymous questionnaire. The questionnaire asked for demographic data (age, sex, country of birth, country of residence, current citizenship), travel history during the previous 5 years, inpatient or outpatient status, major clinical symptoms (>1 per patient possible), pre-travel visit information, reason for most recent travel, and patient classification. Reasons for most recent travel were immigration, tourism, business, research/education, missionary/volunteer work, visit to friends or relatives, and expatriation. Patients were classified as immigrants/refugees, foreign visitors, urban expatriates, nonurban expatriates, students, military personnel, or travelers. Working and final diagnoses were assigned by a physician.

Definitions

An immigrant/refugee was defined as a foreign-born person who had obtained permanent resident status or immigrant/refugee status in Switzerland. Traveler (or traditional traveler) was defined as a resident of Switzerland who crossed an international border and did not previously immigrate to Switzerland. When the purpose of recent travel was VFRs, a traveler was termed VFR. Different patient classifications were possible (i.e., immigrant-VFR, traveler-VFR). The rate of illness was calculated as the number of patients with a specific or a summary diagnosis as a proportion of all VFR or traditional travelers, respectively, expressed as number per 1,000 patients. The percentage of "chief complaints" was expressed as the number of primary symptoms that led to a clinic visit per total patients in each group. More than one chief complaint per patient was possible.

Countries were assigned to 1 of 15 regional classifications [13]. Because of small case numbers, a more simplified regional classification was sometimes used: sub-Saharan Africa, south-central America (South and Central America), Asia (south-central, southeast, east, and north Asia), and Eastern Europe. "All other regions" include those with no assigned travel destination. For travelers or VFR who entered >1 region, the most likely place of exposure during travel was determined to be the single region visited.

Summary diagnosis were defined as follows: "respiratory tract infection" included upper and lower respiratory infections; "malaria" infections included all malaria-causing species; "diarrhea" included acute diarrhea of parasitic, viral, bacterial, or unknown origin; "hepatitis" included chronic or acute viral hepatitis; "viral syndrome" included any nonspecific viral symptoms; and "AIDS/HIV/STI" included asymptomatic human immunodeficiency virus (HIV), acute HIV, acquired immune deficiency syndrome (AIDS), gonorrhea, syphilis, and other sexually transmitted infections (STIs). Syndrome groups such as "dermatologic disorder" were defined as previously described [15].

Statistics

Stata software (version 9.1, Stata Corporation, College Station, TX, USA) was used for statistical analysis. The OR of binary, categorical, or continuous variables were determined by logistic regression (multivariate or univariate) and adjusted to age and sex if indicated. Statistical significance of dichotomous variables was achieved by using χ^2 or nonparametric tests.

General Description and Demographic Data

We analyzed 451 patients included in the database: 181 immigrants, 227 travelers, 25 foreign visitors, and 18 others (expatriates, students, military personnel). Age range was 16–87 years (median 33, interquartile range 27–43); 48% were female, and 20% were inpatients. The median duration of travel was 17.5 days (interquartile range 13–29 days). For these patients, 671 diagnoses were counted. Leading complaints were "fever" (43.0%), "gastrointestinal" (42.7%), "head-ear-nose" (25.2%), "respiratory" (24.3%), "musculoskeletal" (12.8%), and "skin" (11.9%, data not shown). The visits were evenly distributed during the calendar year, with no seasonal abnormities or significant associations.

Comparison of VFR and Traditional Travelers

Our analysis included 217 traditional travelers and 121 VFR travelers. For traditional travelers, the reason for most recent travel was tourism or business. Most VFR travelers (86%) were in the category "immigrants." Birth country regions of VFR travelers were Asia (30%), sub-Saharan Africa (24%), Eastern Europe (17%), and Central or South America (11%). The basic demographic pattern was comparable (Table 1). The VFR travelers traveled on average for a longer period than traditional travelers, were slightly older, were more likely to have inpatient status, and were less likely to seek pre-travel advice. Traveled regions were also comparable (Table 1). Fever and gastrointestinal disorders were the most frequent reasons for seeking treatment (Table 2). Traditional travelers had more gastrointestinal symptoms (53.91% vs. 39.66%, p = 0.03). When the disease spectrums were compared, acute diarrhea was more often diagnosed in traditional travelers (26%) than in VFR travelers (11%). The summary diagnosis HIV/AIDS/STI was more commonly established in VFR travelers (9.9% vs. 4.3%); the same was true for malaria (7.7% vs. 2.7%).

Table 1. Demographic data on persons included in the study whose purpose of travel was visiting friends and relatives (VFR) versus traditional travelers (travelers), Switzerland.

	Travelers, no. (%), n = 217	VFR, no. (%), n = 121	p value
Sex			
Male	119 (54.8)	61 (50.4)	0.43
Female	98 (45.2)	60 (49.6)	
Age (y)			
Median	32	39	0.008
Interquartile range	32–46	26–45	
Patient type			
Outpatient	185 (84.5)	84 (70.6)	0.002
Inpatient	34 (15.5)	35 (29.4)	
Travel duration (d)			
Median	15	21	0.006
Interquartile range	11–24	14–31	
Sought pretravel advice?			
Yes	65 (67)	18 (20)	0.0001
No	32 (33)	70 (80)	
Traveled region			
Sub-Saharan Africa	43 (19.81)	27 (22.31)	
Asia	61 (28.11)	21 (17.35)	
Eastern Europe	6 (2.76)	21 (17.35)	
Central/South America	22 (10.13)	9 (7.43)	
All other regions	85 (39.17)	43 (35.53)	

When comparing VFR with traditional travelers, VFR travelers were more likely to receive a diagnosis of malaria, acute or chronic viral hepatitis, and HIV/AIDS/STI but less likely to receive a diagnosis of acute diarrhea. In contrast, traditional travelers were more likely to receive a diagnosis of diarrhea (OR 2.1, 95% CI 1.2–3.6, p = 0.007; data not shown). Respiratory diseases and viral syndromes were significantly associated with VFR travelers only in the univariate analysis. Traditional travelers were significantly more likely to seek pre-travel advice compared with VFR travelers (Table 1).

A different infectious disease spectrum and a trend toward a distinct pattern in both VFR and traditional travelers were also found when selecting different travel regions (Figure 1). Malaria cases were almost exclusively imported from the sub-Saharan Africa region; 33.3% of diagnoses after travel to this region were attributed to malaria in VFR travelers, compared with 12.3% in traditional travelers. In total, 27 malaria cases were recorded in the GeoSentinel database during the 17-month period: 14 in VFR travelers, eight in tourist travelers, four in recent immigrants, and one in an immigrant/refugee. Of these, 22 cases were imported from sub-Saharan Africa and one from Turkey; for four case-patients, no specified travel region or no data were stratified by VFR versus traditional traveler, the risk for malaria in sub-Saharan Africa was twice as high in the VFR traveler group than in the traditional traveler group (data not shown).

DISCUSSION

The GeoSentinel site based at the University Hospital of Zürich represents a large population in Switzerland. However, GeoSentinel is a health facility–based surveillance system and does not actively screen for certain diseases. Patients included in the database do not necessarily represent the whole population or the epidemiology or frequency of the disease. Besides the unknown number of ill returned travelers going to general practitioners or nonspecialized clinics, the number of travelers returning in good health is also unknown. Incidence rates or relative risks therefore cannot be estimated. Similarly, patients with mild or self-limiting disease are likely to see a general practitioner rather than to go to a specialized center, although many VFR travelers do not have a regular general practitioner. On the other hand, Zürich is a large city with a socioculturally mixed population that offers an opportunity to study immigrant-VFR travelers, and many of these patients may prefer to go to a more anonymous university hospital than to a general practitioner. A limitation of the study is the relatively small number of patients included in the database during the 17-month period, which made it necessary to form summary diagnoses and regions.

Table 2. Primary symptoms of persons seeking treatment at a clinic, frequent summary diagnosis, and syndrome groups in persons whose purpose of travel was visiting friends and relatives (VFR) versus traditional travelers (travelers), Switzerland.

	Travelers, no. (%)*	VFR, no. (%)*
Primary symptom		
Fever	108 (49.76)	57 (47.10)
Gastrointestinal	107 (53.91)	48 (39.99)
Head-ear-nose	54 (24.88)	38 (31.40)
Resiratory	52 (23.96)	34 (28.09)
Musculoskeletal	25 (11.52)	22 (18.18)
Skin	30 (13.82)	14 (11.57)
Fatigue	24 (11.05)	13 (10.74)
Other	18 (8.29)	16 (13.22)
Total	428	242
Summary diagnosis and syndrome groups		
Diarrhea, acute	79 (26.33)	21 (11.53)
Respiratory infection	40 (13.33)	22 (12.09)
HIV/AIDS	12 (4)	15 (8.24)
Malaria, all species	8 (2.67)	14 (7.69)

Table 2. *(Continued)*

	Travelers, no. (%)*	VFR, no. (%)*
Viral syndrome	23 (7.67)	10 (5.49)
Viral hepatitis, acute/chronic	6 (2)	10 (5.49)
Urinary tract infection	3 (1)	3 (1.65)
Febrile illness, unspecified	10 (3.33)	1 (0.55)
Dengue fever (uncomplicated)	4 (1.33)	1 (0.55)
Sexually transmitted infection	1 (0.33)	3 (1.65)
Loa loa	–	2 (1.1)
Cutaneous leishmaniasis	1 (0.33)	–
Typhoid/paratyphoid fever	1 (0.33)	1 (0.55)
Brucellosis	–	1 (0.55)
Extraintestinal amebiasis	1 (0.33)	–
Dermatologic disorder	22 (7.33)	9 (4.95)
Chronic diarrhea	7 (2.33)	5 (2.75)
Healthy	4 (1.33)	2 (1.1)
Adverse drug or vaccine reaction	3 (1)	1 (0.55)
Cardiovascular disorder	2 (0.67)	3 (1.65)
Neurologic disorder	2 (0.67)	2 (1.1)
Lost to follow-up	2 (0.67)	–
Pulmonary embolism	1 (0.33)	2 (1.1)
Psychological disorder	1 (0.33)	2 (1.1)
Death	1 (0.33)	1 (0.55)
Other diagnosis	66 (22)	51 (28.02)
Total	300	182

*Percentage expressed as number of primary symptoms that led to a clinic visit per total patients in each group.

In our analysis, VFR travelers showed a different infectious disease and risk spectrum than did traditional travelers; were more likely to receive a diagnosis of malaria, viral hepatitis, or HIV/AIDS/STI; and were less likely to seek pre-travel advice. Traditional travelers (mainly tourists) were significantly more likely to seek advice before traveling and to have a post-travel diagnosis of acute diarrhea. This is consistent with previous studies from European migrants returning to their home countries [16], as well as a recent review of the global GeoSentinel database [5]. Malaria is most likely to be acquired in the sub-Saharan Africa region, according to our data and those of others [13, 15].

By contrast, acute diarrhea was the greatest problem in traditional travelers, with an illness rate of 364 per 1,000 ill returned travelers compared with 173/1,000 in VFR travelers. Acute diarrhea, or traveler's diarrhea, is known to affect >50% of travelers, depending on the destination [17]. The protective effect in VFR travelers could reflect immunity due to recent exposure or exposure in childhood.

Acute or chronic viral hepatitis was also significantly associated with VFR travel, which correlates with a recent study of hepatitis A virus infections in Swiss travelers during a period of 12 years that identified VFR travelers as a high-risk group, especially children of immigrants [18]. Other significant associations of disease between VFR and traditional travelers were not found; however, this does not necessarily mean that no such relationship exists.

Systemic febrile illnesses, including malaria and typhoid fever, tuberculosis, and respiratory syndromes, are more frequently diagnosed among VFR travelers [5]. In our study, respiratory diseases contributed to the relatively high rate of illness in both VFR and traditional travelers (181 versus 184 per 1,000 ill returnees). No significant association could be established between influenza, long trip duration, and travel involving VFRs as described before [14], probably because of small numbers and very few cases of influenza. Viral syndrome, a rather loosely defined summary diagnosis with unspecific viral symptoms, was also frequently diagnosed and can be interpreted as a flulike syndrome. Other typical tropical infectious diseases, such as typhoid fever, leishmaniasis, dengue fever, or brucellosis, were rarely diagnosed.

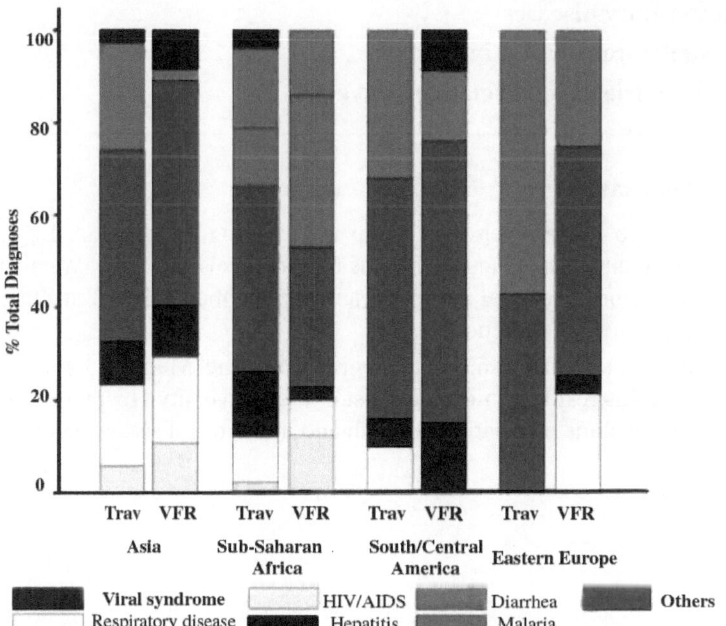

Figure 1. Percentage of disease diagnoses in travelers visiting friends and relatives (VFR) and traditional travelers (trav) who reported illnesses after returning to Switzerland, classified by geographic region visited.

This study shows that VFR travelers are at greater risk for certain infectious diseases and have a disease spectrum distinct from that of traditional travelers. Malaria is the most important, life-threatening imported disease for both nonimmune and VFR travelers, and malaria acquisition is even more likely in VFR travelers. For other infectious diseases, HIV and STIs must also be included in the differential diagnosis, particularly for VFR travelers. VFR travelers are vulnerable because they may visit more rural destinations, live under poor sanitary conditions, and stay away for longer periods [3, 4]. Moreover, the health condition of the immigrant population in Switzerland is poor compared with that of the native population [8]. Prevalence gaps in disease and disparities in access to care exist not only between countries but also between population groups within countries. In addition, VFR travelers often did not seek pre-travel advice. Thus, culturally sensitive strategies for pre-travel contact with VFR travelers are greatly needed. Further surveillance of traveler groups with denominator data is needed, and prospective studies focusing on behavioral aspects of disease prevention would allow for evidence-based interventions as part of a public health strategy.

KEYWORDS

- **Diagnosis**
- **GeoSentinel**
- **Respiratory diseases**
- **Sexually transmitted infections**
- **Visiting friends and relatives travelers**

ACKNOWLEDGMENTS

We are grateful to Elena Axelrod for help in preparing the data set, Leisa Weld for statistical consultancy, and Hanspeter Jauss for technical assistance. We also thank the GeoSentinel network, the local site at Zürich, and the medical staff at Zürich University Hospital for their cooperation.

Dr. Fenner obtained his medical degree from the Medical Faculty of Basel, Switzerland, and is resident microbiologist at the University Hospital, Basel. His research interests include international health and infectious diseases epidemiology.

Chapter 24

Malaria Risk of African Mosquito Movement by Air Travel

Andrew J. Tatem, David J. Rogers, and Simon I. Hay

INTRODUCTION

The expansion of global travel has resulted in the importation of African Anopheles mosquitoes, giving rise to cases of local malaria transmission. Here, cases of "airport malaria" are used to quantify, using a combination of global climate and air traffic volume, where and when are the greatest risks of a *Plasmodium falciparum*-carrying mosquito being imported by air. This priorities areas at risk of further airport malaria and possible importation or reemergence of the disease.

Monthly data on climate at the World's major airports were combined with air traffic information and African malaria seasonality maps to identify, month-by-month, those existing and future air routes at greatest risk of African malaria-carrying mosquito importation and temporary establishment.

The location and timing of recorded airport malaria cases proved predictable using a combination of climate and air traffic data. Extending the analysis beyond the current air network architecture enabled identification of the airports and months with greatest climatic similarity to *P. falciparum* endemic regions of Africa within their principal transmission seasons, and therefore at risk should new aviation routes become operational.

With the growth of long haul air travel from Africa, the identification of the seasonality and routes of mosquito importation is important in guiding effective aircraft disinsection and vector control. The recent and continued addition of air routes from Africa to more climatically similar regions than Europe will increase movement risks. The approach outlined here is capable of identifying when and where these risks are greatest.

Throughout history the opening of travel and trade routes between countries has been accompanied by the spread of diseases and their vectors [1, 2]. Air travel has been identified as a prime factor in the global spread of both infectious and vector-borne diseases [3, 4] and represents a longstanding concern [5]. Many recent disease vector invasions are suspected to have resulted from air travel [6-8] and, with continual rapid expansion in global air travel, the threat of future invasions should not be ignored. The public health and economic impacts of past disease vector invasions [2] are illustrated by *Aedes aegypti's* invasion of the Americas [7] and the escape of *Anopheles gambiae* to Brazil from Africa [9].

The last 30 years has seen air travel to tropical regions of the World rise dramatically. International tourist arrivals to sub-Saharan Africa (SSA) increased from 6.7

million in 1990 to over 17 million in 2000 [10]. Mosquito species, including *Aedes albopictus* and *A. gambiae s.l.,* have been shown to survive long haul flights [11-13]. For example, in one 3-week period in 1994, it was estimated that 2,000–5,000 Anopheline mosquitoes were imported into France at a rate of 8–20 Anopheline mosquitoes per flight [6]. An example of the effects of such importations are the many cases of autochthonous (locally-acquired) malaria, which are principally clustered around international airports: so called "airport malaria" [14, 15]. These occur primarily through the transport of infected Anopheles mosquitoes that can survive for long enough after arrival to transmit malaria [14]. Recent studies suggest that, where used, routine disinsection is proving effective in reducing airport malaria risk [16], although the number of countries implementing such procedures is in decline [17, 18]

Airport malaria cases are rare, with just two cases per year on average recorded (1969–99), all but one of which were *P. falciparum* malaria. However, these cases provide important evidence of sufficient traffic volumes and climatic similarity between origin and destination for the survival of malaria-carrying Anopheles mosquitoes. Here we describe an exploratory approach which makes use of this information derived from airport malaria cases to quantify, in terms of global climate and air traffic, which airports have the greatest risks of local *P. falciparum* malaria transmission through importation from SSA of infected mosquitoes. We estimate (a) the risks based on year 2000 air traffic volumes, (b) how this varies throughout the year, and (c) where the greatest potential future risks would lie through the opening of new routes.

MATERIALS AND METHODS

Data

Flight data on total passenger numbers in the year 2000 moving between the World's top 100 airports by traffic (100% aircraft capacity was assumed), were obtained from OAG Worldwide Ltd [19]. The database includes cargo flights. For full geographical coverage, the database also included data on the principal airports of 143 other countries not represented in this top 100. Data on a total of 7129 routes between 278 international airports in the year 2000 were thus available. To provide an estimate of the most likely months of malaria movement, information on the onset and end of the principal malaria transmission seasons for each African country were obtained from maps of malaria seasonality across Africa [20]. These maps were derived only for *P. falciparum* transmission by *A. gambiae s.l.*, and all results presented here refer only to this parasite and vector combination. The results may be extended to other species, but this chapter concerns itself with the most efficient vector of malaria (*A. gambiae*) and the most pathogenic of the malaria parasites (*P. falciparum*) [21, 22].

Climate Signatures

A 10 × 10 min (~18 × 18 km at the equator) spatial resolution gridded climatology was used to extract mean temperature, rainfall and humidity data for a synoptic year (1961–1990) [23], and these layers were then linearly rescaled to a common range of values by dividing through by the maximum in each layer. Climatic similarity between origin and destination airports was assumed to determine principally whether mosquitoes from originating airports would survive and have the potential to produce local malaria transmission around the destination airports. The locations of the 278 airports were superimposed onto the monthly climatology surfaces and each 10 × 10 min spatial resolution grid square covering the airport location identified. To ensure a representative climate was included, the eight land grid squares surrounding each airport square were also identified, forming a three by three grid square centered on the airport. This was not possible for coastal airports or those on small islands, where reduced numbers of land grid squares were extracted. Airports located on islands too small to be represented by the climatology surfaces were eliminated from the analysis, reducing the sample size to 259 airports. Ideally, data for these airports would have been included in the analysis, but the need to use a global climatology meant this was not possible. Data from the grid squares identified in each of the three climatology surfaces thus formed climate "signatures" for each month, for each airport.

Distance Measures, Clustering, and Dendrograms

The lack of sufficient variance in the climate data constituting the majority of signatures, and the location of many airports on small islands, dictated that only simple Euclidean distance could be used as a measure of climatic similarities between origin and destination airports [24]. Euclidean distance is defined as the shortest straight line distance between two points, in this case, the distance between the environmental signature centroids in three-dimensional climatic space, as defined by the temperature, rainfall, and humidity values. Euclidean distances between each signature centroid and the centroids of every other signature were calculated to derive separate monthly climate "dissimilarity" matrices. The climate dissimilarity matrices were then subject to hierarchical clustering using an agglomerative algorithm. The clustering results were then translated into dendrograms based on centroid linkage using Phylip v3.63 (University of Washington, USA), for each month of the year. The dendrograms are monthly climate-based phenetic trees, and represent the global air transport network remapped in terms of disease vector suitability [2, 24]. Tests using those signatures which did facilitate the use of more sophisticated distance measures (e.g., divergence, Jefferies-Matusita), revealed that the resultant dendrogram architecture was very similar to those developed using Euclidean distances (results not shown).

Climatic Similarity Thresholds

To define how similar airport climates need to be to permit the temporary survival of imported Anopheles and the possible transmission of *P. falciparum* malaria, confirmed examples of where this has occurred were used. These cases of airport malaria confirm that, at the time of year of the case, the climates in the vicinity of the origin and destination airports were similar enough for the survival of malaria-carrying Anopheles, and transmission by them at the destination. In no suspected cases of airport malaria has the origin of imported Anopheles or malaria been confirmed unambiguously, so it was assumed that the origin was the SSA airport or region most climatically similar to the destination and within its primary transmission season. This gives the most conservative estimate of the climatic range within which imported malaria transmission is possible.

Figure 1 shows incoming passenger volumes from malaria-endemic African airports for 2000, where suspected cases of airport malaria have been reported from 1969–1999 and, where details were provided, the month of European airport malaria cases. Figures 2 and 3 show that in the last 30 years the vast majority of probable airport malaria cases have occurred in the months of July and August, in the vicinity of Paris Charles De Gaulle airport, London Heathrow and Gatwick airports, and Brussels airport [6]. All routes linking these destination airports to departure airports in malaria endemic SSA countries with transmission in July and August were identified. The routes were located on the relevant climatic dendrograms and the branch height joining the most similar origin and destination airports in question noted. The height of the highest branch joining airport malaria origin to destination airport was then taken as the climatic similarity limit for temporary Anopheles survival, once imported. This provided an empirically-defined conservative climatic tolerance limit in terms of temperature, rainfall, and humidity. This limit was then applied across all dendrograms.

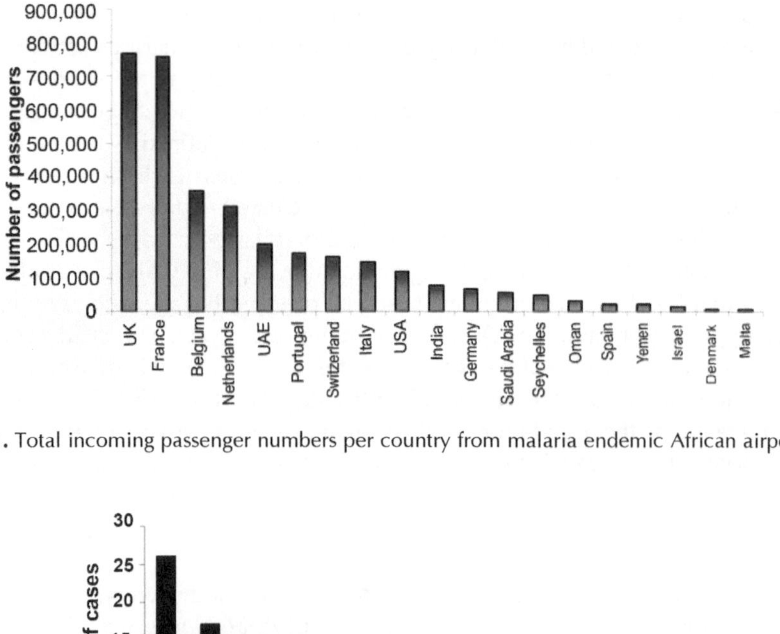

Figure 1. Total incoming passenger numbers per country from malaria endemic African airports for 2000.

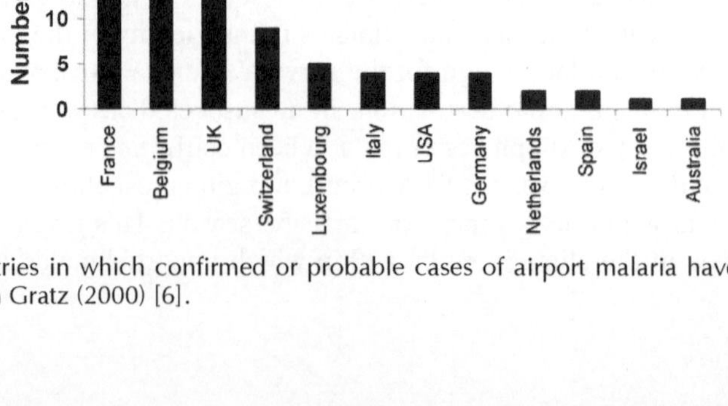

Figure 2. Countries in which confirmed or probable cases of airport malaria have been reported. Data taken from Gratz (2000) [6].

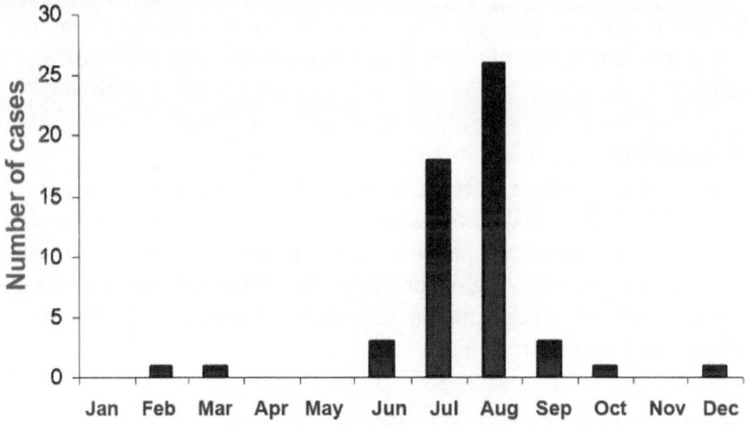

Figure 3. Month in which European airport malaria cases occurred [7, 8, 14, 25] (where date is provided).

The African airports in the database were overlaid on the malaria seasonality maps and classified as either suitable or not for transmission during each month of the year. Those non-malarious airports linked via a dendrogram branch lower than the airport malaria-defined climatic limit to a malarious airport during its transmission season were identified as being sufficiently similar climatically, based on previous airport malaria cases, for there to be a risk of infectious mosquito arrival, survival, and possible consequent local malaria transmission.

Risk Matrices

To obtain a monthly measure of malarial mosquito movement risk to those airports identified as being at risk within the dendrogram in 2000, the monthly Euclidean environmental distances and traffic data were used. The Euclidean distances between malarious airports and other airports were rescaled linearly by dividing through by the maximum Euclidean distance in the climate dissimilarity matrix, and inverted to lie between 0 and 1. Therefore, the most climatically similar airport pairs had a value close to 1 and those distinctly different, a value close to 0. Similarly, the air traffic data were also rescaled, resulting in the airports with the most direct traffic running between them in a year taking a value close to 1, while those direct routes with little or no traffic a value close to or at 0. It was assumed for this analysis that passenger numbers on each route remained consistent year-round. For each month and route between malarious and other airports, the rescaled climatic and traffic matrices were then multiplied together to provide a simple monthly measure of the likelihood of temporary malarious mosquito importation and possible consequent local transmission.

Sensitivity of Results

The results obtained are dependent upon both the accuracy of the seasonality map and the choice of dendrogram threshold. It was therefore essential to assess how sensitive these results were to small alterations in each. The approach, results, and related discussion are provided and demonstrate that the results presented remain relatively insensitive to small changes in the seasonality map and choice of dendrogram threshold.

Year 2000 Situation

Table 1 shows the top 10 air travel risk routes for malaria-carrying Anopheles invasion in operation in 2000 based on dendrogram-thresholding, combined air traffic volumes and climatic similarity between departure and destination airports. All 10 routes fly to European destinations in July, August, or September. Nineteen risk routes were identified in total, with all (n = 8) destination airports having previously reported cases of local *P. falciparum* transmission.

Table 1. Year 2000 top 10 air travel risk routes for *P. falciparum* infected *An. gambiae* invasion and subsequent autochthonous transmission.

	From		To			
Rank	**Airport**	**Country**	**Airport**	**Country**	**Month**	**Annual No. Passengers**
1	Abidjan	Cote d'Ivoire	Paris Charles de Gaulle	France	August	169,188
2	Accra	Ghana	Amsterdam Schippol	Netherlands	July	53,130
3	Entebbe/Kampala	Uganda	Brussels	Belgium	July	42,141
4	Accra	Ghana	Amsterdam Schippol	Netherlands	September	53,130
5	Abidjan	Cote d'Ivoire	Brussels	Belgium	August	58,021
6	Accra	Ghana	Rome Fiumicino	Italy	September	12,420
7	Abidjan	Cote d'Ivoire	Zurich	Switzerland	July	46,495
8	Accra	Ghana	Rome Fiumicino	Italy	September	12,420
9	Abidjan	Cote d'Ivoire	London Gatwick	United Kingdom	August	12,420
10	Cotonou	Benin	Brussels	Belgium	August	14,954

Future Risks

Examination of the monthly climate dissimilarity matrices between SSA airports within principal malaria transmission season and all other airports globally, allowed identification of the most climatically similar airports through the year. Table 2 shows the top 20 airport pairs representing the greatest risks of imported *P. falciparum*-carrying Anopheles survival, should these routes become operational in the future. Utilization of the airport malaria thresholded vector-movement dendrogram allows for the examination of the number of months per year that the climate at each airport is sufficiently similar to its nearest malarious SSA airport climatically for imported *P. falciparum*-carrying Anopheles survival. These results are shown in Figure 4. Figure 5 shows the specific month when the destination airport climate is closest to the malarious origin airport.

Table 2. Top 20 climatically closest linked destination airports with malarious-SSA airports within principal transmission season per-month.

	From		To		
Rank	**Airport**	**Country**	**Airport**	**Country**	**Month**
1	Conakri	Guinea	Bangkok	Thailand	Dec
2	Manzini	Swaziland	Brisbane	Australia	Oct
3	Conakri	Guinea	Managua	Nicaragua	Feb
4	Dar Es Salaam	Tanzania	Fort Lauderdale	USA	May
5	Maputo	Mozambique	Paramaribo	Surinam	Feb
6	Ndjamena	Chad	Santo Domingo	Dominica	Jul
7	Lusaka	Zambia	Guatemala City	Guatemala	Apr
8	Lome	Togo	St Vincent	St Vincent and the Grenadines	June
9	Dar Es Salaam	Tanzania	Miami	USA	May
10	Entebbe	Uganda	Detroit	USA	Aug
11	Accra	Ghana	Grand Cayman	Cayman Islands	May
12	Accra	Ghana	Montego Bay	Jamaica	May
13	Pointe Noire	Congo	Sal	Cape Verde	June
14	Ouagadougou	Burkina Faso	Havana	Cuba	Jul
15	Entebbe	Uganda	Nashville	USA	Sep
16	Maputo	Mozambique	Tampa	USA	Oct
17	Dar Es Salaam	Tanzania	Asuncion	Paraguay	Mar
18	Lilongwe	Malawi	Caracas	Venezuela	Apr
19	Ndjamena	Chad	Jakarta	Indonesia	Sep
20	Abidjan	Cote d'Ivoire	Miami	USA	Oct

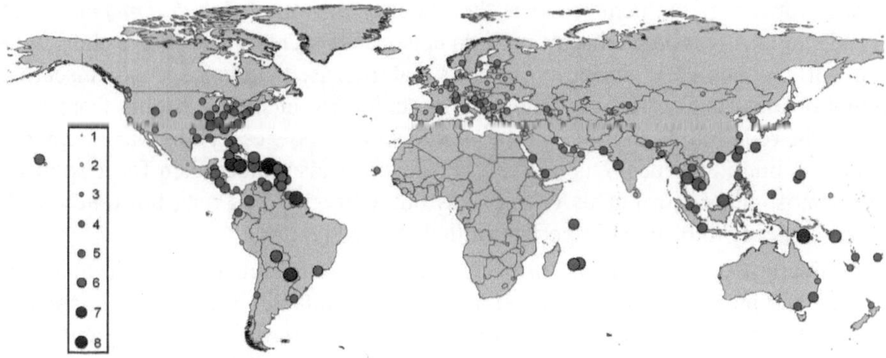

Figure 4. Number of months in a year that the climate at each international airport is sufficiently similar to that of a SSA airport within its primary malaria transmission season for imported *P. falciparum*-carrying *A. gambiae* survival.

Figure 5. Month of peak climatic similarity with climatically closest malaria-endemic SSA airport.

DISCUSSION

Year 2000 Situation

The routes identified in Table 1 as the most likely for temporary malarious mosquito invasion and possible consequent autochthonous transmission in 2000 reflect both the structure of the global air traffic network and sufficient climatic similarities between SSA and Europe in July, August, and September. There is strong correspondence between the risk routes and suspected airport malaria case location (Figure 2) and timing (Figure 3). The predominance of West African airports in Table 1 occurs because the malaria transmission season timing coincides with the European summer. Although many other airports around the World were identified as more similar climatically to malarious SSA airports than the airport malaria examples, the majority of flights originating from SSA have European destinations, with over 100,000 per annum traveling on certain routes (e.g., Abidjan to Paris, see Table 1). Figure 4 shows that European destinations may be sufficiently similar climatically to SSA airports for malarious mosquito survival only 2–4 months a year, yet because almost all air traffic is directed toward Europe, the continent receives the majority of imported *P. falciparum* cases [25] and almost all recorded airport malaria episodes (Figure 1) [6]. Such a short window of sufficient climatic similarity suggests that increased vigilance and disinsection in terms of malaria-carrying Anopheles importation by incoming flights from SSA may only be required during the summer months in Europe, especially during unusually hot and humid periods. Disinsection, however, is also undertaken for arbovirus-carrying mosquito control. This chapter has not addressed this risk, but other work suggests shipping to be most important in their spread [7, 24].

The likelihood of *P. falciparum* or *A. gambiae* establishment through air travel in Europe and many other locations remains low. Unsuitable year-round climate, enforced disinsection measures, *A. gambiaes*' intolerance of urban areas [26] and competition from local mosquitoes that are inefficient vectors of *P. falciparum* all provide barriers to establishment. However, that all destinations identified for 2000 have experienced local malaria transmission within the months shown, is evidence of the existing risks and the need to incorporate climatic information in predictions of future risks.

Although a conservative climatic similarity threshold was chosen, the fact that only 19 risk routes (of a possible 1,032) were identified for 2000, shows that the current air traffic network is restricted climatically, with almost all air traffic from SSA directed to climatically dissimilar European airports. This is perhaps one of the reasons why *A. gambiae* and *P. falciparum* malaria have escaped so few times from Africa.

Evidence of the importance of shipping traffic volume, particularly container shipping, in vector invasion has been outlined elsewhere [2, 24]. While the focus of this analysis has been on passenger flights, this includes thousands of cargo-laden flights, and in terms of cargo-only flights, database interrogation shows that these make up less than 7% of all scheduled flights. The role of passenger air traffic volume is emphasized here through comparison of Figures 1 and 2. The spatial pattern of airport malaria cases is reflected in the annual incoming passenger numbers, with the adjusted $r^2 = 0.704$ ($n = 19$, $p < 0.01$) between the two. The fact that France has received more suspected cases of airport malaria than the UK, despite similar incoming passenger volumes from endemic airports, can be attributed to more routes linking it to West Africa, where transmission season and European summer timings match, though other factors, such as differences in surveillance systems, may play a part. Given that air traffic volumes generally peak in the northern hemisphere summer months, it should be additionally noted that the year round constant traffic volumes assumed here could produce an underestimation of risk levels.

Future Risks

The results show that many airports in regions outside of Europe are climatically more favorable than is Europe for Anopheles survival, and for many more months of the year. The effects of opening up new routes from malaria-endemic SSA countries to non-European destinations could therefore have potentially serious consequences. The accidental introduction of *A. gambiae* into Brazil in 1930, resulted in over 16,000 malaria deaths and a mosquito control program that cost 3 billion USD equivalent today [9, 27]. Recently, new routes have been opening, with long-haul flights from SSA direct to Washington, Beijing, Hong Kong, and Bangkok among others. With more routes planned, and larger planes capable of traveling greater distances in shorter times scheduled, the risk of another *A. gambiae* escape grows [28]. While recent evidence points to the effectiveness of routine aircraft cabin disinsection in flights to the UK from SSA [16], elsewhere in the World disinsection is in decline. The World Health Organization continues to recommend aircraft disinsection [29], but fears over the health effects of the pyrethroid insecticides used [30] and resultant law suits [31] have led to many airlines and governments ceasing the practice [17, 18].

The destinations in Table 2 with climates matched almost perfectly for the month in question to SSA airports home to *P. falciparum* infected Anopheles are all in malarious regions, or those declared malaria-free only recently [32, 33]. Should regular flights commence on any of those routes identified in Table 2, the potential for temporary *A. gambiae* invasion and consequent *P. falciparum* transmission in those months may be considerable. Though many in Table 2 appear to be unlikely routes in the near future, just outside the top 20 are routes of potential future operation or routes which have recently opened (e.g., Addis Ababa to Washington, Dakar to New York). A route for almost every month of the year is identified in the top 20 alone, highlighting that should SSA become better connected by air, a year-round linkage with climatically similar airports would exist, potentially facilitating the escape of *A. gambiae* from SSA. Moreover, the opening of flight routes from south-east Asia to SSA may also speed up the global movement of drug resistant malaria (in humans or mosquitoes) and insecticide resistant mosquitoes [34, 35].

Figure 4 shows, as expected, that the climatic regimes of the airports in the tropical regions of the Americas and south-east Asia are more similar to those of malaria-endemic SSA airports than are the latter to those of most European airports. This is especially true of the airports in Central America and the Caribbean which have the closest match of all airports globally, and for the longest period. This explains the predominance of Caribbean and Central American destination airports in Table 2.

Unsurprisingly the periods of greatest similarity of higher latitude climates to those of SSA airports are the summer months of May–September in the northern hemisphere and November–February in the southern hemisphere (Figure 5); it is, therefore, during these months that airport malaria in these regions is most likely. The equivalent periods of similarity for tropical latitudes are much more variable, with little apparent spatial coherency in peak month. Evidence of this can be seen in Table 2, which includes two routes to Miami, USA, one from Dar Es Salaam in East Africa in May, the other from Abidjan in West Africa in October. In the past, high risk locations and months for temporary Anopheles invasion leading to local transmission have been predictably along specific routes to certain European airports, and solely in the summer months. Figure 5 shows that should routes between *P. falciparum*-endemic SSA countries and other tropical locations continue to open up, the risks, origin, and timing of Anopheles invasion will be much less predictable.

CONCLUSION

The continued occurrence of airport malaria cases and rise in imported *P. falciparum* malaria cases [15, 25] are indicative of an expanding global air transport network and increased travel to malarious countries [36]. It also reflects a decline in aircraft disinsection [17, 18]. The approach presented highlights routes and months within the current global air transport network at risk of importation and temporary establishment of *P. falciparum*-carrying mosquitoes. The development of new air travel routes from SSA suggests that the relative risks identified will continue to increase and that monitoring schemes based on climate suitability methods could be used to optimize Anopheles-specific disinsection and control efforts. The analysis presented here is a first step, and future challenges to refine the predictions will involve incorporating information on temporal variations in passenger numbers, flight stopover risks, intra-species competition, human populations at risk, breeding site availability, possible climate change [37], disinsection and land transport, and quantifying the relative importance of sea and air transport for vectors and diseases.

KEYWORDS

- **Airport malaria cases**
- ***Anopheles gambiae***
- **Dendrograms**
- ***Plasmodium falciparum***
- **Vector-borne diseases**

AUTHORS' CONTRIBUTIONS

Andrew J. Tatem conceived, designed, and implemented the research and wrote the chapter. David J. Rogers provided methodological and editorial input. Simon I. Hay helped conceive the research and aided in the chapter writing and editing. All authors have read and approved the final manuscript.

ACKNOWLEDGMENTS

We thank Abdisalan Noor, Sarah Randolph, Robert Snow, and Briony Tatem for comments on earlier drafts of the manuscript. Andrew J. Tatem and Simon I. Hay are funded by a Research Career Development Fellowship (to Simon I. Hay) from the Wellcome Trust (#069045).

Permissions

Chapter 1: Prevalence Study of *Legionella* Spp. Contamination of Cruise Ships was originally published as "Prevalence study of *Legionella* spp. contamination in ferries and cruise ships" in *BioMed Central 4:18, 2006*. Reprinted with permission under the Creative Commons Attribution License or equivalent.

Chapter 2: Risk of Malaria for Travelers with Stable Malaria Transmission was originally published as "Modeling the risk of malaria for travelers to areas with stable malaria transmission" in *BioMed Central 12:16, 2009*. Reprinted with permission under the Creative Commons Attribution License or equivalent.

Chapter 3: Alcohol Problems in Party Package Travel was originally published as "Party package travel: alcohol use and related problems in a holiday resort: a mixed methods study" in *BioMed Central 10:7, 2008*. Reprinted with permission under the Creative Commons Attribution License or equivalent.

Chapter 4: Cumulative Incidence of Novel Influenza A/H1N1 in Foreign Travelers was originally published as "Use of Cumulative Incidence of Novel Influenza A/H1N1 in Foreign Travelers to Estimate Lower Bounds on Cumulative Incidence in Mexico" in *PLoS ONE 9:9, 2009*. Reprinted with permission under the Creative Commons Attribution License or equivalent.

Chapter 5: Health, Parks, Recreation, and Tourism was originally published as "Research roundtable on health, parks, recreation, and tourism" in *Klenosky, David B.; Fisher, Cherie LeBlanc, eds. Proceedings of the 2008 Northeastern Recreation Research Symposium; 2008 March 30 - April 1; Bolton Landing, NY. Gen. Tech. Rep. NRS-P-42. Newtown Square, PA: U.S. Department of Agriculture, Forest Service, Northern Research Station: 53-58*. Reprinted with permission under the Creative Commons Attribution License or equivalent.

Chapter 6: Eco-medical Tourism was originally published as "Eco-medical tourism: can it be sustainable" in *Klenosky, David B.; Fisher, Cherie LeBlanc, eds. Proceedings of the 2008 Northeastern Recreation Research Symposium; 2008 March 30 - April 1; Bolton Landing, NY. Gen. Tech. Rep. NRS-P-42. Newtown Square, PA: U.S. Department of Agriculture, Forest Service, Northern Research Station: 158-164*. Reprinted with permission under the Creative Commons Attribution License or equivalent.

Chapter 7: Walking Benefits of C&O Canal National Historical Park was originally published as ""Increasing walking at the C&O Canal National Historical Park: an intervention focused on local employees in *Klenosky, David B.; Fisher, Cherie LeBlanc, eds. Proceedings of the 2008 Northeastern Recreation Research Symposium; 2008 March 30 - April 1; Bolton Landing, NY. Gen. Tech. Rep. NRS-P-42. Newtown Square, PA: U.S. Department of Agriculture, Forest Service, Northern Research Station: 44-52*. Reprinted with permission under the Creative Commons Attribution License or equivalent.

Chapter 8: Travel Patterns and Imported *Plasmodium falciparum* Rates Among Zanzibar Residents was originally published as "The use of mobile phone data for the estimation of the travel patterns and imported *Plasmodium falciparum* rates among Zanzibar residents" in *BioMed Central 12:10, 2009*. Reprinted with permission under the Creative Commons Attribution License or equivalent.

Chapter 9: Neglected Tropical Diseases of the Caribbean was originally published as "Holidays in the Sun and the Caribbean's Forgotten Burden of Neglected Tropical Diseases" in *PLoS Neglected Tropical Disease, 5:28, 2008*. Reprinted with permission under the Creative Commons Attribution License or equivalent.

Chapter 10: Small Islands and Pandemic Influenza was originally published as "Small islands and pandemic influenza: Potential benefits and limitations of travel volume reduction as a border control measure" in *BioMed Central 9:29, 2009*. Reprinted with permission under the Creative Commons Attribution License or equivalent.

Chapter 11: Filariasis in Travelers and GeoSentinel Surveillance Network was originally published as "Filariasis in Travelers Presenting to the GeoSentinel Surveillance Network" in *PLoS Neglected Tropical Disease, 12:26, 2007*. Reprinted with permission under the Creative Commons Attribution License or equivalent.

Chapter 12: Travel Restrictions for Moderately Contagious Diseases was originally published as "The effect of travel restrictions on the spread of a moderately contagious disease" in *BioMed Central 12:14, 2006*. Reprinted with permission under the Creative Commons Attribution License or equivalent.

Chapter 13: New *Salmonella enteritidis* Phage Types in Europe was originally published as "Emergence of new *Salmonella* Enteritidis phage types in Europe? Surveillance of infections in returning travellers" in *BioMed Central 9:2, 2004*. Reprinted with permission under the Creative Commons Attribution License or equivalent.

Chapter 14: HIV-related Restrictions on Entry in the WHO European Region was originally published as "HIV-related restrictions on entry, residence and stay in the WHO European Region: a survey" in *Lazarus et al. Journal of the International AIDS Society 2010, 13:2*. Reprinted with permission under the Creative Commons Attribution License or equivalent.

Chapter 15: Seasonal Impact on Orthopedic Health Services in Switzerland was originally published as "Seasonal variation in orthopedic health services utilization in Switzerland: The impact of winter sport tourism" in *BioMed Central 3:3, 2006*. Reprinted with permission under the Creative Commons Attribution License or equivalent.

Chapter 16: Risk of Malaria in Travelers to Latin America was originally published as "The low and declining risk of malaria in travellers to Latin America: is there still an indication for chemoprophylaxis?" in *BioMed Central 8:23, 2007*. Reprinted with permission under the Creative Commons Attribution License or equivalent.

Chapter 17: Tourism Implications of *Cryptococcus gattii* in the Southeastern USA was originally published as "First Reported Case of *Cryptococcus gattii* in the Southeastern USA: Implications for Travel-Associated Acquisition of an Emerging Pathogen" in *PloS ONE 4:22, 2009*. Reprinted with permission under the Creative Commons Attribution License or equivalent.

Chapter 18: Risk Areas for *Cryptococcus gattii*, Vancouver Island, Canada was originally published as "Tourism and Specific Risk Areas for *Cryptococcus gattii*, Vancouver Island, Canada" in *Emerging Infectious Diseases, 2008 November; 14(11): 1781–1783. doi: 10.3201/eid1411.080532* . Reprinted with permission under the Creative Commons Attribution License or equivalent.

Chapter 19: Dogs as Carriers of Canine Vector-borne Pathogens was originally published as "Imported and travelling dogs as carriers of canine vector-borne pathogens in Germany" in *BioMed Central 4:8, 2010*. Reprinted with permission under the Creative Commons Attribution License or equivalent.

Chapter 20: Healthcare Services in Mediterranean Resort Regions was originally published as "Estimation of the real population and its impact on the utilization of healthcare services in Mediterranean resort regions: an ecological study" in *BioMed Central 1:31, 2007*. Reprinted with permission under the Creative Commons Attribution License or equivalent.

Chapter 21: Backpacking Holidays and Alcohol, Tobacco, and Drug Use was originally published as "Effects of backpacking holidays in Australia on alcohol, tobacco and drug use of UK residents" in *BioMed Central 1:2, 2007*. Reprinted with permission under the Creative Commons Attribution License or equivalent.

Chapter 22: Imported Case of Marburg Hemorrhagic Fever, in the Netherlands was originally published as "Response to Imported Case of Marburg Hemorrhagic Fever, the Netherlands" in *Emerging*

Infectious Diseases, 2009 August; 15(8): 1171–1175. doi: 10.3201/eid1508.090051. Reprinted with permission under the Creative Commons Attribution License or equivalent.

Chapter 23: Imported Infectious Disease and Purpose of Travel, Switzerland was originally published as "Imported Infectious Disease and Purpose of Travel, Switzerland" in *Emerging Infectious Diseases, 2007 February;13(2): 217–222. doi: 10.3201/eid1302.060847*. Reprinted with permission under the Creative Commons Attribution License or equivalent.

Chapter 24: Malaria Risk of African Mosquito Movement by Air Travel was originally published as "Estimating the malaria risk of African mosquito movement by air travel" in *BioMed Central 7:14, 2006*. Reprinted with permission under the Creative Commons Attribution License or equivalent.

References

1

1. Gianvenuti A: Verso uno sviluppo sostenibile: il turismo sostenibile, strumento di sviluppo economico e di protezione ambientale. Retrieved from [http://www.runiceurope.org/italian/indicesito/docs_contr.html]
2. World Tourism Organization. Retrieved from [http://www.world-tourism.org/]
3. Fields, B. S., Benson, R. F., and Besser, R. E. (2002). *Legionella* and Legionnaires' disease: 25 years of investigation. *Clin. Microbiol. Rev.* **15**(3), 506–526.
4. Breimen, R. F. and Butler, J. C. (1998). Legionnaires' Disease: Clinical, epidemiological, and public health perspectives. *Semin. Respir. Infect.* **13**(2), 84–89.
5. Woo, A. H., Goetz, A., and Yu, V. L. (1992). Transmission of Legionella by respiratory equipment and aerosol generating devices. *Chest* **102**, 1586–1590.
6. Mattana, A., Biancu, G., Alberti, L., Accardo, A., Delogu, G., Fiori, P. L., Cappuccinelli, P. (2004). *In vitro* evaluation of the effectiveness of the macrolide rokitamycin and chlorpromazine against Acanthamoeba castellanii. *Antimicrob. Agents Chemother.* **48**(12), 4520–4527.
7. Patterson, W. J., Hay, J., Seal, D. V., McLuckie, J. C. (1997). Colonization of transplant unit water supplies with *Legionella* and protozoa: Precautions required to reduce the risk of Legionellosis. *J. Hosp. Infect.* **37**, 7–17.
8. EWGLI: European guidelines for control and prevention of travel associated Legionnaires' disease. [http://www.ewgli.org/guidelinedownload].
9. Gazzetta Ufficiale n. 103 del 5 maggio 2000: Linee guida per la prevenzione e il controllo della Legionellosi. Retrieved from [http://www.guritel.it/free-sum/ARTI/2000/05/05/sommario.html]
10. Gazzetta Ufficiale n. 28 del 4 febbraio 2005: Linee guida recanti indicazioni sulla Legionellosi per i gestori di strutture turistico-recettive e termali. Retrieved from [http://www.guritel.it/free-sum/ARTI/2005/02/04/sommario.html]
11. Gazzetta Ufficiale n. 29 del 5 febbraio 2005: Linee guida recanti indicazioni ai laboratori con attività di diagnosi microbiologica e controllo ambientale della Legionellosi. Retrieved from [http://www.guritel.it/free-sum/ARTI/2005/02/05/sommario.html]
12. Ricketts, K. and Joseph, C. (2004). European Working Group for *Legionella* Infections: Travel Associated Legionnaires' disease in Europe: 2003. *Euro. Surveill* **9**(10):40–43.
13. Cayla, J. A., Maldonado, R., Gonzales, J., Pellicer, T., Ferrer, D., Pelaz, C., Gracia, J., Baladron, B., and Plasencia, A. (2001). Legionellosis study group: A small outbreak of Legionnaire's disease in a cargo ship under repair. *Eur. Resp. Jun.* **17**(6), 1322–1327.
14. Jernigan, D. B., Hofmann, J., Cetron, M. S., Genese, C. C., Nuorti, J. P., Fields, B. S., Benson, R. F., Carter, R. J., Edelstein, P. H., Guerrero, I. C., Paul, S. M., Lipman, H. B., and Breiman, R. (1996). Outbreak of Legionnaire's disease among cruise ship passengers exposed to a contaminated whirlpool spa. *Lancet* **347**, 494–499.
15. Regan, C. M., McCann, B., Syed, Q., Christie, P., Joseph, C., Colligan, J., and McGaffin, A. (2003). Outbreak of Legionnaires' disease on a cruise ship: Lessons for international surveillance and control. Liverpool Health Authority. *Commun. Dis. Pub. Health* **6**(2), 152–156.
16. Doleans, A., Aurell, H., Reyrolle, M., Lina, G., Freney, J., Vandenesch, F., Etienne, J., and Jarraud, S. (2004). Clinical and environmental distributions of *Legionella* strains in France are different. *J. Clin. Microbiol.* **42**(1), 458–60.
17. World Health Organization: Sanitation on ships. Compendium of outbreaks of foodborne and waterborne disease and Legionnaires' diseases associated with ships (1970–2000). Retrieved from [http://www.

who.int/entity/water_sanitation_health/hygiene/ships/en/shipsancomp.pdf].

2

1. WHO. Retrieved from [http://www.who.int/ith/countries/bra/en/]
2. WHO. Retrieved from [http://www.who.int/malaria/wmr2008/malaria.pdf]
3. Ladislaw, J. L. B. (2006). Situação da Malária na Amazônia Legal. Ministério da Saúde. Secretaria de Vigilância em Saúde.
4. Ecobrasil (2008). Retrieved from [http://www.ecobrasil.org.br].
5. Embratur (2006). Retrieved from [http://www.ecoviagem.com.br/].
6. Behrens, R. H., Bisoffi, Z., Björkman, A., Gascon, J., Hatz, C., Jelinek, T., Legros, F., and Mühlberger, N. (2006). TropNetEurop, Voltersvik P: Malaria prophylaxis policy for travellers from Europe to the Indian Sub Continent. *Malaria J.* **5**, 7.
7. Massad, E., Ma, S., Burattini, M. N., Tun, Y., Coutinho, F. A., and Ang, L. W. (2008). The risk of chikungunya fever in a dengue-endemic area. *J. Travel Med.* **15**(3), 147–55.
8. Burattini, M. N., Chen, M., Chow, A., Coutinho, F. A., Goh, K. T., Lopez, L. F., Ma, S., and Massad, E. (2008). Modelling the control strategies against dengue in Singapore. *Epidemiol. Infect.* **136**(3), 309–319.
9. Forattini, O. P., Kakitani, I., Massad, E., and Marucci, D. (1993). Studies on mosquitoes (Diptera:Culicidae) and anthropic environment 4- Survey of resisting adults and synanthropic behaviour in South-Eastern Brazil. *Revista de Saúde Pública* **27**, 398–411.
10. Tadei, W. (1997). Entomologia da malária em áreas de colonização da Amazônia. Chapter 4. *MCT, pPD-Programa de Pesquisa Dirigida*, pp. 157–168.
11. Taylor, J. R. (2001). Introduction to Error Analysis: *The Study of Uncertainties in Physical Measurements*. 2nd edition. University Science Books, Mill Valley, 126.
12. PAHO. Retrieved from [http://www.paho.org/English/AD/DPC/CD/mal-day-08.htm]
13. Askling, H. H., Nilsson, J., Tegnell, A., Janzon, R., and Ekdahl, K. (2005). Malaria Risk in Travelers. *Emerg. Infect. Dis.* **11**, 463–441.
14. Tada, Y., Okabe, N., and Kimura, M. (2008). Travelers' risk of malaria by destination country: A study from Japan. *Travel Med. Infect. Dis.*, **6**, 368–372.
15. House, H. R. and Ehlers, J. P. (2008). Travel-Related Infections. *Emerg. Med. Clin. North Am.* **26**, 499–516.
16. Massad, E., Coutinho, F. A., Burattini, M. N., Lopez, L. F. (2001). The risk of yellow fever in a dengue-infested area. *Trans. R. Soc. Trop. Med. Hyg.* **95**, 370–374.
17. Massad, E., Burattini, M. N., Coutinho, F. A., and Lopez, L. F. (2003). Dengue and the risk of urban yellow fever reintroduction in São Paulo State, Brazil. *Rev. Saude Publica.* **37**, 477–484.
18. Massad, E., Coutinho, F. A., Burattini, M. N., Lopez, L. F., and Struchiner, C. J. (2005). Yellow fever vaccination: How much is enough? *Vaccine* **23**, 3908–3914.
19. Wyse, A. P. P. (2007). Controle ótimo do vetor da malária para o modelo matemático sazonal. *PhD thesis*. Laboratório Nacional de Computação Científica, Brazil.
20. Okell, L. C., Drakeley, C. J., Bousema, T., Whitty, C. J. M., and Ghani, A. C. (2008). Modelling the Impact of Artemisinin Combination Therapy and Long-Acting Treatments on Malaria Transmission Intensity. *PloS Med.* e226.
21. Chen, L. H., Wilson, M. E., and Schlagenhauf, P. (2006). Prevention of malaria in long-term travelers. *JAMA* **296**, 2234–2244.
22. Behrens, R. H., Carroll, B., Beran, J., Bouchaud, O., Hellgren, U., Hatz. C., Jelinek, T., Legros, F., Mühlberger, N., Myrvang, B., Siikamäki, H., and Visser, L. (2007). The low and declining risk of malaria in travellers to Latin America: is there still an indication for chemoprophylaxis? *Malaria J* **6**, 114.
23. Macdonald, G. (1952). The analysis of equilibrium in malaria. *Trop. Dis. Bull.* **49**, 813–828.
24. Santos, R. L. C., Forattini, O. P., and Burattini, M. N. (2002). Laboratory and field observations on duration of gonotrophic cycle of Anopheles albitarsis s.l. (Diptera:

Culicidae) in southeastern Brazil. *J. Med. Entomol* **39**(6), 926–930.

25. Molineaux, L. and Gramiccia, G. (1980). *The Garki Project: Research on the Epidemiology and Control of Malaria in the Sudan Savanna of West Africa*. World Health Organization. Geneva.
26. IBGE (2007). Retrieved from [http://www.ibge.gov.br/english/estatistica/populacao/contagem2007/default.shtm].
27. Molineaux, L. (1988). The Epidemiology of Human Malaria as an Explanation of its Distribution, Including Some Implications for its Control. In *Malaria: Principles and Practice of Malariology*. Chapter 35. W. H. Wernsdorfer, and I. McGregor (Eds.). Churchill Livingstone. Edinburgh, pp. 913–998.
28. Burattini, M. N., Massad, E., Coutinho, F. A. B. (1993). Malaria transmission rates estimated from serological data. *Epidemiol. Infec.* **111**, 503–523.
29. Noronha, E., Alecrim, M. D. G. C., Romero, G. A. S., and Macedo, V. (2000). Clinical study of *falciparum* malaria in children in Manaus, AM, Brazil. *Rev. Soc. Bras. Med. Trop.* **33**(2), 185–190.
30. Santos, R. L. C., Forattini, O. P., Burattini, M. N. (2004). Anopheles albitarsis s.l. (Diptera: Culicidae) survivorship and density in a rice irrigation area of the State of São Paulo, Brazil. *J. Med. Entomol.* **41**(5), 997–1000.

3

1. Hughes, K., Bellis, M., McVeigh, J., and Thomson, R. (2004). A potent cocktail. *Nurs. Stand.* **18**(47), 14–16.
2. Bellis, M. A., Hughes, K., McVeigh, J., Thomson, R., and Luke, C. (2005). Effects of nightlife activity on health. *Nurs. Stand.* **19**(30), 63–71.
3. Dunn, M. S., Bartee, R. T., and Perko, M. A. (2003). Self-reported alcohol use and sexual behaviors of adolescents. *Psychol. Rep.* **92**(1), 339–348.
4. Josiam, B. M., Hobson, J. S. P., Dietrich, U. C., and Smeaton, G. L.: An analysis of the sexual, alcohol and drug related behavioural patterns of students on spring break. *Tour. Manag.* **19**(6), 501–513.
5. Grant, B. F., Stinson, F. S., and Harford, T. C.: Age at onset of alcohol use and DSM-IV alcohol abuse and dependence: A 12-year follow-up. *J. Subs. Abuse* **13**, 493–504.
6. Järvinen, M. and Demant, J. (2006). Constructing Maturity through Alcohol Practice. *Addict. Res. Theo.* **15**(6), 589–602.
7. Bellis, M. A., Hughes, K., and Lowey, H.: Healthy nightclubs and recreational substance use. From a harm minimisation to a healthy settings approach. *Addict. Behav.* **27**(6), 1025–1035.
8. Smeaton, G. L., Josiam, B. M., and Dietrich, U. C. (1998). College students' binge drinking at a beach-front destination during spring break. *J. Am. Coll. Health* **46**(6), 247–254.
9. Segev, L., Paz, A., and Potasman, I. (2005). Drug abuse in travelers to southeast Asia: An on-site study. *J. Travel Med.* **12**(4), 205–209.
10. Bellis, M. A., Hughes, K., Bennett, A., and Thomson, R. (2003). The role of an international nightlife resort in the proliferation of recreational drugs. *Addiction* **98**(12), 1713–1721.
11. Bellis, M. A., Hughes, K. E., Dillon, P., Copeland, J., and Gates, P. (2007). Effects of backpacking holidays in Australia on alcohol, tobacco and drug use of UK residents. BMC *Pub. Health* **7**, 1.
12. Tutenges, S. and Hesse, M. (2008). Patterns of binge drinking at an international nightlife resort. *Alcohol Alcohol*, **43**(5), 595-–599.
13. Goodyear, M. D., Krleza-Jeric, K., and Lemmens, T. (2007). The Declaration of Helsinki. *Brit. Med. J.* **335**(7621), 624–625.
14. Maffesoli, M. and de Dionysos L'Ombre (1982). Contribution à une sociologie de l'orgie. Le Livre de Poche, Paris.
15. Jørgensen, M. J., Curtis, T., Christensen, P. H., and Grønbæk, M. (2007). Harm minimization among teenage drinkers: findings from an ethnographic study on teenage alcohol use in a rural Danish community. *Addiction* **102**(4), 554–559.

4

1. Ghani, A. C., Donnelly, C. A., Cox, D. R., Griffin, J. T., Fraser, C., et al. (2005). Methods for estimating the case fatality ratio for a novel, emerging infectious disease. *Am. J. Epidemiol.* **162**, 479–486.
2. Mexico Ministry of Tourism (2006). *Turismo de Internacion, 2001–2005.* 12 p.
3. Halloran, M. E., Ferguson, N. M., Eubank, S., Longini, I. M. Jr., Cummings, D. A., et al. (2008). Modeling targeted layered containment of an influenza pandemic in the United States. *Proc. Natl. Acad. Sci. U.S.A.* **105**, 4639–4644.
4. Direccion General Adjunta de Epidemiologia; Ministerio de Salud de Mexico (2009). Brote de Influenza Humana A H1N1 Mexico; Boletin Diario No. 14, 09/05/09.
5. Brundage, J. F. and Shanks, G. D. (2008). Deaths from bacterial pneumonia during 1918–19 influenza pandemic. *Emerg. Infect. Dis.* **14**, 1193–1199.
6. Anderson, R. M., Fraser, C., Ghani, A. C., Donnelly, C. A., Riley, S., et al. (2004). Epidemiology, transmission dynamics and control of SARS: The 2002–2003 epidemic. *Philos. Trans. R. Soc. Lond. B. Biol. Sci.* **359**, 1091–1105.
7. Kuri-Morales, P., Galvan, F., Cravioto, P., Zarraga Rosas, L., and Tapia-Conyer, R. (2006). Mortalidad en México por influenza y neumonía (1990–2005). *Salud Publica Mex* **48**, 379–384.
8. Thompson, W. W., Shay, D. K., Weintraub, E., Brammer, L., Cox, N., et al. (2003). Mortality associated with influenza and respiratory syncytial virus in the United States. *JAMA* **289**, 179–186.
9. Moser, M. R., Bender, T. R., Margolis, H. S., Noble, G. R., Kendal, A. P., et al. (1979). An outbreak of influenza aboard a commercial airliner. *Am. J. Epidemiol.* **110**, 1–6.
10. Surveillance Group for New Influenza A(H1N1) Virus Investigation and Control in Spain (2009). New influenza A(H1N1) virus infections in Spain, April–May 2009. *Eurosurveillance*. **14**, 1–4.
11. Fraser, C., Donnelly, C. A., Cauchemez, S., Hanage, W. P., Van Kerkhove, M. D., et al. (2009). Pandemic potential of a strain of influenza A(H1N1): Early findings. *Science* **324**, 1557–61.
12. Ypartnership/Yankelovich, I. (2008). National Leisure Travel Monitor.
13. Lessler, J., Reich, N. G., Brookmeyer, R., Perl, T. M., Nelson, K. E., Cummings, D. A. (2009). Incubation periods of acute respiratory viral infections: A systematic review. *Lancet Infect. Dis.* **9**, 291–300.

5

1. Memorandum of Understanding (MOU). (2002). Department of Health and Human Services, Department of Agriculture, Department of the Interior, Department of the Army. Accessed May 1, 2008, Retrieved from [http://www.cdc.gov/nccdphp/dnpa/physical/health_professionals/active_environments/mou.htm].
2. NRPA (2008). Parks for Physical Activity Research Consortium, PPARC. Information accessed May 15, 2008, Retrieved from [http://www.nrpa.org/content/default.aspx?documentId=6143].
3. Olmsted, F. L. (1968). The value and care of parks. Reprinted in R. Nash, (Ed.). *The American Environment: Readings in the history of conservation.* Reading, MA; Addison-Wesley, pp. 18–24.
4. Ulrich, R. S., Simons, R. F., Losito, B. D., Fiorito, E., Miles, M. A., and Zelson, M. (1991). Stress recovery during exposure to natural and urban environments. *J. Environ. Psychol.* **11**, 201–230.
5. Faber Taylor, A., Kuo, F. E., and Sullivan, W. C. (2001). Coping with ADD: The surprising connection to green play settings. *Environ. Behav.* **33**(1), 54–77.
6. Kuo, F. E. and Faber Taylor, A. (2004). A potential natural treatment for Attention-Deficit/Hyperactivity Disorder: Evidence from a national study. *Am. J. Pub. Health* **94**(9), 1580–1586.
7. Kaplan, S. (1995). The restorative benefits of nature: Toward an integrative framework. *J. Environ. Psychol.* **15**, 169–182.
8. Aitken, S. C. (1991). A transactional geography of the image-event: The films of Scottish director, Bill Forsyth. *Trans., Inst. Brit. Geog.* **16**, 105–118.

9. Kaplan, S. and Kaplan, R. (1989). *The experience of nature: A psychological perspective*. Cambridge University Press, New York.
10. Nasar, J. L. (Ed.). (1992). Environmental Aesthetics: Theory, Research, & Applications. Cambridge University Press, Cambridge.
11. Stewart, W. P. and Hull, R. B. (1992). Satisfaction of what? Post hoc versus real-time construct validity. *Leis. Sci.* **14**(3), 195–209.
12. Sheppard, S. R. J. and Harshaw, H. W. (Eds.) (2001). Forests and Landscapes: Linking Ecology, Sustainability, and Aesthetics. IUFRO Research Series, No. 6. CABI Publishing Wallingford, UK.
13. Havitz, M. E. and Mannell, R. C. (2005). Enduring involvement, situational involvement, and flow in leisure and non-leisure activities. *J. Leis. Res.* **37**(2), 152–177.
14. Jarman, J. W. (2005). Political affiliation and presidential debates: A real-time analysis of the effect of the arguments used in the presidential debates. *Am. Behav. Sci.* **49**(2), 229–242.
15. Pierskalla, C. D., Siniscalchi, J. M., Hammitt, W. E., Smaldone, D. A., and Storck, S. J. (2007). Identifying predictors for quality and quantity restorative character of wilderness: using events as an analysis unit. In R. Burns and K. Robinson (comps.) (Ed.). Proceedings of the 2006 Northeastern Recreation Research Symposium, 2006 April 9–11, Bolton Landing, NY. Gen. Tech. Rep. NRS-P-14. Newtown Square, PA: USDA Forest Service, Northern Research Station, pp. 497–508.
16. Laumann, K., Gärling, T., and Stormark, K. M. (2001). Rating scale measures of restorative components of environments. *J. Environ. Psychol.* **21**, 31–44.
17. Herzog, T. R., Maguire, C. P., and Nebel, M. B. (2003). Assessing the restorative components of environments. *J. Environ. Psychol.* **23**, 159–170.
18. Hammitt, W. E. (2004). A restorative definition for outdoor recreation. In K. Bricker, (comp.) (Ed.) 2005. Proceedings of the 2004 Northeastern Recreation Research Symposium. Gen. Tech. Rep.NE-326. Newtown Square, PA: USDA Forest Service, Northeastern Research Station, pp. 1–5.
19. Chang, C., Hammitt, W., Chen, P., Machnik, L., and Su, W. (2007). Psychophysiological responses and restorative values of natural environments in Taiwan. *Lands. Urb. Plan.* **85**(2), 79–84.

6

1. Associated Press. (2007). Issues Poll. Retrieved April 8, 2008 from [http://www.usatoday.com/news/nation/2007–12–28-issuespoll_N.htm].
2. ABC News/Washington Post Poll. (2008). *ABC News/Washington Post Poll*. Retrieved May 6, 2008 from [http://www.pollingreport.com/prioriti.htm].
3. Rahim, S. (2007). Q&A: Preparing for a surgery Abroad. Retrieved March 8, 2008 from [http://www.npr.org/templates/story/story.php?storyId=16296677].
4. Healism (2008). Universal health care through medical tourism. Retrieved May 26, 2008 from [http://www.healism.com/].
5. Saratoga Spa State Park. (2008). Retrieved April 8, 2008 from [http://www.saratogaspastatepark.org/history.html].
6. Saratoga Spring Water. (2008). Retrieved June 1, 2008 from [http://www.saratogaspringwater.com].
7. English, V., Gardner, J., Romano-Critchley, G., and Sommerville, A. (2001). Ethics Briefings. *J. Med. Ethics* **27**, 284–285.
8. Baldoria, F. and Osana, J. (2007). *Medical Tourism: A Booming Industry*. Philippine Daily Inquirer, June 15, 2007. Business Friday Section.
9. Economist. (March 10, 2007). Sun, sand and scalpels. *Economist* **382**(8519), 62.
10. Alsever, J. (2006). Basking on the Beach, or maybe on the Operating Table. October 15, 2006. Retrieved July 30, 2007 from NYTimes.com
11. Burkhart, L. and Gentry, L. (Jan/Feb 2008). Medical Tourism: What you should know. *The Saturday Evening Post* **280**(1), pp. 52–53, 90, 92, 94.

12. Hanson, F. (2008). A revolution in Healthcare: Medicine meets the marketplace. *Public Affairs Review* 59, p. 4.
13. Oxford Analytica. (2006). Medical Tourism Industry Grows Rapidly. Retrieved July 30, 2007 from [www.forbes.com/business/2006/10/25/health-medical-tourism-biz-cx_1026oxford.html].
14. Mecir, A. and Greider, K. (2007). Traveling for Treatment. Retrieved March 15, 2008 from [http://www.aarp.org/bulletin/yourhealth/traveling_for_treatment.html]
15. U.S. Department of State. (2007). Costa Rica: Country specific information. Retrieved February 8, 2008 from [http://travel.state.gov/travel/cis_pa_tw/cis/cis_1093.html#medical].
16. Borner, T. (2001). *Potholes To Paradise; Living In Costa Rica What You Need To Know*. Silvio Mattacchinone, Port Perry, CA.
17. World Health Tourism Congress. (2008). Third Annual World Health Tourism Congress. Retrieved April 15, 2008 from [http://www.healthtourismcongress.com].
18. United Nations Statistics Division. (2008). Retrieved May 26, 2008 from [http://unstats.un.org/unsd/default.htm].
19. International Ecotourism Society. (2008). Retrieved Feb 15, 2008 from [www.ecotourism.org].
20. Instituto Costarricense de Turismo. (2008). Certification for Sustainable Tourism. Retrieved Feb 15, 2008 from [http://www.turismo-sostenible.co.cr/].
21. Tico Times. (February 29, 2008). *White House Advertisement*. p. 9.
22. Smith, G. (2006). *The Globalization of Health Care: Can Medical Tourism Reduce Health Care Costs?* From a Hearing of the U.S. Senate Special Committee on Aging, June 27, 2006. Retrieved Feb 15, 2008 from [http://aging.senate.gov/hearing_detail.cfm?id=270728&].
23. JCI (Joint Commission International) (2008). Retrieved February 15, 2008 from [http://www.jointcommissioninternational.org].
24. World Mapper. (2008). University of Sheffield. Retrieved March 27, 2008 from [http://www.worldmapper.org].
25. Mirrer-Singer, P. (2007). Medical malpractice overseas: The legal uncertainty surrounding medical tourism. *Law and Contemporary Problems* **70**(2), 211–233.
26. Hamilton, J. (2007). Medical Tourism Creates Thai Doctor Shortage. Retrieved March 8, 2008 from [http://www.npr.org/templates/story/story.php?storyId=16735157].
27. WHO (World Health Organization). (2007). Wastes from Health-Care Activities Fact Sheet. Retrieved April 15, 2008 from [http://www.who.int/mediacentre/factsheets/fs253/en/].
28. Rogers, D. (2007). Faulty control on biowaste creates a lurking health danger. Retrieved March 26, 2008 from [http://www.amcostarica.com/060707.htm#32].

7

1. U.S. Department of Health and Human Services (HHS). (1996). *Physical Activity and Health: A Report of the Surgeon General Executive Summary*. Atlanta, (GA): Centers for Disease Control and Prevention, National Center for Chronic Disease Prevention and Health Promotion, The President's Council on Physical Fitness and Sports.
2. U.S. Department of Health and Human Services (HHS). (1995). *Healthy People 2000: Midcourse Review and 1995 Revisions*. Government Printing Office, Washington, DC.
3. Pate, R., Pratt, M., Blair, S., Haskell, W., Macera, C., et al. (1995). Physical activity and public health: A recommendation from the centers for disease control and prevention and the American college of sports medicine. *J. Am. Med. Associat.* **273**(5), 402–407.
4. Hodges, J. S. and Henderson, K. A. (1999). Promoting the physical activity objectives in the Surgeon General's report: A summary. *J. Phys. Edu. Rec. Dance* **70**(3), 40–41.
5. Iwasaki, Y., Zuzanek, J., and Mannell, R. C. (2001). The Effects of Physically Active Leisure on Stress-Health Relationships. *Revue Canadienne de Santé Publique* **92**(3), 214–218.
6. Ho, C. (2003). Parks, recreation and public health: Parks and recreation improve the

physical and mental health of our nation—Research update. *Parks and Recreation* **38**(4), April, 18–23.

7. Oresega-Smith, E., Mowen, A., Payne, L., and Godbey, G. (2004). Interaction of stress and park use on psycho-physiological health in older adults. *J. Leisure Res.* **36**, 232–257.
8. Giles-Corti, B. and Donovan, R. J. (2002). The relative influence of individual, social, and physical environment determinants of physical activity. *Soc. Sci. Med.* **54**, 1793–1812.
9. Addy, C. L., Wilson, D. K., Kirtland, K. A., Ainsworth, B. E., Sharpe, B., and Kimsey, D. (2004). Associations of perceived social and physical environmental supports with physical activity and walking behavior. *Am. J. Public Health* **94**(3), 440–443.
10. Gordon, P. M., Zizzi, S. J., and Pauline, J. (2004). Use of a community trail among new and habitual exercisers: A preliminary assessment. *Preventing Chronic Disease* **1**(4), 1–11.
11. Libbrett, J. J., Yore, M. M., and Schmid, T. L. (2006). Characteristics of physical activity levels among trail users in a US national sample. *Am. J. Prevent. Med.* **31**(5), 399–405.
12. Kaplan, S. (1995). The restorative benefits of nature: Toward an integrated framework. *J. Environ. Psychol.* **15**, 169–182.
13. Gobster, P. H. (2005). Recreation and leisure research from an active living perspective: Taking a second look at urban trail use data. *Leisure Sciences* **27**(5), 367–383.
14. Ajzen, I. (1991). The theory of planned behavior. *Organ.Human Decision Proc.* **50**, 179–211.
15. Stradling, S. G. and Parker, D. (1996). *Extending the Theory of Planned Behavior: The Role of Personal Norms, Instrumental Beliefs and Affective Beliefs in Predicting Driving Violations.* Presented at the International Conference on Traffic and Transport Psychology, Valencia, Spain.
16. Povey, R. Conner, M., Sparks, P., James, R, and Shepherd, R. (2000). Application of the Theory of planned behavior to two dietary behaviors: Roles of perceived control and self-efficacy. *British J. Health Psychol.* **5**, 121–139.
17. Courneya, K. S., Plotnikoff, R. C., Hotz, S. B., and Birkett, N. J. (2001). Predicting exercise stage transitions over two consecutive 6-month periods: A test of the theory of planned behavior in a population-based sample. *British J. Health Psychol.* **6**, 135–150.
18. Reger, B., Cooper, L., Booth-Butterfield, S., Smith, H., Bauman, A., Wootan, M., Middlestadt, S., Marcus, B., and Greer, F. (2002). Wheeling walks: A community campaign using paid media to encourage walking among sedentary older adults. *Preventive Medicine* **35**, 285–292.
19. Stead, M., Tagg, S., MacKintosh, A. M., and Eadie, D. (2005). Development and evaluation of a mass media theory of planned behavior intervention to reduce speeding. *Health Edu. Res.* **20**, 36–41.
20. Godin, G. (1993). The theories of reasoned action and planned behavior: Overview of findings, emerging research problems and usefulness for exercise promotion. *J. Appl. Sport Psychol.* **5**, 141–157.
21. Blue, C. L. (1995). The predictive capacity of the theory of reasoned action and the theory of planned behavior in exercise research: An integrated literature review. *Res. Nurs. Health* **18**, 105–121.
22. Hagger, M. S., Chatzisarantis, N. L., and Biddle, S. J. H. (2002). Meta-analysis of the theories of reasoned action and planned behavior in physical activity: An examination of the predictive validity and the contribution of additional variables. *J. Sport. Exer. Psychol.* **24**, 3–32.
23. Hausenblaus, H. A., Carron, A. V., and Mack, D. E. (1997). Application of the theories or reasoned action and planned behavior to exercise behavior: A meta-analysis. *J. Sport Exer. Psychol.* **19**, 36–51.
24. Rosen, C. L. (2000). Integrating stage and continuum models to explain processing of exercise messages and exercise initiation among sedentary college students. *Health Psychology* **19**, 172–180.
25. Duncan, T. E., McAuley, E., Stollmiller, M., and Duncan, S. C. (1993). Serial fluctuations in exercise behavior as a function of social support and efficacy conditions. *J. Appl. Soc. Psychol.* **23**(18), 1498–1522.

26. Carron, A. V., Hausenblas, H. A., and Mack, D. (1996). Social influences and exercise: A meta-analysis. *J. Sport Exer. Psychol.* **18**(1), 1–16.
27. Trost, S. G., Owen, N., Bauman, A. E., Sallis, J. F., and Brown, W. (2002). Correlates of adults' participation in physical activity: Review and update. *Med. Sci. Sports. Exer.* **34**(2), 1996–2001.
28. Kahn, E. B., Ramsey, L. T., Brownson, R. C., Heath, G. W., Howze, E. H., Powell, K. E., Stone, E. J., Rajab, M. W., Corso, P., and the Task Force on Community Preventive Services. (2002). The effectiveness of interventions to increase physical activity: A systematic review. *Am. J. Prevent. Med.* **22**(4S), 73–107.
29. Siegel, P., Brackbill, R., and Heath, G. (1995). The epidemiology of walking for exercise: Implications for promoting activity among sedentary groups. *Am. J. Public Health* **85**, 706–10.
30. Brownson, R. C., Baker, E. A., Boyd, R. L., Caito, N. M., Duggan, K., Housemann, R. A., Kreuter, M. W., Mitchell, T., Motton, F., Pulley, C., Schmid, T. L., and Walton, D. (2004). A community-based approach to promoting walking in rural areas. *Am. J. Prevent. Med.*, **27**(1), 28–32.
31. Middlestadt, S. E., Bhattacharyya, K., Rosenbaum, J., Fishbein, M., and Sheperd, M. (1996). The use of theory based semi structured elicitation questionnaires: Formative research for CDC's prevention marketing initiative. *Public Health Reports* **3**(1), 18–27.
32. Ham, S., Brown, T., Curtis, J., Weiler, B., Hughes, M., and Poll, M. (2007). *Promoting Persuasion in Protected Areas: A Guide for Managers*. Sustainable Tourism Cooperative Research Centre.
33. Lackey, B. K. and Ham, S. H. (2003). Contextual analysis of interpretation focused on human-black bear conflicts in Yosemite National Park. *Appl. Envirn. Edu. Comm.* **2**, 11–21.
34. Petty, R., McMichael, S., and Brannon, L. (1992). The elaboration likelihood model of persuasion: Applications in recreation and tourism. In *Influencing Human Behavior*. M. Manfredo (Ed.), Sagamore, Champaign, IL, pp. 77–102.
35. Welk, G. J., Differding, J. A., and Thompson, R. W. (2000). The utility of the digiwalker step counter to assess daily physical activity patterns. *Med. Sci. Sports Exer.* **32**(9), S481–488.
36. Tudor-Locke, C. and Bassett, D. (2004). How many steps/day are enough? Preliminary pedometer indices for public health. *Sports Medicine* **34**(1), 1–8.
37. Texas AgriLife Extension. (1996). *Walk Across Texas*. Retrieved March 3, 2007 from [http://walkacrosstexas.tamu.edu/index.htm].
38. Dillman, D. (2007). *Mail and Internet Surveys: The Tailored Design Method*. John Wiley & Sons, Inc, New Jersey.

8

1. Feachem, R. and Sabot, O. (2008). A new global malaria eradication strategy.*Lancet* **371**, 1633–1635.
2. Roberts, L. and Enserink, M. (2007). Did they really say... eradication? *Science* **318**, 1544–1545.
3. Mendis, K., Rietveld, A., Warsame, M., Bosman, A., Greenwood, B. M., and Wernsdorfer, W. H. (2009). From malaria control to eradication: The WHO perspective. *Trop. Med. Int. Health* **14**, 802–809.
4. Pampana, E. (1963). *A Textbook of Malaria Eradication*. Oxford University Press, Oxford.
5. World Health Organization, (2008). *Global Malaria Control and Elimination: Report of a Technical Review*. World Health Organization, Geneva.
6. Moonen, B., Barrett, S., Tulloch, J., and Jamison, D. T. (2009). Making the decision. In *Shrinking the Malaria Map: A Prospectus on Malaria Elimination*. University of California, San Francisco, pp. 1–18.
7. Zanzibar Malaria Control Program (2008). *Roll Back Malaria Indicator Survey: Survey 2007*. Ministry of Health and SocialWelfare, Zanzibar.
8. Bhattarai, A., Ali, A. S., Kachur, S. P., Martensson, A., Abbas, A. K., Khatib,

R., Al-Mafazy, A. W., Ramsan, M., Rotllant, G., Gerstenmaier, J. F., Molteni, F., Abdulla, S., Montgomery, S. M., Kaneko, A., and Bjorkman, A. (2007). Impact of artemisinin-based combination therapy and insecticide-treated nets on malaria burden in Zanzibar. *PLoS Med* **4**, e309.

9. Hay, S. I., Guerra, C. A., Gething, P. W., Patil, A. P., Tatem, A. J., Noor, A. M., Kabaria, C. W., Manh, B. H., Elyazar, I. R. F., Brooker, S. J., Smith, D. L., Moyeed, R. A., and Snow, R. W. (2009). World malaria map: *Plasmodium falciparum* endemicity in 2007. *PLoS Med* **6**, e1000048.
10. Schapira, A. (2007). *Prospects for Eradication and Elimination of Malaria: Annexe 2. Pportunities, Obstacles and Risks for Elimination of Plasmodium falciparum Malaria in Difference Countries and Regions of the World with Currently Existing Tools*. Department for International Development, London.
11. Julvez, J., Mouchet, J., and Ragavoodoo, C. (1990). Epidemiologie historique du paludisme dans l'archipel des Mascareignes (Ocean Indien). *Ann. Soc. Belg. Med. Trop.* **70**, 249–261.
12. Prothero, R. M. (1961). Population movements and problems of malaria eradication in Africa. *Bull. World Health Organ.* **24**, 405–425.
13. Sivagnanasundaram, C. (1973). Rates of infection during the 1967–68 *P. vivax* epidemic in Sri Lanka (Ceylon). *J. Trop. Med. Hyg.* **76**, 83–86.
14. Hammadi, D., Boubidi, S. C., Chaib, S. E., Saber, A., Khechache, Y., Gasmi, M., and Harrat, Z. (2009). Malaria in Algerian Sahara. *Bull. Soc. Pathol. Exot.* **102**, 185–192.
15. Brockmann, D., Hufnagel, L., and Geisel, T. (2006). The scaling laws of human travel. *Nature* **439**, 462–465.
16. Brockmann, D. and Theis, F. (2008). Money circulation, trackable items, and the emergence of universal human mobility patterns. *Pervasive. Comput.* **7**, 28.
17. Candia, J., Gonzalez, M. C., Wang, P., Schoenharl, T., Madey, G., and Barabasi, A. L. (2008). Uncovering individual and collective human dynamics from mobile phone records. *J. Phys. Math. Gen.* **41**, 1–11.
18. Gonzalez, M. C. and Barabasi, A. L. (2007). From data to models. *Nat. Phys.* **3**, 224–225.
19. Gonzalez, M. C., Hidalgo, C. A., and Barabasi, A. L. (2008). Understanding individual human mobility patterns. *Nature* **453**, 779–782.
20. Zanzibar Commission for Tourism (2008). *Annually Recorded Number of Tourist Arrivals in Zanzibar by Country 2002–2007*. Zanzibar Commission for Tourism, Zanzibar.
21. Zanzibar Ministry of Communications and Transport (2008). *Ferry Passenger Data 2006–2007*. Zanzibar Ministry of Communications and Transport., Zanzibar.
22. Guerra, C. A., Gikandi, P. W., Tatem, A. J., Noor, A. M., Smith, D. L., Hay, S. I., and Snow, R. W. (2008). The limits and intensity of *Plasmodium falciparum* transmission: Implications for malaria control and elimination worldwide. *PLoS Med.* **5**, e38.
23. Guerra, C. A., Hay, S. I., Lucioparedes, L. S., Gikandi, P. W., Tatem, A. J., Noor, A. M., and Snow, R. W. (2007). Assembling a global database of malaria parasite prevalence for the Malaria Atlas Project. *Malar. J.* **6**, 17.
24. Smith, D. L., Dushoff, J., Snow, R. W., and Hay, S. I. (2005). The entomological inoculation rate and *Plasmodium falciparum* infection in African children. *Nature* **438**, 492–495.
25. Smith, D. L. and McKenzie, F. E. (2004). Statics and dynamics of malaria infection in anopheles mosquitoes. *Malar. J.* **3**, 13.
26. Smith, D. L., McKenzie, F. E., Snow, R. W., and Hay, S. I. (2007). Revisiting the basic reproductive number for malaria and its implications for malaria control. *PLoS Biol.* **5**, e42.
27. Tanser, F., Sharp, B., and le Sueur, D. (2003). Potential effect of climate change on malaria transmission in Africa. *Lancet* **362**, 1792–1798.
28. Tatem, A. J., Noor, A. M., von Hagen, C., di Gregorio, A., and Hay, S. I. (2007). High resolution population maps for low income nations: combining land cover and census in East Africa. *PLoS ONE* **2**, e1298.
29. AfriPop Project. Retrieved from [http://www.afripop.org].

30. United Nations Population Division (2009). *World Population Prospects, 2008 Revision.* United Nations, New York.
31. Hay, S. I., Noor, A. M., Nelson, A., and Tatem, A. J. (2005). The accuracy of human population maps for public health application. *Trop. Med. Int. Health.* **10**, 1–14.
32. Tanzania Communications Regulatory Authority (2009). *Telecommunications Statistics as at 31st December 2008.* TCR (Ed.). DarEs Salaam.
33. James, J. and Versteeg, M. (2007). Mobile phones in Africa: How much do we really know? *Soc. Indic. Res.* **84**, 117–126.
34. Vodafone (2005). Africa: The impact of mobile phones. *Vodafone Policy Papers Series: Vodafone Group*
35. Balk, D. L., Deichmann, U., Yetman, G., Pozzi, F., Hay, S. I., and Nelson, A. (2006). Determining global population distribution: Methods, applications and data. *Adv. Parasitol.* **62**, 119–156.
36. Smith, D. L. and Hay, S. I. (2009). Endemicity response timelines for *Plasmodium falciparum* elimination. *Malar. J.* **8**, 87.
37. Stewart, L., Gosling, R., Griffin, J., Gesase, S., Campo, J., Hashim, R., Masika, P., Mosha, J., Bousema, T., Shekalaghe, S., Cook, J., Corran, P., Ghani, A., Riley, E. M., and Drakeley, C. (2009). Rapid assessment of malaria transmission using age-specific sero-conversion rates. *PLoS ONE* **4**, e6083.
38. Okiro, E. A., Hay, S. I., Gikandi, P. W., Sharif, S. K., Noor, A. M., Peshu, N., Marsh, K., and Snow, R. W. (2007). The decline in paediatric malaria admissions on the coast of Kenya. *Malar. J.* **6**, 151.
39. Kaneko, A., Taleo, G., Kalkoa, M., Yamar, S., Kobayakawa, T., and Bjorkman, A. (2000). Malaria eradication on islands. *Lancet* **356**, 1560–1564.
40. Feachem, R. G. A., Phillips, A. A., and Targett, G. A., (Eds.) (2009). *Shrinking the Malaria Map: A Prospectus on Malaria Elimination.* The Global Health Group, Global Health Sciences, University of California, San Francisco.
41. Malaria Atlas Project. Retrieved from [http://www.map.ox.ac.uk].

9

1. CIAT (Centro International de Agricultural Tropical) (2008). United Nations Environment Program (UNEP), Center for International Earth Science Information Network (CIESIN), Columbia University, and the World Bank (2005) Latin American and Caribbean population database, Version 3. Table A.2. Retrieved from [http://gisweb.ciat.cgiar.org/population/download/report.pdf]. Accessed May 5.
2. Jayawardena, C. (October 19, 2000). *The Future of Tourism in the Caribbean.* The Jamaica Gleaner. Retrieved from [http://www.jamaica-gleaner.com/gleaner/20001019/news/news3.html]. Accessed May 5, 2008.
3. Caribbean Tourism Organization (2004). Annual Caribbean tourism statistical report of the Caribbean Tourism Organization. Retrieved from [http://www.onecaribbean.org/content/files/2004visitorexptables.pdf] and [http://www.onecaribbean.org/content/files/2004tables8and9marketdata.pdf]. Accessed May 7, 2008.
4. Hotez, P. J. (2008). *Forgotten People And Forgotten Diseases: The Neglected Tropical Diseases And Their Impact On Global Health And Development.* ASM Press, Washington DC, (in press).
5. World Health Organization (2006). Global programe to eliminate lymphatic filariasis. *Wkly. Epidemiol. Rec.* **81**, 221–232.
6. Steinmann, P., Keiser, J., Bos, R., Tanner, M., and Utzinger, J. (2006). Schistosomiasis and water resources development: Systematic review, meta-analysis, and estimates of people at risk. *Lancet. Infect. Dis.* **6**, 411–425.
7. Schneider, C. R., Hiatt, R. A., Malek, E. A., and Ruiz-Tiben, E. (1985). Assessment of schistosomiasis in the Dominican Republic. *Publ. Health Rep.* **100**, 524–530.
8. Vargas, M., Malek, E. A., and Perez, J. G. (1990). Schistosomiasis mansoni in the Dominican Republic; prevalence and intensity in various urban and rural communities, 1982–1987. *Trop. Med. Parasitol.* **41**, 415–418.
9. De Silva, N. R., Brooker, S., Hotez, P. J., Montresor, A., Engels, D., et al. (2003).

Soil-transmitted helminth infections: Updating the global picture. *Trends Parasitol.* **19**, 547–551.

10. Lammie, P. J., Lindo, J. F., Secor, W. E., Vasquez, J., Ault, S. K., et al. (2007) Elimination of lymphatic filariasis, onchocerciasis, and schistosomiasis from the Americas: Breaking a historical legacy of slavery. *PLoS Negl, Trop. Dis.* **1,** e71.
11. Pan American Health Organization (2007). Leprosy in the Americas, 2007. Retrieved from [http://www.paho.org/English/AD/DPC/CD/lep-sit-reg-2007.pdf]. Accessed May 5, 2008.
12. Pan American Health Organization (2007). 2006: Number of reported cases of dengue & dengue hemorrhagic fever. Retrieved from [http://www.paho.org/english/ad/dpc/cd/dengue-cases-2006.htm]. Accessed May 5, 2008.
13. Beatty, M. E., Hunsperger, E., Long, E., Schurch, J., Jain, S., et al. (2007). Mosquitoborne infections after Hurricane Jeanne, Haiti, 2004. *Emerg. Infect. Dis.* **13**, 308–310.
14. Pan American Health Organization (2007). *Health in the Americas*. Scientific and technical publication no. 622, Regional.
15. Pincus, L. B., Grossman, M. E., and Fox, L. P. (2008). The exanthema of dengue fever: Clinical features of two US tourists traveling abroad. *J. Am. Acad. Dermatol.* **58,** 308–316.
16. Blackwell, V. and Vega-Lopez, F. (2001). Cutaneous larva migrans: Clinical features and management of 44 cases presenting in the returning traveler. *Br. J. Dermatol.* **145,** 434–437.
17. Grady, C. A., Beau de Rochars, M., Diereny, A. N., Orefus, J. N., Wendt, J., et al. (2007). Endpoints for lymphatic filariasis programs. *Emerg. Infect. Dis.* **13**, 608–610.
18. The Global Alliance to Eliminate Lymphatic Filariasis (2008). How can we prevent/eliminate LF? Retrieved from [http://www.filariasis.org/resources/prevent_eliminatelf.htm]. Accessed May 5, 2008.
19. Hotez, P. J., Molyneux, D. H., Fenwick, A., Kumaresan, J., Ehrlich Sachs, S., et al. (2007). Control of neglected tropical diseases. *N. Engl. J. Med.* **357**, 1018–1027.
20. Hotez, P. J. and Ferris, M. (2006). The antipoverty vaccines. *Vaccine* **24**, 5787–5799.

10

1. Berro, A., Gallagher, N., Yanni, E., Lipman, H., Whatley, A., Bossak, B., Murphy, R., Pezzi, C., et al. (2008). World Health Organization (WHO) travel recommendations during the 2003 SARS outbreak: Lessons learned for mitigating pandemic influenza and globally emerging infectious diseases [Poster presentation]. *Atlanta International Conference on Emerging Infectious Diseases (ICEID).*
2. Ministry of Health (2006). *New Zealand Influenza Pandemic Action Plan*. Ministry of Health, Wellington.
3. McLeod, M., Kelly, H., Wilson, N., and Baker, M. G. (2008). Border control measures in the influenza pandemic plans of six South Pacific nations: A critical review. *N. Z. Med. J.* **121**(1278), 62–72.
4. Epstein, J. M., Goedecke, D. M., Yu, F., Morris, R. J., Wagener, D. K., and Bobashev, G. V. (2007). Controlling pandemic flu: The value of international air travel restrictions. *PLoS ONE* **2**, e401.
5. Bell, D. M. (2006). World Health Organization Writing Group: Non-pharmaceutical interventions for pandemic influenza, international measures. *Emerg. Infect. Dis.* **12**, 81–87.
6. Aledort, J. E., Lurie, N., Wasserman, J., and Bozzette, S. A. (2007). Non-pharmaceutical public health interventions for pandemic influenza: An evaluation of the evidence base. *BMC Public Health* **7**, 208.
7. Schwehm, M., Eichner, M., Wilson, N., and Baker, M. (2009). A freely available software tool for assessing aspects of pandemic influenza risk reduction for small islands. *N. Z. Med. J.* **122**(1295), 94–95.
8. Eichner, M., Schwehm, M., Duerr, H., and Brockmann, S. (2007). The influenza pandemic preparedness planning tool InfluSim. *BMC Infect. Dis.* **7**, 17.
9. Berro, A., Gallagher, N., Yanni, E., Lipman, H., Whatley, A., Bossak, B., Murphy, R., Pezzi, C., et al. (2008). World Health Organization (WHO) travel recommendations

during the 2003 SARS outbreak: Lessons learned for mitigating pandemic influenza and globally emerging infectious diseases. [Poster presentation]. *International Conference on Emerging Infectious Diseases (ICEID)*, Atlanta.

10. SPC (Secretariat of the Pacific Community) (2008). Tourism Indicators–Arrivals and Country of Residence–Latest Year. Retrieved from [http://www.spc.int/prism/tourism/arrivals.html].
11. Nishiura, H., Wilson, N., and Baker, M. G. (2009). Quarantine for pandemic influenza control at the borders of small island nations. *BMC Infect. Dis.* **9**, 27.
12. McLeod, M. A., Baker, M., Wilson, N., Kelly, H., Kiedrzynski, T., and Kool, J. L. (2008). Protective effect of maritime quarantine in South Pacific jurisdictions, 1918–1919 influenza pandemic. *Emerg. Infect. Dis.* **14**, 468–470.
13. Scalia Tomba, G. and Wallinga, J. (2008). A simple explanation for the low impact of border control as a countermeasure to the spread of an infectious disease. *Math. Biosci.* **214**, 70–72.

11

1. Steffen, R., deBernardis, C., and Banos, A. (2003). Travel epidemiology—a global perspective. *Int. J. Antimicrob. Agents* **21**, 89–95.
2. Southgate, B. A. (1992). Intensity and efficiency of transmission and the development of microfilaraemia and disease: Their relationship in lymphatic filariasis. *J. Trop. Med. Hyg.* **95**, 1–12.
3. Klion, A. D., Massougbodji, A., Sadeler, B. C., Ottesen, E. A., and Nutman, T. B. (1991). Loiasis in endemic and nonendemic populations: Immunologically mediated differences in clinical presentation. *J. Infect. Dis.* **163**, 1318–1325.
4. McCarthy, J. S., Ottesen, E. A., and Nutman, T. B. (1994). Onchocerciasis in endemic and nonendemic populations: Differences in clinical presentation and immunologic findings. *J. Infect. Dis.* **170**, 736–741.
5. Nutman, T. B., Miller, K. D., Mulligan, M., and Ottesen, E. A. (1986). *Loa loa* infection in temporary residents of endemic regions: Recognition of a hyper-responsive syndrome with characteristic clinical manifestations. *J. Infect. Dis.* **154**, 10–18.
6. Nutman, T. B., Reese, W., Poindexter, R. W., and Ottesen, E. A. (1988). Immunologic correlates of the hyperresponsive syndrome of loiasis. *J. Infect. Dis.* **157**, 544–550.
7. Churchhill, D. R., Morris, C., Fakoya, S. G., Wright, S. G., and Davidson, R. N. (1996). Clinical and laboratory features of patients with Loiasis (*Loa loa* filariasis). *UK J. Infect.* **33**, 103–109.
8. Freedman, D. O., Kozarsky, P. E., Weld, L. H., and Centron, M. S. (1999). GeoSentinel: The global emerging infections sentinel network of the International Society of Travel Medicine. *J. Travel. Med.* **6**, 94–98.
9. Chun, Y. S., Chun, S. I., Im, K. I., Moon, T. K., and Lee, M. G. (1998). A case of loiasis. *Yonsei Med. J.* **39**, 184–188.
10. van Dellen, R. G., Ottesen, E. A., Gocke, T. M., and Neafie, R. C. (1985). *Loa loa*. An unusual case of chronic urticaria and angioedema in the United States. *JAMA* 253, 1924–1925.
11. Encarnacion, C. F., Giordano, M. F., and Murray, H. W. (1994). Onchocerciasis in New York City. The Moa-Manhattan connection. *Arch. Intern. Med.* **154**, 1749–1751.
12. Rakita, R. M., White, A. C. Jr., and Kielhofner, M. A. (1993). *Loa loa* infection as a cause of migratory angioedema: Report of three cases from the Texas Medical Center. *Clin. Infect. Dis.* **17**, 691–694.
13. Connor, D. H. (1978). Current concepts in parasitology: onchocerciasis. *N. Engl. J. Med.* **298**, 379–381.
14. Mahoney, J. L. (1981). Onchocerciasis in expatriates on the Ivory Coast. *South Med. J.* **73**, 295–297.
15. Nutman, T. B. and Kradin, R. L. (2002). Case records of the Massachusetts General Hospital. Weekly clinicopathological exercises. Case 1-2002. A 24-year-old woman with paresthesias and muscle cramps after a stay in Africa. *N. Engl. J. Med.* **346**, 115–122.
16. McCarthy, J. S., Ottesen, E. A., and Nutman, T. B. (1994) Onchocerciasis in endemic and nonendemic populations: Differences

in clinical presentation and immunologic findings. *J. Infect. Dis.* **170**, 736–741.

17. Kumaraswami, V. (2000). The clinical manifestations of lymphatic filariasis. In *Lymphatic Filariasis*. T. B. Nutman (Ed.). Imperial College Press, London, pp. 103–120.
18. Freedman, D. O., Weld, L. H., Kozarsky, P. E., et al. (2006). Spectrum of disease and relation to place of exposure among ill returned travelers. GeoSentinel Surveillance Network. *N. Engl. J. Med.* **354**, 119–130.

12

1. Keeling, M. J., Woolhouse, M. E. J., Shaw, D. J., Matthews, L., Chase-Topping, M., Haydon, D. T., Cornell, S. J., Kappey, J., Wilesmith, J., and Grenfell, B. T. (2001). Dynamics of the 2001 UK foot and mouth epidemic: Stochastic dispersal in a heterogeneous landscape. *Science* **294**(5543), 813-817.
2. Wylie, J. L. and Jolly, A. (2001). Patterns of chlamydia and gonorrhea infection in sexual networks in Manitoba, Canada. Sex. *Trans.* Dis. **28**(1), 14-24.
3. Grenfell, B. T., Bjornstad, O. N., and Kappey, J. (2001). Travelling waves and spatial hierarchies in measles epidemics. *Nature* **414**(6865), 716-723.
4. Sattenspiel, L. and Dietz, K. (1995). A Structured Epidemic Model Incorporating Geographic-Mobility among Regions. *Mathemat. Biosci.* **128**(1–2), 71-91.
5. Pearson, H. (2003). SARS—What have we learned? *Nature* **424**(6945), 121-126.
6. Rvachev, L. A. and Longini, I. M. (1985). A mathematical-model for the global spread of influenza. *Mathemat. Biosci.* **75**(1), 1-1.
7. Grais, R. F., Ellis, J. H., and Glass, G. E. (2003). Assessing the impact of airline travel on the geographic spread of pandemic influenza. *Eur. J. Epidemiol.* **18**(11), 1065-1072.
8. Hufnagel, L., Brockmann, D., and Geisel, T. (2004). Forecast and control of epidemics in a globalized world. *Proc. Nat. Acad. Sci. US Am* **101**(42), 15124-15129.
9. Eubank, S., Guclu, H., Kumar, V. S., Marathe, M. V., Srinivasan, A., Toroczkai, Z., and Wang, N. (2004). Modelling disease outbreaks in realistic urban social networks. *Nature* **429**(6988), 180-184.
10. Andersson, H. and Britton, P. (2000). *Stochastic Epidemic Models and Their Statistical Analysis*. Volume 151. Springer-Verlag, New York.
11. Anderson, R. M., May, R. M., and Anderson, B. (1992). *Infectious Diseases of Humans: Dynamics and Control*. Oxford University Press.
12. Diekmann, O. and Heesterbeek, J. A. P. (2000). *Mathematical Epidemiology of Infectious Diseases: Model Building, Analysis and Interpretation*. John Wiley and Sons Ltd, Chichester.
13. Statens Institut för Kommunikationsanalys SSC (2002). RES 2001. Den nationella reseundersökningen.
14. Lipsitch, M., Cohen, T., Cooper, B., Robins, J. M., Ma, S., James, L., Gopalakrishna, G., Chew, S. K., Tan, C. C., Samore, M. H., et al. (2003). Transmission dynamics and control of severe acute respiratory syndrome. *Science* **300**(5627), 1966-1970.
15. Ferguson, N. M., Cummings, D. A. T., Cauchemez, S., Fraser, C., Riley, S., Meeyai, A., Iamsirithaworn, S., and Burke, D. S. (2005). Strategies for containing an emerging influenza pandemic in Southeast Asia. *Nature* **437**(7056), 209-214.

13

1. World Health Organization Regional Office for Europe (1993–1998). 7th report of the WHO surveillance programme for the control of foodborne infections and intoxications in Europe. Retrieved from [http://www.bgvv.de/internet/7threport/7threp_fr.htm]
2. Poppe, C. (1999). Epidemiology of *Salmonella enterica* serovar Enteritidis. In *Salmonella enterica serovar Enteritidis in Humans and* Animals. A Saed (Ed.). Iowa State University Press, Ames, Iowa, pp. 3-18.
3. Mishu, B., Koehler, J., Lee, L. A., Rodrigue, D., Brenner, F. H., Blake, P., and Tauxe, R. V. (1994). Outbreaks of *Salmonella enteritidis* infections in the United States, 1985–1991. *J. Infect. Dis.* **169**, 547-552.

4. Rodrigue, D. C., Tauxe, R. V., and Rowe, B. (1990). International increase in *Salmonella enteritidis*: A new pandemic? *Epidemiol. Infect.* **105**, 21-27.
5. Isaacs, S., Sockett, P., Wilson, J., Styliadis, S., and Borczyk, A. (1997). *Salmonella enteritidis* phage type 4 in Ontario; Editorial comment. *Can. Commu. Dis. Rep. 23.*
6. European Commission (2001). Trends and sources of zoonotic agents in animals, feedingstuffs, food and man in the European Union and Norway in 2001. Retrieved from [http://europa.eu.int/comm/food/food/biosafety/salmonella/zoonoses_reps_2001_en.htm]
7. Angulo, F. and Swerdlow, D. (1999). Epidemiology of human *Salmonella* enterica serovar Enteritidis infections in the United States. In *Salmonella enterica serovar Enteritidis in Humans and Animals*. A. Saed (Ed.). Iowa State University Press, Ames, Iowa, pp. 33-41.
8. Schmid, H., Burnens, A. P., Baumgartner, A., and Oberreich, J. (1996). Risk factors for sporadic salmonellosis in Switzerland. *Eur. J. Clin. Microbiol. Infect. Dis.* **15**, 725-732.
9. European Commission (2000). Trends and sources of zoonotic agents in animals, feedstuffs, food and man in the European Union in 2000. Retrieved from [http://europa.eu.int/comm/food/fs/sfp/mr/mr08_en.pdf]
10. From the Centers for Disease Control and Prevention (2003). Outbreaks of *Salmonella* serotype enteritidis infection associated with eating shell eggs—United States, 1999–2001. *JAMA* **289**, 540-541.
11. Hogue, A., White, P., Guard-Petter, J., Schlosser, W., Gast, R., Ebel, E., Farrar, J., Gomez, T., Madden, J., Madison, M., McNamara, A. M., Morales, R., Parham, D., Sparling, P., Sutherlin, W., and Swerdlow, D. (1997). Epidemiology and control of egg-associated *Salmonella enteritidis* in the United States of America. *Rev. Sci. Tech.* **16**, 542-553.
12. Olsen, S. J., Bishop, R., Brenner, F. W., Roels, T. H., Bean, N., Tauxe, R. V., and Slutsker, L. (2001). The changing epidemiology of *Salmonella*: Trends in serotypes isolated from humans in the United States, 1987–1997. *J. Infect. Dis.* **183**, 753-761.
13. Engvall, A. and Andersson, Y. (1999). Control of *Salmonella* enterica serovar Enteritidis infections in Sweden. In *Salmonella enterica serovar Enteritidis in Humans and Animals* A. M. Saeed (Ed.).Iowa State University Press, Ames, Iowa, pp. 291-305.
14. Nygard, K., Guerin, P., Andersson, Y., and Giesecke, J. (2002). Detection of a previously uncommon *Salmonella* phage in tourists returning from Europe. *Lancet* **360**, 175.
15. Swedish Civil Aviation Administrationr. Passengers in international traffic by first destination. Swedish CAAs web-site. Retrieved from [http://www.lfv.se/templates/LFV_InfoSida_Bred____4813.aspx]
16. Instituto de Salud Carlos III. Information on infectious intestinal diseases in Spain. Retrieved from [http://www.isciii.es/]
17. Guerin, P., Nygard, K., Vold, L., Kuusi, M., Alvseike, O., Siitonen, A., Lassen, J., Andersson, Y., and Aavitsland, P. (2002). Outbreak of *Salmonella enteritidis* among Scandinavian tourists returning from Greece. In: *Program and Abstracts Book, International Conference on Emerging Infectious Diseases 2002*. Atlanta, p. 102.
18. CDSC (2002). National increase in *Salmonella*: Enteritidis PT14b. 2002. *CDR weekly.* p. 12.
19. Moyer and Nelson, P. (1997). *Salmonella enteritidis* surveillance 1995/1996. *Hotline [serial online]* **36**, 1-5.
20. CDC: U.S. Foodborne Disease Outbreaks. Retrieved from [http://www.cdc.gov/ncidod/dbmd/outbreak/fbo_finals/fbo1994/bacterial94.htm]
21. Kistemann, T., Dangendorf, F., Krizek, L., Sahl, H. G., Engelhart, S., and Exner, M. (2000). GIS-supported investigation of a nosocomial *Salmonella* outbreak. *Int. J. Hyg. Environ. Health.* **203**, 117-126.
22. Meijer, G. and vd Berg, G. (2000). Explosie van *Salmonella enteritidis* faagtype 14b na diner in hotel. *Infect. Bull. [serial online]* **11**, 82-83.
23. Rankin, S. and Platt, D. J. (1995). Phage conversion in *Salmonella* enterica serotype Enteritidis: implications for epidemiology. *Epidemiol. Infect.* **114**, 227-236.

24. Chart, H., Row, B., Threlfall, E. J., and Ward, L. R. (1989). Conversion of *Salmonella enteritidis* phage type 4 to phage type 7 involves loss of lipopolysaccharide with concomitant loss of virulence. *FEMS Microbiol. Lett.* **51**, 37-40.
25. Brown, D. J., Baggesen, D. L., Platt, D. J., and Olsen, J. E. (1999). Phage type conversion in *Salmonella* enterica serotype Enteritidis caused by the introduction of a resistance plasmid of incompatibility group X (IncX). *Epidemiol. Infect.* 122, 19-22.
26. Fadl, A. A. and Khan, M. I. (1997). Genotypic evaluation of *Salmonella enteritidis* isolates of known phage types by arbitrarily primed polymerase chain reaction. *Avian Dis.* **41**, 732-737.
27. Fisher, I. and Crowcroft, N. (1989). Enter-net/EPIET investigation into the multinational cluster of *Salmonella* livingstone. *Eurosurveillance Weekly* 2.
28. Fisher, I. and Lieftucht, A. K. M. (1993). Paratyphoid fever after travel to Turkey. *Eurosurveillance Weekly* 3.
29. Laconcha, I., Baggesen, D. L., Rementeria, A., and Garaizar, J. (2000). Genotypic characterisation by PFGE of *Salmonella* enterica serotype Enteritidis phage types 1, 4, 6, and 8 isolated from animal and human sources in three European countries. *Vet. Microbiol.* **75**, 155-165.
30. Ang-Kucuker, M., Tolun, V., Helmuth, R., Rabsch, W., Buyukbaba-Boral, O., Torumkuney-Akbulut, D., Susever, S., and Ang, O. (2000). Phage types, antibiotic susceptibilities and plasmid profiles of *Salmonella* typhimurium and *Salmonella enteritidis* strains isolated in Istanbul, Turkey. *Clin. Microbiol. Infect.* **6**, 593-599.
31. Glosnicka, R. and Dera-Tomaszewska, B. (1999). Comparison of two *Salmonella enteritidis* phage typing schemes. *Eur. J. Epidemiol.* **15**, 395-401.
32. Schroeter, A., Ward, L. R., Rowe, B., Protz, D., Hartung, M., and Helmuth, R. (1994). *Salmonella enteritidis* phage types in Germany. *Eur. J. Epidemiol.* **10**, 645-648.
33. Ministry of Food Agriculture and Fisheries (1997–2001). Annual report on zoonozes in Denmark. Retrieved from [http://www.dfvf.dk/Default.asp?ID=9202]
34. Karpiskova, R. and Mikulaskova, M. (1995). *Salmonella* phage types distribution in the Czech Republic in 1991–1994. *Cent. Eur. J. Public Health* **3**, 161-162.
35. Nastasi, A. and Mammina, C. (1996). Epidemiology of *Salmonella* enterica serotype Enteritidis infections in southern Italy during the years 1980–1994. *Res. Microbiol.* **147**, 393-403.
36. CDSC (2001). *Salmonella* infections in humans: monthly totals for 1997 to 2000. *Commun. Dis. Rep. CDR Wkly [serial online]* 11.
37. Gado, I., Laszlo, V. G., Nagy, B., Milch, H., Drin, I., Awad-Masalmeh, M., and Horvath, J. (1998). Phage restriction and the presence of small plasmids in *Salmonella* enteritidis. *Zentralbl. Bakteriol.* **287**, 509-519.
38. Hasenson, L., Gericke, B., Liesegang, A., Claus, H., Poplawskaja, J., Tscherkess, N., and Rabsch, W. (1995). [Epidemiological and microbiological studies on salmonellosis in Russia]. *Zentralbl. Hyg. Umweltmed.* **198**, 97-116.
39. Majtanova, L. (1997). Occurrence of *Salmonella* enterica serotype Enteritidis phage types in the Slovak Republic. *Eur. J. Epidemiol.* **13**, 243-245.

14

1. Amon, J. and Todrys, K. (2008). Fear of foreigners: HIV-related restrictions on entry, stay and residence. *J. Int. AIDS Soc.* **11**, 8.
2. United Nations Human Rights Committee (May 31, 2009). General Comment No. 27(67). Retrieved from [http://www.unhchr.ch/tbs/doc.nsf/0/6c76e1b8ee1710e380256824005a10a9?Op endocument] *Freedom of movement (Art. 12 of the International Covenant on Economic, Social and Cultural Rights)* 1999. paragraph 1. Accessed
3. Office of the High Commissioner for Human Rights (November 11, 2009). General Comment No. 15. Retrieved from [http://www.unhchr.ch/tbs/doc.nsf/0/bc561aa81bc5d86ec12563ed004aaa1b?Op endocument] *The position of aliens under the Covenant on Civil and Political Rights* 1986. paragraph 5.

4. Human Rights Watch. The Netherlands: Discrimination in the Name of Integration: Migrants' Rights under the Integration Abroad Act. Retrieved from [http://www.hrw.org/en/node/82373/section/1]
5. World Health Organization (1988). Statement on screening of international travellers for infection with Human Immunodeficiency Virus.
6. World Health Organization (WHO) Regional Office for Europe. Scaling up the response to HIV/AIDS in the European Region of WHO EUR/RC52/R9. Retrieved from [http://www.euro.who.int/Governance/resolutions/2002/20021231_4]
7. Border restrictions and HIV/AIDS (1993). A public health policy disaster. AIDS Health *Promot. Exch.* **1**, 1213.
8. Morris K (2008). USA lifts travel restrictions for HIV-positive people. *Lancet. Infect. Dis.* **8**(9), 532.
9. Plotkin, B. (2007). Human rights and other provisions in the revised International Health Regulations (2005). *Pub. Health* **121**, 840845.
10. International AIDS Society (IAS) (May 31, 2009). HIV-specific travel and residence restrictions. Retrieved from [http://www.iasociety.org/Web/WebContent/File/ias_policy%20paper.pdf] *IAS Policy Paper Geneva*: IAS; 2009.
11. Joint United Nations Programme on HIV/AIDS (UNAIDS), International Organization for Migration (IOM) (2004). UNAIDS/IOM Statement on HIV/AIDS-related Travel Restrictions. Retrieved from [http://www.iom.int/jahia/webdav/site/myjahiasite/shared/shared/mainsite/activities/health/UNAIDS_IOM_statement_travel_restrictions.pdf] Geneva: UNAIDS, IOM.
12. The Global Database on HIV-Related Travel Restrictions Retrieved from [http://www.hivtravel.org]
13. United States Bureau of Consular Affairs: Travel.state.gov: country specific information. Retrieved from [http://travel.state.gov/travel/cis_pa_tw/cis/cis_1765.html]
14. EU HIV/AIDS Civil Society Forum: Call for a European response to remove HIV specific travel restrictions in Europe by 2010. Retrieved from [http://www.hivtravel.org/Web/ WebContentEATG/File/Call%20for%20European%20response%20to%20remove%20HIV%20travel%20restrictions%20in%20Europe%20by%202010.pd f]
15. Office of the United Nations High Commissioner for Human Rights and the Joint United Nations Programme on HIV/AIDS (2006). *International Guidelines on HIV/AIDS and Human Rights.* Joint United Nations Programme on HIV/AIDS (UNAIDS), Geneva.
16. Madhok, R., Gracie, J. A., Lowe, G. D., and Forbes, C. D. (1986). Lack of HIV transmission by casual contact. *Lancet* **328**, 863.
17. International Task Team on HIV-related Travel Restrictions: Denying entry, stay and residence due to HIV status: Ten things you need to know. Retrieved from [http://www.iasociety.org/ Web/ WebContent/File/ travel_restrictions_English_WEB.pdf]
18. European Parliament, Council of the European Union (2004). Corrigendum to Directive 2004/38/EC of the European Parliament and of the Council of 29 April 2004 on the right of citizens of the Union and their family members to move and reside freely within the territory of the Member States amending Regulation (EEC). No 1612/68 and repealing Directives 64/221/EEC, 68/360/EEC, 72/194/EEC, 73/148/EEC, 75/34/EEC, 75/35/EEC, 90/364/EEC, 90/365/EEC and 93/96/EEC (OJ L 158, 30.4.2004). *Official J. L.* **229**(29/06/2004), 3548.
19. World Health Organization (WHO). Influenza A: frequently asked questions: travel. Retrieved from [http://www.who.int/csr/disease/swineflu/frequently_asked_questions/travel/en/ index.html]
20. World Health Organization (WHO) (2005). *International Health Regulations*. 2nd edition. WHO, Geneva, Article 43

15

1. Friedman, E. (1978). A hospital for all seasons. *Hospitals* **52**(18), 101, 104, 108.
2. Fullerton, K. J. and Crawford, V. L. (1999). The winter bed crisisquantifying seasonal

effects on hospital bed usage. *QJM* **92**(4), 199206.

3. Garfield, M., Ridley, S., Kong, A., Burns, A., Blunt, M., and Gunning, K. (2001). Seasonal variation in admission rates to intensive care units. *Anaesthesia* **56**(12), 11361140.
4. Menec, V. H., Roos, N. P., and MacWilliam, L. (2002). Seasonal patterns of hospital use in Winnipeg: Implications for managing winter bed crises. *Health. Manage. Forum*. Suppl, 5864.
5. Afza, M. and Bridgman, S. (2001). Winter emergency pressures for the NHS: contribution of respiratory disease, experience in North Staffordshire district. *J. Public Health Med.* **23**(4), 312313.
6. Boulay, F., Berthier, F., Schoukroun, G., Raybaut, C., Gendreike, Y., and Blaive, B. (2001). Seasonal variations in hospital admission for deep vein thrombosis and pulmonary embolism: Analysis of discharge data. *BMJ* **323**(7313), 601602.
7. Inagawa, T. (2002). Seasonal variation in the incidence of aneurysmal subarachnoid hemorrhage in hospital- and community-based studies. *J. Neurosurg.* **96**(3), 497509.
8. Menec, V. H., MacWilliam, L., and Aoki, F. Y. (2002). Hospitalizations and deaths due to respiratory illnesses during influenza seasons: Acomparison of community residents, senior housing residents, and nursing home residents. *J. Gerontol. A. Biol. Sci. Med. Sci.* **57**(10), M629635.
9. Muroi, C., Yonekawa, Y., Khan, N., Rousson, V., and Keller, E. (2004). Seasonal variations in hospital admissions due to aneurysmal subarachnoid haemorrhage in the state of Zurich, Switzerland. *Acta. Neurochir. (Wien)* **146**(7), 659665.
10. Panagiotakos, D. B., Chrysohoou, C., Pitsavos, C., Nastos, P., Anadiotis, A., Tentolouris, C., Stefanadis, C., Toutouzas, P., and Paliatsos, A. (2004). Climatological variations in daily hospital admissions for acute coronary syndromes. *Int. J. Cardiol.* **94**(2–3), 229233.
11. Rusticucci, M., Bettolli, M. L., and de, A. H. (2002). Association between weather conditions and the number of patients at the emergency room in an Argentine hospital. *Int. J. Biometeorol.* **46**(1), 4251.
12. Saynajakangas, P., Keistinen, T., and Tuuponen, T. (2001). Seasonal fluctuations in hospitalisation for pneumonia in Finland. *Int. J. Circumpolar Health* **60**(1), 3440.
13. Shiloh, R., Shapira, A., Potchter, O., Hermesh, H., Popper, M., Weizman, A. (2005). Effects of climate on admission rates of schizophrenia patients to psychiatric hospitals. *Eur. Psychiatry* **20**(1), 6164.
14. Petridou, E., Gatsoulis, N., Dessypris, N., Skalkidis, Y., Voros, D., Papadimitriou, Y., and Trichopoulos, D. (2000). Imbalance of demand and supply for regionalized injury services: a case study in Greece. *Int. J. Qual. Health Care* **12**(2), 105113.
15. Zilm, F. (2004). Estimating emergency service treatment bed needs. *J. Ambul. Care Manage.* **27**(3), 215223.
16. Klauss, G., Staub, L., Widmer, M., and Busato, A. (2005). Hospital service areasA new tool for health care planning in Switzerland. *BMC Health Serv. Res.* **5**(1), 33.
17. *Schweizerische Operationsklassifikation (CHOP)*, ICD-9-CM 2004, Volume 3 (Version 7.0).
18. *Swiss federal statistic office*, icd-10, cim-10 for Switzerland, Retrieved from [http://www.icd10.ch]
19. Goodman, D. C. and Green, G. R. (1996). Assessment tools: Small area analysis. *Am. J. Med. Qual.* **11**(1), S1214.
20. Heim, D., Weymann, A., Loeliger, U., and Matter, P. (1993). [Epidemiology of winter sport injuries]. *Z. Unfallchir. Versicherungsmed.* Suppl 1, 1631.
21. Crivelli, L. FMMI (2004). Federalism and regional health care expenditures: An emerical analysis for the Swiss cantons. Quaderni della facolta, working papers, university of Lugano 229.

16

1. Rombo, L. (2005). Who needs drug prophylaxis against malaria? My personal view. *J. Travel Med.* **12**, 217–221.
2. PAHO (2003). 44th Directing Council 55th Session of the Regional Committee Status

report on Malaria programs in the Americas (Based on 2002 data). Retrieved from [http://www.paho.org/English/AD/DPC/CD/malaria.htm], Washington, DC, USA, CD44/INF/3 (Eng.), 17.

3. 44th Directing Council 55th Session of the Regional Committee Status Report on Malaria Programs in the Americas (2006). (Based on 2004 data) Retrieved from [http://www.paho.org/English/AD/DPC/CD/mal-status-2004.pdf].
4. Organization WT (2006). International Tourist Arrivals by Country of Destination. Retrieved from [http://www.unwto.org/facts/eng/indicators.htm].
5. Organization WT (2007). World Tourism Highlights 2006 edition. Retrieved from [http://www.unwto.org/facts/menu.html].
6. Causer, L. M., Newman, R. D., Barber, A. M., Roberts, J. M., Stennies, G., Bloland, D. V. M., Parise, M. E., and Steketee, R.W. (2002). Malaria surveillance—United States, 2000. *MMWR Surveill. Summ.* **51**, 9–21.
7. Filler, S., Causer, L. M., Newman, R. D., Barber, A. M., Roberts, J. M., MacArthur, J., Parise, M. E., and Steketee, R.W. (2003). Malaria surveillance—United States, 2001. *MMWR Surveill. Summ.* **52**, 1–14.
8. Shah, S., Filler, S., Causer, L. M., Rowe, A. K., Bloland, P. B., Barber, A. M., Roberts, J. M., Desai, M. R., Parise, M. E., and Steketee, R. W. (2004). Malaria surveillance—United States, 2002. *MMWR Surveill. Summ.* **53**, 21–34.
9. Eliades, M. J., Shah, S., Nguyen-Dinh, P., Newman, R. D., Barber, A. M., Nguyen-Dinh, P., Roberts, J. M., Mali, S., Parise, M. E., Barber, A. M., and Steketee, R. (2005). Malaria surveillance—United States, 2003. *MMWR Surveill. Summ.* **54**, 25–40.
10. Skarbinski, J., James, E. M., Causer, L. M., Barber, A. M., Mali, S., Nguyen-Dinh, P., Roberts, J. M., Parise, M. E., Slutsker, L., and Newman, R. D. (2006). Malaria surveillance—United States, 2004. *MMWR Surveill. Summ.* **55**, 23–37.
11. Thwing, J., Skarbinski, J., Newman, R. D., Barber, A. M., Mali, S., Roberts, J. M., Slutsker, L., and Arguin, P. M. (2007). Malaria surveillance—United States, 2005. *MMWR Surveill. Summ.* **56**, 23–40.
12. US Department of Commerce ITA Tourism Industries. 2004 Profile of U.S. Resident Traveler Visiting Overseas Destinations Reported From: Survey of International Air Travelers. Retrieved from [http://tinet.ita.doc.gov/view/f-2004-11-001/index.html]. ITA. Office of Travel & Tourism Industries.
13. PAHO (2006). Malaria in the Countries and Region of the Americas: Time series Epidemiological Data, 1998–2004. Retrieved from [http://www.paho.org/English/AD/DPC/CD/mal-2005.htm]. Pan American Health Organization World Health Organization.
14. Regional Strategic Plan for Malaria in the Americas 2006–2010 (2006). Retrieved from [http://www.paho.org/English/AD/DPC/CD/mal-reg-strat-plan-06.pdf].
15. Organization WT (Ed.) (2006). *Tourism Market Trends: Americas in Tourism Market Trends.* World Tourism Organization, Madrid, Spain, pp. 1–272.
16. Verret, C., Cabianca, B., Haus-Cheymol, R., Lafille, J. J., Loran-Haranqui, G., and Spiegel, A. (2006). Malaria outbreak in troops returning from French Guiana. *Emerging Infect. Diseas.* **12**, 1794–1795.
17. Behrens, R. H., Bisoffi, Z., Björkman, A., Gascon, J., Hatz, C. F., Jelinek, T., Legros, F., Mühlberger, N., and Voltersvik, P. (2006). Malaria prophylaxis policy for travellers from Europe to the Indian Sub Continent. Retrieved from [http://www.malariajournal.com/content/5/1/7]. *Malaria J.* **5**, 1–7.
18. Roshanravan, B., Kari, E., Gilman, R. H., Cabrera, L., Lee, E., Metcalfe, J., Calderon, M., Lescano, A. G., Montenegro, S. H., Calampa, C., and Vinetz, J. M. (2003). Endemic malaria in the Peruvian Amazon region of Iquitos. *Am. J. Trop. Med. Hyg.* **69**, 45–52.
19. Currie, J., Cabada, M., Campos, B., Bazan, E., Behrens, R. H., and Gotuzzo, E. (2005). Malaria prophylaxis among travelers visiting Peru: Measurement and analysis of compliance: 2005/5/1. *Lisbon, International Society of Travel Medicine*, [CISTM9].
20. CDC (2007). CDC Health Information for International Travel, 2008. *Atlanta* 1–627.

21. International Travel and Health (2007). *Geneva, World Health Organization* 1–227, Retrieved from [http://www.who.int/ith/en/].
22. Chiodini, P. L., Bannister, B., Hill, D. R., Lalloo, D., Lea, G., Walker, E., and Whitty, C. J. (2007). Guidelines for Malaria Prevention in Travellers from the United Kingdom. Retrieved from [http://www.hpa.org.uk/publications/2006/Malaria/guidelines.htm?submit=Accept].
23. Parise, M., Kozarsky, P. E., and Cetron, M. (2003). Delayed onset of malaria—Implications for chemoprophylaxis in travelers. *N. Engl. J. Med.* **349**, 1510–1516.
24. Bottieau, E., Clerinx, J., Van den, E. E., Van Esbroeck, M., Colebunders, R., Van Gompel, A., and Van den, E. J. (2006). Imported non-*Plasmodium falciparum* malaria: A five-year prospective study in a European referral center. *Am. J. Trop. Med. Hyg.* **75**, 133–138.
25. Lehky Hagen, M. R., Haley, T. J., and Hatz, C. F. (2005). Factors influencing the pattern of imported malaria. *J. Travel Med.* **12**, 72–79.
26. Schlagenhauf, P., Tschopp, A., Johnson, R., Nothdurft, H. D., Beck, B., Schwartz, E., Herold, M., Krebs, B., Veit, O., Allwinn, R., and Steffen, R. (2003). Tolerability of malaria chemoprophylaxis in non-immune travellers to sub-Saharan Africa: Multicentre, randomised, double blind, four arm study. *BMJ* **327**, 1078–1081.
27. Hatz, C. F., Beck, B., Blum, J., Bourquin, C., Brenneke, F., Funk, M., Furrer, H., Genton, B., Holzer, B., Loutan, L., Raeber, P. A., Rudin, W., Schlagenhauf, P., Steffen, R., and Stossel, U. (2006). Supplementum 1: Malariaschutz fur Kurzzeitaufenthalter. Retrieved from [http://www.bag.admin.ch/themen/medizin/00682/00684/02535/index.html?lang=de]. Swiss Federal Office of Public Health 2006.

17

1. King, D. A., Peckham, C., Waage, J. K., Brownlie, J., and Woolhouse, M. E. (2006). Epidemiology. Infectious diseases: Preparing for the future. *Science* **313**, 1392–1393.
2. Morens, D. M., Folkers, G. K., and Fauci, A. S. (2004). The challenge of emerging and re-emerging infectious diseases. *Nature* **430**, 242–249.
3. Jones, K. E., Patel, N. G., Levy, M. A., Storeygard, A., Balk, D., et al. (2008). Global trends in emerging infectious diseases. *Nature* **451**, 990–993.
4. Cohen, M. L. (2000). Changing patterns of infectious disease. *Nature* **406**, 762–767.
5. Perfect, J. R. and Casadevall, A. (2006). Fungal molecular pathogenesis: What can it do and why do we need it? In *Molecular Principals of Fungal Pathogenesis*. J. Heitman, S. Filler, J. Edwards, and A. Mitchell (Eds.). ASM Press, Washington DC.
6. Maiden, M. C., Bygraves, J. A., Feil, E., Morelli, G., Russell, J. E., et al. (1998). Multilocus sequence typing: A portable approach to the identification of clones within populations of pathogenic microorganisms. *Proc. Natl. Acad. Sci. USA* **95**, 3140–3145.
7. Frothingham, R. and Meeker-O'Connell, W. A. (1998). Genetic diversity in the Mycobacterium tuberculosis complex based on variable numbers of tandem DNA repeats. *Microbiology* **144**(Pt 5), 1189–1196.
8. Kidd, S. E., Guo, H., Bartlett, K. H., Xu, J., and Kronstad, J. W. (2005). Comparative gene genealogies indicate that two clonal lineages of *Cryptococcus gattii* in British Columbia resemble strains from other geographical areas. *Eukaryot Cell* **4**, 1629–1638.
9. Litvintseva, A. P., Thakur, R., Vilgalys, R., and Mitchell, T. G. (2006). Multilocus sequence typing reveals three genetic subpopulations of *Cryptococcus neoformans* var. grubii (serotype A), including a unique population in Botswana. *Genetics* **172**, 2223–2238.
10. Fraser, J. A., Giles, S. S., Wenink, E. C., Geunes-Boyer, S. G., Wright, J. R., et al. (2005). Same-sex mating and the origin of the Vancouver Island *Cryptococcus gattii* outbreak. *Nature* **437**, 1360–1364.
11. Bovers, M., Hagen, F., Kuramae, E. E., and Boekhout, T. (2008). Six monophyletic lineages identified within *Cryptococcus neoformans* and *Cryptococcus gattii* by

multi-locus sequence typing. *Fungal Genet. Biol.* **45**, 400–421.

12. Li, W., Fenollar, F., Rolain, J. M., Fournier, P. E., Feurle, G. E., et al. (2008). Genotyping reveals a wide heterogeneity of *Tropheryma whipplei*. *Microbiology* **154**, 521–527.
13. Li, W., Raoult, D., and Fournier, P. E. (2007). Genetic diversity of *Bartonella henselae* in human infection detected with multispacer typing. *Emerg. Infect. Dis.* **13**, 1178–1183.
14. Brisse, S., Pannier, C., Angoulvant, A., de Meeus, T., Diancourt, L., et al. (2009). Uneven distribution of mating types among genotypes of Candida glabrata from clinical samples. *Eukaryot Cell*. Online ahead of print January 16, 2009.
15. Casadevall, A. and Perfect, J. (1998). *Cryptococcus Neoformans*. ASM Press, Washington DC.
16. Kwon-Chung, K. J., Boekhout, T., Fell, J. W., and Diaz, M. (2002). Proposal to conserve the name *Cryptococcus gattii* against *C. hondurianus* and *C. bacillisporus* (Basidiomycota, Hymenomycetes, Tremellomycetidae). *Taxon* **51**, 804–806.
17. Sorrell, T. C. (2001). *Cryptococcus neoformans* variety gattii. *Med. Mycol.* **39**, 155–168.
18. Upton, A., Fraser, J. A., Kidd, S. E., Bretz, C., Bartlett, K. H., et al. (2007). First contemporary case of human infection with *Cryptococcus gattii* in Puget Sound: Evidence for spread of the Vancouver Island outbreak. *J. Clin. Microbiol.* **45**, 3086–3088.
19. Kidd, S. E., Hagen, F., Tscharke, R. L., Huynh, M., and Bartlett, K. H., et al. (2004). A rare genotype of *Cryptococcus gattii* caused the cryptococcosis outbreak on Vancouver Island (British Columbia, Canada). *Proc. Natl. Acad. Sci. USA* **101**, 17258–17263.
20. MacDougall, L., Kidd, S. E., Galanis, E., Mak, S., Leslie, M. J., et al. (2007). Spread of *Cryptococcus gattii* in British Columbia, Canada, and detection in the Pacific Northwest, USA. *Emerg. Infect. Dis.* **13**, 42–50.
21. Bartlett, K. H., Kidd, S. E., and Kronstad, J. W. (2008). The emergence of *Cryptococcus gattii* in British Columbia and the Pacific Northwest. *Curr. Infect. Dis. Rep.* **10**, 58–65.
22. Byrnes, E. J. III, Bildfell, R., Frank, S. A., Mitchell, T. G., Marr, K. A., et al. (2009). Molecular evidence that the Vancouver Island *Cryptococcus gattii* outbreak has expanded into the United States Pacific Northwest. *J. Inf. Dis.* Published online February 16, 2009.
23. Byrnes, E. J. III, Bildfell, R. J., Dearing, P. L., Valentine, B. A., and Heitman, J. (2009). *Cryptococcus gattii* with bimorphic colony types in a dog in western Oregon: Additional evidence for expansion of the Vancouver Island outbreak. *J. Vet. Diagn. Invest.* **21**, 133–136.
24. Kwon-Chung, K. J. and Varma, A. (2006). Do major species concepts support one, two or more species within *Cryptococcus neoformans*? *FEMS Yeast Res.* **6**, 574–587.
25. Kwon-Chung, K. J. (1976) A new species of Filobasidiella, the sexual state of *Cryptococcus neoformans* B and C serotypes. *Mycologia* **68**, 943–946.
26. Boekhout, T., Theelen, B., Diaz, M., Fell, J. W., Hop, W. C., et al. (2001). Hybrid genotypes in the pathogenic yeast *Cryptococcus neoformans*. *Microbiology* **147**, 891–907.
27. Perfect, J. R. (1989). Cryptococcosis. *Infect. Dis. Clin. North Am.* **3**, 77–102.
28. Kwon-Chung, K. J. and Bennett, J. E. (1984). Epidemiologic differences between the two varieties of *Cryptococcus neoformans*. *Am. J. Epidemiol.* **120**, 123–130.
29. Stephen, C., Lester, S., Black, W., Fyfe, M., and Raverty, S. (2002). Multispecies outbreak of cryptococcosis on southern Vancouver Island, British Columbia. *Can. Vet. J.* **43**, 792–794.
30. Litvintseva, A. P., Thakur, R., Reller, L. B., and Mitchell, T. G. (2005). Prevalence of clinical isolates of *Cryptococcus gattii* serotype C among patients with AIDS in Sub-Saharan Africa. *J. Infect. Dis.* **192**, 888–892.
31. Chaturvedi, S., Dyavaiah, M., Larsen, R. A., and Chaturvedi, V. (2005). *Cryptococcus gattii* in AIDS patients, southern California. *Emerg. Infect. Dis.* **11**, 1686–1692.
32. Blankenship, J. R., Singh, N., Alexander, B. D., and Heitman, J. (2005). *Cryptococcus*

neoformans isolates from transplant recipients are not selected for resistance to calcineurin inhibitors by current immunosuppressive regimens. *J. Clin. Microbiol.* **43**, 464–467.

33. Miller, W. G., Padhye, A. A., van Bonn, W., Jensen, E., Brandt, M. E., et al. (2002). Cryptococcosis in a bottlenose dolphin (*Tursiops truncatus*) caused by *Cryptococcus neoformans* var. gattii. *J. Clin. Microbiol.* **40**, 721–724.
34. Pfeiffer, T. and Ellis, D. (1991). Environmental isolation of *Cryptococcus gattii* from California. *J. Infect. Dis.* **163**, 929–930.
35. Litvintseva, A. P., Kestenbaum, L., Vilgalys, R., and Mitchell, T. G. (2005). Comparative analysis of environmental and clinical populations of *Cryptococcus neoformans*. *J. Clin. Microbiol.* **43**, 556–564.
36. Chambers, C., MacDougall, L., Li, M., and Galanis, E. (2008). Tourism and specific risk areas for *Cryptococcus gattii*, Vancouver Island, Canada. *Emerg. Infect. Dis.* **14**, 1781–1783.
37. Lindberg, J., Hagen, F., Laursen, A., Stenderup, J., and Boekhout, T. (2007). *Cryptococcus gattii* risk for tourists visiting Vancouver Island, Canada. *Emerg. Infect. Dis.* **13**, 178–179.
38. Lim, S., Notley-McRobb, L., Lim, M., and Carter, D. A. (2004). A comparison of the nature and abundance of microsatellites in 14 fungal genomes. *Fungal. Genet. Biol.* **41**, 1025–1036.
39. Benson, G. (1999). Tandem repeats finder: A program to analyze DNA sequences. *Nucleic Acids Res.* **27**, 573–580.
40. Larkin, M. A., Blackshields, G., Brown, N. P., Chenna, R., McGettigan, P. A., et al. (2007). Clustal W and Clustal X version 2.0. *Bioinformatics* **23**, 2947–2948.
41. Xue, C., Tada, Y., Dong, X., and Heitman, J. (2007). The human fungal pathogen Cryptococcus can complete its sexual cycle during a pathogenic association with plants. *Cell Host Microbe.* **1**, 263–273.
42. Mylonakis, E., Moreno, R., El Khoury, J. B., Idnurm, A., Heitman, J., et al. (2005). *Galleria mellonella* as a model system to study *Cryptococcus neoformans* pathogenesis. *Infect. Immun.* **73**, 3842–3850.
43. Halliday, C. L. and Carter, D. A. (2003). Clonal reproduction and limited dispersal in an environmental population of *Cryptococcus neoformans* var gattii isolates from Australia. *J. Clin. Microbiol.* **41**, 703–711.
44. London, R., Orozco, B. S., and Mylonakis, E. (2006). The pursuit of cryptococcal pathogenesis: Heterologous hosts and the study of cryptococcal host-pathogen interactions. *FEMS Yeast Res.* **6**, 567–573.
45. Fuchs, B. B. and Mylonakis, E. (2006). Using non-mammalian hosts to study fungal virulence and host defense. *Curr. Opin. Microbiol.* **9**, 346–351.
46. Idnurm, A., Walton, F. J., Floyd, A., Reedy, J. L., and Heitman, J. (2009). Identification of ENA1 as a virulence gene of the human pathogenic fungus *Cryptococcus neoformans* through signature-tagged insertional mutagenesis. *Eukaryot Cell.* Online ahead of print January 16, 2009.
47. Fan, W., Idnurm, A., Breger, J., Mylonakis, E., and Heitman, J. (2007). Eca1, a sarcoplasmic/endoplasmic reticulum Ca2+-ATPase, is involved in stress tolerance and virulence in *Cryptococcus neoformans*. *Infect. Immun.* **75**, 3394–3405.
48. Datta, K., Bartlett, K., Baer, R., Byrnes, E., Galanis, E., et al. (2009). *Cryptococcus gattii*: An emerging pathogenic fungus in Western North America. *Emerg. Infect. Dis.* Submitted.
49. Sorrell, T. C., Chen, S. C., Ruma, P., Meyer, W., Pfeiffer, T. J., et al. (1996). Concordance of clinical and environmental isolates of *Cryptococcus neoformans* var. gattii by random amplification of polymorphic DNA analysis and PCR fingerprinting. *J. Clin. Microbiol.* **34**, 1253–1260.
50. Campbell, L. T., Currie, B. J., Krockenberger, M., Malik, R., Meyer, W., et al. (2005). Clonality and recombination in genetically differentiated subgroups of *Cryptococcus gattii*. *Eukaryot Cell* **4**, 1403–1409.
51. Kidd, S. E., Sorrell, T. C., and Meyer, W. (2003). Isolation of two molecular types of *Cryptococcus neoformans* var. gattii from insect frass. *Med. Mycol.* **41**, 171–176.
52. Raboin, L. M., Selvi, A., Oliveira, K. M., Paulet, F., Calatayud, C., et al. (2007). Evidence for the dispersal of a unique lineage

from Asia to America and Africa in the sugarcane fungal pathogen Ustilago scitaminea. *Fungal. Genet. Biol.* **44**, 64–76.

53. Fraser, J. A., Subaran, R. L., Nichols, C. B., and Heitman, J. (2003). Recapitulation of the sexual cycle of the primary fungal pathogen *Cryptococcus neoformans* var. gattii: Implications for an outbreak on Vancouver Island, Canada. *Eukaryot Cell* **2**, 1036–1045.
54. Saul, N., Krockenberger, M., and Carter, D. (2008). Evidence of recombination in mixed-mating-type and alpha-only populations of *Cryptococcus gattii* sourced from single eucalyptus tree hollows. *Eukaryot Cell* **7**, 727–734.
55. Heitman, J. (2006). Sexual reproduction and the evolution of microbial pathogens. *Curr. Biol.* **16**, R711–725.
56. Nielsen, K. and Heitman, J. (2007). Sex and virulence of human pathogenic fungi. *Adv. Genet.* **57**, 143–173.
57. Campbell, L. T. and Carter, D. A. (2006). Looking for sex in the fungal pathogens *Cryptococcus neoformans* and *Cryptococcus gattii*. *FEMS Yeast Res.* **6**, 588–598.
58. Carter, D., Saul, N., Campbell, L. T., Tien, B., and Krockenberger, M. (2007). Sex in natural populations of *C. gattii*. In *Sex in Fungi: Molecular Determination and Evolutionary Implications*. J. Heitman, J. W. Kronstad, J. Taylor, and L. Casselton (Eds.). ASM Press, Washington DC, pp. 477–488.
59. Grigg, M. E., Bonnefoy, S., Hehl, A. B., Suzuki, Y., and Boothroyd, J. C. (2001). Success and virulence in Toxoplasma as the result of sexual recombination between two distinct ancestries. *Science* **294**, 161–165.
60. Su, C., Evans, D., Cole, R. H., Kissinger, J. C., Ajioka, J. W., et al. (2003). Recent expansion of Toxoplasma through enhanced oral transmission. *Science* **299**, 414–416.

18

1. Casadevall, A. and Perfect, J. R. (1998). *Cryptococcus neoformans*: Molecular pathogenesis and clinical management. American Society for Microbiology Press, Washington.
2. Stephen, C., Lester, S., Black, W., Fyfe, M., and Raverty, S. (2002). Multispecies outbreak of cryptococcosis on southern Vancouver Island, British Columbia. *Can. Vet. J.* **43**, 792–794.
3. Kidd, S. E., Chow, Y., Mak, S., Bach, P. J., Chen, H., Hingston, A. O., et al. (2007). Characterization of environmental sources of the human and animal pathogen *Cryptococcus gattii* in British Columbia, Canada, and the Pacific Northwest of the United States. *Appl. Environ. Microbiol.* **73**, 1433–1443.
4. Kidd, S. E., Hagen, F., Tscharke, R. L., Huynh, M., Bartlett, K. H., Fyfe, M., et al. (2004). A rare genotype of *Cryptococcus gattii* caused the cryptococcosis outbreak on Vancouver Island (British Columbia, Canada). *Proc. Natl. Acad. Sci. USA* **101**, 17258–17263.
5. MacDougall, L., Kidd, S. E., Galanis, E., Mak, S., Leslie, M. J., Cieslak, P. R., et al. (2007). Spread of *Cryptococcus gattii* in British Columbia, Canada, and detection in the Pacific Northwest, USA. *Emerg. Infect. Dis.* **13**, 42–50.
6. Duncan, C., Stephen, C., Lester, S., and Bartlett, K. H. (2005). Sub-clinical infection and asymptomatic carriage of *Cryptococcus gattii* in dogs and cats during an outbreak of cryptococcosis. *Med. Mycol.* **43**, 511–516.
7. Lindberg, J., Hagen, F., Laursen, A., Stenderup, J., and Boekhout, T. (2007). *Cryptococcus gattii* risk for tourists visiting Vancouver Island, Canada. *Emerg. Infect. Dis.* **13**, 178–179.
8. MacDougall, L. and Fyfe, M. (2006). Emergence of *Cryptococcus gattii* in a novel environment provides clues to its incubation period. *J. Clin. Microbiol.* **44**, 1851–1852.
9. BC Centre for Disease Control (2007). *Cryptococcus gattii* surveillance summary, British Columbia, 1999–2006. Vancouver (Canada): BC Centre for Disease Control. [Cited August 14, 2008]. Retrieved from [http://www.bccdc.org/topic.php?item=109].
10. Tourism BC (2007). Regional Profile: Vancouver Island, Victoria, and the Gulf Islands. Victoria (Canada): Tourism BC Research Services. [Cited August 14, 2008].

Retrieved from [http://www.tourismbc.com/special_reports.asp?id=2065].

11. Askling, H. H., Nilsson, J., Tegnell, A., Janzon, R., and Ekdahl, K. (2005). Malaria risk in travelers. *Emerg. Infect. Dis.* **11**, 436–441.
12. Ekdahl, K. and Andersson, Y. (2004). Regional risks and seasonality in travel-associated campylobacteriosis. *BMC Infect. Dis.* **4**, 54.
13. Ekdahl, K., de Jong, B., Wollin, R., and Andersson, Y. (2005). Travel-associated non-typhoidal salmonellosis: Geographical and seasonal differences and serotype distribution. *Clin. Microbiol. Infect.* **11**, 138–144.
14. Ekdahl, K. and Anderssonm Y. (2005). The epidemiology of travel-associated shigellosis—Regional risks, seasonality and serogroups. *J. Infect.* **51**, 222–229.

19

1. Shaw, S. E., Day, M. J., Birtles, R. J., and Breitschwerdt, E. B. (2001). Tick-borne infectious diseases of dogs. *Trends Parasitol.* **17**, 74–80.
2. Otranto, D., Dantas-Torres, F., and Breitschwerdt, E. B. (2009). Managing canine vector-borne diseases of zoonotic concern: Part one. *Trends Parasitol.* **25**, 57–163.
3. Glaser, B. and Gothe, R. (1998). Imported arthropod-borne parasites and parasitic arthropods in dogs: Spectrum of species and epidemiological analysis of the cases diagnosed in 1995 and 1996. *Tierärztl Prax.* **26**, 40–46.
4. Glaser, B. and Gothe, R. (1998). Tourism and import of dogs: An inquiry in Germany on the extent as well as on the spectrum and preference of countries concerning stay abroad and origin, respectively. *Tierärztl Prax.* **26**, 197–202.
5. Weise, M. (2004). *Relevant Species of the Canine Parasite Fauna in European Mediterranean Countries and Portugal for Dogs in Germany Concerning Epidemiology and Travel Veterinary Medicine—A Literature Review.* PhD thesis. University Munich, Faculty of Veterinary Medicine.
6. Beelitz, P. and Pfister, K. (2004). Diagnosis and treatment of exotic diseases in travelling dogs. *Tierärztl Prax.* **32**, 158–165.
7. Hirsch, M. and Pantchev, N. (2008). Occurrence of the travel diseases leishmaniosis, ehrlichiosis, babesiosis and dirofilariosis in dogs living in Germany. *Kleintierprax* **53**, 154–165.
8. Defra Department for Environment Food and Rural Affairs. Retrieved from [http://www.defra.gov.uk/wildlife-pets/pets/travel/pets/procedures/stats.htm].
9. Jensen, J., Müller, E., and Daugschies, A. (2003). Arthropod-borne diseases in Greece and their relevance for pet tourism. *Prakt. Tierarzt.* **84**, 430–438.
10. Daugschies, A. (2001). Import of parasites by tourism and animal trading. *Dtsch. Tierärztl. Wschr.* **108**, 348–352.
11. Deplazes, P., Staebler, S., and Gottstein, B. (2006). Travel medicine of parasitic diseases in the dog. *Schweiz. Arch Tierheilk.* **9**, 447–461.
12. Gärtner, S., Just, F. T., and Pankraz, A. (2008). *Hepatozoon canis* infections in two dogs from Germany. *Kleintierprax* **53**, 81–87.
13. Naucke, T. J., Menn, B., Massberg, D., and Lozentz, S. (2008). Sandflies and leishmaniasis in Germany. *Parasitol Res.* **103**(Suppl. 1), 65–68.
14. Jensen, J., Simon, D., Schaarschmidt-Kiener, D., Müller, W., and Nolte, I. (2007). Retrospective assessment of autochthone infection with *Ehrlichia canis* in dogs in Germany. *Tierärztl Prax.* **35**, 123–128.
15. Hermosilla, C., Pantchev, N., Dyachenko, V., Gutmann, M., and Bauer, C. (2006). First autochthonous case of canine ocular *Dirofilaria repens* infection in Germany. *Vet. Rec.* **158**, 134–135.
16. Pantchev, N., Norden, N., Lorentzen, L., Rossi, M., Rossi, U., Brand, B., and Dyachenko, V. (2009). Current surveys on the prevalence and distribution of *Dirofilaria* spp. in dogs in Germany. *Parasitol Res.* **105**, 63–74.
17. Solano-Gallego, L., Lull, J., Osso, M., Hegarty, B., and Breitschwerdt, E. (2006). A serological study of exposure to arthropod-

borne pathogens in dogs from northeastern Spain. *Vet. Res.* **37**, 231–244.

18. Tabar, M. D., Francino, O., Altet, L., Sánchez, A., Ferrer, L., and Roura, X. (2009). PCR survey of vectorborne pathogens in dogs living in and around Barcelona, an area endemic for leishmaniosis. *Vet. Rec.* **164**, 112–116.
19. Torina, A. and Caracappa, S. (2006). Dog tick-borne diseases in Sicily. *Parassitologia* **48**, 145–147.
20. Otranto, D. and Dantes-Torres, F (2010). Canine and feline vector-borne diseases in Italy: Current situation and perspectives. *Parasit. Vectors* **3**, 2.
21. Cardoso, L., Costa, A., Tuna, J., Vieira, L., Eyal, O., Yisaschar-Mekuzas, Y., and Baneth, G. (2008). *Babesia canis canis* and *Babesia canis vogeli* infections in dogs from northern Portugal. *Vet Parasitol.* **156**, 199–204.
22. Alexandre, N., Santos, A. S., Núncio, M. S., Sousa, R., Boinas, F., and Bacellar, F. (2009). Detection of *Ehrlichia canis* by polymerase chain reaction in dogs from Portugal. *Vet. J.* **181**, 343–344.
23. Conceição-Silva, F. M., Abranches, P., Silva-Pereira, M. C. D., and Janz, G. (1988). Hepatozoonosis in foxes from Portugal. *J. Wildl. Dis.* **24**, 344–347.
24. Cortes, S., Afonso, M. O., Alves-Pires, C., and Campino, L. (2007). Stray dogs and Leishmaniasis in Urban Areas, Portugal. *Emerg. Infect. Dis.* **13**, 1431–1432.
25. Breitschwerdt, E. B. (2007). Canine and feline anaplasmosis: Emerging infectious diseases. *Proceedings of the 2nd Canine Vector-Borne Disease (CVBD) Symposium*, April 25–28, Sicily, Italy, pp. 6–14.
26. Otranto, D., Dantas-Torres, F., and Breitschwerdt, E. B. (2009). Managing canine vector-borne diseases of zoonotic concern: Part two. *Trends Parasitol.* **25**, 228–235.
27. Kordick, S. K., Breitschwerdt, E. B., Hegarty, B. C., Southwick, K. L., Colitz, C. M., Hancock, S. I., Bradley, J. M., Rumbough, R., Mcpherson, J. T., and MacCormack, J. N. (1999). Coinfection with multiple tick-borne pathogens in a Walker Hound kennel in North Carolina. *J. Clin. Microbiol.* **37**, 2631–2638.
28. Euzeby, J. (1981). Diagnostic Expérimental des Helminthoses animales livre 1. *Boulevard de Grenelle.* Paris, pp. 277–312.

20

1. Marion Buen, J., Peiro, S., Marquez Calderon, S., and Meneu de Guillerma, R. (1998). Variations in medical practice: Importance, causes, an implications. *Med. Clin. (Barc.)* **110**, 382–390.
2. Hinrichsen, D. (1994). Coasts under pressure. *People Planet* **3**, 6–9.
3. MacPherson, D. W. and Gushulak, B. D. (2001). Human mobility and population health. New approaches in a globalizing World. *Perspect. Biol. Med.* **44**, 390–401.
4. Batisse, M. (1994). Mending the Med. *People Planet* **3**, 17–18.
5. Olive, F., Rey, S., and Zmirou, D. (1998). Industrial waste as indicator of population size: Possible utilization in mountain resort tourist stations? *Rev. Epidemiol. Sante. Publique.* **46**, 299–304.
6. Crocetti, E., Geddes da Filicaia, M., Crotti, N., Dell'Olio, E., and Spigai, R. (1997). The emigration of Italian patients to countries of the European Economic Community. Review of data published by the Ministry of Health. *Epidemiol. Prev.* **21**, 100–105.
7. Sheaff, R. (1997). Healthcare access and mobility between the UK and other European Union states: An 'implementation surplus.' *Health Policy* **42**, 239–253.
8. Gushulak, B. D. and Macpherson, D. W. (2004). Population mobility and health: An overview of the relationships between movement and population health. *J. Travel. Med.* **11**, 171–174.
9. Librero, J. and Garcia Benavides, F. (1995). Validity of the municipality of residence in mortality statistics: Findings based on municipality census update in 2 municipalities of the Valencian community. *Gac. Sanit.* **9**, 232–236.
10. Librero Lopez, J., Garcia Benavides, F., and Godoy Laserna, C. (1993). An analysis of mortality in small areas: The problem of residency. *Gac.Sanit.* **7**, 169–175.
11. Esteva, M., Tamborero, G., Arias, A., Seguí, M., and Llobera, M. (2003). Utilización de

servicios sanitarios por la población flotante en Mallorca. *Rev. Adm. Sanit.* **3**, 441–456.

12. Juaneda, N., Cladera, M., Esteva, M., and Tamborero, G. (2003). Impacto del turismo sobre la demanda de servicios públicos: el caso de los servicios sanitarios públicos. *Ann. Tourism Res.* **5**, 149–162.
13. Instituto Nacional de Estadística (2004). Retrieved from [http://www.ine.es/inebase/index.html]. Censo de Población y Viviendas 2001 INEBASE, Madrid.
14. Consorci per a la Gestió de Residus Sòlids Urbans a Menorca. Consell Insular de Menorca (2002). Retrieved from [http://www.obsam.org/indicadors/residus/sense_seleccio/produccio_RSU_rebuig_municipis.pdf]. Dades de recollida de RSU a nivell municipal i mensual 1997–2001, Menorca.
15. Instituto de Estadística de Andalucía. Consejería de Economía y Hacienda (2004). Retrieved from [http://www.juntadeandalucia.es/institutodeestadistica/sima_web/index.jsp]. Sistema de Información Multiterritorial de Andalucía, Sevilla.
16. Ministerio de Medio Ambiente (2000). Retrieved from [http://www.mma.es/polit_amb/planes/index.htm]. Plan Nacional de Residuos Urbanos (2000–2006), Madrid.
17. Buenrostro, O., Bocco, G., and Bernache, G. (2001). Urban solid waste generation and disposal in Mexico: A case study. *Waste Manag. Res.* **19**, 169–176.
18. EUROSTAT (2004). Retrieved from [http://epp.eurostat.cec.eu.int]. Eurostat Metadata in SDSS format. Municipal Waste, Bruselas.

21

1. Josiam, B. M., Hobson, J. S. P., Dietrich, U. C., and Smeaton, G. (1998). An analysis of the sexual, alcohol and drug related behavioral patterns of students on spring break. *Tourism Manage* **19**, 501–513.
2. Bellis, M. A., Hughes, K., Bennett, A., and Thomson, R. (2003). The role of an international nightlife resort in the proliferation of recreational drugs. *Addiction* **98**, 1713–1721.
3. Bellis, M. A., Hughes, K., Thomson, R., and Bennett, A. (2004). Sexual behavior of young people in international tourist resorts. *Sex. Transm. Infect.* **80**, 43–47.
4. Apostolopoulos, Y., Sönmez, S., and Yu, C. H. (2002). HIV-risk behaviors of American spring break vacationers: A case of situational disinhibition? *Int. J. STD AIDS* **13**, 733–743.
5. Eiser, J. R. and Ford, N. (1995). Sexual relationships on holiday: A case of situational disinhibition? *J. Soc. Pers. Relat.* **12**, 323–339.
6. Traeen, B. and Kvalum, I. L. (1996). Sex under the influence of alcohol among Norwegian adolescents. *Addiction* **91**, 995–1006.
7. Connor, J., Norton, R., Ameratunga, S., and Jackson, R. (2004). The contribution of alcohol to serious car crash injuries. *Epidemiology* **15**, 337-344.
8. Tunbridge, R. J., Keigan, M., and James, F. J. (2001). *The Incidence of Drugs and Alcohol in Road Accident Fatalities*. TRL Report 495, TRL Limited, Wokingham.
9. Soar, K., Turner, J. J. D., and Parrott, A. C. (2001). Psychiatric disorders in Ecstasy (MDMA) users: A literature review focusing on personal predisposition and drug history. *Hum. Psychopharmacol.* **16**, 651–645.
10. Farrell, M., Howes, S., Taylor, C., Lewis, G., Jenkins, R., Bebbington, P., Jarvis, M., Brugha, T., Gill, B., and Meltzer, H. (2003). Substance misuse and psychiatric comorbidity: An overview of the OPCS National Psychiatric Morbidity Survey. *Int. Rev. Psychiatry.* **15**, 43–49.
11. Beny, A., Paz, A., and Potasman, I. (2001). Psychiatric problems in returning travelers: Features and associations. *J. Travel. Med.* **8**, 243–246.
12. Paz, A., Sadetzki, S., and Potasman, I. (2004). High rates of substance abuse among long-term travelers to the tropics: An intervention study. *J. Travel. Med.* **11**, 75–81.
13. Bellis, M. A., Hughes, K., and Lowey, H. (2002). Healthy night clubs and recreational substance use from a harm minimization to a healthy settings approach. *Addict. Behav.* **27**, 1025–1035.
14. World Tourism Organisation (2002). *Youth outbound travel of the Germans, the British*

and the French. World Tourism Organisation, Madrid.

15. Mintel (2005). Youth holidays—UK—July 2005. Mintel International Group Limited, London.
16. Office for National Statistics (2006). *Mid-2004 Population Estimates: UK Estimated Resident Population by Single Year of Age and Sex*. Retrieved from [http://www.statistics.gov.uk/statbase/Expodata/Spreadsheets/D9081.xls]. Accessed November 10.
17. Office for National Statistics (2005). *Travel trends 2004: A report on the International Passenger Survey.* Palgrave MacMillan, Hampshire.
18. Jones, A. (2004). *Review of Gap Year Provision*. Research Report RR555. Department for Education and Skills, London.
19. Richards, G. and Wilson, J. (2003). *New Horizons in Independent Youth and Student Travel*. International Student Travel Confederation, Amsterdam.
20. Hampton, M. P. (1998). Backpacker tourism and economic development. *Ann. Tourism. Res*. **25**, 639–690.
21. Jarvis, J. (1994). *The Billion Dollar Backpackers*. Monash University, Clayton.
22. Tourism Research Australia (2004). *Backpackers in Australia, 2003*. Niche Market Report No. 4. Tourism Research Australia, Canberra.
23. Tourism Tasmania (2006). *Backpacker Profile. 2004*. Retrieved from [http://www.tourismtasmania.com.au/pdf/backpackers2004.pdf]. Accessed November 10.
24. Uriely, N. and Belhassen, Y. (2005). Drugs and tourists' experiences. *J. Travel. Res*. **43**, 238–246.
25. Hellum, M. (2005). Negotiation risks and curiosity: Narratives about drugs among backpackers. In *Drugs and Youth Cultures: Global and Local Expressions*. P. Lalander and M. Salasuo (Eds.). Nordic Council for Alcohol and Drug Research, Helsinki, pp. 105–120.
26. Barton, A. and James, Z. (2003). "Run to the sun": Policing contested perceptions of risk. *Policing and Society* **13**, 259–270.
27. Hughes, K. and Bellis, M. A. (2006). Sexual behavior among casual workers in an international nightlife resort: A case control study. *BMC Public Health* **6**, 39.
28. Shugg, J., Wood, N., Hewitt, H., and Cohen, C. (2006). *Travellers' Pulse Survey. 2005*. Retrieved from [http://directory.istcnet.org/ISTCnet/Publications/LonelyPlanet_TravellerSurvey.pdf]. Accessed November 10.
29. Hudson, J. I., Pope, H. G. Jr., and Glynn, R. J. (2005). The cross-sectional cohort study: An underutilized design. *Epidemiology* **16**, 355–359.
30. Topp, L., Degenhardt, L., Kaye, S., and Darke, S. (2002). The emergence of potent forms of methamphetamine in Sydney, Australia: A case study of the IDRS as a strategic early warning system. *Drug Alcohol. Rev*. **21**, 341–348.
31. Australian Bureau of Statistics. *Regional Population Growth*. Australian Bureau of Statistics 2006. ABS Catalogue number 3218.0, Canberra.
32. SPSS Inc (2001). *SPSS Base 11 0 User Guide*. SPSS Inc., USA.
33. Roe, S. (2005). Drug misuse declared. Findings from the 2004/05 British Crime Survey. *Home Office Statistical Bulletin 16/05*. Home Office, London.
34. Topp, L. and Churchill, A. (2002). Australia's dynamic methamphetamine markets. *Illicit Drug Reporting System Drug Trends Bulletin, June 2002*. National Drug and Alcohol Research Centre, Sydney.
35. [http://www.gogapyear.com/]. Accessed November 13, 2006.
36. Ross, G. F. (1997). Backpacker achievement and environmental controllability as visitor motivations. *J. Trav. Tourism. Market*. **6**, 69–82.
37. Australian Institute of Health and Welfare (2005). *2004 National Drug Strategy Household Survey*. Australian Institute of Health and Welfare, Canberra.
38. Australian Crime Commission (2006). *Illicit Drug Data Report 2004–2005*. Australian Crime Commission, Canberra.
39. Stafford, J., Degenhardt, L., Agaliotis, M., Chanteloup, F., Fischer, J., Matthews, A., Newman, J., Proudfoot, P., Stoové, M., and Weekley, J. (2005). *Australian Trends in Ecstasy and Related Drug Markets 2004: Findings from the Party Drugs Initiative*.

NDARC Monograph 57. National Drug and Alcohol Research Centre, Sydney.

40. National Drug and Alcohol Research Centre (2006). NDARC fact sheet: Amphetamines. Retrieved from [http://ndarc.med.unsw.edu.au/NDARCWeb.nsf/resources/NDARCFact_Drugs5/$file/Amphetamine+fact+sheet.pdf]. Accessed November 15.
41. Sommers, I., Baskin, D., and Baskin-Sommers, A. (2006). Methamphetamine use among young adults: Health and social consequences. *Addict. Behav.* **31**, 1469–1476.
42. Beyrer, C, Razak, M. H., Jittiwutikarn, J., Suriyanon, V., Vongchak, T., Srirak, N., Kawichai, S., Tovanabutra, S., Rungruengthanakit, K., Sawanpanyalert, P., Sripaipan, T., and Celentano, D. D. (2004). Methamphetamine users in northern Thailand: Changing demographics and risks for HIV and STD among treatment-seeking substance users. *Int. J. STD AIDS* **15**, 697–704.
43. Edmonds, K., Sumnall, H., McVeigh, J., and Bellis, M. A. (2005). *Drug Prevention among Vulnerable Young People*. National Collaborating Centre for Drug Prevention, Liverpool.
44. Room, R., Babor, T., and Rehm, J. (2005). Alcohol and public health. *Lancet* **365**, 519–530.
45. Elliott, L., Morrison, A., Ditton, J., Farrall, S., Short, E., Cowan, L., and Gruer, L. (1998). Alcohol, drug use and sexual behaviour of young people on a Mediterranean dance holiday. *Addict. Res.* **6**, 319–340.
46. Gandini, S., Sera, F., Cattaruzza, M. S., Pasquini, P., Picconi, O., Boyle, P., Melchi, C. F. (2005). Meta-analysis of risk factors for cutaneous melanoma: II. Sun exposure. *Eur. J. Cancer* **41**, 45–60.
47. BBC (2006). Youth moves on as Faliraki fades. May 10, 2004 Retrieved from [http://news.bbc.co.uk/1/hi/uk/3700153.stm]. Accessed November 10.

22

1. Crowcroft, N. S., Morgan, D., and Brown, D. (2002). Viral haemorrhagic fevers in Europe—Effective control requires a coordinated response. *Euro. Surveill.* **7**, 31–32.
2. Centers for Disease Control and Prevention (2005). Outbreak of Marburg virus hemorrhagic fever–Angola, October 1, 2004–March 29, 2005. *MMWR Morb. Mortal Wkly. Rep.* **54**, 308–309.
3. Borio, L., Inglesby, T., Peters, C. J., Schmaljohn, A. L., Hughes, J. M., Jahrling, P. B., et al. (2002). Hemorrhagic fever viruses as biological weapons: Medical and public health management. *JAMA* **287**, 2391–2405, doi:10.1001/jama.287.18.2391
4. Leffel, E. K. and Reed, D. S. (2004). Marburg and Ebola viruses as aerosol threats. *Biosecur. Bioterror.* **2**, 186–191.
5. Peters, C. J. (2005). Marburg and Ebola virus hemorrhagic fevers. In *Mandell, Douglas, and Bennett's Principles and Practice of Infectious Diseases.* G. L. Mandell, J. E. Bennett, and R. Dolin (Eds.). Elsevier Inc., Philadelphia, pp. 2057–2059.
6. Siegert, R. (1972). Marburg virus. *Virology Monograph.* Springer-Verlag, New York, pp. 98–153.
7. Gear, J. S., Cassel, G. A., Gear, A. J., Trappler, B., Clausen, L., Meyers, A. M., et al. Outbreak of Marburg virus disease in Johannesburg. *BMJ* **4**, 489–493.
8. Johnson, E. D., Johnson, B. K., Silverstein, D., Tukei, P., Geisbert, T. W., Sanchez, A. N., et al. (1996). Characterization of a new Marburg virus isolated from a 1987 fatal case in Kenya. *Arch. Virol. Suppl.* **11**, 101–114.
9. Smith, D. H., Johnson, B. K., Isaacson, M., Swanapoel, R., Johnson, K. M., Killey, M., et al. (1982). Marburg-virus disease in Kenya. *Lancet.* **1**, 816–820.
10. Khan, A. S., Sanchez, A., and Pflieger, A. K. (1998). Filoviral haemorrhagic fevers. *Br. Med. Bull.* **54**, 675–692.
11. World Health Organization (1999). Marburg fever, Democratic Republic of the Congo. *Wkly. Epidemiol. Rec.* **74**, 145.
12. World Health Organization (1999). Viral haemorrhagic fever/Marburg, Democratic Republic of the Congo. *Wkly. Epidemiol. Rec.* **74**, 157–158.

13. World Health Organization (2007). Outbreak of Marburg haemorrhagic fever: Uganda, June–August 2007. *Wkly. Epidemiol. Rec.* **82**, 381–384.
14. European Network for Diagnostics of Imported Viral Diseases. Management and control of viral hemorrhagic fevers [cited August 13, 2008]. Retrieved from [http://www.enivd.de].
15. Drosten, C., Gottig, S., Schilling, S., Asper, M., Panning, M., Schmitz, H., et al. (2002). Rapid detection and quantification of RNA of Ebola and Marburg viruses, Lassa virus, Crimean-Congo hemorrhagic fever virus, Rift Valley fever virus, dengue virus, and yellow fever virus by real-time reverse transcription-PCR. *J. Clin. Microbiol.* **40**, 2323–2330.
16. Towner, J. S., Pourrut, X., Albarino, C. G., Nkogue, C. N., Bird, B. H., Grard, G., et al. (2007). Marburg virus infection detected in a common African bat. *PLoS One.* **2**, e764.
17. Swanepoel, R., Smit, S. B., Rollin, P. E., Formenty, P., Leman, P. A., Kemp, A., et al. (2007). Studies of reservoir hosts for Marburg virus. *Emerg. Infect. Dis.* **13**, 1847–1851.
18. Filoviruses (2008). In *LCI Guidelines Infectious Disease Control Edition 2008* [in Dutch]. J. E. Steenbergen, A. Timen, and D. J. Beaujean (Eds.). National Institute for Public Health and the Environment, Bilthoven, pp. 478–484.
19. Haas, W. H., Breuer, T., Pfaff, G., Schmitz, H., Kohler, P., Asper, M., et al. (2003). Imported Lassa fever in Germany: Surveillance and management of contact persons. *Clin. Infect. Dis.* **36**, 1254–1258.
20. Borchert, M., Muyembe-Tamfum, J. J., Colebunders, R., Libande, M., Sabue, M., and van der Stuyft, P. (2002). Short communication: A cluster of Marburg virus disease involving an infant. *Trop. Med. Int. Health.* **7**, 902–906.
21. Borchert, M., Mulangu, S., Swanepoel, R., Libande, M. L., Tshomba, A., Kulidri, A., et al. (2006). Serosurvey on household contacts of Marburg hemorrhagic fever patients. *Emerg. Infect. Dis.* **12**, 433–439.
22. Bausch, D. G., Sprecher, A. G., Jeffs, B., and Boumandouki, P. (2008). Treatment of Marburg and Ebola hemorrhagic fevers: A strategy for testing new drugs and vaccines under outbreak conditions. *Antiviral Res.* **78**, 150–161.
23. Conrad, J. L., Isaacson, M., Smith, E. B., Wulff, H., Crees, M., Geldenhuys, P., et al. (1978). Epidemiologic investigation of Marburg virus disease, southern Africa, 1975. *Am. J. Trop. Med. Hyg.* **27**, 1210–1215.
24. Bausch, D. G., Borchert, M., Grein, T., Roth, C., Swanepoel, R., Libande, M. L., et al. (2003). Risk factors for Marburg hemorrhagic fever, Democratic Republic of the Congo. *Emerg. Infect. Dis.* **9**, 1531–1537.
25. Centers for Disease Control and Prevention. Interim guidance for managing patients with suspected viral hemorrhagic fever in US hospitals [cited October 13, 2008]. Retrieved from [http://www.cdc.gov/ncidod/dhqp/bp_vhf_interimGuidance.html].
26. Health Protection Agency. Management and control of VHF (ACDP 1996) [cited October 13, 2008]. Retrieved from [http://www.hpa.org.uk/web/HPAwebFile/HPAweb_C/1194947382005].
27. Wirtz, A., Niedrig, M., and Fock, R (2002). Management of patients in Germany with suspected viral haemorrhagic fever and other potentially lethal contagious infections. *Euro. Surveill.* **7**, 36–42.

23

1. Gushulak, B. D. and MacPherson, D. W. (2004). Globalization of infectious diseases: The impact of migration. *Clin. Infect. Dis.* **38**, 1742–1748.
2. World Tourism Organisation Facts and Figures. [cited Jun 12, 2006]. Retrieved from [http://www.world-tourism.org/facts/menu.html].
3. Bacaner, N., Stauffer, B., Boulware, D. R., Walker, P. F., and Keystone, J. S. (2004). Travel medicine considerations for North American immigrants visiting friends and relatives. *JAMA* **291**, 2856–2864.
4. Angell, S. Y. and Cetron, M. S. (2005). Health disparities among travelers visiting friends and relatives abroad. *Ann. Intern. Med.* **142**, 67–72.

5. Leder, K., Tong, S., Weld, L., Kain, K. C., Wilder-Smith, A., von Sonnenburg, F., et al. (2006). For the GeoSentinel Surveillance Network. Illness in travelers visiting friends and relatives: A review of the GeoSentinel Surveillance Network. *Clin. Infect. Dis.* **43**, 1185–1193.
6. Siem, H. (1997). Migration and health—The international perspective. *Schweiz. Rundsch. Med. Prax.* **86**, 788–793.
7. Statistical Data on Switzerland 2004. Neuchatel, Switzerland: Swiss Federal Statistical Office; April 2004. [cited Jan 10, 2007]. Retrieved from [http://www.bfs.admin.ch/bfs/portal/en/index/dienstleistungen/publikationen_statistik/publikationskatalog.Document.49104.html].
8. Bischoff, A. (1997). Migration and health in Switzerland. Geneva: Swiss Federal Office of Public Health.
9. Loutan, L. and Chaignat, C. L. (1994). Refugees in Switzerland: Which health problems do they encounter? *Swiss J. Mili. Med.* **71**, 105–109.
10. Ferron, C., Haour-Knipe, M., Tschumper, A., Narring, F., and Michaud, P. A. (1997). Health behaviours and psychosocial adjustment of migrant adolescents in Switzerland. *Schweiz. Med. Wochenschr.* **127**, 1419–1429.
11. Egger, M., Minder, C. E., and Smith, G. D. (1990). Health inequalities and migrant workers in Switzerland. *Lancet.* **336**, 816.
12. Freedman, D. O., Kozarsky, P. E., Weld, L. H., Cetron, M. S. (1999). GeoSentinel: The global emerging infections sentinel network of the International Society of Travel Medicine. *J. Travel Med.* **6**, 94–98.
13. Leder, K., Black, J., O'Brien, D., Greenwood, Z., Kain, K. C., Schwartz, E., et al. (2004). Malaria in travelers: A review of the GeoSentinel Surveillance Network. *Clin. Infect. Dis.* **39**, 1104–1112.
14. Leder, K., Sundararajan, V., Weld, L., Pandey, P., Brown, G., and Torresi, J. (2003). Respiratory tract infections in travelers: A review of the GeoSentinel Surveillance Network. *Clin. Infect. Dis.* **36**, 399–406.
15. Freedman, D. O., Weld, L. H., Kozarsky, P. E., Fisk, T., Robins, R., von Sonnenburg, F., et al. (2006). Spectrum of disease and relation to place of exposure among ill returned travelers. *N. Engl. J. Med.* **354**, 119–130.
16. Schlagenhauf, P., Steffen, R., and Loutan, L. (2003). Migrants as a major risk group for imported malaria in European countries. *J. Travel Med.* **10**, 106–107.
17. Al-Abri, S. S., Beeching, N. J., Nye, F. J. (2005). Traveller's diarrhoea. *Lancet Infect. Dis.* **5**, 349–360.
18. Mutsch, M., Spicher, V. M., Gut, C., and Steffen, R. (2006). Hepatitis A virus infections in travelers, 1988–2004. *Clin. Infect Dis.* **42**, 490–497.

24

1. McNeill, W. H. (1979). Plagues and people. Anchor Press, New York.
2. Tatem, A. J., Rogers, D. J., and Hay, S. I. (2006). Global transport networks and infectious disease spread. *Adv. Paras.* **62**, 293–343.
3. Gezairy, H. A. (2003). Travel epidemiology: WHO perspective. *Inter. J. Antimicrob. Agents* **21**, 86–88.
4. Grais, R. F., Ellis, J. H., and Glass, G. E. (2003). Assessing the impact of airline travel on the geographic spread of pandemic influenza. *Eur. J. Epidemiol.* **18**, 1065–1072.
5. Massey, A. (1933). Epidemiology in relation to air travel. H. K. Lewis and Co. Limited, London.
6. Gratz, N. G., Steffen, R., and Cocksedge, W. (2000). Why aircraft disinsection? *Bull. World Health Organ.* **78**(8), 995–1004.
7. Lounibos, L. P. (2002). Invasions by insect vectors of human disease. Ann. Rev. Entomol. **47**, 233–266.
8. Mangili, A. and Gendreau, M. A. (2005). Transmission of infectious diseases during commercial air travel. *Lancet* **365**, 989–996.
9. Soper, F. L. and Wilson, D. B. (1943). *Anopheles gambiae* in Brazil: 1930–1940. Rockefeller Foundation, New York.
10. Franco-Parades, C. and Santos-Preciado, J. I. (2006). Problem pathogens: Prevention of malaria in travellers. *Lancet Infect. Dis.* **6**, 139–149.
11. Misao, T. and Ishihara, M. (1945). An experiment on the transportation of vector

mosquitoes by aircraft (in japanese). *Rinsho to Kenkyu* **22**, 44–46.

12. Russell, R. C. (1987). Survival of insects in the wheelbays of Boeing 747B aircraft on flights between tropical and temperate airports. *Bull. World Health Organ.* **65**, 659–662.
13. Russell, R. C. (1989). Transport of insects of public health importance on international aircraft. *Travel Med. Inter.* 26–31.
14. Isaäcson, M. (1989). Airport malaria: A review. *Bull. World Health Organ.* **67**(6), 737–743.
15. Muentener, P., Schlagenhauf, P., and Steffen, R. (1999). Imported malaria (1985–95): Trends and perspectives. Bull. *World Health Organ.* **77**(7), 560–566.
16. Hutchinson, R., Bayoh, M., and Lindsay, S. (2005). Risk of airport malaria in the UK. *Eur. Mosq. Bull.* **19**, 12–13.
17. The plane truth about disinsection Environmental Health Perspectives (1999). **107**(8), 397–398.
18. Russell, R. C. and Paton, R. (1989). Inflight disinsection as an efficacious procedure for preventing international transport of insects of public health importance. *Bull. World Health Organ.* **67**(5), 543–547.
19. OAG Worldwide Ltd. Retrieved from [http://www.oag.com].
20. Tanser, F. C., Sharp, B., and le Sueur, D. (2003). Potential effect of climate change on malaria transmission in Africa. *Lancet* **362**(9398), 1792–1798.
21. Rogers, D. J., Randolph, S. E., Snow, R. W., and Hay, S. I. (2002). Satellite imagery in the study and forecast of malaria. *Nature* **415**, 710–715.
22. Snow, R. W., Guerra, C. A., Noor, A. M., Myint, H. L., and Hay, S. I. (2005). The global distribution of clinical episodes of *Plasmodium falciparum* malaria. *Nature* **434**, 214–217.
23. New, M., Lister, D., Hulme, M., and Makin, I. (2002). A high-resolution data set of surface climate over global land areas. *Clim. Res.* **21**, 1–25.
24. Tatem, A. J., Hay, S. I., and Rogers, D. J. (2006). Global traffic and disease vector dispersal. *Proc. Natl. Acad. Sci.* **103**, 6242–6247.
25. Toovey, S. and Jamieson, A. (2003). Rolling back malaria: How well is Europe doing? *Travel Med. Infect. Dis.* **1** 167–175.
26. Hay, S. I., Guerra, C. A., Tatem, A. J., Atkinson, P. M., and Snow, R. W. (2005). Urbanization, malaria transmission and disease burden in Africa. *Nat. Rev. Microbiol.* **3**(1), 81–90.
27. Killeen, G. F., Fillinger, U., Kiche, I., Gouagna, L. C., and Knols, B. G. J. (2002). Eradication of *Anopheles gambiae* from Brazil: Lessons for malaria control in Africa? *Lancet Infect. Dis.* **2**, 618–627.
28. Powell, J. R. and Coluzzi, M. (2004). Malarial mosquito: Is *Anopheles gambiae* plotting an escape. *Inter. Herald Trib.*
29. World Health Organisation (1985). WHO recommendations on the disinsecting of aircraft. *Wkly. Epidemiol. Record* **60**(7), 45–47.
30. Das, R., Cone, J., and Sutton, P. (2001). Aircraft disinsection. *Bull. World Health Organ.* **79**(9), 900–901.
31. Woodyard, C. (2001). Fliers fume over planes treated with pesticides. *USA Today*.
32. Guerra, C. A., Snow, R. W., and Hay, S. I. (2006). Defining the global spatial limits of malaria transmission in 2005. *Adv. Parasitol.* **62**, 157–179.
33. Guerra, C. A., Snow, R. W., and Hay, S. I. (2006). Mapping the global extent of malaria in 2005. *Trends Parasitol.* (in press).
34. Okeke, I. (2004). Stopping the spread of drug-resistant malaria. *Science* **306**, 2039.
35. Roper, C., Pearce, R., Nair, S., Sharp, B., Nosten, F., and Anderson, T. (2004). Intercontinental spread of Pyrimethamine-resistant malaria. *Science* **305**(5687), 1124.
36. Loutan, L. (2003). Malaria: Still a threat to travellers. *Inter. J. Antimicrob. Agents* **21**, 158–163.
37. Tatem, A. J., Rogers, D. J., and Hay, S. I. (2006). T8.5: Traffic in disease vectors: 2005, 2015 and 2030. Commissioned as part of the U.K. Government's Foresight project, Infectious Diseases: Preparing for the future. Office of Science and Innovation, London, UK.

Index

I

T